Unveiling Daniel and Revelation

Unveiling Daniel and Revelation

ROY ALLAN ANDERSON

Pacific Press® Publishing Association
Nampa, Idaho
Oshawa, Ontario, Canada
www.pacificpress.com

Book design by Steve Trapero
Cover photo by Steve Trapero

Copyright © 2006 by
Pacific Press® Publishing Association
Printed in the United States of America
All rights reserved

Additional copies of this book are available by
calling toll-free 1-800-765-6955
or by ordering online at
www.adventistbookcenter.com

Unless otherwise indicated,
Scripture references are from the King James Version.

ISBN 13: 978-0-8163-2151-3
ISBN 10: 0-8163-2151-5

06 07 08 09 10 • 5 4 3 2 1

Contents

Unveiling Daniel and Revelation

Revelation

Preface

No book in the field of biblical prophecy could be more timely than this work on the prophetic books of Daniel and the Revelation—for two reasons: First, there is a strong feeling among students of Bible prophecy that Daniel and the Revelation are understood best when studied together. Each needs the other. Second, the times in which we now live demand a restudy of these prophecies.

The great prophetic cinema of the march of the ages moves with gathering speed before our eyes. We need a fresh approach, a restudy of the prophecies of Daniel and Revelation that have been such a blessing to God's people since the days of the prophets themselves. This is what this author has brought to us. Religious confusion reigns in our day; we need a clear understanding of these books. One special strength of this book is the thorough research the author has made into the historical background of the prophecies and their authors.

During his boyhood, Daniel witnessed the collapse of the mighty Assyrian Empire, which had dominated the Near East for centuries. He also saw the rise of the new Babylonian Empire under Nebuchadnezzar the Great. The invasions of the West, the capture of Jerusalem, the forced transfer of the inhabitants to Babylon are graphically pictured. The prophet himself was one of these captives. Thus began the seventy-year captivity of God's people as predicted by Jeremiah. (See Jeremiah 25:11, 12.)

Located at the very center and headquarters of the first prophetic world empire, Daniel wrote his great book on historic prophecy. For several generations now biblical scholars have disputed certain interpretations in the book of Daniel. Dr. Anderson's treatment of these issues is like a breath of fresh air on the subject. The historical credibility for the book of Daniel is especially emphasized in the chapter titled "Daniel in the Critics' Den." Here we see how modern archaeology has helped rescue the book of Daniel from its tormentors. A new understanding, a brilliant light, now penetrates many dark places of the past. Not only the existence but the identity of Belshazzar is clear. Important material on Darius and the friendship of Cyrus with Daniel will intrigue the reader.

Just before the first advent of Christ, the book of Daniel proved of great importance, identifying as it does the long expected Messiah. The prophecy of the seventy weeks found in Daniel chapter 9 positively identifies Jesus of Nazareth as the true Messiah, the Christ of the Holy Scriptures. However, Daniel 9 is only a part of a larger prophecy that actually begins in chapter 8. Its complete fulfillment reaches down to the period just before the second coming of Christ, the period Daniel speaks of as "the time of the end." The author of this volume believes that we are now living in that time.

Again, the book of Daniel becomes important because, while the prophecies of that great book do not give a definite date for Christ's second coming, they do reach down with awe-inspiring accuracy to the very days in which we live. The eleventh chapter of Daniel, with its remarkable fulfillment in history, has always proved a problem to exegetes. This author makes a strong case for his enlarged view. That this prophecy of Daniel 11 has been fulfilled by the literal events of history has been generally accepted by Bible students at least down to verse 36. After presenting the conflict between the rulers of Alexander's broken empire and their followers, the author then shows how the Republic of Rome, with Julius Caesar and other great men from the West, played a prominent part in subsequent history. The words recorded in Daniel have been fulfilled with marvelous accuracy.

Finally, in Daniel 11:36 to 12:4, the author sees a greater fulfillment than have many writers in the past. He envisions a worldwide application of these verses. The Ottoman Empire passed away in 1922 after allied intervention in the Turkish war on Greece. But Islam today is in the news. Mighty world changes are now taking place. New lineups and new divisions presage the time when demon spirits will take possession of human powers. These developments could lead to global government. Then the "dragon," "the beast," and the "false prophet" mentioned in the book of Revelation will have their day challenging the people of God.

Tensions in the East and near East, with growing world confusion, seem destined to lead into world conflict until at last the voice of God in heaven declares, "It is done!" Then His judgments will be poured out in seven-fold affliction that will surely bring the great confederacy of evil to collapse. As Daniel predicted, "He shall come to his end, and none shall help him."

The author wisely urges that we tread softly on unfulfilled prophecy. Remember the words of Jesus in John 13:19, "Now I tell you before it come, that, when it is come to pass, ye may believe that I am he." (See also John 14:29.)

From beginning to end, this book stresses the importance of the study of the prophecies of Daniel and Revelation by everyone privileged to be living in these "latter days." Earnest study of God's Word will bring blessing and spiritual growth through the grace of our Lord Jesus Christ. Only the power of His divine Spirit can give us what is needful in our preparation to meet the King in His glory with peace and joy.

H. M. S. Richards, Sr.

Introduction

Sir Isaac Newton, the great physicist, once said, "To reject Daniel is to reject the Christian religion."

A helpful study guide to the book of Daniel is Uriah Smith's work, *The Prophecies of Daniel and the Revelation.* It was written more than a hundred years ago, and much more is known today. The discoveries of recent times give one a different outlook on the Babylon of Daniel's day. Much light has been shed on that ancient world. Events and geographical places, which earlier critics and liberal theologians declared must be fictitious, have today been proved accurate and true.

Knowledge concerning Babylon has increased, thus giving us an overview not available to people of previous generations. But Daniel wrote more than history; half of his book is prophecy. And next in importance to a saving knowledge of our Lord and Savior is a knowledge of His prophetic program for our age and the coming age.

The world is being shaken to its foundations; civilization balances on the brink; "men's hearts [are] failing them for fear, and for looking after those things which are coming on the earth." For these times our Lord admonishes us to study "Daniel, the prophet." He said, "Whoso readeth, let him understand" (Matthew 24:15). Only those who understand the prophecies of Daniel and the Revelation can comprehend the issues we face in our generation. Daniel is the outstanding apocalypse of the Old Testament, as Revelation is of the New Testament.

Three times Daniel was called "greatly beloved" by Gabriel, the messenger of the God of heaven. One whose inspired counsel has meant much to us has well observed that "the book of Daniel is unsealed in the revelation to John, and carries us forward to the last scenes of this earth's history." "The light that Daniel received from God was given especially for these last days." "There is need of a much closer study of the word of God; especially should Daniel and the Revelation have attention as never before in the history of our work" (*Testimonies to Ministers,* pages 112, 113, 115).

"The Holy Spirit has so shaped matters, both in the giving of the prophecy and in events portrayed, as to teach that the human agent is to be kept out of sight, hid in Christ, and the Lord of heaven and His law are to be exalted. Read the book of Daniel. Call up, point by point, the history of the kingdoms there represented. Behold statesmen, councils, powerful armies, and see how God wrought to abase the pride of men, and lay human glory in the dust" (ibid., page 112).

To deal with every facet in the book of Daniel and keep within the scope of these chapters is not possible. But I hope that those who read these pages will do so with hearts bowed in humility and prayer, asking that the Holy Spirit, whom the author believes has guided in the research, may lead the reader to a deeper knowledge of Daniel's God. Praise be to His name!

Roy Allan Anderson

Unveiling the Prophecies of Daniel

1. Who Was Daniel the Prophet?

Daniel holds a place of unusual honor in sacred history. Of all the ancient Hebrew writers, this prophet-statesman stands out as unique. Not only did he profoundly influence his own generation, but his prophecies still have influence. His messages can mean even more to our own generation, living as we do just prior to our Lord's return.

Guided by the Holy Spirit, Daniel introduced a new type of revelation, which we speak of as apocalyptic prophecy. Rather than giving glimpses of isolated events, this kind of prediction takes in the whole sweep of history from ancient times to the end of the age. The book of Daniel is up-to-date; certain parts read like the headlines in our morning papers. Truly Daniel is the prophet for our day.

Jesus referred to him as "Daniel the prophet" and added, "Whoso readeth, let him understand." As Fenton translates it, "Let the reader comprehend" (Matthew 24:15).

To comprehend the message of Daniel we need to know something of the international scene of his day. The opening words of his book are significant: "In the third year of the reign of Jehoiakim king of Judah came Nebuchadnezzar king of Babylon unto Jerusalem, and besieged it. And the Lord gave Jehoiakim king of Judah into his hand" (Daniel 1:1, 2). Note that "the Lord *gave* Jehoiakim into his hand."

The year was 605 B.C., and this was the first of three invasions of Judah by Chaldean conquerors. Daniel and his companions, the only exiles mentioned by name, were among those first taken to Babylon. The second invasion occurred in 598 B.C., when a much larger group was deported. Among them was a young priest, Ezekiel, who later wrote the book that bears his name. In the final invasion, in 586 B.C., the last large group of exiles, together with the remaining temple treasures, were taken to Babylon. Then the invading army destroyed Solomon's magnificent temple and the city of Jerusalem.

TRAGEDY IN JERUSALEM

Those were tragic days for the Jews. What would we have thought had we been there witnessing wave after wave of heathen armies carrying away the strongest of the people as slaves and leaving the city of Jerusalem a heap of ruins? Fear and grief filled the hearts of the Jewish people as they saw their lavish house of worship, probably one of the most ornate and beautiful buildings the world had ever known, leveled to the ground. Such a thing need never have happened had the nation heeded the messages of God through the prophets, especially Jeremiah. Daniel was not more than eighteen years old—just a teenager—when he was snatched from his home and marched at least eight hundred miles to Babylon, the capital of idolatry. As far as we know, none of those first exiles ever saw his homeland again. The date of Daniel's birth could not have been later than 623 B.C. This coincided with the rise of the Neo-Babylonian kingdom, which, having conquered the warring empire of the Assyrians, quickly gained world renown.

SUNSET OF ASSYRIAN RULE

The last strong king of Assyria was Ashurbanipal, who died in 626 B.C. or possibly as early as 631 B.C. The last remnants of Assyrian power collapsed during the reign of the weak king Ashur-uballit, when the Babylonians marched against Syria to quiet a revolt there. Later they attacked Egypt in order to overthrow all opposition to the establishment of Babylon's universal rule.

These campaigns against Syria and Egypt were entrusted to Nebuchadnezzar, the crown prince of the expanding Neo-Babylonian Empire. Right at the time he was ready to invade Egypt, word reached him that his father, Nabopolassar, had died. He therefore hurried home to Babylon by the shortest route in order to secure to himself the throne, leaving some of his generals to superintend the march of the captives, including Daniel, over the long, eight-hundred-mile journey to Babylon.

Three years earlier, in 608 B.C., King Josiah, one of Judah's greatest leaders, had been fatally wounded on the field of battle close to Megiddo. During his long reign this noble king had done much to lead the nation back to God. He sought diligently to undo the trend toward heathenism of the fifty-seven shameless years of the two kings before him—his grandfather Manasseh and his father Amon.

THE LOST BOOK SPARKS A GREAT REVIVAL

Josiah came to the throne when but a boy of eight years. At sixteen he was soundly converted, and two years later he led one of the most far-reaching revivals in the history of the nation. He then gave orders to repair the temple, which had then stood for four centuries. While the workmen performed their tasks, they found the "book of the law." It had evidently been placed in one of the pillars of the temple. They brought it to Shaphan, the scribe, who took it to the king. Hearing the reading of the word of the Lord, Josiah was alarmed. In humility he called a convocation of the leaders of the nation. As they came together and listened to the book of the covenant, they, too, were convicted; and, following the lead of the king, they laid plans that resulted in the greatest Passover service ever recorded. (See 2 Kings 23:21–23; 2 Chronicles 35:1–9.)

Daniel was but a child at the time of this national revival, the effect of which, under King Josiah's leadership, carried over for many years. When this leader fell on the field of battle in 608 B.C. and his body was brought home for burial, Daniel was a youth of fifteen years. It is not hard to imagine the impression this tragedy had on his adolescent mind. A short time later, the whole nation entered into a memorial lament in Josiah's honor. Their sorrow was deep and lasting. But, sad to say, the effect of Josiah's devotion had little or no influence on his own sons.

A remnant of the nation's youth, however, remained true. Among these were young men of royal birth. Daniel and his companions were probably students in the Jerusalem school of the prophets and may have studied the Hebrew Scriptures under the guidance of leaders like Habakkuk, Jeremiah, Zephaniah, and Nahum. At any rate, they were "skilful in all wisdom" (Daniel 1:4).

The godly prophets and teachers bore witness for God and warned the people of coming national calamity. But apostate kings and false prophets opposed the messengers of the Lord and led the nation deeper into sin and idolatry until there was no remedy. (See 2 Chronicles 36:14–16.) Picture faithful Jeremiah going up and down the streets of Jerusalem wearing a yoke around his neck—a symbol of the tragedy that awaited the nation because of its defiant disobedience. He knew that the flower of its youth was destined to be captives and slaves in an alien land. But the leaders of the people gave little heed.

Daniel and his friends probably knew of the experiences of Hezekiah as recorded in Isaiah 39. Because of that king's vanity in showing the ambassadors from Babylon the treasures of his kingdom when he should have been giving glory to God and leading these visitors to a knowledge of Jehovah, Isaiah declared that his posterity would be "eunuchs in the palace of the king of Babylon" (Isaiah 39:7). We can almost hear godly teachers like Habakkuk saying, "Young men, this could and may well happen to you. But if you determine to be true and faithful to God, no matter what happens, He will make you strong witnesses for truth and righteousness, even in wicked Babylon."

Separation from families and teachers

When at last the Chaldeans came, we can imagine these earnest teachers throwing an arm around these boys as they said farewell, wishing them God's blessing as they witnessed for Him in an alien land. Try to imagine these young men, under the cruel command of their captors, beginning their long trek to the great metropolis. That surely would have been a tragic sight. But for Daniel and his three dedicated friends the challenge became their opportunity.

Their parents and teachers had prepared them well for whatever awaited them. Josiah's godly influence was, unfortunately, lost on his own sons, Jehoahaz, Jehoiakim, and Zedekiah, and his grandson, Jehoiachin, each of whom became king for a short time and each of whom chose to follow his own wicked way. While the effects of Josiah's revival were lost on his own sons, they were not lost on Daniel, Hananiah, Mishael, and Azariah, all of whom moved on to leadership even in the land of their servitude. The record of their fidelity to principle while facing sentences of death is recorded not only in the Old Testament; these men are mentioned by inference in Hebrews 11:33, 34 as men of faith.

Shortly after the death of Ashurbanipal, Nabopolassar, father of Nebuchadnezzar and commander-in-chief of the Chaldean armies in Babylonia, sensing the weak leadership of Ashurbanipal's sons, saw an opportunity to build up the ancient kingdom of Babylon. Having seceded from the Assyrian command, he set himself up as the new king of Babylonia. Later he entered into an alliance with Cyaxares I, king of the Medes. And that alliance was sealed by the king giving his daughter, Princess Amuhia, in marriage to the young Prince Nebuchadnezzar.

A few years prior to his first attack on Judah, Nabopolassar laid siege to the city of Ninevah, one-time capital of Assyria. It fell before the armies of Babylon and Media in 612 B.C. This marked the end of Assyria's ruthless rule, which for three centuries had terrorized surrounding nations.

Ashurbanipal's famous library was buried in the ruins and lay undiscovered for almost twenty-five hundred years, until Layard and others found it over a century ago. This ruin yielded a rich booty, especially the former library. Few other places have given so much aid to the science of archaeology.

The final collapse of the Assyrian kingdom left the whole area open. It was divided between Media and Babylonia. Cyaxares took all the northern section, while Nabopolassar laid claim to all the south, including Syria, Egypt, and Palestine. Judah, therefore, came under the jurisdiction of Babylon. Jehoiakim, king of Judah, was definitely pro-Egyptian, however, and foolishly felt that the nation's security depended upon Egypt rather than upon the living God. When Nebuchadnezzar besieged Jerusalem in 605 B.C., it was really to overthrow Egypt's influence in that area. Had Judah heeded the message of the prophets, how different would have been the history of the Jews. The Scripture records that the Lord gave Jehoiakim into the hand of Nebuchadnezzar, who reduced Judah to the status of a vassal state.

GOD'S PURPOSE WORKED OUT THROUGH BABYLON

International intrigues and rebellions were well known to young Daniel. When he and his royal companions were taken as hostages and made eunuchs in the service of the king of Babylon, it was no surprise but rather a fulfillment of Isaiah's prophecy uttered a hundred years earlier. Habakkuk, a decade or more earlier, had expressed his deep concern that the Lord seemed to be doing nothing to thwart the rising power of the Chaldeans. He reminded the Lord that spoiling and violence occurred everywhere and that wicked armies compassed the righteous. (See Habakkuk 1:2, 3.) But the Lord said to him, "Behold . . . I will work a work in your days, which ye will not believe, though it be told you. For, lo, I raise up the Chaldeans, that bitter and hasty nation, which shall march through the breadth of the land, to possess dwellingplaces that are not their's" (verses 5, 6). The prophet could not understand this. He wondered why it was permitted. But the Lord said He had "ordained them [the Chaldeans] for judgment" and "established them for correction" (verse 12).

Habakkuk was shown that what was to happen was in the purpose of an all-wise God. He doubtless passed on this message to the young people in his classes; when Nebuchadnezzar arrived at the gates of Jerusalem, young Prince Daniel understood why. How greatly he prized the words of Isaiah, Micah, Habakkuk, Jeremiah, and the other prophets. If he did not actually have the writings, he knew the contents of the prophets' messages.

Although exposed to the vice and corruption of an oriental court—and no other city was more vice-ridden than Babylon—Daniel maintained an unblemished life of practical holiness. And he lived a long life, extending from Nebuchadnezzar to Cyrus the Great. Jeremiah, Ezekiel, Ezra, and Zerubbabel were all his contemporaries. We do not know the year of his death, but he was at least eighty-eight years old when he read the handwriting on the wall of the Babylonian palace the night of Belshazzar's feast. He witnessed the invasion of the Persian army and was in his ninetieth year at least when thrown into the lions' den. He was honored with high office under Cyrus, king of Persia, and doubtless played an important role in influencing Cyrus to make the decree that permitted the Jews to return and rebuild the temple in Jerusalem. He may have watched the first caravan of rejoicing fellow countrymen as they left for the land of their fathers under the leadership of Zerubbabel and Joshua the high priest.

DANIEL THROUGH THE EYES OF CONTEMPORARIES

Ezekiel mentions Daniel as an outstanding example of righteousness, coupling his name with Noah and Job (see Ezekiel 14:14, 20). He also speaks of Daniel as a man of exceptional intelligence (see Ezekiel 28:3).

Josephus, the Hebrew historian, refers to Daniel's skill in architecture. His book is written partly in Aramaic and partly in Hebrew, there being six chapters in each language. He may well have lived to be a hundred years old. Today, the traveler to the acropolis of Susa (Shushan), one of the capitals of Elam (Daniel 8:2), is shown the supposed tomb of Daniel. While he was a great prophet, he did not come with a denunciation of specific sins and a plea for repentance as did others. But he did speak to his nation in an authoritative way. Never once did he use the regular formula, "Thus saith the Lord," for he spoke for God to a foreign court. He was statesman, prophet, and prime minister, first of Babylon and later of Media-Persia.

We can learn wonderful lessons from this spiritual giant. His life spanned almost a century, and nothing in his long and active life reveals more clearly his character than when, as a youth of eighteen, he "purposed in his heart that he would not defile himself with the portion of the king's meat, nor with the wine which he drank" (Daniel 1:8).

Eager to impress these brilliant young Judean captives and hasten their Chaldeanization, Nebuchadnezzar personally ordered their diet. This was, of course, part of a plan to change their lifestyle. To hasten this change, the four were given idolatrous names. Daniel, which means "God is my judge," was named Belteshazzar, "Bel protect his life"; Hananiah, "God is gracious," became Shadrach, "worship of the moon"; Mishael, "God has no equal," was given the name Meshach, "devotee of the moon god"; and Azariah was renamed Abednego, "a servant of Nego" (or "Nebo"). For some reason, Daniel's friends are subsequently known by these heathen names.

ROYAL CUISINE REFUSED

Sharing the bounties from the royal table was really a gracious act on the king's part. But these young men courteously refused it. They had been well trained at home and at school. To accept this provision would be to violate the food laws of Leviticus. Furthermore, they knew it was first offered to idols, perhaps to Marduk (Bel or Merodach), the chief god of Babylon. As spokesman for the group, Daniel requested Melzar, the chief steward, that they be given water instead of wine and "pulse," or vegetables, in place of the king's meat. The Hebrew word *zero'im*, "pulse," is rendered "vegetables" or "grains" in other translations. In Isaiah 61:11 the word reads "things that are sown."

God brought Daniel into favor and tender love with the prince of the eunuchs. The tactful approach of Daniel is a wonderful example of godly humility and wisdom. "Prove thy servants . . . ten days," he said. "Then let our countenances be looked upon before thee . . . : and as thou seest, deal with thy servants" (Daniel 1:12, 13). It was actually a case of clinical nutrition. And it worked. Their countenances were fairer; they were well nourished and alert. But it was not only the radiance of good health; it was the outshining of God's presence. Their bodies were, indeed, the temples of the Holy Spirit.

GOD-GIVEN KNOWLEDGE AND SKILL

No wonder Melzar permitted them to continue their plain diet. What a demonstration of living a life of restraint and temperance rather than sensual indulgence! With what result? God gave these four young men "knowledge and skill in all learning and wisdom" (verse 17). They underwent three years of study, and at the end of that time, when they stood before the king to be examined, Nebuchadnezzar, himself a trained Chaldean, "found them ten times better than all the magicians and astrologers that were in all his realm" (verse 20).

At eighteen, Daniel was a man of leadership, a fact he early proved. Had he not taken the lead, one might never have heard of the other three. He possessed an "excellent spirit" (Daniel 5:12), and because of his integrity and unswerving loyalty he proved he could be trusted with the secrets of kings. He served as Nebuchadnezzar's prime minister for perhaps forty years, and when Babylon fell, he became prime minister of Media-Persia. Daniel's strength was the strength of righteousness. What man in all history can equal this statesman-prophet in spiritual and political leadership?

2. Daniel at the Court of Babylon

In the Old Testament nothing adverse is recorded against either Joseph or Daniel. Both of them were taken from their homes at the tender age of seventeen or eighteen, and neither ever saw his homeland again. Both endured hardships as slaves, yet both rose to become prime minister of the empire in which they served.

Because these young men were destined for great leadership, God permitted hard experiences to help mold their characters. No one has better expressed the principles so essential in shaping great lives than has Angela Morgan:

WHEN GOD WANTS A MAN

When God wants to drill a man
And thrill a man and skill a man;
When God wants to mold a man
To play the noblest part;
When He yearns with all His heart
To create so great and bold a man
That all the world shall praise—
Watch His method, watch His ways!
How he ruthless perfects
Whom He royally elects;
How He hammers him and hurts him
And with mighty blows converts him
Into trial shapes of clay which only God can understand—
While his tortured heart is crying and he lifts beseeching hand!
How He bends, but never breaks,
When his good He undertakes—
How He uses whom he chooses
And with every purposes fuses him,
By every art induces him

To try his splendor out—
Yes, God knows what He's about.
When God wants to name a man
And fame a man and tame a man;
When God wants to shame a man
To do his heavenly best;
When He tries the highest test
That His reckoning may bring;
When He wants to make a king—

When the force that is divine
Leaps to challenge every failure and his ardor still is sweet
And love and hope are burning in the presence of defeat—

When the people need salvation
Doth he come to lead the nation.
Then to all God shows His plan
When the world has found—a man!

—Angela Morgan, adapted.

While Daniel served in positions of high service in a foreign land, he embodied truth and loyalty, adhered to principle, and was recognized even by his enemies as a master in statecraft.

- He was of royal birth through the line of King Hezekiah. Daniel 1:3; 2 Kings 20:17, 18.
- Neither money nor power could corrupt him. Daniel 5:17.
- King Nebuchadnezzar recognized his brilliance as a scholar. Daniel 1:18, 20.
- He permitted nothing to interfere with his regular periods of prayer. Daniel 6:10.
- He carried on his heart the spiritual needs of his whole nation. Daniel 9:3, 17, 18.
- Three times Gabriel bore witness that he was a man "greatly beloved." Daniel 9:23; 10:11, 19.

- Even jealous enemies testified to his blameless character. Daniel 6:4, 5.
- His courage and spiritual endowments were known to all. Daniel 5:10, 11; 6:10.
- Those closest to him recognized his "excellent spirit." Daniel 5:12; 6:3.
- During his lifetime his righteousness and wisdom were proverbial. Ezekiel 14:20; 28:3.
- Scripture ranks him with such stalwarts as Noah and Job. Ezekiel 14:19, 20.
- While serving in the court, he personally wrote part of the book that bears his name. Daniel 7:1.
- His messages influenced tremendously the later prophecies of Zechariah, Haggai, Paul, and John.
- His prophecies were recognized as authentic by Jesus, the greatest teacher of all time. Matthew 24:15.
- He was a student of "science" and a competent scholar when but a youth. Daniel 1:4.
- He was made chief of the foremost group of scholars in Babylon. Daniel 2:48.

In the school of science were also astrologers, magicians, and philosophers. They were later known as the magi. The magician school continued for many centuries. The wise men who came from the East to Bethlehem were evidently students of nature and were led to worship the newborn King. "They belonged to a large and influential class that included men of noble birth. . . . upright men who studied the indications of Providence in nature" (*The Desire of Ages*, page 59).

While Daniel was promoted as overseer of the wise men, there is no intimation that he ever participated in the superstitious rites of the Chaldeans. Never did he compromise his faith in God. In *A Manual of the Ancient History of the East,* Lenormant describes this elite group of priests, astrologers, and Chaldeans as "the absolute governing class in politics. . . . At the head of this hierarchy and cast was Archi-Magus . . . ; he was, next to the king, the chief personage in the empire."

Nebuchadnezzar elevated Daniel to this preeminent and authoritative position, as is made clear in Daniel 5:11.

Some readers may have the impression that Babylonian "wisdom" was little more than the pseudoscience of astrology and did not also include true astronomy. On this point George Stephen Goodspeed says of the Babylonians:

> The heavens were mapped out, and the courses of the heavenly bodies traced to determine the bearing of their movements upon human destinies. . . . The year of three hundred sixty-five and one-fourth days was known, though the common year was reckoned according to twelve months of thirty days each, and equated with the solar year by intercalating a month at the proper times. Tables of stars and their movements, of eclipses of moon and sun, were carefully prepared. The year began with the month Nisan (March-April); the day with the rising of the sun; the month was divided into weeks of seven days; the day from sunrise to sunrise into twelve double hours of sixty minutes. The clepsydra [water clock] and the sundial were Babylonian inventions for measuring time (*A History of the Babylonians and Assyrians,* pages 93, 94).

Two outstanding Babylonian astronomers were Nabu-rimannus and Kidinnu. The former collected records covering two hundred years and compiled tables of the sun's motions in relation to the moon. He also calculated the daily revolutions of the earth and measured the length of the year as 365 days, 6 hours, 15 minutes, 41 seconds. Two thousand years later the telescope revealed that his measurement of the year was only 26 minutes, 55 seconds too long. This splendid timetable is the earliest known recorded great constructive piece of astronomical science.

A little over a century later, Kidinnu made similar tables, which have been proven even more accurate. It has been said that these scientists from about the time of David "are entitled to a place among the greatest astronomers. . . . They became founders of astronomical science." Without a doubt some very remarkable scientific deductions were made in ancient Babylonia.

Morey, in his *Ancient Peoples,* says,

As they discovered the regular movements of the heavenly bodies, they acquired some knowledge of astronomical science. They marked out the constellations and gave names to the stars. They divided the year into months, weeks, days, hours, minutes, and seconds. They measured the hours of the day by the sundial, and they adopted the decimal notation; but they also used another system of notation, that is, a system based on the number sixty—which we have inherited from them in our division of the hour and the minute into sixty parts. Besides acquiring considerable knowledge of mathematics, the Babylonians were the first to devise a regular system of weights and measures.

The progress made by the early Babylonians in architecture, science, and the mechanic arts exercised a great influence upon later nations. Indeed, it would be difficult to overestimate the importance of these early steps in the world's civilization (pages 26, 27).

DANIEL'S PLACE AMONG THE SCIENTISTS OF HIS DAY

As we noticed, Daniel headed this group of Chaldean "wise men." In fact, he remained chief counselor to King Nebuchadnezzar for about forty years. The king himself was a Chaldean—a scholar. That is why he was able to examine Daniel and his companions.

In Daniel, then, we see not only a great statesman recognized by both the Babylonian and the Medo-Persian Empires but also a talented representative of the God who reveals secrets. With all the honors the world could give, however, he was also a humble servant of the Most High God. The messages he wrote and taught in his own generation were important, but those messages are even more vital to the present generation, for the things he foretold would happen in the "time of the end" are either in process of fulfillment now or will be in the very near future, for the end of all things is at hand.

EZEKIEL'S ESTIMATE OF DANIEL

Ezekiel, a contemporary of Daniel, was another Jewish captive in

Babylon. He belonged to the priestly line, while Daniel was of the royal line. Ezekiel, who was younger than Daniel, had the unusual opportunity to observe him at close range. Ezekiel was called of God to the office of both prophet and priest. He began his ministry some fourteen years after Daniel's arrival in Babylon, so at the time Ezekiel began to write Daniel was about forty years old. At the time Ezekiel wrote of him, Daniel could have been close to fifty. Certain critics declare Daniel would have been too young to have earned such a reputation as we find recorded in Ezekiel 28:3. Writing of Lucifer, Ezekiel says, "Behold thou art wiser than Daniel; there is no secret that they can hide from thee." But as a chosen messenger of God, Daniel had plenty of time to demonstrate his wisdom and knowledge. Moreover, he earned that reputation in a land that boasted greater wisdom than any previous generation. The Chaldean wise men, of whom Daniel proved wiser than any, were recognized as the most famous and knowledgeable in the ancient world. We can well imagine what it meant to the Jewish captives, slaves, for the most part, to know of Daniel's presence in the highest councils of the empire. To know that at the head of the state and the "university" stood one of their own must have been wonderfully reassuring. He was their representative, their influential patron, loved by God and by the people.

As a priest (also a prophet) among the exiles, Ezekiel was probably settled in the community of Tel-abib on the canal Chebar, a short distance from the capital. (See Ezekiel 3:15.) Delivering his divine warnings (verse 17), he too probably heard of what Daniel was doing at the administrative headquarters. And it was this younger messenger of God who linked the name of Daniel with the great righteous men of other days—Job and Noah. (See Ezekiel 14:14, 20.) True, Daniel was young when he became chief counselor to the king, but that was because he demonstrated so wonderfully his unusual God-given gifts when but twenty-one years old. However, when Ezekiel wrote of him he had reached the zenith of his power and fame. Ezekiel may have had opportunity to see personally the evidence of Daniel's greatness and esteem.

CAPTIVE JEWS REBUILD BABYLON

The Jewish exiles played a great part in the rebuilding of the city of Babylon. It became the most ornate city of the ancient world, with its temples and palaces planned and inspired by Nebuchadnezzar. While he was their conqueror, he permitted the exiles to live in colonies of their own, where they could carry out their religious customs. In fact, during these captivity years the synagogue came into being. There were no such places as synagogues before the Babylonian captivity. Ezekiel speaks of a "little sanctuary" that many believe has reference to the synagogue.

Jeremiah was not numbered among these exiles. He still lived in Jerusalem when he urged the exiles to build their own houses and serve their masters. (See Jeremiah 29:5–7.) He foretold that they would remain in captivity for seventy years. (See verse 10.) Yet while living in a foreign land, they were still permitted to live as families. Daniel and his companions, however, had no such privilege.

Although living at the court, they, like the whole nation of Judah, were victims of God's judgment. But the judgments upon these young men were especially severe. The Scripture declares that Daniel and his three companions were princes, members of the royal family. They were born to rule and, as fathers of families, to guide their children in the ways of God. But instead they were destined to live as eunuchs in the service of their captors. When divine wrath is visited on a nation, the innocent suffer with the guilty. It has often been so.

More than a hundred years before Nebuchadnezzar came to power, Isaiah told King Hezekiah that because of his failure to represent the God of heaven rightly, when the ambassadors came to him from Babylon, his sons would be "eunuchs in the palace of the king of Babylon" (Isaiah 39:7). And this is exactly what Daniel and his companions were—emasculated men with no hope of family or posterity. Think of what this meant to a genius like Daniel. Bred in the expectation of princely responsibility and sovereignty, he at last found himself destined to spend his life in the service of a heathen monarch in a foreign land!

The tragedy of Judah's national sin was compounded a thousand times as the parents were forced to see what happened to the flower of their youth. But with it all, these four young men, of whom Daniel was leader, remained noble examples of true knowledge and righteous living. By diligent study they prepared themselves for whatever places of trust they might be called to fulfill, and all four of them rose to positions of responsibility.

Unveiling Daniel and Revelation

During Nebuchadnezzar's invasion of the Holy Land, Jeremiah was left in Jerusalem. He continued as the great prophetic figure to the nation already suffering divine judgments. On the other hand, Ezekiel prophesied to the exiles already in Babylon while Daniel served as prophet-statesman at this seat of political power. What a tremendous role he played in keeping the vision of the future clear to the captives! And not to them alone but also to the Babylonians themselves, many of whom will no doubt inhabit the kingdom of glory because of Daniel's faithful witness.

Did Daniel write the book of Daniel? Jesus spoke of him as the "prophet." (See Matthew 24:15.) The Lord did not refer to him as a forger or a deceiver. Nor did He imply that some other person had written the book that bears Daniel's name.

In his book *Observations Upon the Prophecies of Daniel and the Apocalypse of St. John,* Sir Isaac Newton says, "Whoever rejects the prophecies of Daniel does as much as if he undermined the Christian religion, which so to speak, is founded on Daniel's prophecies of Christ."

Josephus, the noted Jewish historian, declared that the prophet-statesman himself wrote the book. In *Antiquities of the Jews,* 10:11:7, he says: "All these things did this man leave in writing, as God had showed them to him, insomuch that such as read his prophecies, and see how they have been fulfilled, would wonder at the honour wherewith God honoured Daniel."

DANIEL'S INFLUENCE ON GREEK HISTORY

Josephus relates a moving incident in the life of Alexander that involved the book of Daniel. After telling how the nation was filled with fear when the Jewish people heard that Alexander was making his way to Jerusalem, Josephus says, "Now Alexander, when he had taken Gaza, made haste to go up to Jerusalem; and Jaddua the high priest, when he heard that, was in an agony, and under terror, as not knowing how he should meet the Macedonians. . . . [But] God warned him in a dream . . . that he should take courage, and adorn the city, and open the gates; that the rest should appear in white garments, but that he and the priests should meet the king in the habits proper to their order, without the dread of any ill consequences, which the providence of God would prevent. . . . Alexander, when he saw the multitude at a distance, in white garments, while the priests stood clothed with fine linen, and the high priest in purple and scarlet clothing, with his mitre on his head, having the golden plate whereon the name of God was engraved, he approached by himself, and adored that name, and first saluted the high priest." In explanation of his act, he said, " 'I saw this very person in a dream, in this very habit, when I was at Dios in Macedonia. . . . [And] I believe that I bring this army under the Divine conduct, and shall therewith conquer Darius.' . . . And he came into the city. And when he went up into the temple, he offered sacrifice to God, according to the high priest's direction, and magnificently treated both the high priest and the priests. And when the Book of Daniel was shown him, wherein Daniel declared that one of the Greeks should destroy the empire of the Persians, he supposed that himself was the person intended." (*Antiquities of the Jews,* 11:8.)

The prophecies of Daniel (chapters 7 and 8) so impressed Alexander, the Macedonian conqueror, that he became the protector of the Jews throughout his whole realm. And this occurred a century and a half before the date (165 B.C.) which Porphyry and the critics of our day assign to the writing of the book of Daniel!

While Daniel was writing his prophecies, he was prime minister of the empire that ruled the world and the acknowledged head of the Chaldean hierarchy, next to the king. Yet all the while that he was carrying such tremendous responsibility as a statesman, he remained a loyal, dedicated messenger of the living God, one who, though exalted, did not forget his Hebrew companions.

"Then the king gave Daniel high honors and many great gifts, and made him ruler over the whole province of Babylon, and chief prefect over all the wise men of Babylon. Daniel made request of the king, and he appointed Shadrach, Meshach, and Abednego over the affairs of the province of Babylon; but Daniel remained at the king's court" (Daniel 2:48, 49, RSV).

It has been truly said, "History follows the mold set for it by Daniel." The events of thousands of years have verified that his prophecies were truly of God.

3. Daniel in the Critics' Den

About two hundred years ago certain scholars of the rationalistic school attacked the book of Daniel. They said it is unreliable, both historically and prophetically. Because of a lack of correlative evidence concerning certain events recorded by Daniel, and also because of the prophet's predictions, they claimed the book could never have been written as prophecy, for no man knows the future. It must, therefore, have been written as history, and the writer, in order to gain prestige, used the name of Daniel.

The argument was not new. Porphyry, a neoplatonic philosopher and Greek historian born in Tyre in A.D. 233, had made the same claim.

PORPHYRY'S ATTACK ON CHRISTIANITY

Enamored with the teachings of Plotinus, Porphyry gave himself to special study and later became a lecturer on philosophy in Rome. Defending polytheism and the worship of the popular gods, he set himself to the task of destroying all that opposed it. Christianity, therefore, he violently attacked. He wrote on many subjects, but his best known works are fifteen books under the title *Adversus Cristianos (Against the Christians)*. Books 12 and 13 of this set are a bitter criticism of Daniel. And, strange as it may seem, his arguments still form the basis of theologians' attacks on Daniel.

His ideas were not accepted by all. This is evident from the fact that Emperor Theodosius II ordered, in A.D. 435 and again in A.D. 448, Porphyry's books to be destroyed publicly. From that time until the rise of German rationalism, around the middle of the eighteenth century, little was heard of this anti-Christian philosopher. However, when renewed attacks were made to discredit divine revelation—with claims that naturalism and reason are the only safe sources of knowledge—Porphyry's arguments were early picked up. In a few years his ideas echoed again in the classrooms. It was claimed, for example, that the book is really a forgery, a kind of religious novel, unreliable as history and impossible as prophecy. No man can foretell the future, declared Porphyry and his followers. Poor Porphyry! How little he and those who accepted his false teachings knew of the multiplied evidences that were to be unearthed in our day!

Theologians who deny the authenticity of the book of Daniel say that it must have been written about 165 B.C. during the Maccabean period. They assign it a place in the Jewish pseudepigrapha—a group of doubtful writings by unknown, uninspired authors, such as *The Fourth Book of Ezra, The Testament of the Twelve Patriarchs, The Assumption of Moses, The Ascension of Isaiah, The Odes of Solomon, The Testament of Abraham, The Testament of Adam,* and *The Apocalypse of Baruch.* The writers of these books used the names of Old Testament worthies in order to get their works accepted. They claimed to have visions and used apocalyptic symbols.

To place Daniel in this group reveals a pathetic ignorance of both the man and his message. Evidence in the book itself shows that the prophet Daniel wrote the book in the sixth century B.C. But "liberal" theology declares that it did not appear until the second century B.C., four hundred years later.

What is the purpose behind these claims? Certain critical scholars are desirous of stripping the Bible of everything supernatural or miraculous, leaving it merely a human production. To them, the book of Daniel is the most vulnerable book of the sacred canon because it contains so much of the supernatural—so many visions, so many miracles, so many unusual happenings. These critical scholars, of course, rule out predictive prophecy.

We would not condemn all biblical criticism. Much good has come as men have sought to understand the true history of the writers and their writings. In recent years we note with appreciation a new trend toward a reverent, believing approach rather than the virtual abandonment of the sacred Scriptures. Every Bible-believing Christian can appreciate this. But in spite of these trends, many scholars still cling to the claims of earlier writers. Many sincerely believe that the book of Daniel is a product of the second century B.C. rather than of the sixth.

The things which most challenged Porphyry some 250 years after Christ were the prophecies of Daniel. They were so accurate up to the time of his writing that he said they could not possibly have been written in advance. But what about all the centuries since? These, too, were foretold in Daniel's prophecies, some much more remarkable than those preceding Porphyry. In fact, prophecy is found in many books of the Word of God. Not only is prophecy predictive; it is also exhortative. While it unveils the future, it also leads men to live lives of justice and righteousness.

THE BIBLE, A BOOK OF PROPHECY

Genuine prophecy is, however, unique to the Word of God. Other religions have their sacred books or scriptures; and, while some contain fine exhortations, none accurately foretells the future. If they did, their mistakes and guesses would soon reveal them to be spurious, for only the living God, the God of the Bible, knows the future. In fact, He stakes His deity on His ability to predict what is yet to happen. These words written by the prophet Isaiah, more than a hundred years before Daniel's day, set forth the claims of the living God: "Remember the former things of old: for I am God, and there is none else; I am God, and there is none like me, Declaring the end from the beginning, and from ancient times the things that are not yet done, saying, My counsel shall stand, and I will do all my pleasure" (Isaiah 46:9, 10). Again: "Who hath declared this from ancient time? who hath told it from that time? have not I the LORD? and there is no God else beside me; a just God and a Saviour" (Isaiah 45:21). As we pursue our study of Daniel's book, we will see how clearly the Lord foretold the future.

When Daniel, the young Hebrew captive, stood before Nebuchadnezzar, he declared, "There is a God in heaven that revealeth secrets, and maketh known to the king . . . what shall . . . come to pass hereafter" (Daniel 2:28, 29). The Judeo-Christian religion is either a revealed religion recording the past and foretelling the future or it is nothing at all. The ancient Hebrew prophets—Daniel, Jeremiah, Moses, and Isaiah—possessed both insight and foresight. They were both forthtellers and foretellers. Peter says, "For the prophecy came not in old time by the will of man: but holy men of God spake as they were moved by the Holy Ghost" (2 Peter 1:21). Daniel was one of these "holy men" who spoke and wrote under the guidance of the Holy Spirit.

In that same letter the apostle Peter refers to his experience with James and John in the holy mount when Christ was transfigured before them. They saw His glory and heard the Father's voice declaring, "This is my beloved Son, . . . hear ye him" (Matthew 17:5). But Peter says, "We have also a more sure word of prophecy; whereunto ye do well that ye take heed, as unto a light that shineth in a dark place" (2 Peter 1:19). What! More sure than what one sees and hears? Yes. The testimonies of the prophets are more sure than our senses. Yet certain critics seem determined to destroy the prophetic elements of the Bible.

Our Savior proved His messianic ministry not only by His miracles but by the prophecies of the Old Testament. And in Gabriel's message to Daniel, the very time when our Lord was to begin His miraculous ministry was clearly revealed. Moreover, Jesus knew it, for we read in Mark 1:14, 15, "Jesus came into Galilee, preaching the gospel of the kingdom of God, And saying, The time is fulfilled, and the kingdom of God is at hand." What time was fulfilled? The time specified in Daniel 9:25, 26. (This prophecy is the basis of chapter 12 of this book.) In His first sermon in Nazareth after returning from His baptism by John, Jesus declared that He was fulfilling prophecy. (See Luke 4:21.) Then, on the evening of His resurrection, having made a surprise entrance to the upper room where His disciples huddled together for fear of the Jews, the Savior said, "These are the words which I spake unto you, while I was yet with you, that all things must be fulfilled, which were written in the law of Moses, and in the prophets, and in the psalms, concerning me" (Luke 24:44).

Our Lord's first advent was foretold in marvelous detail in scores of prophecies. But Porphyry and the naturalistic critics of our time cannot accept prophecy as a possibility. So they reject the books of prophecy, such as Daniel and the Revelation, in the name of scholarship.

They reject Daniel not only because of the prophecies but also because they allege that the history is unreliable. Let us examine just a few of the claims of these critics. The opening verses of Daniel speak of Nebuchadnezzar, king of Babylon, besieging Jerusalem in the reign of Jehoiakim. The critics used to say this is an error, for the event took place before Nebuchadnezzar's father, Nabopolassar, died. Therefore Nebuchadnezzar was not king of Babylon. But Jeremiah speaks of Nebuchadnezzar in the same way (see Jeremiah 27:6). Daniel wrote his opening verses using his knowledge of current history at a time when Nebuchadnezzar *was* king.

Another criticism of Daniel's historic record concerns the spelling of the name Nebuchadnezzar. The critics say it should have been spelled *Nebuchadrezzar,* with an "r" as it is in Ezekiel. (See Ezekiel 29:19; 30:10.) But Daniel spells it exactly as it is found in the books of Kings, Chronicles, Ezra, and Jeremiah. In fact, Jeremiah sometimes spells it as in Daniel and sometimes as in Ezekiel. A number of ancient history names in Scripture are spelled in varied forms. As an example, take the Syrian monarch mentioned in 2 Kings 15:29. There his name is spelled *Tiglath-pileser.* But in 1 Chronicles 5:26 he is called *Tiglath-pilneser.* Other examples could be given. The critics themselves know that the transliteration of names from the Babylonian cuneiform into Hebrew or Aramaic sometimes varies. Literally, *Nebuchadnezzar* is *Nabu-kudarri-ussar,* meaning "Nabu protect the succession rights." In any case, the change from an "r" to an "n" is insignificant, giving no evidence for late authorship of Daniel's book as Porphyry claimed.

ARCHAEOLOGY CONFIRMS DANIEL'S RECORD

The critics also question Daniel's use of the word "Chaldeans." Daniel speaks of them as astrologers and magicians, but critics have claimed that the word "Chaldean" referred to the nation of Babylon, not to a class of astrologers. Let us look at the facts. About a century after Daniel wrote, Herodotus visited Babylon, and he referred to the Chaldeans just as Daniel did. The critics must surely have overlooked Daniel's own words in chapter 5, verse 30, and chapter 9, verse 1, where he also refers to the king or the realm of the Chaldeans. Archaeological evidence shows the Chaldeans as a priestly caste, the elite of Babylon, and dedicated to the worship of the god Bel (Marduk).

What we know of the Chaldeans today corroborates Daniel's description in detail.

As we noted before, part of Daniel's book was written in Hebrew and part in Aramaic. This fact gave critics another occasion to place its writing in the second century, alleging that the Aramaic of Daniel is late Palestinian, not sixth century. But when the records of Qumran were discovered, they contained scrolls written in Aramaic of the Maccabean period, at which time the critics declare Daniel was written. But the second century Aramaic in the scrolls is quite different from that of Daniel. Even more convincing are the Elephantine papyri, dated in the fifth century B.C., shortly after Daniel wrote. The Aramaic of these documents corresponds closely to Daniel's.

One of the critics' strongest points related to the four empires of Daniel's prophecies. Building on Porphyry's premise that Daniel is history, not prophecy, they claim that the succession of empires is not Babylon, Media-Persia, Greece, and Rome, but Babylon, Media, Persia, and Greece. Rome, they argue, had not become a world empire in Daniel's day, whereas Greece was the dominant power in the second century B.C. But they overlook the fact that Media and Persia were actually one empire when Babylon was overthrown. It was Media-Persia that took the stage of world dominion in 539 B.C. The Medes joined the Persians in 550 B.C., and the two became a united empire years before they marched against Babylon. Media-Persia was indeed the second of the world empires outlined in Daniel, chapters 2, 7, 8, and 11.

BELSHAZZAR EMERGES FROM BURIED CITIES

Daniel's mention of Belshazzar as the last king of Babylon has provided a major point of attack by the critics. Until recent years no other historical evidence confirmed the existence of a king named Belshazzar. This, the critics said, betrayed the ignorance of the writer and exposed the book as fiction. Ancient secular sources, known to scholars, indicated that Nabonidus, not Belshazzar, was the last king of Babylon. And Nabonidus was not killed; Cyrus captured him in Tema, northern Arabia. So Belshazzar was Exhibit A in the case against Daniel. But archaeologists have turned the tables. Today, evidence shows not only that Belshazzar lived but that he fulfilled the exact role recorded by Daniel. True, Nabonidus was his father, but from the third year of his reign, 553 B.C., Nabonidus shared the sovereignty with his elder son, Belshazzar, until the night Belshazzar died at the hands of the Persians. (See Daniel 5.)

A crowning piece of evidence is a clay tablet bearing the names of both Nabonidus and Belshazzar as reigning kings.

Belshazzar's name in Babylonian cuneiform is *Bel-shar-usur,* "Bel, protect the king." He was still a young man when he gathered his nobles for a blasphemous banquet. He had been a mere lad when he had witnessed Nebuchadnezzar's return to the throne after seven years of insanity.

During these years Nabonidus, later to become king, was an officer in the court of Babylon, so from his earliest years Belshazzar was accustomed to the throne and the protocol of royalty. When Belshazzar was twenty years old, Nabonidus, after some intrigue, ascended the throne and for the next seventeen years reigned as king of Babylon. For thirteen of those years he shared rulership with his son Belshazzar.

Just prior to the entry of the invading army, Daniel was brought in to read the letters of fire, so boldly traced on the wall, that told the doom of the kingdom. The wise men, the astrologers, the Chaldeans, together with the soothsayers or spiritualists, were unable to interpret the writing. When God's prophet appeared, the king told him that if he could interpret the message he would be made "the third ruler in the kingdom" (Daniel 5:16). Why not the second ruler? The answer is simple. Belshazzar himself was already the second, as co-ruler with his father, Nabonidus.

Yes, the evidence concerning Belshazzar is so convincing today that no well-informed student of Babylonian history would doubt either his existence or his kingship. He was, in truth, the last king of Babylon, his father having gone to Tema at an earlier time.

Cyrus moved with his army toward the seat of the empire and overran the kingdom. The events of his conquest were recorded on the Nabunaid Chronicle. We should note in passing that when a heavenly messenger wrote on the palace wall, the interpretation said that the kingdom is "given to the Medes and Persians," (verse 28), not to the Medes alone as the critics claim. We have already noted the attempt to make Media the second of the four successive empires outlined by Daniel. But history shows that the Persians were united with the Medes in their conquest. In fact, the Persians were the stronger of the two kingdoms. This was clearly indicated in chapter 7 in the symbol of the bear that raised itself up on one side. Also, in chapter 8 we have the symbol of the ram with two horns, one higher than the other. If, as the critics claim, Persia was the third empire in the succession, how could it have been represented in chapter 7 by a leopard with four heads or in chapter 8 by a goat with four horns? Was Persia ever so divided? Strange the lengths to which men will go in their efforts to prove that Daniel did not write prophecy but only recorded history under the guise of prophecy.

Dr. E. B. Pusey, in the introduction to his work *Lectures on Daniel the Prophet,* says, "The book of Daniel is especially fitted to be a battle field in faith and unbelief. It admits no half measures. It is either Divine or an imposture." The tragedy is that the assailants, the critics, are not usually avowed enemies of Christianity but often professors in seminaries who train the preachers of tomorrow.

FOUR CHALLENGING QUESTIONS

It is tragic how far some critics will go in the name of scholarship until every prophecy, every miracle, and almost every historic event recorded in the book of Daniel is either ridiculed or ripped from the record. We would like to ask four questions that demand clear answers:

1. If the book of Daniel was a forgery, how did it get into the Old Testament canon? References from the books of Maccabees (*c.* 165 B.C.) indicate that Daniel was then a part of the canon of Scripture. (See 1 Maccabees 2:51–60; cf. Daniel 1:7; 3:26; 6:23.)

2. If the book of Daniel was not written until 165 B.C., how was it ever included in the Septuagint? This great translation has been assigned by some to the third century B.C., long before 165 B.C., the date some scholars ascribe to Daniel.

3. Why do the critics say Daniel's reference to the doctrine of the resurrection dates the writing? According to their claim, this doctrine was not known in the sixth century. Yet, one of the clearest statements in Scripture concerning the resurrection is found in Job 19:25, 26, possibly the oldest book in the Bible. Then what about Isaiah 26:19? "Thy dead men shall live, together with my dead body shall they arise." Isaiah wrote at least 150 years before Daniel.

4. Who was the man of genius who penned this book foretelling the future of our planet and declaring the year the Messiah would begin His ministry? Daniel also predicted the scattering of the Jews by the Romans and the apostasy of a great anti-Christian power of later centuries. If this was not Daniel, who was it?

In the days of the Maccabees, when the critics say the book was written, the people lamented that there was no prophet in the land and that there was great tribulation in Israel, and "no prophet appeared" (1 Maccabees 9:27). Yet, critics say this book of Daniel appeared to be written in 165 B.C.! We ask, Who wrote it? An "unknown, pious Jew" writing in the days of Antiochus Epiphanes?

W. A. Criswell has stated it well: "They [the critics] cannot hold up their heads in the white light of the historic past."

And Joseph P. Free gives this lucid statement:

> There is no first rate liberal today, as far as the writer knows, who urges the old objection concerning Belshazzar. . . .
>
> The detailed facts are that Nabonidus, in one sense the last king of Babylon, was not killed by the invading Persians, but was given a pension by his conquerors. On the other hand, Belshazzar, elevated to the position of ruler of Babylon by his father, was killed when the city of Babylon was taken, as indicated in Daniel 5:20. The matter concerning Belshazzar, far from being an error in the Scriptures, is one of the many striking confirmations of the Word of God which have been demonstrated by archaeology (*Archaeology and Bible History*, page 235).

When Daniel served as prime minister of Media-Persia after Babylon's fall, the critics of his day had him thrown into the lions' den in order to get rid of him. He was, at that time, about ninety years old. Can we imagine what it would be like to spend the night with great hungry cats? The next morning when the king asked, "Is thy God . . . able to deliver thee from the lions?" Daniel answered with assurance: "My God hath sent his angel, and hath shut the lions' mouths, that they have not hurt me" (Daniel 6:20–22).

The same God who shut the mouths of those savage beasts and spared the life of His prophet lives still, and in many ways He exposes the crumbling foundation upon which the critic's arguments rest. He who delivered His faithful servant long ago is again delivering Daniel from his "enemies" as archaeology and history confirm the accuracy of his writings. The stones of a hundred buried cities shout in the ears of an unbelieving world, "God's Word is truth!" All the critics put together, from Porphyry's time until now, could never produce one chapter of Daniel's book. God gave him the vision and then guided his mind as he wrote the prophecies.

4. Prophetic Panorama of History to Be

As we begin the study of the second chapter of Daniel, let us note again the second verse of chapter 1. "The Lord *gave* Jehoiakim king of Judah into his [Nebuchadnezzar's] hand." Why did Israel's God make such a gift? Obviously to punish His people for their continued blasphemous iniquity. But there was an even deeper purpose. God delivered Israel from Egyptian slavery and placed them in Canaan that they might be His light bearers to the world. "I have endowed him with my spirit," said Jehovah, "to carry true religion to the nations" (Isaiah 42:1, Moffatt). But Israel never measured up to that responsibility. Instead, they hedged themselves about in the Land of Promise, caring little about the surrounding nations who, in their darkness and superstition, continued their idolatrous worship.

ISRAEL'S FAILURE TO FULFILL GOD'S PURPOSE

When Israel failed to carry out its God-given responsibility, the Lord permitted a heathen monarch to invade Jerusalem and take His people captive. Seeing the finest of Judah's youth, such as Daniel and his companions, wrenched from their homes and taken as slaves into Babylon was a terrible shock to the Jews. Doubtless many asked if God had forgotten His promise. No, He had not forgotten, but He had to adapt His plan so as to carry out His original purpose. An all-seeing providence has, through the centuries, been at work permitting the rise and fall of nations and even the overthrow of His own people as a nation.

In the annals of human history, the growth of nations, the rise and fall of empires, appear as if dependent on the will and prowess of man; the shaping of events seems, to a great degree, to be determined by his power, ambition, or caprice. But in the word of God the curtain is drawn aside, and we behold, above, behind, and through all the play and counterplay of human interest and power and passions, the agencies of the All-merciful One, silently, patiently working out the counsels of His own will (Ellen G. White, *Prophets and Kings,* pages 499, 500).

In no other portion of the Bible are these principles more profoundly portrayed than in the second chapter of Daniel. There the whole sweep of history from Daniel's day to our own time and beyond is clearly presented. This fascinating story focuses on a confrontation between two young men—one a slave, the other a king. And this confrontation came about in a strange, but simple, way. The king had a dream; not an unusual thing, especially in that land where the meaning of dreams meant so much. But the impression on the mind of this monarch was profound, so much so that he determined to know its meaning.

FAILURE OF BABYLON'S WISE MEN

A whole retinue of "wise men"—astrologers, magicians, spirit mediums, clairvoyants—peopled the court of Babylon. The king employed them for the very purpose of unraveling mysteries. Sure, they insisted that they could tell Nebuchadnezzar the meaning of his dream. But there was one big problem—the king had forgotten the dream, although he was sure it was important. The God of heaven had made his mind a blank to the details of the dream in order that these so-called "wise men" could not give Nebuchadnezzar a false interpretation.

When the frustrated king summoned his counselors, these educators, these mind readers, these stargazers, all failed. They assured him, however, that if he told them what he had seen they would be able to give the interpretation. The more these men hedged, the more impatient the king became. But they continued to tell him that his demand was not only unreasonable but impossible. Only "the gods, whose dwelling is not with flesh" (Daniel 2:11), could give him the answer. In that they were right. But their failure infuriated the king, who charged them with speaking "lying and corrupt words" (verse 9). The limitations of these palace aides had become all too evident. In his rage the king blurted out, in essence, "There is only one end for all of you. I will have you destroyed." It was a brutal decision, but in keeping with the practice of ancient dictators. So the executioners made ready to carry out the order.

Daniel and his companions, as comparatively recent arrivals, were evidently not consulted, but they were numbered among the Babylonian wise men. When the executioners came to inform Daniel of the situation, he asked, "Why is the decree so hasty from the king?" (verse 15). He then requested an audience with the monarch. Daniel promised that if given time he would tell the dream and also the interpretation. Thus he staked his life upon God's promise to hear his prayer. Failure to keep his word would, he knew, bring terrible retribution. He told the king he had not the slightest notion concerning the dream, but he knew Someone who did know. He had faith. His request was granted.

And what did Daniel do? He called his companions, and together they laid the matter before the living God—One who never fails to honor those who put their trust in Him. They spent the night in prayer, and during the silent watches the Lord revealed the dream to Daniel in a vision. He also gave him its meaning and its message.

Before sharing it with the king, Daniel remembered to thank God:

> Blessed be the name of God for ever and ever: for wisdom and might are his: And he changeth the times and the seasons: he removeth kings, and setteth up kings: he giveth wisdom unto the wise, and knowledge to them that know understanding: He revealeth the deep and secret things: he knoweth what is in the darkness, and the light dwelleth with him. I thank thee, and praise thee, O thou God of my fathers, who hast given me wisdom and might, and hast made known unto me now what we desired of thee: for thou hast now made known unto us the king's matter (verses 20–23).

Some have seen in Daniel's prayer the influence of Habakkuk's revelation of God. Godly teachers can leave lasting impressions on young men. Fellowship and communion in prayer is one of life's richest experiences. When the apostles of the New Testament came together and prayed, the very walls of the building were shaken. True prayer can be the greatest power known to man. Daniel could have prayed alone, but he sought the companionship of his friends. There is great power in prayer fellowship.

DANIEL MEETS THE KING'S DEMAND

The next day, instead of being brought before the executioners, Daniel stands before the king. Erect in the presence of royalty, he unfolds the message that changes the whole atmosphere. Without the slightest indication of boasting, Daniel tells God's message to the ruthless ruler of much of the then-known world.

"Art thou able to make known unto me the dream which I have seen," asks Nebuchadnezzar, "and the interpretation thereof?" (verse 26).

Quickly turning the question from himself to his Lord, Daniel reminds the king that the astrologers, the magicians, even the whole retinue of soothsayers have been unable to meet his demand. "But," Daniel declares, "there is a God in heaven that revealeth secrets, and maketh known to the king Nebuchadnezzar what shall be in the latter days" (verse 28). He also makes clear to the king that "this secret is not revealed to me for any wisdom that I have more than any living" (verse 30). Then young Daniel focuses the monarch's mind on the God of heaven, but before revealing the dream he has one request: "Destroy not the wise men of Babylon" (verse 24).

Nothing more completely reveals the character of Daniel. As did the Savior he represented, he prays for those who do not worship the true God. The wise men naturally were jealous of Daniel's wisdom, for Nebuchadnezzar had already pronounced him and his companions "ten times better" in matters of wisdom and understanding "than all the magicians and astrologers that were in all his realm" (Daniel 1:20).

Picture the king listening spellbound to this twenty-one-year-old wise man who says, "Thou, O king, sawest, and behold a great image," a mighty colossus, "whose brightness was excellent, . . . and the form thereof was terrible. This image's head was of fine gold, his breast and arms of silver, his belly and his thighs of brass, His legs of iron, his feet part of iron and part of clay" (verses 31–33). Then he tells the king, "While you looked, a stone was hewn from a mountain, not by human hands; it struck the image on its feet of iron and clay and shattered them" (verse 34, NEB). And the king's memory reconstructs the scene as this mighty metal-and-mud man crumbles to pieces; he sees the shattered remains swept away by a strong wind, leaving the place as clean as a summer threshing floor.

THE KING LISTENS SPELLBOUND

But this is not all. "The stone that smote the image became a great mountain, and filled the whole earth" (verse 35). We can almost hear the king saying to himself, "Yes, that is exactly what I saw. Nothing added. Nothing left out. But does it have any meaning?"

Yes, it certainly has meaning, and not only for Nebuchadnezzar but for every ruler and every person down to the end of time. Entranced, the king listens as Daniel continues. "This is the dream; and we will tell the interpretation thereof" (verse 36). The young prophet tactfully tells the king that his empire came into being not because of the strength of his well-trained armies, but because it was all in the purpose of God. "Thou . . . art a king of kings," he says, "for the God of heaven hath given thee a kingdom, power, and strength, and glory" (verse 37). In other words, Nebuchadnezzar's power and glory were a given power, a given glory. "Wheresoever . . . men dwell, the beasts of the field and the fowls of the heaven hath he given into thine hand, and hath made thee ruler over them all. Thou art this head of gold" (verse 38).

A smile of satisfaction is seen on the king's countenance, but Daniel continues. "After thee shall arise another kingdom inferior to thee"—not greater, but inferior—"and another third kingdom of brass, which shall bear rule over all the earth" (verse 39).

Before Nebuchadnezzar fell asleep on the night of his dream, he had been pondering the future. He wondered what would happen to his expanding empire after he died. "As you lay in bed," said Daniel, "came thoughts of what would be hereafter, and he who reveals mysteries made known to you what is to be" (verse 29, RSV). There will be other empires, Daniel stated; in fact, three others—no more, no less. And each succeeding empire will be inferior to the one before; inferior in concentrated wealth, but superior in strength and territory. Then, as the image stood in all its glory, suddenly a stone struck the colossus on the feet—not the head, but the feet—and the whole thing crumbled to pieces. Then a great wind came and carried everything away; not a fragment was left. But the stone that smote it began to grow until it filled the whole earth. "The God of heaven [will] set up a kingdom," said Daniel, and that kingdom of glory "shall not be left to other people, . . . and it shall stand for ever" (verse 44). And the youthful prophet concluded his exposition with the emphatic declaration: "The dream is certain, and the interpretation thereof sure" (verse 45).

No wonder the king was troubled. No wonder he wanted someone to give the meaning. Was it a nightmare or a revelation? He did not know. What Nebuchadnezzar needed was "an interpreter, one among a thousand" (Job 33:23), and Daniel proved to be such an interpreter. This mighty colossus in the form of a man was actually a forecast of man's attempt to govern himself apart from God.

"THE TIMES OF THE GENTILES"

When Israel was delivered from Egypt and was established as a nation at the crossroads of the world, God designed that it should teach the nations true religion. Instead, Israel followed the world into idolatry. Instead, the world led Israel into corrupting ways of witchcraft. So the Lord permitted Nebuchadnezzar to invade the Israelites' land, to destroy their city, and to overthrow the throne of Judah. That was the beginning of Gentile rulership. Because of Israel's failure, the Lord may well have permitted the overthrow of Jerusalem in order to teach His people to depend on the living God for their protection and not on alliances with the world. Israel, instead of taking its place as the head of nations as God intended, now found itself in the hands of Gentile powers.

God's original purpose for Jerusalem was that it would stand as a great administrative center, an example to the world. Had His people obeyed Him, the city of Jerusalem would have stood forever. (See Jeremiah 17:25.) But the nation failed to live up to its high destiny, and this led the prophet to mourn that "the sin of Judah is written with a pen of iron, . . . it is graven upon the table of their heart" (Jeremiah 17:1). As a last appeal, Jeremiah was told to stand by the gate where the kings of Judah came in and out and deliver this message: "Thus saith the LORD; Take heed to yourselves, and bear no burden on the sabbath day, nor bring it in by the gates of Jerusalem; . . . neither do ye any work, but hallow ye the sabbath day, as I commanded your fathers. . . . Then there shall enter into the gates of this city kings and princes sitting upon the throne of David . . . : and this city shall remain for ever" (verses 21, 22, 25).

What was the people's response? "They obeyed not, . . . but made their neck stiff, that they might not hear, nor receive instruction" (verse 23). The time came when there was no remedy. (See 2 Chronicles 36:14–17.) True to the prophecy, the city was invaded and overthrown. Since then the Jews have never had a king or a throne. For some two thousand years they have been a scattered people among the nations while Gentile nations have led and ruled the world. This will continue until the coming of the King of kings who will reign forever.

BABYLON GATHERS WEALTH OF THE NATIONS

The sweep of history was outlined before Nebuchadnezzar and emphasized by the contrasting metals of the image. Now let us note the significance of these successive empires. The head of gold pictured Babylon. Under Nebuchadnezzar, Babylon was the recognized center of wealth and glory. Gold flowed into it from all the provinces of the empire. The immense treasures gathered by King Solomon and brought to Jerusalem were later confiscated and carried to Babylon. Tremendous quantities of gold and bronze made Babylon the wealthiest city of its time.

When Herodotus, the ancient historian, visited Babylon a century after Nebuchadnezzar's day, he found an abundance of gold still there. Temples, altars, shrines—all were plated with this precious metal. Jeremiah says, "Babylon hath been a golden cup in the LORD's hand" (Jeremiah 51:7). Isaiah spoke of Babylon as "the glory of kingdoms, the beauty of the Chaldees' excellency" (Isaiah 13:19).

The Babylon of Nebuchadnezzar was not this city's beginning. It was probably the first city built after the Flood. (See Genesis 10:10.) It flourished for hundreds of years. But after the reign of Hammurabi, king of ancient Babylon, it declined until it was little more than a wayside town. Sennacherib of Assyria thoroughly destroyed the ancient city in 689 B.C., but Nabopolassar, father of Nebuchadnezzar, rebuilt it, again making it a great center of trade and industry.

In his book *The Bible As History,* Dr. Werner Keller says of Babylon that "its ancient power and glory had no equal in the ancient world" (page 289). Not only was the city the center of wealth and industry but also the center of religion. The name *Babylon* came from the word *Babili,* meaning "gate of the gods." It was first built by Nimrod, who founded the Babylonian mystery religion at the time of the building of the tower of Babel. The Scriptures speak of Nimrod as "a mighty hunter" (Genesis 10:9). He was not only politically powerful but a rebel against heaven. The name *Nimrod* means "he shall rebel." *The Jewish Encyclopedia* states that Nimrod was "he who made all the people rebellious against God." He was the priest-king of devil worship, and Babylon became the headquarters of the mystery cults, a counterreligion.

The antithesis of all this was Jerusalem, which means "city of peace." This makes all the more remarkable the statement of Daniel 1:2: "The Lord *gave* Jehoiakim king of Judah into his [Nebuchadnezzar's] hand." God designed this disciplinary action on His part to teach Israel lessons they could learn no other way. Even when the seventy years of the Jews' Babylonian exile ceased and they returned to their homeland, Jerusalem failed to regain the greatness it had formerly enjoyed.

Babylon's glory was also short lived. After only seventy years, it passed into the hands of the Persian conqueror. The last king of Babylon was slain in the midst of a royal banquet.

MEDIA-PERSIA MOVES INTO WORLD LEADERSHIP

Those words, "after thee shall arise another kingdom inferior to thee" (Daniel 2:39), must have sounded strange to the king, for usually the superior conquers the inferior. But just as silver is inferior to gold in value, so the next universal kingdom, Media-Persia, was inferior to Babylon in wealth and luxury. What Daniel actually said in Aramaic was, "After thee shall arise another kingdom downward from thee, earthward from thee." It would be downward in quality, but earthward in extent, occupying more land surface.

Persia, however, was known for her treasures of silver. Xerxes, a prominent king of Persia, inherited immense hoards of silver from his father, Darius Hystaspes. In Hebrew, as in all Semitic languages, the word for money, *keseph,* is the same as is used for silver. In the Medo-Persian Empire, reputedly, all taxes had to be paid in silver. Consequently, the kings of this second empire grew extremely wealthy in silver. The empire lasted abut two hundred years, from 539 to 332 B.C.

Then came a third kingdom of brass, or bronze. (The "brass" of the KJV should be "bronze.") This was the Greek Empire, which, by a rapid series of conquests, replaced Media-Persia. The thighs and abdomen of the image were of this material—a forecast of the "brazen coated Greeks" as they were called. This was the third Gentile power to "bear rule over all the earth" (Daniel 2:39). The Greeks were experts in the molding of bronze. The soldiers wore breastplates of bronze, helmets of bronze, and carried shields of bronze. They carried bronze swords.

ALEXANDER BUILDS THE GREEK EMPIRE

Alexander the Great, son of King Philip of Macedon, showed signs of genius even when a teenager. His father procured for him the best possible tutor, the great philosopher Aristotle. Alexander kept in close touch with his teacher throughout all his military campaigns. By the time he was twenty-five he had the world at his feet, but he never really conquered himself.

Returning with his troops from India, he reached Babylon, intending to make that city his world capital. His men were active in a great building program when one of his favorite generals died. This so grieved Alexander that it is said he drank the intoxicating "cup of Hercules." This brought on a very high fever, and he died in his wife's arms in 332 B.C. He conquered the world in eight short years but slipped into silence at the age of thirty-three.

Realizing that their leader had only hours to live, his generals asked, "To whom will you give the kingdom?"

"To the strongest," he replied.

The leading generals tested their strength against each other. "So Alexander . . . died. And his servants bore rule every one in his place. And after his death they all put crowns upon themselves. So did their sons after them many many years; and evils were multiplied in the earth" (1 Maccabees 1:7–9). The Greek Empire was plunged into a state of turmoil and civil war lasting about three decades. The kingdom finally disintegrated and later succumbed to the armies of the emerging power of Rome.

ROME RULES THE WORLD

The Battle of Pydna, June 22, 168 B.C., marks the time when Alexander's homeland fell before the Romans. Thus the empire of Alexander, which had already begun to crumble before Roman pressure, was whittled down, piece by piece, until Rome ruled the Mediterranean world and beyond to Britain in the north.

"The fourth kingdom shall be strong as iron: forasmuch as iron breaketh in pieces and subdueth all things: and as iron that breaketh all these, shall it break in pieces and bruise" (Daniel 2:40).

For more than five hundred years Rome seemed almost unconquerable. Her standards waved from the British Isles to the Arabian gulf, from the North Sea to the Sahara Desert, from the Atlantic to the Euphrates. Her Caesars were worshiped as gods, and by her invincible will she made every country under her influence a prison house for those who disagreed. The historian Edward Gibbon says, "To resist [Rome] was fatal, and it was impossible to fly." (*The Decline and Fall of the Roman Empire,* vol. 1, page 190.)

"Three-fifths of the population of the city of Rome were slaves," says Schlegel in his *Philosophy of History,* page 261. They were just chattels with a voice. It was as if the iron-shod god of war actually bestrode the globe; with every step new currents of blood poured forth. It was a regime of force and brute strength, but God can cause "the wrath of man" to praise Him (Psalm 76:10). So in spite of man's roughshod cruelty, God was working out His plan.

ROMAN ROADS AID CHRISTIANITY

While the Greeks carried their language throughout the Near and Middle East in preparation for the spread of the gospel, Rome built roads from Palestine to Britain, making travel possible for the messengers of Christianity. Her enforcement of law, with her expensive postal system, also aided the carrying of the news of salvation. Her Pax Romana, with two centuries of relative stability in the Mediterranean world, facilitated Christian evangelism. Paul wrote that the message of Jesus had reached "every creature which is under heaven" (Colossians 1:23).

The iron element in the metal image was not to last forever. It stood on feet of clay with a mixture of iron. Daniel emphasized the feet and toes, stating that the fourth empire would not be overthrown by another universal empire but would be replaced by a collection of smaller nations warring among themselves. How accurately history fulfills prophecy!

EMPIRE DIVIDED INTO TEN PARTS

"The iron monarchy of Rome," to use Gibbon's expression, was broken into fragments by barbarian tribes, so that by A.D. 476 the strong empire was broken and western Europe was divided into ten parts. These were the Lombards, the Alemanni, the Anglo-Saxons, the Ostrogoths, the Burgundians, the Franks, the Suevi, the Vandals, the Visigoths, and the Heruli. These were actually the progenitors of the nations of modern Europe—some strong, others weak, as indicated by the mixture of iron and clay. But the most important feature of this strange combination was their inability to adhere or unite. During fifteen centuries, strong dictators have tried to weld them and build a facsimile of the old Roman Empire. While at times they neared their goal, they always failed. Think of Charlemagne, Charles V, Louis XIV, Napoleon, Kaiser Wilhelm II, Adolph Hitler—all of whom tried and failed. Something mysterious seemed to block the way. Seven words of prophecy stood between them and success. The Scripture

52

says, "They shall not cleave one to another" (Daniel 2:43). Treaties, peace pacts, agreements of all kinds have been signed, sealed—and broken. As many as 4,568 treaties and international agreements were submitted before the old League of Nations between May 10, 1920, and May 19, 1939. But the treaties did not prevent World War II.

ATTEMPTS TO AVERT WAR

Daniel said to the astonished king, "As you saw the iron and clay mixed, so shall they be mixed in marriage, but they will not hold together, just as iron does not mix with clay" (verse 43, Berkeley Revised). Before the global war of 1914–1918 most European monarchs were related by marriage, but that, too, proved an ineffectual amalgam. The alliances based on marriage bonds dissolved in the crucible of war.

Today we witness ongoing attempts to weld fragmented Europe, the nations that once formed the Roman Empire. The Common Market was one such effort, as is the European Union of the present day. These have tried to unify the monetary systems, weights and measures, and military equipment of the different European nations. They have made efforts to establish a central government similar to the federal government of the United States of America. The hope of many leaders in Europe has been that sweeping changes together with the standardizing of antitrust laws, transport rates, wage levels, and business and consumer taxes will lead to a politically united Europe.

The Vatican, world headquarters of the Roman Catholic Church, has been prominent in these attempts to weld the nations of Europe into a common union. Centuries ago, when the Roman Empire broke up into fragmentary kingdoms, the Holy See soon saw an unusual opportunity to exercise political control. Through the Holy Roman Empire, a totally artificial conglomerate, and by interference in other national governments, the papacy dominated European affairs for more than a thousand years. However, the Protestant Reformation in the sixteenth century and weaknesses within the church began to erode papal control. So when General Berthier of Napoleon's army took Pope Pius VI prisoner in 1798, the era of papal Rome's political supremacy came to an end. As John the revelator foretold, this religio-political power received a "deadly wound" or death stroke (Revelation 13:3). But the same verse also said that the wound would be healed and then all the world would wonder with great admiration. We see today the recovery of that power. It was Napoleon who said, "There will be no repose in Europe until it is under one emperor whose officers would be kings."

Napoleon actually planned to bring this about. But as H. M. S. Richards, Sr., said, "He was smashing his fists against God's prophecy. 'They shall not cleave one to another' " (*One World,* page 179). Napoleon met his Waterloo and died in exile a crushed and defeated man as were all the others who tried unite Europe into a single empire and thus prove Daniel's prophecy false.

When this great prophetic outline was first interpreted to Nebuchadnezzar, he was looking into the future, scarcely any of which had been fulfilled. But today we look back over twenty-five hundred years and see each segment of the prophecy remarkably fulfilled. How accurately history has met the prophetic forecast! All that is left is the last great event—the ushering in of the eternal kingdom of glory. Our next chapter unfolds the climactic events which will bring an end to human history and usher in the promised new heaven and new earth where disease and death, lawlessness and war, will never be known. Would you be ready if that kingdom were to come today? Right now you can be quietly accepting Jesus Christ as your Savior and coming King.

5. The Mystic Stone Kingdom

How impressive are the words of Daniel, the Hebrew captive, to the young King Nebuchadnezzar:

"As you looked, a stone was cut out by no human hand, and it smote the image on its feet of iron and clay, and broke them in pieces; then the iron, the clay, the bronze, the silver, and the gold, all together were broken in pieces, and became like the chaff of the summer threshing floors; and the wind carried them away, so that not a trace of them could be found. But the stone that struck the image became a great mountain and filled the whole earth.

"This is the dream; now we will tell the king its interpretation. You, O king, the king of kings, to whom the God of heaven has given the kingdom, the power, and the might, and the glory, and into whose hand he has given, wherever they dwell, the sons of men, the beasts of the field, and the birds of the air, making you rule over them all—you are the head of gold. After you shall arise another kingdom inferior to you, and yet a third kingdom of bronze, which shall rule over all the earth. And there shall be a fourth kingdom, strong as iron, because iron breaks to pieces and shatters all things; and like iron which crushes, it shall break and crush all these. And as you saw the feet and toes partly of potter's clay and partly of iron, it shall be a divided kingdom; but some of the firmness of iron shall be in it, just as you saw iron mixed with the miry clay. And as the toes of the feet were partly iron and partly clay, so the kingdom shall be partly strong and partly brittle. As you saw the iron mixed with miry clay, so they will mix with one another in marriage, but they will not hold together, just as iron does not mix with clay. And in the days of those kings the God of heaven will set up a kingdom which shall never be destroyed, nor shall its sovereignty be left to another people. It shall break in pieces all these kingdoms and bring them to an end, and it shall stand forever; just as you saw that a stone was cut from a mountain by no human hand, and that it broke in pieces the iron, the bronze, the clay, the silver, and the gold. A great God has made known to the king what shall be hereafter. *The dream is certain, and its interpretation sure"* (Daniel 2:34–45, RSV, emphasis supplied).

Imagine the thoughts that must have surged through the mind of Nebuchadnezzar as Daniel came to the climax of his interpretation— "after thee . . . another kingdom" and "yet a third kingdom" until the mighty monarchy of Rome appears. But even that great empire was not to last. Just as the prophecy indicated, it broke up as the barbaric invasions divided Europe into ten major fragments.

Then the king saw a stone coming from somewhere and smashing against the feet of clay and iron. Afterward the whole thing crumbled to pieces, and a hurricane carried it away. Strangest of all, the stone that struck the image "became a great mountain and filled the whole earth" (verse 35).

What can it all mean? What is the stone cut out of the mountain without hands that grew until it filled the whole earth? The coming universal kingdom will not be founded by ingenious men, but by the mighty God. It is called the stone kingdom, and the Scriptures have much to say about this stone. When Jacob, in God's name, blessed his son Joseph, he said, "His bow abode in strength, and the arms of his hands were made strong by the hands of the mighty God of Jacob: (from thence is the shepherd, the stone of Israel)" (Genesis 49:24).

Here the stone is linked with the Shepherd of Israel. And when our Lord answered a question put to Him by the chief priests and scribes, He quoted Psalm 118:22, 23, saying, "What is this then that is written, The stone which the builders rejected, the same is become the head of the corner?" Then He added, "Whosoever shall fall upon that stone shall be broken; but on whomsoever it shall fall, it will grind him to powder" (Luke 20:17, 18).

56

CHRIST, THE STONE

More than a hundred years before Daniel's day the prophet Isaiah wrote, "Therefore thus saith the Lord GOD, Behold, I lay in Zion for a foundation a stone, a tried stone, a precious corner stone, a sure foundation: he that believeth shall not make haste" (Isaiah 28:16). Or as Moffatt translates it, "will never flinch." The apostle Paul includes that scripture in his discourse to the Romans, speaking of Christ as "a stumblingstone and rock of offence." But he adds, "Whosoever believeth in him shall not be ashamed" (Romans 9:33). Peter also quotes Isaiah, applying the same text to Christ, doubtless remembering the occasion when Jesus asked the disciples for their definition of Him. Peter had replied, "Thou art the Christ, the Son of the living God." To which our Lord replied, "Upon this rock I will build my church" (Matthew 16:16–18). That is, upon the deity of the Son of God so clearly confessed by Simon Peter. Upon that solid rock of truth the church is established.

Writing to the Corinthian believers, Paul reminds them that Israel "did all eat the same spiritual meat; And did all drink the same spiritual drink: for they drank of that spiritual Rock that followed them: and that rock was Christ" (1 Corinthians 10:3, 4). Yes, our Lord is the rock, or the stone, cut out "without hands." Human generation neither fashioned His substance nor caused His appearing in the flesh. He had a human mother, but no human father. He was sired not by a human male, but by the Spirit of God and conceived by the virgin Mary. Seven hundred years before His birth Isaiah wrote, "Therefore the Lord himself shall give you a sign; Behold, a virgin shall conceive, and bear a son, and shall call his name Immanuel" (Isaiah 7:14).

CHRIST BORN OF A VIRGIN

Matthew, the inspired narrator of the "kingdom messages" of Jesus, applies this prophecy to Christ. And why not? Thousands of years before our Lord's birth, the promise of God to Adam and Eve was that the woman's seed would bruise the head of Satan; victory would come through Him. (See Genesis 3:15.) How the old rabbis pored over this statement of Scripture. What could it mean—the seed of a woman? God, to our first parents, said clearly, "The seed of the woman will crush Satan's head." Not until Jesus was born of a virgin could we fully understand that promise.

Paul emphasizes that supreme miracle when he says, "But when the fulness of the time was come, God sent forth his Son, made of a woman" (Galatians 4:4). Note how precise the Scripture is; not made of a man and a woman like the rest of us, but "made of a woman." The human male had nothing to do with our Lord's birth. It was a physiological miracle to meet a physiological, psychological, and desperate spiritual need—the redemption of a lost race.

That One born of Mary whose father is the Almighty God is "the stone of Israel," the spiritual rock, "a stone . . . cut out without hands" (Daniel 2:34). That stone will strike the image on the feet, dashing it to pieces, and then fill the whole earth.

Let us return to Daniel's interpretation: "Whereas thou sawest the feet and toes; part of potters' clay, and part of iron, the kingdom shall be divided; but there shall be in it of the strength of the iron, forasmuch as thou sawest the iron mixed with miry clay. And as the toes of the feet were part of iron, and part of clay, so the kingdom shall be partly strong, and partly broken [brittle, RSV]" verses 41, 42).

We have already noted the significance of that expression, "they shall mingle themselves with the seed of men: but they shall not cleave one to another, even as iron is not mixed with clay" (verse 43). Those words have stood the test of centuries. Time was when Queen Victoria of England was the grandmother, and King Christian of Denmark was the grandfather, of most of the crowned heads of Europe. But after World War I, nearly all the monarchies of Europe had vanished. Europe is still divided, some nations strong, others weak. Nothing on earth can weld them into a permanent unity. They will remain divided until the appearing of our Lord Jesus, who comes to reign forever as a King of kings and Lord of lords.

WHEN MAY WE EXPECT CHRIST'S RETURN?

Is there any way of knowing when we might expect our Lord to come? Yes, there is. The same great prophecy of Daniel says that "in the days of these kings [the divided nations of Europe] shall the God of heaven set up a kingdom, which shall never be destroyed" (verse 44).

When the prophet speaks of "these kings," he makes himself quite clear. Some commentators suggest it might be the kings of the four universal empires—Babylon, Media-Persia, Greece, and Rome. But the stone does not strike the Babylonian head nor the Medo-Persian breast and arms. It does not strike the Grecian thighs of brass or the iron legs of Rome. It is to strike the *feet and toes* at the very time the nations are trying desperately to unite divided Europe. It could well be that in our generation the stone will strike and the kingdom of God will come. Many other prophecies reveal that these are indeed the latter days.

This prophecy thunders its message in our ears: *There will be no more world empires.* Several times during the last two centuries it seemed likely that the kingdoms of Europe would be welded together, but every such effort has failed.

> It looked as if Napoleon would conquer the civilized world and the prophecy prove to be untrue. But the waters of the Berezina engulfed his battalions and the silent, soft falling snow was a winding sheet around half of his army that perished on the steppes of Russia. The other half of his noble and gallant men lay with their bones bleaching or their bodies buried on the plains of Waterloo. The august invincible emperor . . . [became] a refugee and an exile to die alone on the rocky island of Helena. Why? Because God had said 600 years before Christ and 2,500 years before Napoleon was born, that after the Roman empire there would never be another universal dominion (W. A. Criswell, *Expository Sermons on the Book of Daniel,* vol. 2, page 77).

Napoleon was not the stone that would shatter the kingdoms. But there is a stone, a mystic, destroying stone, that will strike, leaving nothing.

WHEN THE STONE STRIKES

Bible prophecy not only makes clear *when* the stone shall strike, but also *how* and *what* will happen. "It shall break in pieces and consume all these kingdoms," said the prophet, "and it shall stand for ever" (verse 44). It will not be a gradual, imperceptible breaking. The psalmist says, "Our God shall come, and shall not keep silence: a fire shall devour before him, and it shall be very tempestuous round about him. He shall call to the heavens from above, and to the earth, that he may judge his people" (Psalm 50:3, 4). The prophet John, catching a vision of that glorious event, writes:

> And the heaven departed as a scroll when it is rolled together; and every mountain and island were moved out of their places. And the kings of the earth, and the great men, and the rich men, and the chief captains, and the mighty men, and every bondman, and every free man, hid themselves in the dens and in the rocks of the mountains; And said to the mountains and rocks, Fall on us, and hide us from the face of him that sitteth on the throne, and from the wrath of the Lamb: For the great day of his wrath is come; and who shall be able to stand? (Revelation 6:14–17).

Some, however, will be able to stand, for we read:

> God is our refuge and strength, a very present help in trouble. Therefore will not we fear, though the earth be removed, and though the mountains be carried into the midst of the sea. . . . The heathen raged, the kingdoms were moved: he uttered his voice, the earth melted. . . . Come, behold the works of the LORD, what desolations he hath made in the earth. He maketh wars to cease unto the end of the earth; he breaketh the bow, and cutteth the spear in sunder; he burneth the chariot in the fire. . . . The LORD of hosts is with us; the God of Jacob is our refuge (Psalm 46:1, 2, 6, 8, 9, 11).

How relevant are the words of our Lord, who said to the scribes and Pharisees, "Whosoever shall fall on this stone shall be broken: but on whomsoever it shall fall, it will grind him to powder" (Matthew 21:44).

The apostle Paul says,

> The Lord Jesus shall be revealed from heaven with his mighty angels, . . . taking vengeance on them that know not God, and that obey not the gospel of our Lord Jesus Christ: Who shall be punished with everlasting destruction from the presence of the Lord, and from the glory of his power; When he shall come to be glorified in his saints (2 Thessalonians 1:7–10).

In his dream, Nebuchadnezzar saw what was left of all the earthly powers blown away and no place found for them. "And the stone that smote the image became [grew into] a great mountain and filled the whole earth" (Daniel 2:35).

No more striking symbol could have been selected to impress the Chaldean monarch. Centuries before Nebuchadnezzar and his illustrious father Nabopolassar came to power and rebuilt the ancient city of Babylon, making it the capital of the Neo-Babylonian Empire, Nippur was one of the chief cities of Babylonia; there was the shrine of the Sumerian god Enlil, "god of the lands," sometimes called "the stone god." The Amorite kings, of whom Hammurabi was chief, replaced the god Enlil with Marduk, or Merodach, who then became the supreme god of Babylon. Enlil was no longer the god of lordship and the lands. In fact, he is pictured as bestowing on Marduk his favor and place of honor and "his own title, 'Lord of the lands.' . . . From this time forward Merodach was looked upon as the 'Enlil of the gods.' " (Charles Boutflower, *In and Around the Book of Daniel*, page 95.)

Digging in the ruins of Babylon, archaeologists found the name *Shadu Rabu* on many cuneiform inscriptions. This name was originally associated with Enlil, and his main temple in the ancient city of Nippur meant "a great mountain." This was known as "the house of the great mountain of the land." Nippur was recognized as the religious center of Babylonia. When Nebuchadnezzar's armies, centuries later, overran Nippur, they interpreted that as evidence that Marduk, or Merodach, was stronger than Enlil. So Nebuchadnezzar applied the name *Shadu Rabu* to Marduk, the supreme god of Babylon.

Another meaning of Enlil was "lord of the storm" or "storm of terrible strength." In Babylonian mythology, Tiamat, the dragon of chaos, was overcome by Marduk, who launched an attack against her, sending against this god a "sevenfold wind or a whirlwind." So when Daniel spoke to Nebuchadnezzar about a great wind and a great mountain, this was familiar language to the king. The young Hebrew's interpretation had a peculiar significance not only to the king but also to any others who heard the explanation. The language was most appropriate. No figures could possibly have been used that could have had a greater influence. According to Jastrow, "the sacred edifices of Babylonia were intended to be imitations of mountains." Even "the earth itself" was pictured as a "great mountain" (*Religion of Babylonia and Assyria,* M. Jastrow, 1898 ed., page 614).

Mystic stone kingdom soon to be established

The political sovereignty of the world, residing at that time in Babylon, the head of gold, was to pass to others and then to still others until at last the sovereignty of the God of heaven would replace the powers of the whole world. The stone kingdom will be an everlasting kingdom that shall never be destroyed, said Daniel. It will fill the whole earth and stand unchallenged forever and ever.

King Nebuchadnezzar bowed before Daniel in reverent worship, recognizing that Daniel's God was indeed the God of the universe. He said, "Of a truth it is, that your God is a God of gods, and a Lord of kings, and a revealer of secrets" (Daniel 2:47). Daniel was made "regent over the whole province of Babylon and chief prefect over all the wise men of Babylon" (verse 48, NEB).

Think of this brilliant young Chaldean king, master of a great empire, bowing reverently in worship because of what had been revealed to him. Is the same kind of reverent response in our hearts as we review this prophecy? We are twenty-five centuries removed from the scene, and the stone kingdom that will replace the kingdoms of this world is about to be established. If that kingdom of glory were to be ushered in now, would we be ready? Could we take our place as citizens of heaven, members of the family of God? If not, then let us settle that question right now, before we read any farther.

In these tremendous days when thousands are turning from darkness to light and accepting our Lord as Savior and coming King, let us decide that at all costs we will be among those to whom the Lord will say, "Come, ye blessed of my Father, inherit the kingdom prepared for you from the foundation of the world" (Matthew 25:34).

6. Treason, Trial, and Triumph

The story of the Babylonian protestors who were thrown into the furnace is well known. While many today regard the story as legend, yet the writer of the New Testament epistle to the Hebrews includes it in his list of evidences of faith. Referring to Daniel and his three companions, the writer mentions those "who through faith . . . quenched the violence of fire" and also "stopped the mouth of lions." These individuals of faith also "wrought righteousness, [and] obtained promises" (Hebrews 11:33, 34). An inspired New Testament record, therefore, seals these accounts as true.

These are more than children's stories. They are revelations of God's power to deliver His servants who put their trust in Him. The central figure in the story of the fiery furnace is neither the king nor the courageous Hebrews, but the Son of God, whom the king saw walking in the fire. What marvelous overtones there are in this narrative! Paul probably had such experiences in mind when he wrote, "For whatsoever things were written aforetime were written for our learning, that we through patience and comfort of the scriptures might have hope" (Romans 15:4).

When the king of Babylon set up his golden image on the plain of Dura, his reputation as conqueror and ruler had been established. No date is known for the episode of the great image, but it certainly occurred after Nebuchadnezzar was firmly established on his throne. Earlier the king had heard the interpretation of the dream of the metallic image, showing that the head of gold represented Nebuchadnezzar and his kingdom.

During the years since the dream Nebuchadnezzar had conquered other kingdoms. He was a real success. There is no record that he ever lost a battle. Pride and ambition now urged him to erect a monument to his own greatness, which would impress the world that Babylon would be indestructible—a kingdom that would break in pieces other kingdoms and stand forever.

A few years ago archaeologists discovered a mound on which are found the remains of a rectangular brick structure. Some believe this might well have been the base of this huge golden image. The measurements recorded in Daniel are given in the sexagesimal system. It was sixty cubits (about ninety feet) high including the base, and six cubits (nine feet) broad. The Babylonians used this system founded on the number sixty. It is divisible by twelve factors, in contrast with our system founded on the number one hundred, which is divisible by only nine factors. We still follow the sexagesimal system in the measurement of time (and angles)—sixty seconds make a minute, sixty minutes an hour (or a degree).

GATHERING OF ADMINISTRATORS

Administrative leaders attending this great ceremony came from many parts of the growing empire. The occasion was a dedication ceremony. Although not primarily a religious gathering, religion played an important role in almost everything the Babylonians did. No priests or philosophers or astrologers are mentioned as being present, but the governors, captains, judges, treasurers, counselors, and rulers of provinces were required to attend. This pageant was designed to impress everybody with the glory of Babylon.

At the time of the dream of Daniel 2, Shadrach, Meshach, and Abednego, the three Hebrews mentioned in the story, had been appointed as administrative leaders. (See Daniel 2:49.) Thus they were present at the ceremony. And there was no mistaking the royal order: " 'When you hear the sound of the horn, pipe, lyre, trigon, harp, bagpipe, and every kind of music, you are to fall down and worship the golden image that King Nebuchadnezzar has set up; and whoever does not fall down and worship shall immediately be cast into a burning fiery furnace' " (Daniel 3:4–6, RSV).

Refusal to obey the king's order was treason. The situation was important, and the atmosphere tense. To understand the real issues involved, we must see this as one of the unusual ways God chose to reveal truth to Babylon.

That day on the plain of Dura two invisible powers met head on—the power of earthly ambition inspired by the prince of darkness and the power of love revealed in the lives of men dedicated to truth and righteousness. The charge brought against these men as recorded in verse 12 is revealing. It is easy to see a spirit of jealousy moving some to say to the king, "Certain Jews whom thou hast set over the affairs of the province . . . have not regarded thee." A herald had summoned all "people, nations, and languages" (verse 4) to heed the mandate and bow in homage before the golden image, a symbol of man's greatness. This the loyal Hebrews could not conscientiously do. They held in respect the king, as is shown in their reply. But they had to protest.

Nebuchadnezzar was embarrassed and outraged. He ordered the three men to appear before him. He had never had cause to doubt their loyalty before. He knew, of course, that they did not worship his gods. From his point of view he was not really asking them to abandon the worship of their God. All that he required was that they bow in recognition of his symbol of the fact that Babylon was the greatest and most enduring power on earth. But these men recognized a greater power—that of Jehovah.

To disobey the king's order was treason punishable by death. But Nebuchadnezzar, eager to spare their lives, offered to give them another chance. They did not need another chance. The issue was perfectly plain to them. So they courteously replied, "We would not make any defense in this matter; for the God whom we serve is able to save us" (verse 16, 17, Berkeley). They knew that God would deliver them either *from* death or *in* death.

What a marvelous example of faith in the living God! They rested their case with Him. More than a hundred years earlier the prophet Isaiah had penned the promise, "When thou passest through the waters, I will be with thee; . . . when thou walkest through the fire, thou shalt not be burned; neither shall the flame kindle upon thee" (Isaiah 43:2). Wrapped in such a promise, they could give their witness confidently.

If we put ourselves in the place of Nebuchadnezzar, we can appreciate his problem. To have permitted these men to defy him would have seriously affected his standing as ruler. His position before the world was at stake. He commanded the furnace to be heated seven times hotter than usual, and that these men dressed in all their regalia—their trousers, shirts, mantles, and turbans—be bound and hurled into the flames. Moreover, the strongest men of the army were chosen for the grim execution. Picked up like living logs, these protestors were tossed into the blazing furnace. The flame "slew those men who took up Shadrach, Meshach, and Abed-nego" (verse 22).

That has put an end to the matter, Nebuchadnezzar no doubt thought. But when man has done his worst, God can always add a final chapter. And what a chapter it was! In his fury Nebuchadnezzar had challenged Jehovah: "Who is that God that shall deliver you out of my hands?" (verse 15). But he did not realize the power he was opposing. In a matter of minutes this autocratic king got the revelation of his life. He saw the God that he had defied walking in the fire with His three faithful servants. That was a theophany, a preincarnate appearance of our Lord who later was born in Bethlehem.

Not only did the king see this miracle, but so also did his administrative leaders—governors, rulers, treasurers, counselors. The fire that slew the executioners had no power over the men they thought to destroy. Not a hair of their head was singed, nor was the smell of fire upon them (verse 27). Only the cords that bound them were burned.

Moving nearer the furnace, Nebuchadnezzar called to them, "Ye servants of the most high God, come forth, and come hither" (verse 26). "The most high God" was a reverent name evidently well known to the king. The term "most high" is found eight times in the first five chapters of Daniel. Nebuchadnezzar had heard also about angels, for later he confessed that God had "sent his angel, and delivered his servants that trusted in him" (verse 28). These men had yielded their bodies but not their wills. We get a glimpse of Nebuchadnezzar as a man with a certain greatness of soul, for he even rejoiced that his own word had been changed. "There is no other God that can deliver after this sort" (verse 29).

So overwhelmed was Nebuchadnezzar by this revelation of divine power that he decided to go into partnership with this God. He even made a decree granting recognition to the Hebrew religion, and he pledged protection for the God of Shadrach, Meshach, and Abednego. Any who opposed Him should be "cut in pieces" (verse 29), as if Jehovah needed human protection! The king published a royal document telling of this marvelous deliverance, and he sent this throughout the empire. Thus the name and power of Jehovah were proclaimed. This was God's second message to Babylon.

The story ends in a doxology of praise, in an atmosphere of toleration that prepared the way for God's third message to Babylon. This we will note in our next chapter. These brave men, instead of being destroyed, were promoted. Their humble courage in the face of bitter opposition has inspired countless thousands throughout the centuries. We do well to study the example of these noble men in these days when loyalty is often regarded as obstinacy.

John Chrysostom was one of the great Greek church fathers. Born in A.D. 347, he was brought before the emperor at an early age to answer for his faith.

"If you persist in being a Christian," said the emperor, "I will banish you from your father's land."

Chrysostom replied, "Your Majesty, you cannot; the whole world is my Father's land."

"Then I will take away all your property."

"You cannot do that either. My treasures are in heaven."

"Then I will send you to a place where there will not be a friend to speak to."

"You cannot do that, for I have a Friend that sticketh closer than a brother. I shall have my Brother Jesus Christ forever."

The emperor said, "I will take away your life."

"You cannot do that either. My life is hid with Christ in God," Chrysostom replied.

That was not blind obstinacy. It was faith—"the faith of Jesus" (Revelation 14:12) that will characterize the last witness of God's true church on earth. We need such faith today.

As boys, Shadrach, Meshach, and Abednego had been brought up on the Ten Commandments, the first of which says, "Thou shalt have no other gods before me" (Exodus 20:3). The second is an expression of the first. "Thou shalt not make unto thee any graven image. . . . Thou shalt not bow down thyself to them, nor serve them: for I the LORD thy God am a jealous God" (verses 4, 5). Now they were men—governors of provinces in the empire of Babylon.

When they had arrived in Babylon, the king changed their names, but he could not change their devotion to the living God. They were members of a conquered race, and, when they appeared before Nebuchadnezzar, they realized that they were standing before the conqueror. Yet they were unconquerable. Having seen by faith the face of God, they need not fear the face of man. As we read the story in Daniel, chapter 3, we note that their names are repeated thirteen times in this one chapter. There was no mistaking the three to whom the king was speaking. Everyone present knew who these men were. All eyes turned to witness men who would dare to disobey the king. But before the day ended, the whole retinue of Babylonian leaders knew that with these Hebrews there was no compromise.

It is easy in such a situation to rationalize. Some might have reasoned that a simple genuflection was little enough to do for a king who had treated them so kindly. Others might say in the words of Solomon, "A living dog is better than a dead lion" (Ecclesiastes 9:4). But these men could not compromise, for they were first God's servants, and second servants of Nebuchadnezzar. We can almost hear them reciting the words of Joshua, "As for me and my house, we will serve the LORD" (Joshua 24:15). Or the words of David, "My heart is fixed, O God, my heart is fixed" (Psalm 57:7).

They knew God could deliver them; however, they went on to add, "But if not—" (Daniel 3:18). How hard those words are to say! God does not always intervene in such a miraculous way. And we can well imagine the emotions of these men as the fire was heated seven times hotter, and the assembled host expected the end of these "stubborn" Jews. What a surprise awaited that crowd!

In setting up this image, all of gold, Nebuchadnezzar was challenging God's plan of history as revealed in the dream of four successive empires and the final establishment of God's everlasting kingdom. Babylon's king was determined that his kingdom would continue; the golden kingdom was to endure forever.

But God's deliverance of His servants "changed the king's word" (verse 28), as He can change any and all who challenge His right to rule.

7. Maniac King Regains His Kingdom

We have already noticed that the book of Daniel is an apocalyptic book, divided equally between history and prophecy. It is not a complete history of Babylon or the captive Jews, for it touches only those events that definitely affected the people of God. The whole Bible follows this pattern. The first eleven chapters of Genesis cover the creation of the world, the fall of man, the destruction of the world by flood. Then the record touches the development of philosophies such as that which led to the building of the tower of Babel, which led men far away from God. Chapters 12 to 28 trace the history of Abraham and Isaac. The last twenty-two chapters give the history of Jacob and his family, especially of Joseph.

Secular history is not usually presented this way. While there is much history in the Bible, the whole purpose of the sacred Book is to reveal the gospel of salvation to men. God's purpose through Abraham's posterity was "to carry true religion to the nations" (Isaiah 42:1, Moffatt). To accomplish this, the Lord used not only the faithful witness of His people but even the scattering of Israel and Judah.

Gentile nations overran Palestine during the sixth and seventh centuries B.C., Assyria taking Israel into captivity and Babylon overthrowing Judah. We might wonder if anything good could come out of such conquests. But wherever Israel and Judah were scattered, they carried with them some knowledge of the true God.

NEBUCHADNEZZAR IN VARIED ROLES

In the first three chapters of Daniel, King Nebuchadnezzar is portrayed as a *conqueror,* an *autocrat,* and a *builder.* But in the fourth chapter we find him a *converted servant* of the most high God. More is recorded in sacred history about this man than perhaps any other Gentile ruler. In Daniel, chapter 3, we saw Nebuchadnezzar as an autocrat defying the God of heaven. But the monarch's word was changed. Years later in the document preserved in Daniel, chapter 4, he says, "I . . . was at rest, . . . flourishing in my palace" (verse 4). And that was no mere figure of speech. This proud conqueror and prouder architect had accomplished much. The royal document recorded in chapter 4 he sent throughout the lands under his authority. In this he related his own experience.

His conquests were at an end. The empire was consolidated. The city of Babylon was adorned with lofty palaces. He had created one of the seven wonders of the ancient world—the hanging gardens, built in his wife's honor. The city contained 53 dedicated temples, 955 smaller sanctuaries, and 384 altars. Werner Keller describes "Babylon as an international center of trade, industry, and commerce" (*The Bible as History,* page 297).

NEBUCHADNEZZAR, THE BUILDER

Nebuchadnezzar's last campaign against Egypt ended his military career. God gave him Egypt as "wages for his army" because of the service he rendered against Tyre. His siege against Tyre lasted thirteen years. The Scripture says:

> Nebuchadnezzar king of Babylon caused his army to serve a great service against Tyrus: every head was made bald, and every shoulder was peeled: yet he had no wages, nor his army, for Tyrus, for the service that he had served against it: There-fore thus saith the Lord GOD; Behold, I will give the land of Egypt unto Nebuchadnezzar king of Babylon; . . . and it shall be the wages for his army. I have given him the land of Egypt for his labour wherewith he served against it, because they wrought for me, saith the Lord GOD (Ezekiel 29:18–20).

Apparently Nebuchadnezzar invaded Egypt and carried away rich booty. From all the conquered countries, including Judah and the other nations of that area, he brought gold and art treasures to adorn the city of Babylon, hailed as "the golden city" and "the glory of the kingdoms" (Isaiah 14:4; 13:19). There was much to admire in Nebuchadnezzar. To those who accepted his rule, he was beneficent. The Jewish captives he treated kindly. Jeremiah, the prophet of God, counseled the refugees to "build . . . houses" and "plant gardens" and to "seek the peace of the city" (Jeremiah 29:5–7).

The area around Babylon was devoid of stone. Nebuchadnezzar therefore made Babylon the center of the greatest brick-making industry of his times. This ruler became one of the greatest builders of antiquity. Boutflower says, "He seems to have been possessed with a perfect rage for building" (page 68).

NEBUCHADNEZZAR AS WOODSMAN

One of Nebuchadnezzar's royal inscriptions reads, "I made the inhabitants of the Lebanon live in safety together and let nobody disturb them" (James B. Pritchard, *Ancient Near Eastern Texts,* page 307).

The monarch of Babylon was particularly fond of great cedars, which he brought all the way from the mountains of Lebanon. He regarded the forests of Lebanon as the possession of his Babylonian god Marduk. He tells us that he "cut through steep mountains" to open up the way for "mighty cedars, high and strong" to be transported into Babylon (ibid.).

In the document preserved in Daniel, chapter 4, he says, "I . . . was at rest" (Daniel 4:4). No longer was he leading his armies to victory, nor was he building beautiful palaces. His developing days were over. Probably no single man ever left behind him as his memorial upon the earth one-half the amount of building that was erected by this king.

Now for the story: The king again had an impressive dream. As before, the dream left him deeply troubled. Calling the magicians, the astrologers, the Chaldeans, and the soothsayers, he related the dream to them. But again he was disappointed. They could give no interpretation. Then "at the last Daniel came" (verse 8). Nebuchadnezzar's attitude toward Daniel is quite touching. He called him "master of the magicians," saying, "The spirit of the holy gods is in thee, and no secret troubleth thee" (verse 9).

The important events of this dream "made me afraid," he said (verse 5, RSV). Nebuchadnezzar afraid? He had conquered nations, and yet this dream left him staggered. In the dream (see verses 10–17) he saw an immense tree that seemed to reach to the end of the earth. And under its branches the beasts of the field and the fowls of heaven found shelter. Then he heard a voice saying, "Hew down the tree, and cut off his branches, shake off his leaves, and scatter his fruit: . . . Nevertheless leave the stump of his roots in the earth, even with a band of iron and brass . . . : Let his heart be changed from man's and let a beast's heart be given unto him; and let seven times pass over him" (verses 14–16). This declaration was to inform everyone that "the most High ruleth in the kingdom of men, and giveth it to whomsoever he will, and setteth up over it the basest of men" (verse 17).

When Daniel heard the dream, he too was troubled. A whole hour passed in silence. While the king was concerned, Daniel was even more concerned, for during the two or three decades of working together, these two men, the king and the prime minister, had become close associates. At last the king said, "Let not the dream, or the interpretation thereof, trouble thee" (verse 19). But Daniel knew the interpretation would come as a shock, and thus his silence.

Daniel Interprets the Dream

The prophet begins: "My lord, the dream be to them that hate thee, and the interpretation thereof to thine enemies" (verse 19). He has a solemn message with a very personal application, and he must give it to one for whom he has great regard. "It is thou, O king, that art grown and become strong: for thy greatness is grown . . . to the end of the earth." Respectfully he adds, "And whereas the king saw a watcher and an holy one coming down from heaven, and saying, Hew the tree down, and destroy it; . . . and let his portion be with the beasts of the field, till seven times pass over him; This is the interpretation, O king, and this is the decree of the most High" (verses 22–24).

Continuing, the statesman-prophet unfolded God's message: "They shall drive thee from men, and thy dwelling shall be with the beasts of the field, and they shall make thee to eat grass as oxen, . . . and seven times [seven years] shall pass over thee, till thou know that the most High ruleth in the kingdom of men, and giveth it to whomsoever he will" (verse 25).

It was not easy to bear a clear prophetic message to this proud, autocratic ruler. Daniel loved Nebuchadnezzar and doubtless had been praying for many years that in some way this great general, this

73

great builder, this outstanding leader of men, would come to know that the God of heaven rules. What a different world this would be if the rulers of all nations recognized that, in spite of their greatness, their power and prestige, a greater power is still in charge! The everlasting God rules earth and heaven.

DANIEL AS FRIEND, PROPHET, AND EVANGELIST

Now Daniel the prophet becomes Daniel the evangelist. Listen as he pleads for this man's soul: "Wherefore, O king, let my counsel be acceptable unto thee, and break off thy sins by righteousness, and thine iniquities by shewing mercy to the poor; if it may be a lengthening of thy tranquility"—or as Moffatt says, "perhaps your prosperity may be prolonged" (verse 27).

Many today, after hearing bad news, are sobered for a while. But as the months pass, the Holy Spirit's impressions are brushed aside. So it was with Nebuchadnezzar—his heart was not transformed. He still indulged a spirit of self-glorification, and perhaps even jested about his former fears. To himself he said, "Babylon was built by me alone, by my might, for my majesty."

THE KING'S MIND SNAPS

Exactly one year after Daniel's appeal, while boasting of his greatness, the king's mind suddenly snapped; he was a maniac. Unexpectedly, God struck down his proud impiety. His greatness and glory meant nothing now. Said the voice, "The kingdom is departed from thee" (verse 31).

Despite his position and his regal glory, he fled from the palace to the field, smitten with madness, suffering from a disease known to medical science as "lycanthropy" (*lukos*, "wolf," and *anthropos*, "man"), "a delusion that one has become or has assumed the characteristics of a wolf or other predatory animal." Is such a strange illness possible? The *Dictionary of Psychological Medicine* declares, "The complete loss of personal identity and the conviction of being changed into one of the lower animals . . . is one of the most remarkable facts in psychological history that the race reveals" (quoted in *Studies of the Book of Daniel*, by Dr. Robert Dick Wilson, pages 286, 287).

NEBUCHADNEZZAR RETURNS TO THE THRONE

Daniel was probably there when the king lost his reason, and thus was able to counsel those responsible for affairs of state. He knew just how long it would be until the king's mind would be restored. But let Nebuchadnezzar tell the story. One of the most remarkable passages in all the Bible is Daniel 4:34–37, where the king says, "At the end of the days I Nebuchadnezzar lifted up mine eyes unto heaven, and mine understanding returned unto me, and I blessed the most High, and I praised and honoured him" (verse 34). What a change! No longer did he consider himself a beast; he was a man!

How did Nebuchadnezzar know he had reached "the end of the days"? During those years he had had no knowledge of time or human responsibilities. In his royal document he says, "My counsellors and my lords sought unto me" (verse 36). Naturally, his counselors would surround him after he was reinstated, but let us imagine the part Daniel must have played in the affairs of the government during those long years of waiting!

THE KING COMES HOME

Knowing the purpose of God, the prophet-statesman doubtless looked forward to the time when the king would return in his right mind. The queen also may have helped preserve the nation. She was a princess from the mountain region of Media, and on this lady the king had lavished much. He built the "hanging gardens" for her pleasure. But now "at the end of the days," what can the queen and the counselors expect? Will the king return? If so, how? It does not take much imagination to see Daniel at the head of a chosen group going to the field or the forest in search of his friend.

Knowing the king's haunts, Daniel makes his way till he finally locates him. With a prayer of praise to God that the seven years are at an end, he walks up to this creature who, though human, has thought of himself as an animal. Daniel lifts his eyes heavenward as he addresses God, the same God who has answered his prayers during the twenty or thirty years since he first faced King Nebuchadnezzar. But what a contrast now! This beastlike human is covered with filth, his matted hair dangling on the ground, and his nails grown like birds' claws—a repulsive sight. But now Nebuchadnezzar lifts his eyes to heaven and opens his heart to the God of gods whose "dominion is an everlasting dominion . . . : And all the inhabitants of the earth are reputed as nothing" (verses 34, 35). He begins to realize that the living God "doeth according to his will in the army of heaven [the angels], and among the inhabitants of the earth: and none can stay his hand, or say unto him, What doest thou?" (verse 35).

Having been exposed to the elements for years, Nebuchadnezzar is a strange sight. But his heart is radiant and joyful. "Now I Nebuchadnezzar praise and extol and honour the King of heaven, all whose works are truth, and his ways judgment: and those that walk in pride he is able to abase" (verse 37).

How wonderful that a heathen autocrat could learn the saving truth of righteousness by faith! Daniel, who had prayed for this man's salvation for many years, now has the joy of witnessing his conversion.

BABYLON'S SPIRIT IN TODAY'S WORLD

In the dream Nebuchadnezzar had seen the stump of the tree bound by two bands, one of iron, the other of brass. In the metallic image of chapter 2, we reflect that the brass represented Greece, and the iron, Rome. The tree Nebuchadnezzar saw in his dream represented not only the king as a person, but Babylon as a system. Daniel's interpretation emphasized that the influence of Babylon's kingdom reached "to the end of the earth" (verse 22). The spirit of Babylon that began under Nimrod's rulership some sixteen centuries earlier with the building of the tower of Babel, and also a number of important cities (see Genesis 10:12; 11:1–9), had spread out and gripped the whole world. And that spirit did not die with Nebuchadnezzar. Even today's world is under the strong influence of the mystery religions of ancient Babylon.

Nebuchadnezzar's royal document was sent to "all people, nations, and languages" (verse 1). This may be thought of as hyperbole, but the influence of Babylon was doubtless felt in many of the unconquered lands. The king said, "For the glory of my kingdom, mine honour and brightness returned unto me; . . . I was established in my kingdom, and excellent majesty was added unto me" (verse 36).

Concluding, he gives his own personal testimony, a doxology, "Now I Nebuchadnezzar praise and extol and honour the King of heaven, all whose works are truth, and his ways judgment: and those that walk in pride he is able to abase" (verse 37). Not only does he recognize the justice of his affliction, but he praises the God of truth for His mercy and justice. This sobered, converted king ruled for perhaps two years before he passed to his rest.

The genuineness of his conversion is seen by his willingness to tell the story, including the details of his own folly and the marvelous grace of the everlasting God. How wonderful that God by His grace could take a seemingly hopeless case like this proud king and make him a member of the family of God! When God undertakes to abase our pride and lay human glory in the dust, that is truly a work of creation just as when He brought this earth from chaos to beauty. All this is portrayed in this unusual royal document. Will it not be a privilege in the coming kingdom of glory to fellowship with Nebuchadnezzar and hear from the man himself the story of God's patience and love?

WORLDLY WISDOM REJECTS THE GOSPEL

Twenty-seven years after Nebuchadnezzar died, the empire of Babylon passed away forever. The Babylonian principles, however, were not uprooted when the empire fell, but were preserved by the Greeks and the Romans. Greece became the home of great philosophers, educators, artists, and sculptors, but God as Creator and Sustainer was not recognized in it all. The Greeks sought to develop a super race. Sculpture reached its highest point in Athens, with special reverence for the human form. "A mutilated body is an impertinency," the Greeks said. No wonder it was so difficult to reach the Greek mind with the gospel of a crucified Christ. How, they reasoned, could One who permitted Himself to be taken by His enemies be man's Savior? So the people of Paul's day turned away from the saving grace of Christ. The apostle Paul observed that "the world by wisdom knew not God" (1 Corinthians 1:21).

Rome's contribution to culture was more in the field of law and government. What philosophy they had came largely from Greece. Like Babylon's rule, Rome's rule was also autocratic. The world became a prison from which there was no escape.

"History repeats itself," we say, and that seems to be true. Much that characterized ancient Babylon is being reenacted in our day. In Revelation 13:15 we read of the "beast" (modern Babylon) and its "image" (apostate Christianity) uniting to oppose God's people in the last days. In the name of human development and international peace, demands will be made on all the world to worship the beast and its image. Those who refuse will face a death decree. But the same God who delivered His ancient servants who put their trust in Him will deliver His people in the final worldwide test.

DANIEL SPEAKS TO OUR DAY

Not only the prophecies of Daniel but also the historic sections have special meaning for us in these days. Well did the apostle Paul say, "Whatsoever things were written aforetime were written for our learning, that we through patience and comfort of the scriptures might have hope" (Romans 15:4). This counsel from Ellen White should challenge every lover of God's Word:

> There is need of a much closer study of the word of God; especially should Daniel and the Revelation have attention as never before in the history of our work. We may have less to say in some lines, in regard to the Roman power and the papacy; but we should call attention to what the prophets and apostles have written under the inspiration of the Holy Spirit of God. The Holy Spirit has so shaped matters, both in the giving of the prophecy and in the events portrayed, as to teach that the human agent is to be kept out of sight, hid in Christ, and that the Lord God of heaven and His law are to be exalted. Read the book of Daniel. Call up, point by point, the history of the kingdoms there represented. Behold statesmen, councils, powerful armies, and see how God wrought to abase the pride of men, and lay human glory in the dust. . . .
>
> The light that Daniel received from God was given especially for these last days. The visions he saw by the banks of the Ulai and the Hiddekel, the great rivers of Shinar, are now in process of fulfillment, and all the events foretold will soon have come to pass (*Testimonies to Ministers,* pages 112, 113).

May the Spirit of God, who inspired these records, guide us as we further study these prophecies.

8. Belshazzar and Babylon's Fall

Was there ever such a man as Belshazzar, or is he just a legendary figure? For many years some regarded him as a fictitious character. But today, thanks to archaeology, we know not only that he existed but that he and his father Nabonidus were vital characters in the unfolding story of nations.

The fall of Babylon, one of the greatest and most beautiful cities of ancient times, has left an indelible mark on history. The overthrow of this Chaldean Empire by the Persians fulfilled a number of prophecies well known to Daniel. Nothing that happened on that tragic night recorded in Daniel 5 came as a surprise to him. He knew what Isaiah and Jeremiah had foretold concerning the city. Some of these prophecies we will notice in detail later, but first the story of Babylon's fall.

Nabonidus, Belshazzar's father, ascended the throne in 555 B.C.; he made Belshazzar a co-ruler in about 553 B.C. Nabonidus, more of a scholar than a military leader, has been called "the first archaeologist." His inscriptions indicate that he was also deeply religious. Belshazzar was reckless and defiant. At the time the city fell he was engaging in a wild party with a thousand of his lords. Babylon's fall brought an end to a dynasty that had started so promisingly.

BELSHAZZAR'S DEFIANT FEAST

That hilarious night of drunkenness and idolatry was, according to the famous Nabonidus Chronicle in the British Museum, the eve of the great day of celebration—the sixteenth of Tishri. Belshazzar's defiance of the God of heaven reached an all-time high on that occasion. When liquor had dethroned reason, he commanded that the sacred vessels of Jehovah, which his grandfather Nebuchadnezzar had brought from Jerusalem, be produced for use at the drunken celebration. From these holy vessels of God, Belshazzar and his guests drank the unholy wine of Babylon. The number of these gold and silver vessels, according to Ezra 1:7, 8, 11 was fifty-four hundred.

Entrenched behind tremendously high walls and surrounded by a deep moat, as described by Herodotus after his visit to the ruined city, Belshazzar felt confident that no enemy could possibly enter. He may have planned this feast to express his defiance of the advancing army of the Persians. Why should he be concerned? This city was invincible, so he thought. It had an endless supply of water from the broad River Euphrates, which flowed through the center of the city. It had endless supplies of grain. It could grow ample produce inside the city, aided by irrigation. With alluvial soil and wonderful weather, the gardens could produce three crops each year.

But while Belshazzar drank and praised the gods of gold and silver and wood and bronze, he did not know that his father Nabonidus was fleeing precipitously toward Arabia. For a kingdom to last, it must be established on justice and righteousness. This orgiastic festival of impiety and immorality brought divine judgment with a suddenness that threw the whole party into consternation. Never till the moment when men or nations have filled the cup of their iniquity does God strike. Israel's possession of the land of Canaan had been delayed because "the iniquity of the Amorites was not yet full" (Genesis 15:15, 16). But Babylon's cup was full to overflowing.

LETTERS OF FIRE ON THE PALACE WALL

God bore long with the wickedness of this land, but the fateful moment came when Belshazzar stood before his lords and raised one of God's sacred cups, drinking to the gods of Babylon. While all eyes were upon the king, the assembled crowd witnessed the most startling spectacle. Out of the sleeve of darkness appeared fingers like those of a man's hand, which wrote on the wall, "MENE, MENE, TEKEL, UPHARSIN" (Daniel 5:25).

The revelers hushed into silence. Was this a message of doom from another world? Was it a token of ill omen? The king called loudly for the magicians, the astrologers, the soothsayers, and the Chaldeans to explain. But they could neither read the writing nor interpret its message.

In the midst of the consternation, in came the queen mother, possibly Nitocris, daughter of Nebuchadnezzar. She reminded her blasphemous son that while the wise men could not read the writing, one in the realm could not only read the writing but also interpret it. "Let Daniel be called," she said. She remembered the part this messenger of God had played during the long reign of Nebuchadnezzar and how he had led him at last to accept the most high God. She also knew that more than sixty years earlier Daniel had stood before Nebuchadnezzar and unfolded the future of the world, declaring that Babylon would pass away and another kingdom take its place.

DANIEL INTERPRETS THE MESSAGE

When Daniel appeared, the terrified monarch promised him gifts and honor. Politely, the aged statesman-prophet told the king to give his rewards to another. But "I will read the writing," he said (verse 17). Before doing so, he reminded Belshazzar that it was the most high God who had given his grandfather, Nebuchadnezzar, a kingdom that extended to "all people, nations, and languages" (verse 19). "But when his heart was lifted up, and his mind hardened in pride, he was deposed from his kingly throne, and they took his glory from him: And he was driven from the sons of men; and his heart was made like the beasts, . . . till he knew that the most high God ruled in the kingdom of men, and that he appointeth over it whomsoever he will" (verses 20, 21). Then, fixing his eyes on the trembling king, Daniel delivered his message in the presence of the assembled nobles. "And thou his son, O Belshazzar, hast not humbled thine heart, *though thou knewest all this;* But hast lifted up thyself against the Lord of heaven" (verses 22, 23, emphasis supplied).

Belshazzar was well aware of the family history. He must have been about fourteen years old when Nebuchadnezzar died. But he had stifled his conscience. Daniel continued, "They have brought the vessels of his [the Lord's] house before thee, and thou, and thy lords, thy wives, and thy concubines, have drunk wine in them; . . . and the God in whose hand thy breath is, and whose are all thy ways, hast thou not glorified. . . . Thou art weighed in the balances, and art found wanting. . . . Thy kingdom is divided, and given to the Medes and Persians" (verses 23–28).

Even while Daniel was reading the writing, the Persian armies were marching up the riverbed ready to enter the palace. Belshazzar's day had already passed. He had crossed the unseen barrier between God's mercy and His wrath and did not know it. He had sinned away his day of grace.

How true are the words of the wise man, "Pride goeth before destruction, and an haughty spirit before a fall" (Proverbs 16:18).

THE KING IS DEAD

The Medo-Persian troops entered the banquet hall, and soon the red blood of royalty mingled with the red wine of Babylon on the pavement of the banquet hall. Edward Arnold's well-known words fit the occasion:

> That night they slew him on his father's throne,
> The deed unnoticed and the hand unknown.
> Crownless and scepterless, Belshazzar lay,
> A robe of purple around a form of clay.

Why could not the brilliantly educated Chaldeans read the writing? The medieval Jews believed the letters were probably placed in the form of a rectangle like this:

M N A
M N A
T Q L
P R S

The words are *mene*, "to number"; *tekel*, "to weigh"; *peres*, "dividing," or *paras*, "Persian." Whatever the reason, the God of heaven planned it in order that Daniel might give his final message. That night Babylon fell to rise no more. How true are those words: "The wicked shall be turned into hell, and all the nations that forget God" (Psalm 9:17).

Two of Israel's greatest prophets, Isaiah and Jeremiah, had not only predicted the downfall of Babylon, they had enumerated many of the details as to how it would be accomplished. More than a hundred years before Cyrus was born, God said through the prophet Isaiah, "I will dry up thy rivers" (Isaiah 44:27). "Thus saith the LORD to his anointed, to Cyrus, . . . I will go before thee; . . . I will give thee the treasures of darkness, . . . I have even called thee by thy name: I have surnamed thee, though thou hast not known me" (Isaiah 45:1–4).

Jeremiah, a century later than Isaiah, delivered this message from God: "A drought is upon her waters; and they shall be dried up: for it is the land of graven images, and they are mad upon their idols" (Jeremiah 50:38). And again, "Babylon hath been a golden cup in the LORD's hand, that made all the earth drunken: the nations have drunken of her wine; therefore the nations are mad. Babylon is suddenly fallen and destroyed. . . . We would have healed Babylon, but she is not healed. . . . the LORD hath raised up the spirit of the kings of the Medes: for his device is against Babylon, to destroy it" (Jeremiah 51:7, 9, 11). The prophet further added, "A rumour shall both come one year, and after that in another year shall come a rumour, and violence in the land" (verse 46). These predictions were fulfilled in minute detail. Guided by two deserters—whom Xenophon calls Gadatus and Gobryas—the Persian conquerors made their way up the riverbed without resistance.

CYRUS DELAYS HIS INVASION

A "rumour" did come in one year that Cyrus was marching toward Babylon, but he did not arrive. The reason? It is said that while Cyrus was crossing the River Gyndes, one of his sacred white horses drawing the chariot of Ormazd (or Ahura Mazda) was drowned. Cyrus took revenge on the river, draining it into 360 channels. This took months. Not until the following year did the Persian conqueror arrive at the borders of Babylon. Then he found the conquest very different from the normal pattern. Werner Keller says, "It was without a parallel in the military practice of the ancient Orient; for this time there were no columns of smoke rising from behind shattered walls, no temples or palaces razed to the ground, no house plundered, no man was butchered or impaled" (*The Bible as History,* page 301).

In his own record Cyrus says, "As I entered Babylon in peace, and established my royal residence in the palace of the princes amid jubilation and rejoicing, Marduk [Babylon's chief god], the great lord, warmed the hearts of the Babylonians towards me." Then Cyrus tells how he freed the people from the yoke of bondage and repaired their houses, healing their afflictions. He closes by saying, "I am Cyrus, king of all, the great king, the mighty king, king of Babylon, king of Sumer and Akkad, king of the four corners of the earth" (ibid.).

WHO WAS "DARIUS THE MEDIAN"?

Cyrus the Persian is not named in chapter 5 of Daniel, but "Darius the Median" is. Who was Darius the Mede? There has been considerable discussion as to his identity. In the words of Josephus, he "had another name among the Greeks" (*Antiquities,* X.11.4). Some say he was Astyages, the last ruler of Media. Others say he was Gobryas, the governor of Babylonia under Cyrus; or even Gubaru, another governor. Still others believe he must have been Cyaxares II, son of Astyages. Whoever he was, Daniel's God recognized him and honored him, for Gabriel on one occasion was sent to Darius to "confirm and strengthen him" (Daniel 11:1).

Frederick Tatford, D.D., has written that "the name Darius is not itself a proper name, but an appellative which was borne by several kings and means 'the subduer' " (*The Climax of the Ages,* page 93). In Daniel 9:1 he is called the son of Ahasuerus. Bishop Lowth comments on this: "This is the same person who was called Cyaxares, the son of Astyages by heathen historians with whom Josephus agrees. . . . Astyages had the name Ahasuerus among the Jews as appears by the passage in Tobit XIV, verse 15, where the taking of Ninevah is ascribed to . . . Nabopolassar, Nebuchadnezzar's father, and Astyages." Xinophon, the Greek writer, in his *Cyropaedia,* declares that Darius the Mede was Cyaxares II and therefore the son of Astyages, after whose death he became heir of the Median throne and was the last ruler, in which case his sister was Mandane, the mother of Cyrus.

Keller informs us that Astyages, Cyrus's grandfather, had two dreams that greatly troubled him. He saw water flowing from his daughter and covering great areas of the country. Fearing this to be an ill omen, he called his counselors, who assured him that the daughter's offspring was destined to overrun the whole land. Hearing that the child born to Mandane was a boy, Astyages sent Harpagus, "the most faithful of the Medes," to destroy the baby. But this man did not have the heart for murder. The child grew and was none other than Cyrus, son of Cambyses, descendant of the royal race of Achaemenes. This royal son was greatly admired from his boyhood. "His unparalleled swift and brilliant rise to power was marred by no deed of violence," says Keller. "His able and humane policy made him one of the most attractive figures in the ancient orient. . . . Despotic cruelty was foreign to this Persian" (*The Bible as History,* page 299). He not only issued the decree permitting the Jews to return and rebuild their temple in Jerusalem but also bore the cost of the Jews' transportation and later of the actual construction itself.

If Cyrus was the son of Mandane, daughter of King Astyages, then her brother was Cyaxares II or Darius. This would make Darius the uncle of Cyrus, with whom the latter became well acquainted during the years he spent as a youth in the court of the Medes. After Cyrus's conquest of Babylon, he visited his uncle, presenting him with gifts. Cyaxares II, or Darius, in return gave Cyrus his daughter in marriage as well as his kingdom, according to *Cyropaedia* VIII, 5.17, 18. It would seem, then, that Darius was not only the uncle of Cyrus, but also his father-in-law. We can therefore understand the great conqueror's inviting Darius to Babylon to act as king of that area.

CYRUS LEARNS OF DANIEL'S GOD

Both Cyrus and Darius came to recognize Daniel's God as the God of gods. Imagine the surprise of Cyrus when, after entering the city, he learned that the God of heaven had foretold the important details of this very conquest. Daniel's influence upon the new regime must have been considerable.

The Scripture comment on the conquest is brief: "That night was Belshazzar the king of the Chaldeans slain. And Darius the Median took the kingdom, being about threescore and two years old" (Daniel 5:30, 31).

Darius set up 120 princes or "satraps" over the kingdom. "And over these, three presidents; of whom Daniel was first" (Daniel 6:1, 2). Jealousy soon arose among the two subordinate presidents and the princes, and they "sought to find occasion against Daniel concerning the kingdom" (verse 4). But the only cause they could find was concerning his religion.

After much discussion they approached Darius in a spirit of flattery and persuaded him to sign a decree according to "the law of the Medes and Persians, which altereth not" (verse 8). This was actually a design against Daniel, although Darius did not realize the subtlety of the plan. The wording of the decree was very clear: "Whosoever shall ask a petition of any God or man for thirty days, save of thee, O king, he shall be cast into the den of lions" (verse 7).

The Persians, like other Orientals, regarded the king as divine and worshiped him as the representative of Ormazd, or Ahura Mazda. So the plan was not unusual. But it was all a trap for Daniel, and Daniel knew it. But he could not be intimidated. He still carried out his regular worship, "his windows being open." He knelt "three times a day, and prayed" (verse 10). Had he closed the windows, that would have shown cowardice. Of course he could have rationalized, "Well, I can pray in my heart. God will understand." But Daniel was no compromiser. He knew that those men were waiting and watching, and they soon had a clear case.

Coming to Darius, they reminded him of the decree he had signed. Then they made the charge, saying, "That Daniel, which is of the children of the captivity of Judah, regardeth not thee, O king, nor the decree that thou hast signed, but maketh his petition three times a day" (verse 13).

It was then that Darius realized what his perfidious courtiers had done. He was alarmed and deeply grieved. He knew he had been trapped. All day long he labored, hoping to find a way out, consulting with lawyers and politicians, but without success. The statute could not be changed or favoritism shown. The king was bound by his own law. So Daniel was arraigned before Darius. We could wish that all the conversation between the king and Daniel had been recorded, but the last words of Darius to Daniel are most moving. "Thy God whom thou servest continually, he will deliver thee" (verse 16).

DANIEL LOWERED TO THE LIONS

With feigned loyalty, the accusers lowered Daniel into the den of lions, closed the mouth of the pit with a stone, and saw to it that it was sealed with the king's seal, as well as that of his lords. That night Darius, in deep despondency, could not sleep. Nor would he tolerate any entertainment. He even refused food.

"Then the king arose very early in the morning, and went in haste unto the den of lions. And . . . he cried with a lamentable voice unto Daniel: . . . O Daniel, servant of the living God, is thy God, whom thou servest continually, able to deliver thee from the lions?" (verses 19, 20).

Daniel called back, "My God hath sent his angel, and hath shut the lions' mouths, that they have not hurt me" (verse 22).

The king's heart bounded with joy. Here was the answer not only to Daniel's prayer, but also to the prayers of Darius. When Daniel was taken up, not even a scratch was found upon him. Those wild, hungry cats had been under the control of a higher decree than that of an earthly king. An angel from God had been Daniel's companion all the long night. Perhaps the prayer of King David had been on his lips that night: "My soul is among lions: and I lie even among them that are set on fire. . . . My heart is fixed, O God, my heart is fixed" (Psalm 57:4, 7).

Did somebody suggest that the lions were not hungry? The next part of the story is almost too terrible to contemplate. Those men who had accused Daniel were thrown into the den and their families with them. The record says that the lions tore them to pieces before they reached the bottom.

DARIUS RECOGNIZES THE GOD OF ISRAEL

The story of Daniel's deliverance became known throughout the land, for Darius sent a royal letter to "all people, nations, and languages, that dwell in all the earth" (verse 25). In this letter he gave his testimony to the living God who "delivereth and rescueth," declaring that he "worketh signs and wonders in heaven and in earth" (verse 27). What was to be the execution of one man became a bloodbath for his accusers. After the deliverance, the God of Israel was again proclaimed to the people throughout that vast empire. This was the third royal document that proceeded from the city of Babylon as a testimony to the God of heaven. The first was sent by Nebuchadnezzar telling the story of the fiery furnace and the deliverance of the three Hebrews. The second was Nebuchadnezzar's portrayal of his insanity, recovery, and restoration. The third came from this Median king, and again it was a tribute to God's power to save those who trust in Him. The same God who delivered Daniel and his three companions is the God we serve today. If, while reading this, you feel that subtle intrigue surrounds your life, that there seems no way through, then let the example of these heroes of old inspire you to be true to the living God. He has a thousand ways to meet your need. Trust Him fully. He will bring you through. David said, "Mine enemies would daily swallow me up: for they be many that fight against me." But he then added, "What time I am afraid, I will trust in thee. . . . I will not fear what flesh can do unto me" (Psalm 56:2–4). Isaiah was even more confident. He said, "I will trust, and not be afraid" (Isaiah 12:2). Find your strength, dear friend, where these men found theirs. We can be more than conquerors through Christ Jesus our Lord.

This thrilling story of faith and victory finds us halfway through the book of Daniel. The first six chapters deal largely with history; the last six with prophecy. This latter section is, without doubt, the more fascinating part of the book. The visions Daniel received from the Lord cover the whole history of the world from his day to our own. In the earlier chapters, Daniel was heaven's ambassador at earthly courts. In the last chapters he is God's spokesman to the world, opening up the future, especially that which affects the people of God.

In these chapters we will discover that the living God not only predicts what will happen but foretells the movements of men and nations hundreds, even thousands, of years before the events. One of the impressive things about the book of Revelation, the last book of the Bible, is that it is really a commentary on the last six chapters of Daniel. Recognizing the importance of prophecy, let us turn to these chapters with reverence, praying that the Holy Spirit who moved Daniel to write these visions will guide us as we seek to comprehend God's last message of grace in these troublous days.

9. Cartoon Prophecies of World Empires

One of the most comprehensive prophecies of all the Bible is found in Daniel, chapter 7, which portrays the rise, development, and collapse of human governments from Babylon to the end of the age—"until the times of the Gentiles be fulfilled" (Luke 21:24).

God had revealed the succession of history's great empires nearly fifty years earlier, when Daniel had interpreted Nebuchadnezzar's dream. The Chaldean king had seen the future unfolded in the form of a metallic man. That vision has well been called the "ABC of apocalyptic prophecy." But later Daniel himself saw in vision the shape of things to come in the form of fierce beasts.

It was Belshazzar's first year when this vision appeared. (See Daniel 7:1.) Nabonidus had made his son Belshazzar coregent of the empire in the year 553 B.C. Fourteen years before the festival when the Persian armies overthrew the city, the glory of the empire was already waning.

Nabonidus may have felt that bringing his eldest son into a place of rulership would strengthen the empire. Actually, this change in the leadership proved to be one of the reasons why Cyrus found the conquest of this great city comparatively easy. The father of Belshazzar, as we have already noticed, spent most of his time in the city of Tema in northern Arabia, being more interested in archaeology and history than in politics. He therefore left his son in charge of Babylon, in an administrative office for which Belshazzar was ill prepared.

Now let us look at this great apocalyptic prophecy, noting how much more detail the Lord gave to Daniel than to Nebuchadnezzar. Apocalyptic prophecy is one of the most unique forms of literature, conveying its message in signs or symbols.

> I saw in my vision by night, and, behold, the four winds of the heaven strove upon the great sea. And four great beasts came up from the sea, diverse from one another. The first was

like a lion, and had eagle's wings: I beheld till the wings thereof were plucked, and it was lifted up from the earth, and made stand upon the feet as a man, and a man's heart was given to it (Daniel 7:2–4).

In the following verses the prophet describes three more strange creatures.

What are we to understand by these great beasts? No need to use our imagination here, for the Bible is its own interpreter. Said the angel, "These great beasts, which are four, are four kings, which shall arise out of the earth" (verse 17). "The fourth beast shall be the fourth kingdom upon earth" (verse 23). So these beasts are not four individual kings but rather four successive kingdoms or world empires.

INTERPRETING THE LANGUAGE OF SYMBOLS

While symbolic language may appear bewildering at first, the meaning soon becomes clear and also fascinating. What are we to understand by the "winds" striving on the sea? Jeremiah, a contemporary of Daniel, prophesied, "The LORD hath a controversy with the nations; . . . he will give them that are wicked to the sword. . . . A great whirlwind shall be raised up from the coasts of the earth" (Jeremiah 25:31, 32). Wind in symbolic prophecy, therefore, is used to represent strife and war. But what does the "sea" represent? Isaiah indicates that water in prophecy symbolizes a multitude of people. (See Isaiah 17:12, 13.) And in Revelation 17:15 we read: "The waters which thou sawest . . . are peoples, and multitudes, and nations, and tongues."

The beasts represent great kingdoms or empires. With the winds representing strife and war, the sea representing peoples and multitudes, and the beasts representing empires, we can put the picture together. Daniel saw a succession of world empires that arose and fell as the result of war. That has been the pattern of our world from the beginning of recorded history.

The same succession of empires that was portrayed in Nebuchadnezzar's image now appears as fierce beasts with many added details. Babylon is not just a head of gold, but a lion with eagle's wings. The lion (king of beasts) and the eagle (king of birds) denote both strength and speed of conquest—a fitting symbol of Babylon under the rule of Nebuchadnezzar. In recent years archaeologists have unearthed a number of sculptured winged lions among the ruins of ancient Babylon. Daniel saw something strange happening to the lion, however. The wings were plucked off, and a man's heart was given to it. Could anything better express the change that came into the Babylonian Empire before it collapsed? In English history we read of Richard the Lion-Hearted. King Richard was a lion-hearted man, full of courage and strength. But here we have a man-hearted lion.

MEDIA-PERSIA REPLACES BABYLON

The kingdom of Babylon was not to endure for long, for another kingdom, represented by a bear, was soon to arise. "And behold another beast, a second, like to a bear, and it raised up itself on one side, and it had three ribs in the mouth of it between the teeth of it: and they said thus unto it, Arise, devour much flesh" (Daniel 7:5).

More ponderous, but strong and rapacious, the bear was a fitting symbol of Media-Persia, corresponding to the silver kingdom of chapter 2. Something else important—the bear "raised up itself on one side" (verse 5). History records that the Persian element of this dual empire was much the stronger.

The "three ribs" between the teeth of the bear were also significant; also the words, "Arise, devour much flesh." Unlike Cyrus, the later kings of Persia were notably intolerant and cruel. Since the second century of the Christian Era, the three ribs have been interpreted as Babylon, Lydia, and Egypt. These three kingdoms were not to last. Their humiliating defeat on the battlefield of Gaugamela (or Arbela) in 331 B.C. ushered in a new empire represented by the leopard with four heads and four wings. It was easy to understand the bronze of the metallic image as representing Greece, but what is symbolized by the four wings and four heads of the leopard? If the two wings of the eagle represented Babylon's speed of conquest, then these four wings would denote exceptional celerity of movement. This was certainly true of Greece under Alexander. In the brief space of eight years he welded the Greek city-states into a universal power.

Born of royal blood, this son of Philip of Macedon was a pupil of the great philosopher Aristotle. Throughout his conquests, Alexander kept in touch with his mentor. In one lightning campaign following another, he quickly conquered most of the known world. But he could not conquer himself. He is said to have died of a fever brought on by a drunken debauch at the age of thirty-three. When asked on his deathbed to whom he would leave the kingdom, he replied, "To the strongest."

Twenty years of internal strife and civil war followed Alexander's death, until after the Battle of Ipsus in 301 B.C. four of his generals divided the empire among themselves. Lysimachus took the north with Thrace and part of Asia Minor. Cassander took the west, including Macedonia and Athens. Seleucus took the east with most of Syria, Mesopotamia, and Persia, while Ptolemy took the south, including Egypt and Palestine. The four heads of the leopard beast were indeed significant. These divisions, however, weakened the empire and paved the way for the rising power of Rome.

THE STRANGE TEN-HORNED BEAST

While every beast differed from the others, this fourth creature defied description. It was so hideous compared with the preceding creatures that the prophet received a second vision to describe it. The prophet described this crushing power as "dreadful and terrible, and strong exceedingly; and it had great iron teeth: it devoured and brake in pieces, and stamped the residue with the feet of it: and it was diverse from all the beasts that were before it; and it had ten horns" (verse 7).

The prophet was particularly eager to "know the truth of the fourth beast, which was diverse from all the others"(verse 19). With ferocious iron teeth and nails of brass, it would devour and break in pieces all before it and would stamp the residue with his feet; nothing could stand before his power.

This fourth best unquestionably symbolized the empire of the Caesars. This power crucified our Lord and martyred the apostles. A high point during a "Roman holiday" was the slaughter of Christians either as burning torches in the Coliseum or as food for ravenous beasts. But what about the ten horns, and especially "that horn that had eyes, and a mouth that spake very great things" (verse 20)? The angel explained that the ten horns were "ten kings that shall arise: and another shall rise after them; and he shall be diverse from the first, and he shall subdue three kings" (verse 24). While the Roman Empire was strong, cruel, and crushing, it was not all bad. Besides its network of fine roads, which aided Christians in carrying the gospel to their world, Rome also developed a comprehensive legal system.

ROMAN EMPIRE DIVIDED

But the time came when the empire was divided. Weakened by warfare and barbarian invasions, it finally fell. Then the "little horn" pushed its way into leadership, uprooting three of the ten kingdoms. Several centuries later the Holy Roman Empire arose. While neither holy, nor Roman, nor an empire, it held sway for a thousand years.

On occasion interpreters of prophecy have alleged that at no period of Roman history was the empire composed of precisely ten kingdoms. However, it is well documented that the ten kingdoms appeared *after* the decline and fall of the empire of the Caesars. Gibbon, as well as other authoritative historians, make it clear that the ten kingdoms did indeed come into being after Rome's collapse. In his *Horae Apocalypticae,* Elliott lists these as Anglo-Saxons, Alemanni, Franks, Visigoths, Suevi, Burgundians, Bavarians, Heruli, Vandals, and Ostrogoths. (Some were known by other names at different times, and some other lists suggest various different kingdoms.)

The angel told Daniel that the little horn, "whose look was more stout than his fellows" (verse 20), would uproot three horns, or kingdoms. How completely this was fulfilled when the popes came to power! Three kingdoms were uprooted: the Heruli, the Vandals, and the Ostrogoths. And it was because they were Arians in their belief— that is, they did not recognize Christ as eternal, but claimed that He was created. In A.D. 493 the Heruli met their fate; in A.D. 534 the Vandals; and in A.D. 538 the Ostrogoths' power was broken, but they continued until A.D. 552.

EUROPE DOMINATED BY THE CHURCH

The little horn, though small at first, became strong, "more stout than his fellows" (verse 20). This power "made war with the saints, and prevailed against them," as the angel said, and would continue until heaven's great judgment would settle his destiny and "take away his dominion" (verses 21, 26).

The papacy dominated Western Europe during the medieval centuries and later extended its control to the new lands of the Western Hemisphere. Not only did the angel describe this power in specific ways, he also showed what his work would be. This prophecy was well understood by the great Protestant Reformers of the sixteenth century. In fact, their interpretations of the prophecies of Daniel and Revelation led them to break from the apostate medieval church. They called the people back to the Bible, showing clearly from God's Word how the papacy fulfilled Daniel's prophecies. "He shall speak great words against the most High," said the angel, "and shall wear out the saints of the most High, and think to change times and laws: and they shall be given into his hand until a time and times and the dividing of time" (verse 25).

Leaders such as Luther, Calvin, Knox, and Cranmer pointed to Daniel 7 and Revelation 17, identifying the great apostasy with headquarters in Rome. The scriptural message of Revelation 18:4 formed the basis of many of their sermons: "Come out of her, my people, that ye be not partakers of her sins."

POWERFUL PREACHERS WITH A MIGHTY MESSAGE

These men were mighty preachers, and Paul's message in 2 Thessalonians 2:3, 4 concerning "that man of sin . . . Who opposeth and exalteth himself above all that is called God, or that is worshipped," who "sitteth in the temple of God, shewing himself that he is God," moved the Reformers to action. They not only proclaimed the truth, but they were willing to die for it. And many did.

Some of the most brutal persecutions of all history, such as the Inquisition, were inspired by leaders of the church. The little-horn power did indeed wear out the saints of the most High. Millions of God's faithful men and women suffered martyrdom, many by fire, others by the sword, the ax, drowning, flaying, and the rack.

CHANGING GOD'S TIMES AND LAWS

The angel further declared that this power would "think to change times and laws" (verse 25). Rome's attack on God's Ten Commandments is vital, but the changing of "times" is also deeply significant. Great prophetic time prophecies relating to our Lord's first advent— His ministry, death, and resurrection—are clearly delineated in Daniel's prophecies. But these have been changed and reinterpreted, as we shall see in our next chapter. Also, important prophecies concerning our Savior's return, particularly those that focus on this apostate power, outlining its work, have been changed so that the great antichrist of the centuries has been disguised. (We shall consider this point in more detail when we come to the prophecy of Daniel 9.)

Not only would this power attempt to change the great chronological prophecies, the prophetic "times," but this power would even dare to lay his hand upon God's holy law. On this the Reformers were also very clear. Two commandments, particularly the second and the fourth, are clear evidences of this. The second commandment, which forbids the making of graven images, in most Roman Catholic catechisms is attached to the first and reads: "I am the Lord thy god. Thou shalt have no strange gods before me." This, of course, omits all reference to bowing to graven images.

Concerning the Sabbath commandment, Luther said, "They [Roman Catholics] allege the change of the Sabbath into the Lord's day, contrary, as it seemeth to the Decalogue; and they have no example more in their mouths than the change of the Sabbath. They will needs have the Church's power to be very great, because it hath dispensed with a precept of the Decalogue" (*Creeds of Christendom*, vol. 3, page 64).

One of the ablest of the Reformers, Philip Melanchthon, a close associate of Luther, was even more specific. He said, "He changeth the tymes and lawes that any of the six work dayes commanded of God will make them unholy and idle dayes when he lyste, or of their own holy dayes abolished make work dayes again, or when they changed ye Saturday into Sonday" (*Exposition of Daniel the Prophet*, gathered from Melanchthon's writings by George Joye, 1545).

A COUNTERFEIT REST DAY

Some years ago Dr. Edward T. Hiscox, a Baptist scholar and theologian who authored *The Baptist Manual,* addressed a large group of ministers in New York on this question. Concerning Sunday as a day of worship he said, "What a pity that it comes branded with the mark of paganism christened with the name of the sun god when adopted and sanctioned by the papal apostasy, and bequeathed as a sacred legacy to Protestantism." What a pity indeed! But all this was foretold in the prophecies of Daniel, Paul, and John. Eusebius, church historian in the time of Constantine, states it this way: "All things whatever it was our duty to do on the Sabbath, these we [the apostate church] have transferred to the Lord's day" (*Commentary on Psalm 92*).

These claims were later emphasized by the Counter-Reformation, which grew out of the Council of Trent. This council was convened in an effort on the part of the papacy to meet the challenge of the Protestant Reformation. Note these words from the first session of that important council: "The celebration of the Sabbath should be transferred to the Lord's Day" *(Catechism of the Council of Trent).*

The angel also told how long this power was to be in control—"a time and times and the dividing of time" (Daniel 7:25). A "time" was a year; "times" would be two years; and "the dividing of time" would be half a year (see Daniel 12:7), making a total of three and a half years. A Jewish year, recognized by Bible scholars, is 360 days, this being the mean average between a lunar year of 356 days and a solar year of 365 days. Let us add these figures together:

$$1 \text{ time} = 360 \text{ days}$$
$$2 \text{ times} = 720 \text{ days}$$
$$\tfrac{1}{2} \text{ time} = \underline{180 \text{ days}}$$
$$1{,}260 \text{ days}$$

In symbolic prophecy a day may stand for a literal year, as in Ezekiel 4:6 and Numbers 14:34—"each day for a year." Then 1,260 prophetic days would be 1,260 literal years. This measurement of time is brought to view in Revelation 12:6, which reads "a thousand two hundred and threescore days." In Revelation 13:5 the same prophetic period is stated in a little different way: "forty and two months." A Jewish month is 30 days, so 42 months multiplied by 30 brings the same total—1,260 days or years. In Revelation 12:14 the same period is differently stated: "a time, and times, and half a time." In the year A.D. 538 the rule of the Ostrogoths was definitely broken, leaving the papacy free to develop her political and ecclesiastical power. This she did, and for 1,260 years she exercised great authority in Europe, crowning kings and deposing them.

THE REFORMERS CHALLENGE THE CHURCH

The Protestant Reformers of the sixteenth and seventeenth centuries challenged the church's power, but by 1798 papal power in Europe had severely weakened. That year, in the Napoleonic Wars, Pope Pius VI was taken prisoner in Rome by General Berthier of France. The pope died in exile a year and a half later. From A.D. 538 to A.D. 1798 is, we repeat, 1,260 years.

The arrest of Pope Pius made dramatic news. Many Protestants, recognizing in the arrest the fulfillment of prophecies of Daniel and Revelation, felt that the event both confirmed the truths they had proclaimed and inspired an intensive study of the prophecies. Especially they studied the eschatological prophecies—those relating to the second advent of our Lord. The result was a great spiritual awakening in Europe, in the Middle East, in India, in North and South America, even as far away as the new land of Australia.

The words of the angel, "the judgment shall sit, and they shall take away his dominion, to consume and to destroy it unto the end" (verse 26), came with new meaning. "The kingdom and dominion, and the greatness of the kingdom under the whole heaven, shall be given to the people of the saints of the most High, whose kingdom is an everlasting kingdom, and all dominions shall serve and obey him. Hitherto is the end of the matter" (verses 26–28). This could mean nothing more or less than the end of the age, which would be ushered in by the second advent of Christ.

THE "ADVENT AWAKENING" IS BORN

The reaction was tremendous. With new confidence, men and women by hundreds of thousands pored over the prophecies. This was the prelude to the Great Awakening.

When the angel came to the climax of his message, Daniel was speechless. But he says, "I kept the matter in my heart" (verse 28). Are we stirred by this revelation? Does the knowledge of the Lord's return sober us and inspire us? The prophecy reveals that no other world empire will arise until our Lord returns. What courage that should bring to our hearts! While definite attempts are being made today to establish a new world order, we can know that if such a world government were to be established, it would be short lived.

The next great event on this planet will be the ushering in of the eternal kingdom of glory. And that kingdom will be established not by human councils and legislation but by our Lord Himself. What a contrast it will be from all the kingdoms of the past and the present. It will be a kingdom of peace and love—no armies, no navies, no police, no prisons. Riots, demonstrations, poverty, and hunger will be no more. The citizens of that kingdom shall never say, "I am sick," for pain and death will be banished forever.

This is the kingdom for which God's people through all the ages have waited and prayed. Are you, dear friend, a citizen of God's kingdom of grace now? If you are, you will also be a citizen of the kingdom of glory then. Christ loved us so much that He died in our place, so that you and I might live with Him eternally. Not only did He die, He rose again and ascended to His Father's throne from whence He sends forth His Spirit to deliver us from sin and rebellion and to make us members of His family.

Each of us must make a decision individually. Jesus said, "He that is not with me is against me" (Matthew 12:30). As we close this chapter, we simply ask, Are you with Him or against Him?

10. Antichrist and Heaven's Judgment

Scripture refers to God's great judgment more than a thousand times. Almost every Bible writer makes some reference to it. But no more sublime description is given than in Daniel 7:9–14. The nature of the scene demands our serious consideration. The expression "thrones were cast down" (verse 9) is unfortunate. "Thrones were placed" is more correct, as the Revised Standard Version translates the text. Daniel was given a vision of the coming judgment when "the Ancient of days" (verse 9) would take His place, surrounded by a group sitting on lesser thrones. Ten thousand times ten thousand angels, plus thousands more, joined the scene. The prophet John describes the same scene in Revelation 5:11: "I beheld, and I heard the voice of many angels round about the throne: . . . and the number of them was ten thousand times ten thousand, and thousands of thousands."

We usually think of the judgment as a scene with a judge, a prisoner in the dock, and a defense attorney pleading his case. However, a judgment scene in the days of John was quite different. When one who was to preside took his place, then a group of associates took their places in a semicircle. These were special seats, or judgment thrones, and those who occupied those places were representatives. An interesting allusion to this is found in Psalm 122:1–5, where the psalmist says, "I was glad when they said unto me, Let us go into the house of the Lord." Then he goes on to tell about some things he finds there. Berkeley's version of verse 5 reads, "For there seats are placed for judging."

Daniel was given a view of the Ancient of days, God the Father, taking His place. It is He who *presides* in the judgment. Then in verse 13 the Son of man appears to *perform* the work. This is sometimes called the investigative judgment because there the evidence is presented. A more illuminating title would be the

99

pre-Advent judgment, for this takes place before the Son of man returns for His people. And the prophecy says that earthly powers are still struggling for supremacy while this judgment is in session. When our Lord returns in glory, He brings His rewards with Him (see Revelation 22:12)—a statement that indicates that the destiny of every soul will have been settled before the Second Advent. In this pre-Advent judgment, the God of the universe will give a full account of His work in the salvation of men. He will uncover the sinister influences of Lucifer, who has charged God with being unjust.

Sin did not begin on earth. In heaven the highest of the angels led a rebellion against God. He said, "I will exalt my throne above the stars of God: I will sit also upon the mount of the congregation, in the sides of the north: I will ascend above the heights of the clouds; I will be like the most High" (Isaiah 14:13, 14). When Lucifer challenged God's rulership, one-third of the heavenly hosts joined in that rebellion, and they were all cast out of heaven. (See Revelation 12:4, 7–9.)

GOD VINDICATED IN THE JUDGMENT

The judgment Daniel describes in verses 9 and 10 of Daniel 7 is the same as that pictured in Revelation 14:7. The central issue in the judgment is the vindication of the character of God before the whole universe. Thus it is called "the hour of his [God's] judgment" (Revelation 14:7). Part of that judgment will be the presentation of the records. This is the crisis hour of the universe, when God puts Himself on trial.

"When thou speakest thou shalt be vindicated, and win the verdict when thou art on trial" (Romans 3:4, NEB). Not only are *we* on trial, but God Himself is on trial. He planned it that way so that the whole universe can study the story of sin and finally participate in the vindication of His character. When that judgment ends, every creature in the universe will stand on one side or the other of the issue. The Bible does not teach that all will be saved, but it does teach that "we must all appear before the judgment seat of Christ; that every one may receive the things done in his body, according to that he hath done, whether it be good or bad" (2 Corinthians 5:10). When God uncovers all the records, he will reveal to the universe not only His patience and forgiving love, but also who of the human family will have accepted His grace and therefore be candidates for immortality, which will be bestowed on the righteous at the second advent of our Lord.

God, of course, does not have to study record books to discover who will be saved. "The Lord knoweth them that are his" (2 Timothy 2:19). But the judgment reveals God's justice and mercy to the universe.

At the conclusion of that heavenly assize, the Son of man comes before the Ancient of days, God the Father. Then "there was given him dominion, and glory, and a kingdom, that all people, nations, and languages, should serve him: his dominion is an everlasting dominion, which shall not pass away, and his kingdom that which shall not be destroyed" (Daniel 7:14).

OUR REPRESENTATIVE IN THE JUDGMENT

The coming of the Son of man before the Ancient of days is full of meaning, and the term *Son of man* is also significant. Some translations read "one human in form," emphasizing His humanity. As repentant sinners, we have a representative, one like ourselves, before the Father. Jesus evidently took the term *Son of man* from the seventh chapter of Daniel, and the New Testament records more than eighty occasions when He used it.

He concludes His ministry of reconciliation by this work of judgment. While He is our advocate, He is also our judge. Christ Himself said, "The Father judgeth no man, but hath committed all judgment unto the Son. . . . And hath given him authority to execute judgment also, because he is the Son of man" (John 5:22, 27).

While it is the Father who *presides* in this august assembly as the Ancient of days, yet it is the Son who *performs* the judgment. God has "appointed a day, in the which he will judge the world in righteousness by that man whom he hath ordained; whereof he hath given assurance unto all men, in that he hath raised him from the dead" (Acts 17:31). This can be none other than Jesus Christ.

CHRIST, OUR JUDGE

Note these important words: "It is He [Jesus] who has encountered the deceiver, and who through all the ages has been seeking to wrest the captives from his grasp, who will pass judgment upon every soul" (Ellen White, *The Desire of Ages,* page 210). The same author has written: "Christ Himself will decide who are worthy to dwell with the family of heaven. He will judge every man according to his words and his works" (Ellen White, *Christ's Object Lessons,* page 74). And again: "Christ has been made our Judge. The Father is not the Judge. The angels are not. He who took humanity upon Himself, and in this world lived a perfect life, is to judge us. He only can be our Judge. Will you remember this, brethren? Will you remember it, ministers? Will you remember it, fathers and mothers? Christ took humanity that He might be our Judge" (Ellen White, *Testimonies for the Church,* vol. 9, page 185).

It was our Lord who said, "The Father . . . hath committed all judgment unto the Son" (John 5:22). This refers not only to the pre-Advent judgment but also to the pronouncement of the sentence and the execution of that sentence.

At the very time that the pre-Advent judgment is in session, the "little horn" power, which we have noticed in the previous chapter, is heard to speak "great words against the most High" (Daniel 7:25), uttering his most blasphemous claims. An even clearer picture of what that means to us is presented in Daniel 8, which deals particularly with the sanctuary and God's provisions of salvation for sinners.

To understand the messages of Daniel fully we must understand something of the Hebrew sanctuary, for the prophecy declared that the truths of that sanctuary would be "cast down . . . to the ground" and trodden under foot (Daniel 8:10, 11).

How and when was all this to happen? This eighth chapter could well be called the key to understanding Daniel. In this chapter we are introduced to a most important vision of a ram, a goat, and a little-horn power that would seek to destroy the truths of salvation. This vision was given to Daniel two years after the vision of the great beasts recorded in chapter 7. That vision came in "the first year of Belshazzar king of Babylon" (Daniel 7:1), but the events of chapter 8 were brought to Daniel's notice "in the third year of the reign of king Belshazzar" (Daniel 8:1). The prophet received this vision when he was at Shushan in the province of Elam, or Elymias, in Persia. This was a mountainous region occupied originally by a Cushite race. In Genesis 14, we read of Chedorlaomer who founded an extensive empire including Elam, which, according to some historians, became independent as early as 2280 B.C. Later Elam's king attacked Babylon, transported many spoils to Shushan, or Susa, including the famous code of Hammurabi. Susa lay on the direct route from Babylon to India.

In Daniel's day there was evidently a large canal that connected the two rivers, the Coprates and the Choaspes. The canal was called Eluacus or Ulai. Daniel was probably on official business for Babylon when God gave him this very important vision. He says, "I lifted up mine eyes, and saw, and, behold, there stood before the river a ram which had two horns: and the two horns were high; but one was higher than the other, and the higher came up last. I saw the ram pushing westward, and northward, and southward; so that no beasts might stand before him, neither was there any that could deliver out of his hand; but he did according to his will, and became great" (Daniel 8:3, 4).

GABRIEL INTERPRETS THE SYMBOLS

There is no need to guess concerning the interpretation of this vision, for the angel Gabriel made it very clear: "The ram which thou sawest having two horns are the kings of Media and Persia" (verse 20). Under Cyrus the Great, Persia became the stronger force in the dual kingdom, the "higher horn" coming up last. The ram was the symbol of Persia at that time, just as the lion today represents Britain or the eagle symbolizes the United States. In fact, the Persian kings were crowned with a ram's head of gold, jeweled with precious stones. Moreover their coins carried the figure of a ram. In this prophecy the ram pushed westward, taking Babylonia, Mesopotamia, and Syria; northward, taking Armenia and the area of the Caspian Sea; and southward, engulfing Egypt, the Holy Land, Libya, and Ethiopia.

"No beasts [powers] might stand before him" (verse 4). The

advance of the Medo-Persian Empire was overwhelming. Then the prophet said, "As I was considering, behold, an he goat came from the west on the face of the whole earth, and touched not the ground: and the goat had a notable horn between his eyes" (verse 5).

Gabriel interpreted this symbol as well. "And the rough goat is the king of Grecia: and the great horn that is between his eyes is the first king" (verse 21). That king, of course was Alexander the Great, who in a little less than a decade conquered the ancient world. The goat king in the prophecy "came from the west, . . . and touched not the ground" (verse 5). Conquering Asia Minor, Syria, Phoenicia, Cyprus, Egypt, Babylonia, Persia, and the mountains north of India, he took his troops as far east as the Indus River. But the soldiers, having been away from home more than seven years, forced Alexander to return. He traveled as far back as Babylon, where he intended to make his headquarters. But mourning the loss of a favorite friend, it is reported he was seized by a sudden illness ("swamp fever"), perhaps malaria, which was complicated by heavy drinking. Though only thirty-three years old, he died in a few days. This conquering genius left a military record rarely, if ever, surpassed. How true is the prophecy!

The symbol of Greece was the goat. Tradition has it that Caremus, the first king of Macedon, followed a herd of wild goats to Edessa, where he set up his capital, calling it Aege, "the goat city," from whence the national symbol sprang. The prophecy indicated a dramatic change—"when he was strong, the great horn was broken" (verse 8). In its place four horns appeared. It is said that when Alexander lay dying, Perdiccas, his faithful friend, asked to whom he would leave the kingdom. He replied, "To the strongest." Upon his decease, the empire was thrown into a state of strife until it was completely broken. The army scattered, and the cities were plundered. At last four of Alexander's generals divided the empire between them as noted earlier. Lysimachus took the north, including Cappadocia, Thrace, and northern Asia Minor. Ptolemy took the south—Egypt, Cyprus, and Palestine. Cassander claimed Macedonia, Thessaly, and Greece. Seleucus took the east, including Babylonia, Persia, and Syria.

Note carefully the language in the rest of the prophecy, because there is perhaps more confusion on this than on any other part of the book. Scripture says, "And out of one of them came forth a little horn, which waxed exceeding great, toward the south, and toward the east, and toward the pleasant land. And it waxed great, even to the host of heaven" (verses 9, 10).

Then he "shall destroy the mighty and the holy people," and "he shall also stand up against the Prince of princes" (verses 24, 25).

Many commentators see in these verses a description of Antiochus Epiphanes, eighth king in the Seleucid dynasty. While this man certainly was a tyrant and a persecutor, having done all he could against the Jews, yet he certainly was not this little-horn power described in the text. True, he profaned the temple in Jerusalem by sacrificing a sow at the altar of burnt offering and then sprinkling its broth over the temple walls. And while doing all that, he tried to enforce the worship of Olympus and massacred more than a hundred thousand Jews who refused such idolatrous worship. Because of his frightful acts of sacrilege, he was despised not only by the Jews but also by his own people. However, Antiochus was only one of a line of kings and by no means the strongest. When we have said the worst we can about him, he comes short of the prophetic description.

WHO WAS THE "EXCEEDING GREAT" POWER?

Note these important points—the ram representing Persia was to become "great;" the goat representing Greece was to become "very great." But this new power, symbolized by the little horn, was to become "exceeding great." Surely neither Antiochus Epiphanes nor any other of his line was greater than Cyrus or Alexander. Actually, Antiochus was anything but great. He was forced to pay tribute to Rome constantly; he was killed trying to raise more money to pay tribute. It would be hard to find in history a ruler that was more eccentric. Today we might call him paranoid. Even his own people sometimes referred to him as Antiochus *Epimanes* (the "madman") instead of Antiochus *Epiphanes.* He did not enlarge his territory. He was simply one among many kings. If it were left to historians alone to select a man to fill the role, it certainly would not be Antiochus Epiphanes. The choice of this man is part of a design to shift the focus from the power clearly indicated. And we do well to probe this.

The prophecy says, "Out of one of them came forth a little horn, which waxed exceeding great, toward the south, and toward the east, and toward the pleasant land. And it waxed great, even to the host of heaven. . . . Yea, he magnified himself even to the prince of the host" (verses 9–11).

The power introduced here was to do things Antiochus Epiphanes could never do. How could Antiochus stand up against the Prince of princes when the former died in 164 B.C., long before our Lord was born? Some suggest that Antiochus was only a type of a greater power—the antichrist—who will appear in the end time. The real fulfillment, they say, lies in the future, after Christ's second advent. But what right does anyone have to throw this prophecy off into the future (as do many interpreters of prophecy) when the Scripture indicates no such gap?

Note carefully: This new power was to come "out of one of them [the four horns]" (verse 9), that is, out of one of the four divisions of the Greek Empire. It would be small at the beginning but would wax "exceeding great" toward the south (the Egyptian kingdom), and toward the east (the Seleucid kingdom), and toward the pleasant land (Palestine). The kingdom that Antiochus ruled was already in the east. It could not, therefore, refer to him. It must be some other power. We must then look for a power greater than Persia or Greece. Only one fulfills the prophecy, and that is Rome, the fourth in the succession of empires. Egypt was made a province of Rome in 30 B.C. Rome had conquered Syria some years earlier in 65 B.C., and in 63 B.C. Palestine was incorporated into the Roman Empire. More than a century later the wrath of Rome fell upon the Jews with great violence. In response to untold provocations, Rome's armies marched against Jerusalem in A.D. 66, and the war dragged on for four years. Finally, in A.D. 70 the legions under the command of Titus stormed the walls. They completely destroyed the city and the temple and scattered the Jews throughout the empire.

Rome was graphically portrayed as the "iron kingdom" in chapter 2 and also as the indescribable beast with ten horns in chapter 7. Chapter 8 portrays this power also and gives many more details. The Roman Empire bitterly persecuted both the Jewish nation and the

Christian church, having previously ordered the crucifixion of an innocent man, Christ Jesus. But the iron empire was not to last forever. It broke up into ten kingdoms, and another power moved in to take its place. In the previous chapter we noticed that the little-horn power pushed its way into the forefront, uprooting three of the ten kingdoms. It is not merely the political power but the religious power, the apostate church, that is portrayed in Daniel, chapters 7 and 8.

ECCLESIASTICAL ROME CORRUPTS THE GOSPEL

Concerning the little horn, the prophecy said, "Yea, he magnified himself even to the prince of the host, and by him the daily sacrifice was taken away, and the place of his sanctuary was cast down" (Daniel 8:11). To grasp the full meaning of this verse, we need to realize that the word *sacrifice* is not in the original text. It was supplied by the translators. The word translated "daily" is from the Hebrew *tamid,* which occurs 103 times in the Old Testament. It means "continual" or "continually" and is used generally in connection with the ancient sanctuary services such as the "continual burnt offering," "continual shewbread," "continual incense," etc. These services foreshadowed the continual mediation of our Lord on behalf of sinners. For hundreds of years a priestly ministry was carried out in the Mosaic sanctuary. Later it was continued in the temple.

The burnt offering foreshadowed our Lord's death on the cross as the Lamb of God; the shewbread and the incense were types of His ministry as High Priest and Intercessor in the heavenly sanctuary. (See Hebrews 7:3; 4:15; 8:1, 2; 9:11, 12.) The prophecy in Daniel revealed that these central truths of the gospel would be cast down to the ground and stamped upon. Even "the place of his sanctuary was cast down" (Daniel 8:11). This happened first when Rome destroyed Jerusalem and erected a temple to Jupiter on the temple's former site.

THE EMPEROR JOINS THE CHURCH

Two and a half centuries later the apostate church had become so popular that Emperor Constantine became a nominal Christian and, just prior to his death, a baptized member. Soon bishops became

government officers, carrying out the dictates of the state. State offi-
cials were also appointed to high positions in the church, regardless
of their qualifications either morally or spiritually. This not only corrupted the church but paved the way for the introduction of pagan
practices into the worship services. Little by little, the gospel of salvation by grace alone was buried beneath a plethora of ceremonies,
rituals, and penances.

In A.D. 800 Charlemagne, the king of the Franks, created the
Holy Roman Empire, in which the church joined the state in many
areas. Those were dark days for true Christianity and also for the Jews,
who were forced into ghettos with no civil rights and little justice. The
light of truth in many places was almost obliterated. Moffatt's translation of verse 11 reads: "It even magnified itself to match the Prince of
the starry host, and deprived him of the daily sacrifice."

In rabbinical literature, the "daily" included the evening and
morning sacrifices, which became the "center and core of public worship" (Dr. J. A. Herts, *The Pentateuch and Hoftorahs*, page 694).

These sacrifices were designated by the Hebrew word *tamid*, translated "daily" in English. We have already noticed that this word stood
for the continual manifestation of Christ at the throne of grace. But
the prophecy tells how this new power would "magnify himself" and
"prosper and practice," corrupting the gospel and taking glory from
the "prince of the host." (See verses 11, 12.)

Instead of the pure gospel centering in the finished sacrifice of
Christ on Calvary, now ministering as our High Priest in the heavenly sanctuary, a false gospel insinuated itself. This centered in an
earthly sanctuary with headquarters in Rome and manned by an
earthly priesthood. No matter how sincere these priests may be, the
church has declared that "Christ is offered on our altars every day." In
Faber's *Catechism for the Catholic Parochial Schools*, page 72, #359, we
read: "Question: Is the sacrifice of Christ on the cross still offered?
Answer: The sacrifice of Christ on the cross is still offered in every
mass."

While not questioning the sincerity of any, we would point out
that the very heart of the New Testament message is that Jesus Christ
has been offered "once for all" on the cross (Hebrews 10:10). And by

virtue of that finished sacrifice, He is now at the throne of grace ministering for us. The system of an earthly priesthood and the sacrifice of the mass is really alien to the gospel of Christ. Through the mass, the confessional, and the doctrine of salvation by works, this religious system has indeed "cast down the truth to the ground" (Daniel 8:12).

HOW LONG UNTIL THE SANCTUARY TRUTH WOULD BE PROCLAIMED?

While Daniel was watching the activities of the little horn, he heard a dialogue between two heavenly beings. A question was asked, "For how long will the period of this vision last? . . . How long will impiety cause desolation?" (verse 13, NEB). The answer came, "And he said unto me, Unto two thousand and three hundred days; then shall the sanctuary be cleansed" (verse 14). The Hebrew word here translated "cleansed" means "justified" or "made right." A volume could be written on this statement. "The justification of the sanctuary is the vindication of its cause," says A. Bevan, "for as long as it is polluted it lies under condemnation" (*A Short Commentary on the Book of Daniel*).

This period of 2,300 days has presented a real challenge to commentators. Some suggest that *ereb boqer,* translated "days," should read "evenings and mornings" as in the Revised Standard Version. Therefore, they say, it is only 1,150 actual days. To this Keil replies, "A Hebrew reader could not possibly understand this period of 2,300 evenings and mornings as 2,300 half days or 1,150 whole days, because evening and morning at creation consisted not of half days but of whole days" (*The Book of the Prophet Daniel,* quoted in Edward J. Young, *The Prophecy of Daniel,* page 174).

The time period in this vision is very specific, but at this point the precise time for the beginning was not indicated. Daniel was naturally concerned and sought earnestly for the meaning. Gabriel was then told to make the matter clear to Daniel. He informed the prophet that the vision belonged to "the time of the end" (verse 17). And "at the time appointed the end shall be" (verse 19).

"The period determined was long." Dr. Bung, a Jewish writer, declares the prophet understood the expression, "then shall the sanctuary be cleansed," for that occurred every year on the Day of Atonement, on the tenth day of the seventh month. When Daniel received this vision, the sanctuary and the holy city of Jerusalem had already been destroyed by the Babylonians. Even had the temple been standing, the long period of 2,300 days could not be fitted into the regular pattern; and being a prophetic period, the days represented actual years. No wonder Gabriel said, "Shut thou up the vision; for it shall be for many days" (verse 26). "It is far distant," as Fenton translates it.

The angel's explanation of all that was to happen proved too much for the aging prophet. He fainted and was sick for a time. When he recovered, he carried out his governmental responsibilities. But neither he nor any of his associates could understand the vision. The symbols of the ram and the goat were clear; the angel had explained that portion of the vision. But concerning the "sanctuary and the host" and the power that would stand up against the "Prince of princes," as well as the long period of 2,300 days, these concerned the prophet greatly, but none understood it.

DANIEL RECEIVES THE EXPLANATION

Considerable time elapsed between the receiving of this vision and its interpretation. Not until the overthrow of the Babylonian Empire some years later did Daniel receive the explanation of these points. Sometimes we get impatient for God's answer to our problems, but let us remember than even Daniel, a prophet and a man greatly beloved of God, had to wait years for God's answer.

The explanation of the vision we find in the next chapter, Daniel 9, verses 21–27. This is the most precise outline prophecy in the Bible. It provides the master key to the correct understanding of our Lord's first advent and the conditions leading to His second advent. We will note this in detail in our next chapter.

Before leaving chapter 8, we should note that the 2,300-days prophecy of Daniel 8:14 seems to have been given by Christ Himself, called in the marginal reference (in some King James Version Bibles) of verse 13 "the numberer of secrets" or "the wonderful numberer." In Isaiah 9:6, He is called "Wonderful, Counselor, the mighty God, the everlasting Father, the Prince of Peace." The description of Daniel 10:5, 6 is repeated in Revelation 1:13–16. So important is this prophecy concerning the cleansing of the sanctuary that it was not left for lesser beings to describe. It came to the prophet from the One who is "the Judge of all the earth" (Genesis 18:25). But even His truth would be attacked by the one described as of "fierce countenance, and understanding dark sentences" (Daniel 8:23) whom the angel said would "magnify himself" (verse 25) and "destroy the mighty and the holy people" (verse 24).

The clash between the Prince of princes and this corrupting power would reach its climax in the teachings and work of the antichrist, and this would happen prior to the second advent of our Lord. In this context, Jesus urged His people to study the prophecies of Daniel. Tragic as this hour of history is, it is nevertheless full of wonderful meaning for those with eyes to see and ears to hear—those anointed by the Holy Spirit to discern the signs of the times. This generation is destined to witness tremendous things in the near future. Are we ready?

11. Daniel's Key Theme— The Sanctuary and Salvation

We now come to what may be considered the most important chapter in Daniel's unique book. Chapter 9 contains one of the greatest prophecies in the Bible. It opens up areas concerning the Messiah, His matchless ministry, His vicarious death, and His subsequent ministry as our High Priest at the throne of grace.

This marvelous revelation came in direct answer to the prophet's importunate prayer recorded in Daniel 9:4–19. Daniel tells us that he had been studying the books of Jeremiah and was greatly concerned about the fulfillment of the prophecy of seventy years of captivity. (See Jeremiah 25:9, 11.) He also found predictions in the writings of Isaiah concerning events at the close of the seventy years. The more the prophet pondered the writings of these prophets, the greater the sin of Israel appeared. In calculating the seventy years' captivity prophesied by Jeremiah, Daniel realized that the time had almost expired. Did he just let things take their course? No. He took the whole situation on his heart and gave himself to earnest intercessory prayer. With deep concern for his people he unburdened his soul to God.

DANIEL'S MOVING PRAYER

In humiliation and confession, this statesman-prophet, this confidant of kings, poured out his petitions in one of the greatest prayers ever recorded. This was no ordinary supplication; it was sacrificial prayer. He tells how he garbed himself in sackcloth, sprinkling ashes on his head, thus bearing the marks of mourning. "I prayed," he says, ". . . and made my confession" (Daniel 9:4). What did this man of God have to confess? It was not his sin that brought the Jews into slavery. But as a true intercessor he made the nation's guilt his own.

Addressing Jehovah as the covenant-keeping God, he says, *"We* have sinned: . . . Neither have *we* hearkened unto thy servants the prophets. . . . O Lord, righteousness belongeth unto thee, but unto *us*

confusion of faces. . . . To the Lord our God belong mercies and for-
givenesses, though *we* have rebelled against him; Neither have *we*
obeyed" (verses 5–10, emphasis supplied). He continues in the same
vein: "For *our* sins, and for the iniquities of our fathers, Jerusalem and
thy people are become a reproach to all that are about *us*. Now therefore, O our God, hear the prayer of thy servant, . . . and cause thy face
to shine upon thy sanctuary" (verses 16, 17, emphasis supplied).

Some of his expressions he gathered from the psalms: "Cause thy
face to shine; and we shall be saved" (Psalm 80:3, 7, 19). Also Aaron's
priestly benediction contains this expression: "The LORD make his
face shine upon thee" (Numbers 6:25).

With these thoughts in mind, Daniel pleads with Jehovah to cause
His face to shine on His sanctuary. The temple, of course, had been
destroyed long years before, but the time had come for it to be rebuilt.
For the Lord's sake, Daniel presented his petition. As a true intercessor, Daniel, who for almost seventy years had been Heaven's ambassador in an alien land, says, "O Lord, hear; O Lord , forgive; O Lord,
hearken and do" (verse 19). Such intense earnestness should stir the
heart of every Christian, leading us to ask ourselves, Are we as concerned in our petitions as was this man of God? Are our prayers
earnest intercessions, or are they mere formalities by reason of habit?
The prophet's greatest concern was for the honor and reputation of
Jehovah.

GABRIEL APPEARS WHILE DANIEL PRAYS

"And whiles I was speaking, and praying, and confessing my sin
and the sin of my people," said the prophet, "even the man Gabriel,
whom I had seen in the vision at the beginning, being caused to fly
swiftly, touched me about the time of the evening oblation" (verses
20, 21). Although the temple no longer existed, and the Levitical
ritual had long since ceased, yet the prophet, believing the promise of
God concerning the return of His people to Jerusalem and the restoration of the temple worship, made his prayer at the time of the evening sacrifice, about three o'clock in the afternoon.

In answer to Daniel's petition Gabriel made haste to be at the
prophet's side. He came to give special instruction concerning the

vision that Daniel had seen a few years earlier. At that time no one, not even Daniel himself, understood it. So Gabriel began by saying, "I am come to shew thee; . . . therefore understand the matter, and consider the vision" (verse 23). Then to make the matter clear, he introduced another prophecy concerning Daniel's people—the Jews— and especially the coming Messiah. He said, "Seventy weeks are determined upon thy people and upon thy holy city, to finish the transgression, and to make an end of sins, and to make reconciliation for iniquity, and to bring in everlasting righteousness, and to seal up the vision and prophecy, and to anoint the most Holy" (verse 24).

Newer versions such as the Revised Standard Version and James Moffatt's translation are more exact in their wording: "anoint a most holy place;" "consecrate a most sacred Place." The consecration of this sacred place was, without doubt, referring to the heavenly sanctuary, where the Messiah would officiate after giving His life as a sacrifice for us. And to confirm the promise, six tremendous events were to happen, all of them bound up with the Messiah. These were to be fulfilled during the last week of the seventy weeks.

In Daniel 7 we noticed the prophetic period—time, times, and a half, or 1,260 days. We also discovered that when we deal with prophetic time, a day stands for a literal year. (See Numbers 14:34 and Ezekiel 4:6.) These seventy weeks, then, would be weeks of years, a total of 490 years. Moreover, this period would be separated into three parts: 7 prophetic weeks, or 49 years, allotted for the rebuilding of the city; 62 weeks, or 434 years, to reach to "Messiah the Prince;" and one final week. These are vital measurements, but we must be certain when these seventy weeks begin. On this point Gabriel was emphatic, giving the event that would mark the beginning. He said it would be "from the going forth of the commandment to restore and to build Jerusalem" (verse 25).

Daniel did not live to see the issuance of that third decree, authorizing the rebuilding of the city. He did see the result of the first decree, by King Cyrus in 536 B.C., allowing the Jews to return to their homeland and rebuild their temple. Opposition from the Samaritans, however, hindered the work on the temple, making necessary another decree by Darius Hystaspes in 519 B.C.

THE LEGAL LANGUAGE OF THE DECREE

The first proclamation that Cyrus put in writing reads, "The LORD God of heaven hath given me all the kingdoms of the earth; and he hath charged me to build him an house at Jerusalem, which is in Judah. Who is there among you of all his people? his God be with him, and let him go up to Jerusalem, which is in Judah, and build the house of the LORD God of Israel" (Ezra 1:2, 3).

Seventeen years later Darius made a second proclamation, which was really a confirmation of the one issued by King Cyrus. Darius's decree reads, "I make a decree what ye shall do to the elders of these Jews for the building of the house of God: that of the king's goods . . . forthwith expenses be given unto these men, that they be not hindered" (Ezra 6:8).

We emphasize again that wonderful as these decrees were, they concerned only the reconstruction of the temple, the "house at Jerusalem." Another decree was issued by Artaxerxes Longimanus in 457 B.C., sixty-two years after that of Darius. This third decree authorized further rebuilding and restoration, the temple having been finished fifty-eight years earlier, in 515 B.C. (See Ezra 6:15.)

In his decree, Artaxerxes gave, in effect, a blank check to Ezra. Note again the language: "Artaxerxes, king of kings, unto Ezra the priest, a scribe of the law of the God of heaven. . . . I make a decree, that all they of the people of Israel . . . which are minded of their own freewill to go up to Jerusalem, go with thee." "And I, even I Artaxerxes the king, do make a decree to all the treasurers which are beyond the river, that whatsoever Ezra the priest . . . shall require of you, it be done speedily" (Ezra 7:12, 13, 21).

FULL AUTONOMY GIVEN THE JEWS

This third decree included more than the restoration of the city, as Ezra 7:24–26 shows. It gave the Jews as a nation autonomy in the matter of legal judgments, even to the death penalty if necessary. The restoration of Jerusalem meant not merely the laying of stone and bricks, but the establishment of a nation with headquarters in the rebuilt city of Jerusalem.

It was the decree of Artaxerxes that gave the Jews their political existence. Many Jews had already returned as pilgrims and sojourners, but this last decree changed the situation, giving us the beginning date for Daniel's prophecy. The commencement of the seventy weeks, then, was 457 B.C., which date is now accepted by many scholars. (See *The Chronology of Ezra 7,* by S. H. Horn and L. H. Wood.)

Thirteen years later, in 444 B.C., Nehemiah, the king's cupbearer, was granted special permission to go to Jerusalem to join with and encourage the builders. Nehemiah accomplished a wonderful work in a very short time. But he was on leave of absence from the king; this was not a decree, and the permit was granted thirteen years after the royal decree for the rebuilding of the city had been issued. The Scriptures show that the temple had been completed about seventy years before Nehemiah's visit. In Ezra 6:14, 15 we read, "The elders of the Jews builded, and they prospered through the prophesying of Haggai the prophet and Zechariah the son of Iddo. . . . And this house [the temple] was finished on the third day of the month Adar, which was in the sixth year of the reign of Darius the king." This was the year 515 B.C. Artaxerxes's decree made provision for the services of the temple, but it did not provide for the building of the temple.

ARTAXERXES'S DECREE ISSUED FOR EZRA, NOT NEHEMIAH

We repeat that the decree or commandment from Artaxerxes was given, not in 445 B.C. or 444 B.C., but in 457 B.C. This is the date for the beginning of the seventy-weeks prophecy, or the 490 years. It is unfortunate that so many Bible teachers take 445 B.C. or 444 B.C. for the date of the decree, when no decree was given then, nor was it needed, for it had been issued and put into effect thirteen years earlier.

Now note Gabriel's message to Daniel: "Seventy weeks are determined upon thy people" (Daniel 9:24). The word *determined* (*chathak,* in Hebrew) has been variously translated as "decreed," "divided," "shortened," "fixed," "cut off," "apportioned," and "allotted." These variations are significant. Seventy prophetic weeks were allotted to the Jews, during which certain definite things were to happen. Their period of time was "cut off" or "shortened" from the longer period of the 2,300 prophetic days (literal years) of chapter 8, which the prophet said no one understood. Now Gabriel tells Daniel that he has come to give him special instruction concerning the previous vision, saying, "Know therefore and understand, that from the going forth of the commandment to restore and to build Jerusalem unto the Messiah the Prince shall be seven weeks, and threescore and two weeks: the street shall be built again, and the wall, even in troublous times" (verse 25).

THE TEMPLE IS FINISHED

The seven-week (forty-nine-year) period, reaching to 408 B.C., was specified by the angel Gabriel, but present archaeological evidence has not revealed its full significance.

The period of sixty-nine prophetic weeks, 483 actual years, brings us to the year A.D. 27. Now what should we expect at that time? The prophecy says "unto Messiah the Prince" (verse 25). Did He appear then? Yes. The word *Messiah* means "anointed," and the Scripture says, "God anointed Jesus of Nazareth with the Holy Ghost and with power: who went about doing good, and healing all that were oppressed" (Acts 10:38). But when was Jesus anointed? Not at His birth. He was Spirit-born, but not Spirit-baptized until He went to John, who baptized Him in the Jordan River.

CHRIST BAPTIZED AND SPIRIT-ANOINTED

In Luke 3:21, 22 we read: "Now when all the people were baptized, it came to pass, that Jesus also being baptized, and praying, the heaven was opened, And the Holy Ghost descended in a bodily shape like a dove upon him, and a voice came from heaven, which said, Thou art my beloved Son; in thee I am well pleased." Following His baptism, he went up into the wilderness, where He met the devil face to face. Afterward He "came into Galilee, preaching the gospel of the kingdom of God, And saying, The time is fulfilled" (Mark 1:14, 15). To what *time* was He referring? Surely it was the prophetic time of which Daniel wrote—the sixty-nine prophetic weeks, or 483 years, that were to reach to "Messiah the Prince." He had indeed come, and with His own lips He announced that the time had expired; that period foretold by the prophet, which was to mark His manifestation as the Messiah, had arrived.

Daniel foretold not only the appearance and ministry of the Messiah but also His death. The Messiah shall be "cut off, but not for himself" (verse 26). Moffatt says, "leaving no successor." The Amplified Bible, speaking of the anointed one, says, He shall be "cut off or killed, and shall have nothing [and no one belonging] to [and defending] him."

How true that was of the Messiah, the Christ! Isaiah 53:8 says, "He was cut off out of the land of the living: for the transgression of my people was he stricken." Then Gabriel tells how "the people of the prince that shall come shall destroy the city and the sanctuary" (Daniel 9:26). This certainly was not Messiah the Prince, for He destroyed nothing. He gave His life to save His people from destruction. But another prince came thirty-nine years after our Lord's death who did indeed destroy the city and the sanctuary. This was Prince Titus, son of the Roman emperor Vespasian. Following the attack on Jerusalem by Cestius, who later retreated, Titus came to Jerusalem near the end of the Jewish war of A.D. 66 to 70. During the awful siege every detail of Jeremiah's prophecy was fulfilled, even to parents eating their own sons and daughters. (See Jeremiah 19:9.)

JESUS WEEPS OVER JERUSALEM

Knowing what awaited Jerusalem and the Jews, our Lord with a heavy heart "beheld the city, and wept over it, Saying, If thou hadst known . . . the things which belong unto thy peace! but now they are hid from thine eyes. For the days shall come upon thee, that thine enemies shall cast a trench about thee, . . . And shall lay thee even with the ground, and thy children within thee; and they shall not leave in thee one stone upon another" (Luke 19:41–44). "For these be the days of vengeance, that all things which are written may be fulfilled. . . . And they shall fall by the edge of the sword, and shall be led away captive into all nations: and Jerusalem shall be trodden down of the Gentiles, until the times of the Gentiles be fulfilled" (Luke 21:22–24). Josephus claims that more than a million Jews perished during that terrible siege. Those not killed were sold into slavery. A monument to this brutal siege and the success of the campaign can still be seen on the Arch of Titus in Rome on which are carved representations of the spoils of the temple, such as the golden candlestick and the table of showbread. A medal was struck eulogizing the deeds of Rome in overthrowing the Jewish nation, with the legend, "Judaea Capta." The Roman senate gave high praise to the victory, honoring "the divine Titus, son of the divine Vespasian the Emperor."

THE PRINCE WHO DESTROYED THE CITY

Gabriel made reference to this when he told Daniel that the prince who would come would "destroy the city and the sanctuary," by a devastating war resulting in the "overspreading of abominations" (Daniel 9:26, 27). Our Lord was even more specific: "When ye therefore shall see the ABOMINATION OF DESOLATION, spoken of by Daniel the prophet, stand in the holy place, (whoso readeth, let him understand:) Then let them which be in Judaea flee into the mountains" (Matthew 24:15, 16). The "abomination of desolation" to which Jesus referred was the pagan symbols of the Roman army, and they did stand on the holy ground of the temple area.

Some interpreters make this part of Gabriel's prophecy apply to some antichrist of the future. However, the statement of our Lord, later confirmed by history, identifies the "abomination" as the pagan symbols of the ancient Roman army. It is regrettable that some, apparently unacquainted with the facts of history, take this portion of the prophecy and throw it far off into the future. They look for this verse to be fulfilled by one they call the great antichrist, whom they declare will appear *after* the second advent of our Lord and the "secret rapture" of the church. Such interpreters actually make a mistake similar to the one the Jews made two thousand years ago, when they failed to recognize that the prophecies concerning the Messiah were being fulfilled before their eyes. The Jews are still looking for a future Messiah, when actually the Messiah of which the Scriptures speak has already appeared in the person of our Lord Jesus Christ. He fulfilled every feature of this prophecy concerning His ministry. He was finally "cut off" when He died the cruel death of the cross in our place. Why look for some future prince to come and destroy the city of

Jerusalem when everything the prophecy called for happened between A.D. 31 and 70? The details our Lord gave have met their fulfillment exactly as He said.

ABOMINATION OF DESOLATION STANDS IN THE "HOLY PLACE"

Now, note one or two important details. Jesus said that the "abomination of desolation" would "stand in the holy place." "Then let them which be in Judaea flee into the mountains" (Matthew 24:15, 16). This is exactly what the faithful Christians did. They fled and saved their lives, whereas the unbelieving Jews remained in the city, and most of them perished in the awful siege.

Why do some interpreters overlook the facts of history and look for some future "abomination of desolation" or antichrist after our Lord's return for His church? Why? We will seek the answer in our next chapter.

12. Messiah's Ministry and Predicted Day of His Death

Our Lord Jesus knew He would die a cruel death, but more, He knew the year, day, and hour when His death would occur. He left heaven not only to be a great teacher but to be a great sacrifice, to die the death we deserved. Because we all have sinned, we needed someone to take the penalty of our transgression. But more, we needed One who could represent us and intercede for us at the throne of grace. The second Person of the Godhead pledged Himself to do this for us; therefore, "when the fulness of the time was come, God sent forth his Son, . . . To redeem them that were under the law, that we might receive the adoption of sons" (Galatians 4:4, 5).

Christ died at the exact time specified in Daniel's prophecy. Six months before Christ began His marvelous ministry, John the Baptist came preaching, and saying, "Repent ye: for the kingdom of heaven is at hand" (Matthew 3:2). How did he know? He, like Jesus, was a student of the Scriptures. He knew the great time prophecies that related to both Christ and the coming antichrist, for Gabriel told Daniel about the "little horn" power that would attempt to change prophetic times and God's law—the Ten Commandments.

Prophecy inspired the Protestant movement

Those same prophecies inspired the Protestant Reformers of the sixteenth century. Those Reformers applied them to the papal apostasy. The books of Daniel and the Revelation were their special study, and as a writer says, they "found from our sacred books [the Scriptures] that the Pope was Antichrist, and the Church of Rome the harlot of Babylon" (Rev. A. Nampon, S. J., *Catholic Doctrine as Defined by the Council of Trent,* pages 103, 104).

In a tremendous endeavor to meet the challenge of these mighty preachers and teachers, two spurious interpretations were devised in order to lift the stigma from Roman Catholicism. These were known as the preterist and futurist interpretations. They were developed by Alcazar and Ribera. Ribera, a Jesuit theologian of the Roman Catholic Counter-Reformation, actually applied the prophecy concerning our Lord Jesus Christ to the antichrist. Speaking of the Messiah who was to be "cut off" or crucified, Gabriel said He "shall confirm the covenant with many for one week: and in the midst of the week he shall cause the sacrifice and the oblation to cease" (Daniel 9:27).

Christ began His public ministry in A.D. 27, at the end of the sixty-nine prophetic weeks, or 483 years. Gabriel said that seventy weeks, 490 years, were given especially for the Jews. "Seventy weeks of years are decreed concerning your people" (verse 24, RSV). And there was still one "week" of seven years yet to be fulfilled. "In the midst" of that week, three and a half years after he began His ministry, our Lord was crucified, or "cut off out of the land of the living" (Isaiah 53:8).

During those three and a half intensive years of preaching, teaching, and healing the sick, He was confirming the everlasting covenant. Moreover He knew how long He had left in which to minister, for He was working to a timetable. Many times He said, "my time is not yet come" (John 7:6). But when that time arrived, he knew it. He reminded those who came to arrest Him that He had been in the temple daily and they had not laid hands on Him. But "this is your hour," He said, "and the power of darkness" (Luke 22:53).

CHRIST DIED AT THE EXACT MOMENT

Nothing that happened that night came as a surprise to the Savior. He knew not only the day and the hour He was to die, but also the very moment of time. While hanging on the cross that Passover day, He realized that the hour of the evening sacrifice had arrived, and that the sacrificial priest with knife upraised was about to take the life of the little lamb. At that moment the crucial cry came from the cross, "It is finished" (John 19:30). Instantly, the veil in the temple was ripped from ceiling to floor by an unseen hand. The knife dropped from the nerveless hand of the priest, and the little lamb ran away unhurt. A greater Lamb, the Lamb of God, had taken away the sin of the world! The Scripture says "in due time Christ died for the ungodly" (Weymouth, third edition: "at the right moment," Romans 5:6).

He paid the debt of our transgressions, bearing the whole world's sin, even the awful sin of His betrayal and rejection. Some who turned against Him that day accepted Him later as their sin offering, recognizing that the One whom they crucified had paid the price of their forgiveness and by His grace had reconciled them to God.

Our Lord's ministry lasted just three and a half years, and on that Passover day, A.D. 31, Jesus fulfilled all the elaborate services of the Hebrew ritual. His sacrifice did indeed "cause the sacrifice and the oblation to cease" (Daniel 9:27). It was the exact time—"in the midst of the week" (verse 27).

But there were still three and a half years remaining of that last prophetic week. During that time the disciples preached with great power in Jerusalem, and thousands responded to their message, including many of the priests. (See Acts 6:7.) At the end of that prophetic week, Stephen, a deacon and an eloquent preacher, was summoned to appear before the Sanhedrin because his presentation of Jesus as the Messiah was so eloquent that the people "were not able to resist the wisdom and the spirit by which he spake" (verse 10).

STEPHEN'S DEATH ENDS THE SEVENTY WEEKS

In his defense, Stephen unfolded the history of the nation, emphasizing the salient points, bringing it right down to their own day. That powerful sermon, recorded in Acts 7, is one of the high points in the New Testament story. Bu the elders of the Jews rushed upon him, "cast him out of the city, and stoned him" (Acts 7:58). Stephen was the first recorded Christian martyr. The date of that tragic event was A.D. 34, just three and a half years after the crucifixion. This brought to an end the seventy weeks "determined" or "allotted" to the Jewish people.

As we have already seen, both the 490 years and the 2,300 years began in 457 B.C. The exact fulfillment of the details given by the angel Gabriel should give every Bible student renewed confidence in the "sure word of prophecy" (2 Peter 1:19).

Now let us pause to note again verses 26 and 27 of Daniel 9. That portion needs to be studied with particular care. It is well for us to remember that there were no punctuation marks in the original writing; all such markings having been added by translators. But for clarity let us recognize that a couple of clauses, which obviously deal with the "prince" who was to come, should be treated for what they really are—a parenthetical element: ["And the people of the prince that shall come shall destroy the city and the sanctuary; and the end thereof shall be with a flood, and unto the end of the war desolations are determined"] (Daniel 9:26). By placing this portion between brackets, the whole matter is clarified. For the "he" mentioned at the beginning of verse 27 properly belongs to "Messiah the Prince," not to Titus, the prince of Rome, who came later and destroyed the city. To misapply that part of the Scripture and apply it to some antichrist of the future really makes Christ and antichrist change places. Could we imagine a greater misfortune than this?

HISTORY CONFIRMS THE SEVENTY-WEEK PROPHECY

Six important predictions, mentioned in Daniel 9:24, were all fulfilled during the seventieth week. These six points establish without question the timing and the relationship of this great prophecy to our Lord, for not one of these occurred during the preceding sixty-nine weeks of years. The first three had to do with the blight of sin, stating that our Lord would (1) "finish the transgression," (2) "make an end of sins [sin offerings]" through His perfect atonement, and (3) "make reconciliation for iniquity" by a substitutionary sacrifice of the Son of God. The last three deal with the glorious realities of the gospel. These are (4) "to bring in everlasting righteousness" as God's free gift of grace to all who will accept it, (5) "to seal up the vision and prophecy," and (6) "to anoint the most Holy" (Berkeley: "to consecrate the Holy of Holies"). This our Lord did following His ascension, when He entered "into heaven itself; now to appear in the presence of God for us" (Hebrews 9:24).

The completion of our Lord's sacrifice and victory climaxed in the outpouring of the Holy Spirit on the Day of Pentecost. This confirmed the truth that Christ is now our great High Priest at the throne of grace. Moffatt's translation reads, "Seventy weeks of years are fixed for your people and for your sacred city, to end guilt, to complete sins, to expiate iniquity, to bring in everlasting purity, to ratify the prophetic vision, and to consecrate a most sacred Place" (Daniel 9:24).

While some attempt to separate the seventieth week from the sixty-nine, looking to the future for its fulfillment in the coming of the antichrist, yet there seems no good reason for such an interpretation. Philip Mauro declares that "when a definite measure of time or space is specified by the number of units composing it, within which a certain event is to happen, . . . the units of time or space which make up the measure are to be understood as meaning continuously and successively." This he declares to be "an absolute rule" (*The Seventy Weeks and the Great Tribulation*).

While common sense and sound exegesis emphasize the wisdom of this, history also proves the accuracy of such an interpretation.

In Exodus 30:26–30 and Exodus 40:9–13 we have the account of the anointing and consecration of the Mosaic tabernacle before the services began. And in Hebrews 8:1, 2; 9:11, 15 we have the record of the heavenly sanctuary where Christ ministers, which was consecrated at the beginning of His priestly work there.

CHRIST'S MINISTRY OF RECONCILIATION AND JUDGMENT

Just as in the type there were two phases of ministry, reconciliation and judgment, so our heavenly High Priest has a ministry that begins with reconciliation and will climax in the work of judgment. The two apartments in the earthly sanctuary, the "holy place" and the "most holy place," represent these two vital phases of our Lord's ministry. While the earthly sanctuary was small in its construction, it typified great realities in His sacrifice and priestly ministry. When Gabriel said, "Unto two thousand and three hundred days; then shall the sanctuary be cleansed" (Daniel 8:14), he had reference not to a Day of Atonement (Yom Kippur) of the earthly sanctuary but to the Day of Atonement of the heavenly sanctuary.

Just as there came a day in ancient Israel when the high priest performed the ceremonial service of cleansing, so in the heavenly sanctuary there is also a cleansing, and this will be by "better sacrifices" than those offered in the earthly sanctuary (Hebrews 9:23). The Scripture says plainly that "without shedding of blood is no remission" or forgiveness (verse 22). The earthly sanctuary was cleansed by the blood of animals, but the "heavenly things themselves with better sacrifices than these" (verse 23). In ancient Israel the day of cleansing, the Day of Atonement, was a very solemn occasion. If anyone on that day refused to confess his sins, he was "cut off" from the congregation. It was therefore a day of judgment and is so regarded by orthodox Jews even to this day. Gabriel could just as easily have said, "Unto two thousand three hundred years; then shall judgment day begin," for that is what the statement implies.

TERMINATION OF THE PROPHECY OF 2,300 DAYS

We have already noted the marvelous accuracy of the shorter prophecy of seventy prophetic weeks, or 490 years, which ended in A.D. 34. Subtracting 490 years from the longer period of 2,300 years leaves 1,810 years. Finding the termination of the longer period is very easy. Just add 1,810 to 34, and we come to the year 1844, when the sanctuary would be "cleansed." At that time our great High Priest, "Messiah the Prince," entered upon His closing work as our Mediator.

The everlasting gospel going to all the world today is, "Fear God, and give glory to him; for the hour of his judgment is come" (Revelation 14:7). The apostle Paul preached about a judgment to come, declaring that God "hath appointed a day, in the which he will judge the world in righteousness by that man whom he hath ordained; whereof he hath given assurance unto all men, in that he hath raised him from the dead" (Acts 17:31). Messiah, the Prince, who was raised from the dead, is the appointed One to judge the world.

HOW SHALL WE STAND IN THE JUDGMENT?

When the Ancient of Days took His place to preside over that august assembly, "the judgment was set, and the books were opened" (Daniel 7:10). In those books is a record of every life lived on earth; and in the closing work of our Lord in the heavenly sanctuary these records are examined, decisions reached, and rewards apportioned. When our Lord appears in glory, He comes bringing His rewards with Him (See Revelation 22:11, 12.) These words of Scripture in Ecclesiastes 12:13, 14 are relevant and sobering! "Let us hear the conclusion of the whole matter: Fear God, and keep his commandments. . . . For God shall bring every work into judgment, with every secret thing, whether it be good, or whether it be evil."

When we think of the Judge of all the earth reviewing the cases in that judgment, it is reassuring to recall the words of Jesus: "He that heareth my word, and believeth on him that sent me, hath everlasting life, and shall not come into condemnation" (John 5:24). If we are living the life of overcomers, we can claim our Lord's promise that we shall be "clothed in white raiment." His assurance is, "I will not blot out his name out of the book of life, but I will confess his name before my Father" (Revelation 3:5).

Sad to say, some will have their names blotted out of the book of life because they are not living the life of victory through God's grace. As we noticed earlier, the great Judge opens before the intelligent universe all the records of His dealings with men and angels. Thus he vindicates His own character, "that every mouth may be stopped" (Romans 3:19). No word can ever be justly spoken against the justice and the mercy of our great God and Savior.

Sensing what is going on now in the heavenly sanctuary, every one of us should examine our lives, making sure that we are living victoriously by the power of the indwelling Spirit of God.

13. Divine Intervention in International Politics

We have now reached the closing section of the book of Daniel. The last three chapters belong together. Chapter 10 is an introduction to the largest, most involved prophecy in the whole Bible, reaching from Daniel's day to the end of time.

The revelation came to him in the third year of the reign of King Cyrus, 535 B.C. The prophet is specific in his description of what happened. He uses his own Hebrew name, Daniel, as well as Belteshazzar, the name given him by Nebuchadnezzar. The Babylonian Empire has passed; and, although Daniel was about ninety years of age, he was still an officer of state, but now in the empire of Persia. He had already received visions vital to his nation, but what was now revealed was tremendously important. He had been "mourning three full weeks" (Daniel 10:2).

During that long fast he had taken "no pleasant bread" (verse 3) and had abstained from the normal comforts of life. He was greatly burdened for his nation. Cyrus had issued a decree permitting the Jews to return and begin rebuilding the temple in Jerusalem. The builders had met with such stern opposition from their neighbors, the Samaritans, however, that the work that had begun with such enthusiasm had temporarily stopped. This weighed heavily on Daniel's heart, and he gave himself to prayer and fasting. He had chosen some place of retirement on the bank of the River Hiddekel or Tigris, probably close to where it joins the Euphrates, about a hundred miles north of the Persian Gulf. It being the Passover season, followed by the Feast of Unleavened Bread, he was vividly reminded of Israel's deliverance from Egyptian bondage nearly a thousand years earlier. He was certain that the same God who so miraculously worked for His people in the past was able to meet the opposition of present enemies. Thus the prophet prayed.

DANIEL BEHOLDS DEITY

Looking up, he saw a mighty celestial Being in dazzling brightness wearing a golden girdle. The Being's eyes appeared like flaming torches, and His limbs were like burnished brass. The sight was overwhelming. He spoke with a voice as of a multitude. Here was One who surpassed in splendor even the angel Gabriel.

Comparing the words of Daniel 10:5, 6 with Ezekiel 1:24–28 and Revelation 1:13–16, we cannot doubt that Daniel, Ezekiel, and John were each describing the same Being. The Lord of all the earth had come in person to His praying servant on the bank of the river. Little wonder the prophet was overcome with fear.

Daniel tells us that he was alone when he received his vision of majestic splendor. As he swooned and fell to his knees, he heard a reassuring voice saying, "O Daniel, a man greatly beloved, understand the words that I speak unto thee, and stand upright" (Daniel 10:11).

This was not the voice of the celestial Being he had just seen in vision, but the familiar voice of Gabriel who had appeared to him on other occasions. The angel continued, "Fear not, Daniel: for from the first day that thou didst set thine heart to understand, . . . thy words were heard, and I am come for thy words" (Berkeley: " 'I have come in response to your prayers' ") (verse 12). How wonderful to know that when we seek God in earnest prayer as did Daniel, heavenly angels bring the answer.

Three weeks had passed since the prophet began his prayer vigil. Why the long delay? We now enter into one of the most profound revelations in all the Bible. In verse 13 we catch a brief glimpse of the unseen struggle between God's loyal angels and Satan's rebel hosts. The Scriptures picture these forces as real and substantial. The apostle Paul said: "For our fight is not against any physical enemy: it is against organisations and powers that are spiritual. We are up against the unseen power that controls this dark world, and spiritual agents from the very headquarters of evil" (Ephesians 6:12, Phillips). The same apostle reveals that behind the idols of the heathen are demons to whom they make their sacrifices. (See 1 Corinthians 10:20.)

DEMON POWERS SEEK TO THWART GOD'S PLANS

So real are these demonic powers that they delayed even the mighty Gabriel from changing the circumstances to make possible the favorable answer to Daniel's prayer. Notice the angel's words: "The prince of the kingdom of Persia withstood me" (verse 13). The word "prince," *sar* in Hebrew, occurs over four hundred times in the Old Testament. It means "ruler," "governor," or "military commander." The prince of whom Gabriel speaks could well have been Cyrus. But influencing him was another unseen power—"the prince of the power of the air" (Ephesians 2:2), one who seeks to control this dark world of sin, the author of evil, Satan himself. The meaning of the word *Satan* is "adversary."

Gabriel disclosed now to Daniel that not until Michael came to his aid was he able to move upon the heart of King Cyrus to deal with the enemies of the Jews and permit the rebuilding program to proceed. Who is this "Michael"? He is "one of the chief princes" (or "the first of the princes," Daniel 10:13). The name appears three times in the book of Daniel. The earliest occurrence in the Bible story is when "Michael the archangel" contended with the devil about the body of Moses. In that contention, Michael said to the devil, "The Lord rebuke thee" (Jude 9). *Michael* means "who [is] like God?"

It is the Archangel who calls the dead to life at the Second Advent, and Jesus declared that all who are in their graves shall hear His (Jesus') voice and come forth. (See John 5:28, 29.) In Daniel 12, Michael is called "the great prince which standeth for the children of thy people" (verse 1). Putting these scriptures together, we must agree with Melanchthon, the great Reformer, who insisted that Michael should be identified with Christ Himself. Certainly Christ is the One who has stood for Daniel's people through all their struggles. As Redeemer, Deliverer, Sustainer, and coming King, he will at last lead His people through the pearly gates into the Holy City.

WHO IS MICHAEL?

Gabriel told Daniel, "There is none that holdeth with me in these things, but Michael your prince" (Daniel 10:21). This has led some to believe that Michael is in a special sense the guardian angel of the Jews.

But He is the One who calls not only Jews back to life, but all who have died in the hope of the resurrection. Michael "the great prince," (Daniel 12:1) is also called the "Prince of life" (Acts 3:15), the "Prince of princes" (Daniel 8:25), "Messiah the Prince" (Daniel 9:25), the "Prince of Peace" (Isaiah 9:6), and the "prince of the kings of the earth" (Revelation 1:5). He is greater than Gabriel, for He created the angels and every other creature in the universe. Significantly, the only time He is called Michael is when he is matching His power against the prince of evil, and each time he emerges the mighty Conqueror.

In warfare it is vital to know the strategy of the enemy. So in our warfare against Satan and his hosts we need to know something of the strategy of those forces of evil. We need even more than knowledge; we need "the whole armour of God" (Ephesians 6:11). Speaking of his victory, the angel told Daniel that he remained at the Persian court and, according to the Knox translation, "was left master of the field" (Daniel 10:13).

"I am come to make thee understand what shall befall thy people in the latter days: for yet the vision is for many days," said Gabriel (verse 14). Moffatt translates this, " 'Now I am here to let you know what is to befall your people at the end of the ages; for this vision relates to the far future.' "

Daniel's people, of course, were the Jews. According to the angel, something special would happen to these people in the "latter days," that is, "at the end of the ages." The long prophecy of chapter 11 traces the events which lead to the final crisis for the Jews and the whole world. Many nations are introduced in this prophecy, not because of their importance nationally, but simply because of their relationship to Israel through the centuries, either as persecutors or deliverers. This will continue through all time, and at "the end of the ages," "the latter days," "thy people shall be delivered, every one that shall be found written in the book" (Daniel 12:1). In that great day, race will mean nothing. To be found written in the book will mean everything.

Daniel—prophet "greatly beloved"

The presence and appearance of the celestial Being had left the prophet speechless and in a state of prostration. After Gabriel had tried to encourage Daniel and had disclosed to him what was happening behind the scenes, the prophet was overwhelmed still by the revelation. He needed to be not only encouraged but supernaturally strengthened—this time by a being described as one who appeared as a man, saying, "O man greatly beloved, fear not, . . . be strong" (Daniel 10:19). Now Daniel was ready for the full revelation of that which "is noted in the scripture of truth" (verse 21).

Prophets had written, and other prophets were still to write, concerning the long ages of suffering and oppression, not only for Israel, but for all God's people. But in "the time of the end" (Daniel 12:9 [" 'the crisis at the close,' " Moffatt]) God's character will be vindicated in all His children. His purpose will be fully understood, and His people delivered eternally.

This is the theme of all revelation, but especially of this vision of the eleventh chapter, this most interesting prophecy which the angel was about to unfold. Before he did, he asked Daniel, " 'Do you know why I have come unto you?' " (Daniel 10:20, RSV). It was not only to give the prophet a wonderful revelation, but also " 'to fight with the prince of Persia' " (verse 20). Read these words with particular care. In the Septuagint (a Greek translation of the Old Testament), the Hebrew word *im* ("with") is translated by the Greek word *meta,* meaning not "against," but "in common with," "alongside." In other words Gabriel was not fighting *against* the prince of Persia, but "alongside" him, "in common with" him. For three weeks the king of Persia had been influenced by demonic powers, which Gabriel helped him to withstand. But it was not until Michael, the preexistent Son of God, came to Gabriel's aid that the angel was able to visit Daniel. Now, Gabriel said that as soon as he had delivered his full message he would return to the king of Persia, thus helping him to carry out God's purpose in the rebuilding of Jerusalem.

Gabriel also foretold, "When I am gone forth," (that is, when he would withdraw his support from Persia), "lo, the prince [or ruler] of Grecia shall come" (verse 20). So long as it was in the plan of God, Persia would stand. But at last Greece would become a world kingdom, the detailed history of which the angel was about to reveal.

We will study this in the next chapter.

14. Political Intrigue Divides Greek Empire

The last two chapters of Daniel are a fascinating forecast of history. So plain is this prophecy that Porphyry, Syrian sophist of the third century A.D., claimed it could not possibly have been written before the events occurred, but that it must be the work of some "pious Jew" pretending to be a prophet. "No man could forecast history with such exactitude," he said. Following his lead, the critics of our day make the same claim.

While Daniel 11 is both remarkably intricate and precise, it is not beyond our understanding. The prophecies presented in early chapters are now more fully developed as Gabriel unfolds the details of this, the most complex prophecy in God's Word. When the Babylonian Empire collapsed, Cyrus, the Persian conqueror, apparently had appointed Darius the Mede, probably his uncle and father-in-law, as king of Babylon, where he reigned for two years until his death. The angel Gabriel, who had been working so definitely in influencing King Cyrus to suppress the enemies of the Jewish rebuilding program in Jerusalem, now tells Daniel he had also stood by Darius the Mede to strengthen him. (See Daniel 11:1.)

The essence of the prophecy begins with these words: " 'Three more kings will appear in Persia, and the fourth will far surpass all the others in wealth; and when he has extended his power through his wealth, he will rouse the whole world against the kingdom of Greece' " (verse 2, NEB).

The Medo-Persian Empire was well established with Cyrus as the ruling king when Daniel received this vision. The four kings therefore are Cambyses, son of Cyrus, who ruled from 530 to 522 B.C.; Smerdis, the imposter, who ruled only seven months; Darius Hystaspes, also known as Darius the Great, 522–486 B.C.; and Xerxes, the Ahasuerus of Esther 1:1, who ruled from 486 to 465 B.C.

Xerxes was both wealthy and self-assured. Having amassed an army that Herodotus says consisted of more than five million men (a modern estimate puts the figure at 250,000), he declared war on Greece, but suffered a humiliating defeat at Salamis in 480 B.C. Persia never really recovered from it. After Xerxes came nine minor kings, but the prophecy takes no account of them.

Alexander builds a new empire

The next outstanding ruler, destined to "do according to his will," was Alexander the Great, who in eight years welded the Greek city-states into an empire. The angel described him as a "mighty king" who would "do according to his will" (verse 3). " 'But as soon as he is established,' " the angel said, " 'his kingdom will be shattered and split up north, south, east, and west. It will not pass to his descendants, nor will any of his successors have an empire like his' " (verse 4, NEB).

Alexander advanced as far as the plains of northern India. But his soldiers, having been away from home for years, begged him to return. He did, expecting to set up his world headquarters in Babylon. But in the midst of his conquests he contracted a severe fever following a drunken spree. He could conquer the world, but not himself, and he died in 323 B.C. His ambitious projects collapsed and went into eclipse, as we have seen. The empire was rent by civil strife for the next twenty years. The words of the prophecy are exact: The kingdom would be divided, but "not to his posterity" (verse 4).

Alexander's four leading generals, after long and complicated struggles, divided the empire "toward the four winds of heaven" (verse 4). In 301 B.C. Lysimachus took the north; Ptolemy, the south; Seleucus, the east; and Cassander, the west. These were later reduced to three; Seleucus having swallowed up the domains of Lysimachus. That enlarged kingdom then became, in the language of the prophecy, the "king of the north" (verse 6), with Egypt and its environs being the "king of the south" (verse 5). Throughout the centuries, in spite of wars and revolutions that brought changes in boundaries and rulers, the prophecy refers to them by these terms—the "king of the north" and the "king of the south." Historians call the continual conflicts of these times the Syrian Wars, Judea being a buffer state between the two.

A PATCHED-UP PEACE

At last the king of the north and the king of the south made peace when Ptolemy II, called Philadelphus, gave his daughter, Berenice, in marriage to Antiochus Theos, grandson of Seleucus. "They shall join themselves together," says the prophecy, "for the king's daughter of the south shall come to the king of the north to make an agreement" (verse 6). To seal the agreement, Laodice, wife of Antiochus, was divorced and her children declared illegitimate—a poor foundation for a lasting peace. A large dowry accompanied Berenice. Later, when her father died, Antiochus divorced her and took back his former wife, Laodice. Fearing further disgrace, this reclaimed wife had her husband poisoned and her own son placed on the throne. Not long afterward she had her rival, Berenice, assassinated together with Egyptian friends who had come with her.

The remarkable accuracy of the prophecy is evident. "She shall be given up, and they that brought her, and he that begat her [" 'her child,' " NEB]" (verse 6). " 'Then another shoot from the same stock as hers will appear in his father's place,' " says the prophecy (verse 7, NEB).

Ptolemy Euergetes, who came to the Egyptian throne upon the death of his father Philadelphus, determined to avenge the death of his sister Berenice. With a large army he invaded the north and marched eastward as far as Babylon. He was compelled to return to Egypt because of an insurrection, but he brought with him from the kingdom of Seleucus a large booty, including two thousand gold and silver images and four thousand talents of gold, forty thousand talents of silver, and precious vessels which Cambyses of Persia had carried into Syria 280 years earlier. It was then that the people named him "Euergetes," meaning "benefactor." These ruling and warring families were not Syrians or Egyptians; they were Greeks, descendants of Alexander's generals.

During all these wars, Daniel's people, the Jews, knew little peace. But despite the warfare and intrigue surrounding them they remained in the Holy Land. Moreover, they were able to check constantly the accuracy of Daniel's prophecies. More important still, during these decades of intrigue, they gave to the world the famous Greek translation of the Old Testament, the Septuagint (LXX). The Hebrew religion and literature was thus made available to the nations around them.

After Ptolemy's crushing defeat of the Syrians, the area enjoyed a few years respite from war. But Seleucus Callinicus, having reestablished his power in Asia, made a foolhardy expedition into Egypt in 242 B.C. His forces were routed, and he lost his fleet in a severe storm. He was then obliged to return to his own land, thus fulfilling in detail the prophecy of verse 9.

Not long afterward, Callinicus, Seleucus II, fell from his horse and died. He was succeeded by his son Ceraunus, Seleucus III, who reigned only three years, and then his brother Antiochus III came to the throne. These brothers shared their father's determination to repair the national fortunes and avenge their humiliating defeat.

Antiochus commenced with such a show of strength that he was called Antiochus Magnus, "the Great." His reign was marked by incessant warfare. He took advantage of the weak and indecisive king of Egypt, Ptolemy IV, Philopater. Having raised a great force, he launched an offensive against the king of the south. The Syrians seemed irresistible, and as the prophecy declares, he did "overflow, and pass through" (verse 10) Gaza, Phoenicia, and Judea. With perhaps as much as seventy thousand infantry and five thousand cavalry, Antiochus advanced to the Egyptian border. At the frontiers of Raphia, in 217 B.C., his forces were surprisingly defeated and his army routed, leaving ten thousand slain and four thousand taken prisoner.

KING OF THE SOUTH PROFANES THE JEWISH TEMPLE

Ptolemy, elated over his success, continued to fulfill prophecy by annexing Palestine. The Jews were thus forced again to change their allegiance from Syria to Egypt. Instead of moving on to consolidate his gains, the Egyptian ruler, the king of the south, made peace with Antiochus, the king of the north. He insulted the Jews by entering the temple area and attempting to offer sacrifice, a rite reserved for consecrated priests only. When he insisted on entering the Holy of Holies he "fell speechless to the ground," according to legend, and was carried out half dead. Disgraced and furious, he returned to Alexandria. In this city, a stronghold for the Jews, he instituted a murderous persecution against these unfortunate people, demanding that they worship his idols. More than forty thousand Jews preferred death to idolatry. The prophecy said he would "cast down many ten thousands" (verse 12).

Such slaughter God could not let go unpunished. So "after certain years," the king of the north, Antiochus, after strengthening himself, brought many elephants from India and again invaded Egypt, This time his attack was indeed "greater than the former" (verse 13). Many others joined the forces of the Syrian king, including some violent Jews who called themselves "the sons of Tobias." These refractory Jews seemed to think they might establish this vision of Daniel and ultimately regain their independence as a nation. They found their hopes frustrated, however, and their plans overthrown. Many perished in the ensuing conflicts. Antiochus, using Judea as a station from which to menace Egypt, left his armies there, and the little land of Judea, the scene of bitter hostilities between north and south, was laid waste.

"And in those times there shall many stand up against the king of the south," says the prophecy (verse 14). With the death of both the king and the queen of Egypt, probably by poisoning, and a four-year-old son being placed on the throne, Antiochus, the master tactician, saw the possibility of revenge for his overthrow at Raphia.

To make sure of victory, he made an alliance with Philip V of Macedonia, and together these kings gathered a greater army than before, intending to divide the territory between them. But they failed to recognize that the child king of Egypt was under the legal guardianship of the Roman Senate, which promptly declared war on Philip V and forced Antiochus to make peace with Egypt, king of the south.

Verse 15 speaks of "the most fenced cities" (" 'a fortified town,' " NEB). This city was Gaza, which bravely stood out against Antiochus. But at last it, too, was forced to surrender as the prophecy had declared: "The arms of the south shall not withstand" (verse 15). Moreover, Hannibal, the veteran enemy of Rome, joined his forces with Antiochus. Next we find Rome declaring war against Syria in 191 B.C. Defeated by this rising world power, Antiochus was forced to accept the terms the Romans offered him, which included the payment of a large yearly tribute to the Senate. In addition, his young son, later to become the notorious Antiochus Epiphanes, had to go to Rome as a hostage. Thus Rome, the fourth world empire, comes into the prophetic picture. From this point on, until the end of time, this power will have a prominent place both in prophecy and history.

THE RISING POWER OF ROME

The Scripture introduces this new power under the description "He that cometh against him shall do according to his own will" (verse 16). This expression was also used in reference to Alexander the Great. (See verse 3.) But the context shows that here it alludes neither to him nor to Antiochus Epiphanes, as some commentators suggest, though it would be hard to find a more accurate description of Rome than in the last part of the verse: "And none shall stand before him: and he shall stand in the glorious land, which by his hand shall be consumed" (verse 16).

Although the king of the north had conquered the Egyptian forces, neither he nor any other kingdom could stand before the growing power of Rome. Syria eventually became a Roman province under Pompey in 65 B.C. Judea came under the full jurisdiction of Rome in 63 B.C. Nearly a century earlier, in 161 B.C., the Jews had entered into an alliance, called "the League." By this they hoped to protect themselves against the Syrian persecutions under Antiochus Epiphanes, son of Antiochus the Great, who, as mentioned above, had been a hostage in Rome. His rule was marked by cruelties and indignities.

In the end, that alliance with Rome proved to be the Jews' undoing. This is invariably the result when the people of God line up with the world. Had the Jewish leaders heeded the counsel of Isaiah and Jeremiah, history would have been written differently.

Every sentence in verses 17 to 22 adds to the prophetic picture. It is an accurate forecast of the great events in Rome's march to world empire. It is strange that certain interpreters fail to see the great events in the history of Rome, so accurately predicted in this prophecy. Instead, they go in search of incidents in the life and work of Antiochus Epiphanes. An example of this is found in the voluminous notes in this chapter in the RSV Annotated Bible. If one did not know better, he would be led by such commentators to regard this weak and half-witted king, who reigned only a few years, as the central figure in this long and wonderful prophecy. It would be strange if we did not know that this whole system of interpretation is a design on the part of the great enemy of truth and righteousness to lead men's minds from a true understanding of history in order to lift the stigma from the antichrist of the centuries.

Thomas Newton's rendering of verse 17 is, "He [that is, Rome] shall set his face to enter by force the whole kingdom" (*Dissertations on the Prophecies,* vol. 1, page 356). All that was left of the "whole kingdom" of Alexander was Egypt, Thrace, Macedonia, and Judea. Syria had already been conquered by the Romans, who then set out to force Egypt, the king of the south, into subjection. Our next chapter will trace briefly Rome's rulership in the light of this prophecy.

15. Prophecy's Forecast of Rome's Rulership

When Ptolemy Auletes died in 51 B.C. he left the throne to his daughter Cleopatra and her brother Ptolemy XII, a lad of ten years. The king's will provided that they should marry each other—then a common practice in Egyptian royalty—and reign jointly. Because they were young, the guardianship of Rome was sought. The people appointed Pompey as overseer of the court. Three years later, trouble broke out between Pompey and Julius Caesar, which ended in the Battle of Pharsalus. Pompey was defeated and fled to Egypt. Caesar followed him there. Pompey was killed, and Caesar found Egypt in commotion. Ptolemy and Cleopatra were quarreling. She claimed that he had deprived her of her share in the government. Caesar gave orders that the armies of each had to disband and that both Ptolemy and Cleopatra appear before him and then abide by his decision. Advocates were appointed for each side to plead for their respective parties. Cleopatra determined to conquer Caesar by feminine wiles rather than by military force or advocate's arguments. She had the right to be heard if Caesar was to be the judge. So she arranged for a boatman to take her to him.

To reach his presence undetected she had Apollodonum, her Sicilian slave, wrap her up in a cloth and tie the package with thongs. Then raising it to his "Herculean shoulders," he sought Caesar's apartments, claiming to have a special present for the Roman general. Being admitted into Caesar's presence, he laid the burden at his feet and made a speedy exit. When this animated bundle was unbound, there stood the beautiful and voluptuous Cleopatra before him.

The prophecy of chapter 11 could well refer to this, where we read in verse 17: "And he shall give him the daughter of women, corrupting her [margin: 'to corrupt']." While Caesar was past fifty and Cleopatra merely twenty-two, she was as ambitious as he. She became his mistress and bore him a son. His infatuation for the

140

queen kept him much longer in Egypt than his affairs asked for. This may have been a contributing factor in the plot to assassinate him at the zenith of his power. The next verse seems to express this thought: "A prince . . . shall cause the reproach . . . to turn upon him" (verse 18). And is that not what happened? As he passed into the Senate chamber, Cassius and Brutus, outwardly friends of Caesar, signaled to the conspirators, and almost instantly twenty daggers were buried in his body, leaving the greatest general in Rome's history silent in death in the Forum.

Caesar returns to Italy

Before that murder, however, many other details in the prophecy were to be fulfilled. Verse 18 says, "Shall he turn his face unto the isles, and shall take many." Some see in the expression, "the isles," nothing more than the coastlands of northern Africa, but Caesar had conquered more than Egypt; his aim was to rule the world. When trouble broke out in the Cimmerian Bosporus, Julius Caesar was called into action. Later he landed in Sicily with legions of men and six thousand horses. He then set sail for Africa, appearing at the Republican's camp, and summoned them to surrender to "Caesar the Imperator." They refused, saying they acknowledged no imperator but Scipio. War ensued, which Caesar won. He then claimed the north coast of Africa.

One of the tragic losses of Caesar's war was the destruction of the famous Alexandrian library of nearly four hundred thousand volumes, a tremendous collection for those days. It happened this way. Pothimus, chief minister of state for Egypt, was afraid of Caesar's influence. Fearing that Julius might give Cleopatra complete power, he instigated a sedition that resulted in an attempt to burn the Roman fleet. Caesar responded by burning the Egyptian's fleet. Some of the burning vessels were driven by the wind near the quay, and the fire spread to some of the city's buildings, including the grand library.

The prophecy also mentions that the "upright ones" would be with him (verse 17). Antipater of Idumea joined Caesar against Egypt, bringing with him three thousand Jews. The Jews held the frontier gateways into the country through which the Roman armies were permitted to pass without interruption. All of this had a bearing on the outcome. Commenting on this, Uriah Smith says, "A decisive battle was fought near the Nile by the fleets of Egypt and Rome, resulting in complete victory for Caesar. Ptolemy, attempting to escape, was drowned in the river. Alexandria and all Egypt then submitted to the victor. Rome had now entered into and absorbed the entire original kingdom of Alexander" (*Daniel and the Revelation,* 1944 ed., page 251).

JULIUS CAESAR ASSASSINATED

Having accomplished so much for the empire, Julius Caesar, as the prophecy said, turned "his face toward the fort of his own land" (verse 19). Upon arriving in Rome, he was made dictator for life. Having been granted many other honors, he was, in fact, absolute sovereign of the empire. But the same Scripture says, "He shall stumble and fall, and not be found" (verse 19). How true that was! This man who had fought and won fifty battles, taken more than a thousand cities at the cost of 1,192,000 of his soldiers, fell—not amid the strife of the battlefield—but just when he thought all was well.

The night before his assassination in 44 B.C. he was dining with Lepidus and a group of his friends. In casual conversation Caesar was asked, "What is the best way to die?" "Suddenly," he replied as he continued to sign letters. The next day, at noon, the mighty Caesar, the man who had done "according to his own will" (verse 16), lay dead at the foot of Pompey's statue in the Roman Forum.

As Julius Caesar had no legitimate sons, Octavius, his nephew whom he had adopted, became his heir and succeeded him. Announcing publicly his adoption by his uncle, he immediately took his name, which from that time became the title for the Roman emperors. He joined Mark Antony and Lepidus to avenge the death of Caesar. The three formed the *triumvirate* form of government. When the other two members died, Octavius became emperor. The Senate also conferred on him the title Augustus.

For some years the so-called Republic of Rome was torn with internal strife and war, but at length discipline and peace were established. The Battle of Actium in 31 B.C. left Augustus sole ruler. He proved both wise and strong. He replaced chaos and anarchy by imperial organization that lasted, with varying vicissitudes, for the next four centuries. He possessed the unusual ability to levy taxes without upsetting the populace too much. His taxes were light, but universal, and they supplied the funds for the imperial government. He was both clever and efficient. As an empire-wide enroller for taxation, he comes prominently into the Bible story. Note the exact description in Daniel 11:20: "Then shall stand up in his estate [Julius Caesar's place] a raiser of taxes in the glory of the kingdom."

CAESAR AUGUSTUS ENROLLS THE WORLD

The special importance of this prophecy is manifested by its remarkable place in the history of salvation. "It came to pass in those days, that there went out a decree from Caesar Augustus, that all the world should be taxed" (Luke 2:1). It was that decree which brought Joseph and Mary to Bethlehem. While they were there, Jesus was born. "All the world" is a sweeping statement, and the one who enforced such a worldwide decree should surely have the title "a raiser of taxes" above all others. Again we pause to comment on the strange lengths to which some commentators go, seeking for other incidents and personalities to fit the prophecy differently, simply to avoid applying these verses to Rome. Thus unwittingly perhaps, they corrupt the truth and lose the real message that Gabriel gave to Daniel especially for the last days. They attempt to make Heliodorus, the Syrian treasurer, this "raiser of taxes," because he hated the Jews and inflicted very heavy taxes on them. However, this happened more than a century earlier than the context justifies. It also ignores the fact that Luke 2:1 seems to be a direct allusion to Daniel's prophecy. Besides, the taxing of Heliodorus was limited to the Jews, whereas that of Augustus extended to "all the world," including Palestine. Moreover, this "raiser of taxes" appeared "in the glory of the kingdom" (Daniel 11:20).

Rome reached the pinnacle of her greatness during the Augustan age. It was a time of peace and comparative justice. Unlimited luxury was reigned in, and law and order were established. The temple of Janus at Rome was shut for the first time since 235 B.C. This signified that all the world was at peace. How does this compare to the rather insignificant kingdom of Syria, with its even less illustrious Heliodorus, which some commentators see as the fulfillment of this great prophecy?

Augustus died, as the prophecy foretold, "neither in anger, nor in battle" (verse 20). Julius Caesar met his death in anger, but Augustus died peacefully in bed at the high age of seventy-six, his wife being by his side.

He had gone to the quiet resort town of Nola for health reasons and while there suffered a heart attack. His wife, Livia, did not notify the Senate, as she was eager for her son to become emperor. She knew the well-deserved contempt in which her son was held by many, but she was determined to prevent any attempt to place someone else on the throne.

Tiberius was a contrast in every way to Augustus. The prophecy says plainly, "In his estate shall stand up a vile person, to whom they shall not give the honour of the kingdom: but he shall come in peaceably and obtain the kingdom by flatteries" (verse 21).

Tiberius was indeed a vile person ("contemptible person," RSV). Seneca declared that Tiberius was intoxicated only once in his life, and that was all the time! He showed few qualities of a ruler. When Livia urged Augustus to nominate Tiberius, her son by a former marriage, to succeed him as emperor, he replied, "Your son is too vile to wear the purple of Rome." Agrippa, a highly respected man, was nominated instead, but he died before the death of Augustus.

Not to be outdone, Livia gained her end by "flatteries" as the prophecy declared. She organized a royal party in honor of the emperor. When things were at their height, and after a flattering speech about her husband's fine qualities, she repeated her request for Tiberius's nomination for the throne. Augustus, unwilling to hurt her feelings, made the official announcement. His sudden demise left no time to change anything. So Tiberius, the "vile person" (verse 21), came to the throne. To him, however, they did "not give the honour of the kingdom" (verse 21), for he lost the respect of the citizens of Rome.

CHRIST CRUCIFIED DURING REIGN OF TIBERIUS

The next verse (verse 22) tells of " 'overwhelming forces' " (Berkeley) being swept away. The reign of Tiberius was marked by frequent

144

revolutions and violence. " 'Armies shall be utterly swept away before him and broken, and the prince of the covenant also' " (verse 22, RSV). This is "Messiah the Prince," who was to "confirm the covenant with many for one week" (Daniel 9:25, 27). During the reign of Tiberius, our Lord was crucified. Pilate owed his governorship of Judea only to the favor of Tiberius, the uncle of his wife. So, when someone in the crowd shouted, "If thou let this man go, thou art not Caesar's friend" (John 19:12), he gave in to the demands of the Jewish leaders. This settled the verdict. Pilate, the vacillating princeling who knew that Jesus was innocent, gave the order for Him to be scourged and crucified.

Christ, the Prince of the covenant, began His ministry in the autumn of A.D. 27, which terminated three-and-a-half years later in the spring of A.D. 31. The power responsible for our Lord's crucifixion was the one that 192 years earlier had entered into the league, the alliance with Judah, in 161 B.C. At that time the Romans were a "small people" as the prophecy says, but they began to work deceitfully, as Daniel 11:23 foretold.

Having traced the story of Rome from verses 14–22 until the most important, the substitutionary death of the Messiah, "the prince of the covenant," the angel, in order to impress the significance of that event, now reaches back to another milestone for the Jewish people, the entering into the league, that is, the alliance of friendship and mutual assistance between Judah and Rome. Josephus tells how the Jews, led by the high priest, entered into this league with enthusiasm (*Antiquities,* XII, chap. 10).

The prophecy predicted that "he shall enter peaceably even upon the fattest places of the province; and he shall do that which his fathers have not done" (verse 24). Posing as defenders of the weak, the Romans were the first in a large way to capitalize on the hopes of oppressed peoples. They soon became "the world's national referee," as one writer expressed it. By offering a sense of security, they extended their authority from Northern Africa to England, and from Spain to Palestine. Whole countries were bequeathed to the Roman Senate. Pax Romana extended to the civilized world.

The last part of verse 24 says, "even for a time." If we regard that "time" as prophetic, it would be 360 years, according to biblical reckoning as noted in earlier chapters. Counting from September 2, 32 B.C., when the decisive Battle of Actium was fought, from which Augustus dated his reign, a prophetic "time" of 360 years would bring us to A.D. 330. In this year Constantine removed the capital of the empire from Rome to Constantinople, an event regarded by many as a fulfillment of verse 24.

During most of those 360 years the empire was marked by intrigue. Before Octavius (Caesar Augustus) came to power, there was keen rivalry between him and his brother-in-law, Mark Antony, who also had come under the spell of Cleopatra. These two rivals are described in verses 26 and 27. While formerly in alliance, Antony and Octavius each aspired to complete dominion. While they could outwardly enjoy " 'sitting at the same table, they will lie to each other with advantage to neither' " (verse 27, NEB). Octavia, sister of Octavius, declared she had married Antony in the hope of keeping these two men as friends. True to the prophecy, however, it did not "prosper" (verse 27). In a very short time Antony and Cleopatra, for whom he had divorced his wife, were both dead—he by a self-inflicted dagger and she by the bite of an asp (probably an Egyptian cobra) smuggled into her presence in a basket of fruit.

One of the last campaigns of Octavius, by the authority of the Senate, was his war against Cleopatra, which also meant war with Antony. The latter, sensing the impending crisis, set sail for Athens, issuing orders everywhere for men and ships. Antony's fleet was anchored in the Ambracian Gulf, while his land forces were encamped on the north shore of the inlet, a most unhealthful spot, and one that caused the death of many troops. Some of his chief officers were won over to Octavius. The rest, disgusted by Cleopatra's influence on Antony, deserted him.

Antony, urged by Cleopatra, made his attack from the sea. Soon the wind fell, however, and his large, nearly unmanageable vessels proved no match for Octavius's light oar-propelled ships. When at last the wind sprang up, the Egyptian queen with sixty ships set sail for the south. Antony, realizing that the situation was hopeless, sprang from his ship onto a light galley and followed. By nightfall the remnants of the Egyptian fleet were destroyed. Rome had conquered, and Octavius was the hero.

If we are right in applying these verses to Rome, then we should note with care two uses of the word *return* in verse 28. The first is related to Octavius. Returning after his conquest of Egypt, he came back "with great riches," so valuable, it is claimed, that the value of money dropped 50 percent while the price of products increased 100 percent.

Yet there was another, more significant "return" when Titus returned "to his own land" covered with glory, having overthrown Judah and scattered the Jews everywhere. It certainly is true that his heart was "against the holy covenant."

JERUSALEM DESTROYED BY ROME

The destruction of Jerusalem under orders from Vespasian was the next great enterprise of Rome. Daniel's people, the Jews, had been given unusual liberty by Augustus. This was lost under Vespasian and his son, Titus, however. Rome did as it pleased with the Jewish nation. The Jewish war broke out in A.D. 66, and when it concluded four years later, the magnificent temple was no more. Many items of sacred furniture were taken to Rome as trophies of war.

The siege of Jerusalem by Titus was a tragic fulfillment of the prophecy of Moses in Deuteronomy 28:52–55. The Roman general swore "the extermination of the accursed city and people." Jesus said, "There shall not be left here one stone upon another, that shall not be thrown down" (Matthew 24:2). Titus, however, was so charmed by the grandeur of the temple that he gave orders to spare it. In the heat of war, however, a soldier seized a brand and, climbing on the shoulders of a comrade, thrust it into a window. Soon the temple, the pride of the Jews, was ablaze. Realizing the tragedy, the Roman prince and general of the army groaned, and "spreading his hands toward heaven, called God to witness that this was not his doing" (*Historian's History of the World,* vol. 2, page 196).

Titus rushed in personally and bore away the golden candlestick, the table of showbread, and the volume of the law. The candlestick was later deposited in Vespasian's Temple of Peace in Rome. A copy of this is still to be seen on the inside wall of the Arch of Titus, erected to celebrate his victory over the Jews. How accurate was the prophecy,

"He shall do exploits, and return to his own land" (Daniel 11:28). These exploits included the obliteration of the Jewish temple. To show their anger "against the holy covenant" the Romans erected a temple to Jupiter, "the father of the gods," on the site of the Jewish temple, sacred since Solomon's great dedication a thousand years earlier.

The destruction of Jerusalem affected tremendously not only the Jews and Christians, but also the empire itself. Three centuries later, Rome, "the eternal city," was the object of barbarian invasions, which continued intermittently until the imperial power of the empire expired in A.D. 476. Strange as it may seem, the Roman Senate at that time sent the official emblems of government to the Eastern Empire in Constantinople, saying they had no further use for them. Do we see in this the beginning of the transition from the pagan Rome of the Caesars to the papal Rome of the popes? Verse 30 says this power would "forsake the holy covenant," which the papacy surely did by the introduction of such doctrines as transubstantiation and the sacrifice of the mass into the worship services of the church.

Important as these parts of this great prophecy are, that which follows is even more vital.

16. Daniel Views Rise of Persecuting Power

What tremendous vistas of history are packed into a few verses of prophecy! We have already noticed the exactness of this long prophecy of Daniel 11, and some important events in the experience of Julius, Augustus, and Tiberius. It appears that Gabriel goes back into Jewish history in order to outline the movements of Rome in general, which so definitely influenced God's people. In verse 23 reference is made again to the "league" into which the Jews entered with the Romans in 161 B.C. That was an unfortunate step they took, because Judea, a century later, became a mere province of Rome.

It is not unusual for Bible prophecy to double back and repeat certain events, in order to unfold them more definitely. We find the same events recorded in Daniel chapters 7, 8, and 9 and in several places in Revelation. So, having brought the reader down to our Lord's death (see Daniel 11:22), the prophet then carries us back to the time when Rome, then a "small people," began to grow into an empire. From this point the prophecy leads us in a direct line to events that presage the final triumph of God's people and the establishment of the kingdom of glory.

Nothing else is as important to Daniel's people, or to any other people, as the substitutionary death of the Messiah, "the Lamb of God, which taketh away the sin of the world" (John 1:29). In order to emphasize the importance of the part Rome would play in these world-shaping events, the angel reaches back to the time when the Romans entered into this league in response to a definite request from the Jewish high priest, Judas, in 161 B.C. Having heard that the Romans had conquered Galatia, Iberia, Carthage, and Libya, and that three kings had been subdued—Perseus, Phillip, and Antiochus the Great—the Jews felt they should enter into a "league of friendship" with this rising power. The pact was made in the name of the Roman Senate, says Josephus, and while it looked attractive at first, it proved to be a tragic move for the Jews. (See *Antiquities,* bk. XII, chap. X.)

Rome's method of conquest, first promising peace then confiscating "the fattest places," is brought to our notice in Daniel 11:24. Under the pretense of offering protection, the Romans gradually moved in to steal the liberties of the world. But as we noticed before, it was "even for a time" (verse 24). Recognizing that a "time" in prophecy equals a year of 360 days, it is interesting to note that from 31 B.C., the year in which Egypt capitulated to Rome, until Constantine moved his seat of government from the city of Rome to Constantinople in A.D. 330, is exactly 360 years.

Dramatic changes were taking place in the Roman Empire. A truce between Constantine in the west and Lucinius in the east lasted from A.D. 314 to 323, and then war broke out anew. Lucinius was defeated in 324, and this left Constantine the head of the empire. Byzantium was now in the hands of Constantine, who decided to make this his capital. He practically rebuilt the city, beautifying it in every way. He intended to call it New Rome, but he was urged to insert his own name; so it became the metropolis of Constantine, Constantinople.

Verse 29 says, "it shall not be as the former, or as the latter." Rome had conquered Egypt, "the former," and Judea, "the latter." The setting up of this new seat of authority was unique and certainly did not help to stabilize the empire, because on Constantine's death the empire was divided among his three sons—Constantine II, Constantius, and Constans. In the ensuing two centuries this contributed to the collapse of the five-hundred-year empire of Rome.

CONSTANTINE ACCEPTS CHRISTIANITY

With the so-called conversion of Constantine, a new era began for the church. The emperor bestowed favors on the bishops, for he was eager to secure their power for the state. The church and the state united, and paganism insinuated itself into the church. An observer watching the worship service could scarcely realize it was a Christian worship, for many forms of pagan ritual were carried out. Against this apostasy, the Arian Goths rose up and invaded the city of Rome. Gibbon says, "Their arms spread desolation or terror from the columns of Hercules [the Straits of Gibraltar] to the south of the Nile."

While Constantine professed to accept Christianity, apparently he was never really a Christian at heart. While a member of the church, his attitude to the church seemed to be motivated solely by political ambitions. It was a sad day for Christianity when the emperor became the chairman of church councils as Constantine was at the Council of Nicea. Though appearing under the cloak of friendship, his heart was really "against the holy covenant" (verse 30).

"The ships of Chittim shall come against him" (verse 30). Chittim ("Kittim," RSV) doubtless refers to the strong maritime power that began to develop in North Africa. Genseric, the clever admiral of the never-defeated navy of the Vandals, was for fifty years their hero. He was the terror of Constantinople and Rome. Carthage became a stronghold from whence he ventured forth with his ships to attack what he said were "the dwellings of men with whom God was angry." Twice Genseric destroyed the Roman fleet, once in the harbor of Cartagena, Spain, and another time off the coast of Carthage itself. Rome was eventually taken and sacked in A.D. 455.

The breakup of the empire of the Caesars opened the way for the establishment of the papacy, which did indeed "pollute the sanctuary of strength" (verse 31). In other words, papal worship corrupted the true understanding of Christ as our Intercessor in the heavenly sanctuary. Many teachings such as the doctrine of transubstantiation undermined the doctrine of the finished sacrifice of Christ on the cross. Roman Catholicism claims that "Christ is offered every day on our altars."

The prominent powers of Europe exchanged their paganism for another type of paganism under the name of Christianity. As an example, in 498 Symmachus, a recent convert from paganism, ascended the papal throne. His advance to the pontifical chair was stained with the murder of his opponent. Once on the seat of authority, his first act was to excommunicate Emperor Anastasius. This was hailed by the crowd as evidence that he was now judge in the place of God, vicegerent of the Most High. This language is familiar to those who have read papal decrees. In place of the continual ministry of Christ,

151

a human priesthood was established, which claimed the power to forgive sins and open the gates of heaven to the transgressor. This was indeed "the abomination that maketh desolate" (verse 31).

" 'He will win over by plausible promises those who are ready to condemn the covenant' " (verse 32, NEB). In A.D. 533 the Eastern Emperor Justinian, eager to make war against the Vandals, sought for the approval and cooperation of the Bishop of Rome. In that year he wrote a letter, which later became official, to Epiphanius. In this letter he called the Bishop of Rome "the Head of All the Holy Churches," and later, "the Corrector of Heretics." The Arian Goths, having conquered Rome, were determined to rule. They were subdued, however, by armies ordered by the pope in A.D. 538. This marks the date for the beginning of the long prophetic period of 1,260 years—538 to 1798—which has been recognized by Bible scholars for almost 200 years.

FAITHFUL CHRISTIANS AND JEWS

During those dark years the Jews were persecuted and driven into ghettos, deprived of personal liberty and citizenship. Christians, too, were persecuted. Thousands of them remained faithful to God and His Word and fled into places of seclusion. Many Jews also were faithful to the teaching of their fathers.

The Waldenses trained their own ministers, who went out disguised as carpenters, tinsmiths, and even surgeons. They carried portions of the Bible all over Europe, sharing their faith with those who would listen. They paved the way for such early Reformers as Wycliffe, Huss, and Jerome. As the Scripture said, "The people that do know their God shall be strong, and do exploits" (verse 32).

"And they that understand among the people shall instruct many" (verse 33). How true that was! The same verse also says, "Yet they shall fall by the sword, and by flame, by captivity, and by spoil." These terrible persecutions were instituted not by pagans, but by so-called Christians—the apostate church under the leadership of prelates and bishops.

The sixteenth-century Reformation followed the introduction of printing into Europe, and the first book printed was the Bible in A.D. 1456.

In this great prophecy of Daniel 11 we see that mighty conflict between good and evil, between the children of light and the powers of darkness. In this we can see the brave deeds of the Waldenses in maintaining the purity of the faith and in spreading the light of truth over Europe amid the spiritual and moral darkness of their time. We can recognize the courage of the Bohemians in maintaining their faith in the face of huge German armies under papal influence. Here is portrayed the endurance of the Lollards, and later the Lutherans, and the martyrdom of the Huguenots of France. The marvelous story of these and other exploits will never be fully told until that great day when the faithful of all ages shall be gathered into the kingdom of our Lord.

Now, " 'when they fall, they shall receive a little help' " (verse 34, RSV). New legislation began to be passed in a number of countries, which brought some respite. But some, like Tyndale, in order to complete his work of translating the Bible, were compelled to flee to Holland. Persecuted peoples began to leave Europe for America, which became a haven of refuge. But during those terrible years of persecution, the church was being purged and made white, "even to the time of the end" (verse 35). This is the second mention in Scripture of the time of the end. In Daniel 7:25 we notice that the apostate church would hold the dominant position in Europe for 1,260 years. This time period lasted from 538 to 1798. The Napoleonic wars brought an end to papal dominance, for on February 11, 1798, Pope Pius VI was taken prisoner by General Berthier of France. In that same year, 1798, the French Revolution came to an end. After two terrible years of the "Reign of Terror," during which time much blood was shed, tremendous change came into the government of France. The American Revolution had occurred a few years before, and those two revolutions sounded the death knell of "the divine right of kings." The papal power, which for more than a thousand years had been leading into captivity, was now itself taken into captivity, fulfilling the prophecy of Revelation 13:10.

In the previous chapter of Revelation, the same period of papal persecution is brought to view, where the church, symbolized by a woman, fled into the wilderness and was sustained by the Lord. In this very prophecy we notice that the earth helped the woman, opening its mouth and swallowing up the flood which the dragon, or the devil, cast after her. Led by Martin Luther, the Protestant Reformation inflicted wounds in this apostate system by "the sword of the Spirit, which is the word of God" (Ephesians 6:17). The Protestant cause was espoused by some of the German states, which gave protection to the Reformers. The work of persecution was also restrained. Queen Mary of England, "Bloody Mary," was a mortal enemy of the Protestant cause, and her relentless persecutions were responsible for the death of many, including the Reformers burned at Smithfield.

A NEW ERA OF TOLERATION AND ENLIGHTENMENT

Certain decrees of toleration were passed in a few countries in Europe prior to 1798. Yet is was not until the nineteenth century dawned that multitudes began to enjoy toleration and even freedom of religion. The Scriptures call this the "time of the end." And it was indeed the end of wholesale European persecutions and the beginning of a more free society. During the later decades of the eighteenth century, under the impact of the evangelical revival, a new world opened up to hundreds of thousands. John Wesley and his brother Charles, George Whitefield, John Fletcher, and others brought about prison reform and education for children. Sunday Schools where children could learn the truth of salvation were opened. This time also marked the beginning of a world mission program, which aimed to carry the gospel to every land of earth.

In 1793 William Carey, "pioneer of modern missions," arrived in India. A few years later, in 1804, the British and Foreign Bible Society had its beginning. Within a few years Robert Moffatt went to Africa, Robert Morrison to China, Adoniram Judson to Burma, John Williams to Polynesia, Allan Gardiner to South America, and David Livingstone to Africa. Thus began the great program of world evangelism so well known today. The tremendous changes that took place around the end of the eighteenth century and the beginning of the nineteenth century have played a great part not only in the world's culture but also in our understanding of the Word of God.

17. The Atheistic Revolution

The section of Daniel's prophecy to which we now turn is the most challenging portion of chapter 11. Many sincere interpreters have attempted to resolve these verses, but each interpretation seems defective. Take, for example, our futurist friends, among whom are some of the most dedicated evangelical Christians. They put almost everything into the future, looking for fulfillment *after* our Lord's return, which they believe will be a secret and silent coming. They speak of "the king [that] shall do according to his will" (verse 36) as "the willful king," whom they believe will appear as a Jew, but who in reality will be "the very incarnation of Satan"—the terrible coming antichrist. They say he will make a covenant with the Jews, but will later persecute them.

Others see in these verses the restored power, the antichrist of the centuries, whose influence and machinations will assume worldwide influence just before Christ's second advent. They point to the similarity of language in Paul's description of the "man of sin" in 2 Thessalonians 2:2–5, and also in John's prophecy of a worldwide apostate power in Revelation 13:5–8. It seems clear that Daniel, Paul, and John all described the same power. Therefore, they say, it must be the papacy. Still others believe it refers to Russia, or maybe even to Islam. Are all these wrong? Or could all be right in some degree?

We do well to observe that Daniel 11:36 introduces a powerful personality who, at the time of the end, "shall do according to his will." Twice previously this prophecy tells of one who will do "according to his will," and each time it signals a dramatic change in the international scene and introduces a *new power*. The first was the lightning rise of the Grecian power under Alexander the Great. (See Daniel 11:3.) The second was the coming of Rome to world rulership, led by Julius Ceasar. (See verse 16.) Now we meet another who is to do "according to his will."

155

Unveiling Daniel and Revelation

Who is this one? Some say it is the papacy. While having the greatest respect for those who hold this interpretation, yet there are at least four important questions we must face if we read the papacy into these verses: (1) Was the papacy a *new* power at "the time of the end"? (2) Was the papacy a godless power? (3) Was the papacy ever a military power? (4) Was the papacy able "to do according to his will" at the time of the end, 1798?

Concerning the first question, it is sufficient to say that the papacy was already over a thousand years old at the time and had a long record of persecution and intrigue. Moreover, the ruling pope, Pius VI, was taken prisoner in 1798. He died in Valence, France, on August 29, 1799. Not till March 14 of the following year was a new pope elected.

On the second question the prophecy says, "Neither shall he regard the God of his fathers, . . . nor regard any god" (verse 37). Despite the fact that the papacy corrupted the truth, it was not a godless power.

On the third question, while we admit that certain popes were very active militarily, yet the papacy was not primarily a military power as the prophecy suggests. The Scripture says, " 'He shall honor the god of fortresses . . . a god whom his fathers did not know' " (verse 38, RSV). Such words could scarcely be applied to a church. But no words could better describe the atheistic revolution in France during the latter part of the eighteenth century.

The fourth question almost answers itself, for the one power that *could not* do "according to his will" at that time was the papacy. The pope was incarcerated, the forces of atheism having curtailed his power. Atheistic France confiscated the property of the church. The sacred vessels of worship were often melted down for coins, while lead coffins were turned into bullets.

The same atheistic principles that brought to fruition the godless revolution in France are today, however, being taught in schools and colleges everywhere. Ellen White, commenting on conditions at the end of the nineteenth century, listed several threats to stable government: (1) centralization of wealth and power; (2) combinations for increasing the wealth of the few; (3) combinations of the poor to defend their interests; (4) "the spirit of unrest, or riot and bloodshed"; (5) "the world-wide dissemination of the same teaching that led to the

French Revolution." Then she said of these influences, "All are tend-ing to *involve the whole world in a struggle similar to that which con-vulsed France.*" (*Education,* page 228, emphasis supplied.) Note that this speaks of a coming worldwide revolution. At the time these words were written there was little evidence of any such power arising. But a decade and a half later Russia was plunged into her revolution. Since then, the principles of the French Revolution have spread to every land of earth. Rather than think of Daniel 11:36–45 as dealing with just the work of the papacy, would it not be wiser to make a wider application? The new world power predicted here and which will fi-nally come to its end will doubtless include the papacy as it will every other apostate and false system of religion. The prophecy also indi-cates it will be more than just a religious power; it will have to do with commerce and industry as well as with false philosophy. Revela-tion 18, which is an enlargement of Daniel 11:45, portrays the final collapse of all human government arraigned against God.

Not only is a new and dominant leader introduced in Daniel 11:36, but the prophecy forecasts a new and revolutionary type of government. While the French Revolution with all its horror was confined to one nation, it could well be a miniature illustration of the world's final challenge to the living God. That France, the richest, most cultured, and most densely populated country in Europe at that time, could ever become the scene of such brutal disorder and ven-geance as stained her record under the later Louis kings seemed im-possible. But the unbelievable happened.

The French Revolution, however, was but the culmination of two centuries of suppression of the Scriptures, carried out under the guise of religion. Most frightful, heart-rending slaughters had been perpe-trated, such as the St. Bartholomew Massacre in 1572, which was definitely the work of priests and prelates. Commenting on this, Henry White says: "When the news of the massacre reached Rome, the exultation among the clergy knew no bounds. . . . A medal was struck to commemorate the massacre and in the Vatican may still be seen three frescoes of Tasari, describing the attack" (*The Massacre of St. Bartholomew,* ch. 14, par. 34, quoted in Ellen White, *The Great Controversy,* page 273). Ultimately many voices demanded that in the name of reason, religion be abolished. "God does not exist!" they shouted, and the nation through its legislators turned atheistic.

If anyone wonders whether God would bother to mention France in prophecy, the evidence is clear, for the greater part of Revelation 11 deals with the rise of atheism and the French Revolution. "In many of the nations of Europe the powers that ruled in church and state had for centuries been controlled by Satan through the medium of the papacy. But here is brought to view a new manifestation of satanic power" (*The Great Controversy,* pages 268, 269). And "this prophecy has received a most exact and striking fulfillment in the history of France" (ibid., page 269).

Daniel's prophecy describing the new power that was to arise and do its work in "the time of the end" declares that he would not "regard the God of his fathers," but would "honour the god of forces [or fortresses, or munitions]" (Daniel 11:37, 38). In other words, military power would predominate. Then we should look for some powerful personality, a military genius, who at the "time of the end" would assume authority. Naturally, many see this fulfilled in that military genius Napoleon Bonaparte. Not only did he try to reshape Europe, but he was determined to weld the nations into a single empire. It is said that the word *conscription* was first applied to the armed forces in September 1798, making men legally liable for service. This made possible a new system of war.

Napoleon was also responsible for many social and economic changes. And historians agree that modern history begins with Napoleon. His rise marked two great revolutions—one in America and the other in France.

The French Revolution had sought to abolish religion, especially the Christian religion, and the Bible. Fouché declared from the pulpit of the cathedral at Vevers that the worship of Reason "should in future be the national religion" (Louis Madelin, *The French Revolution,* page 388). Here surely was "a god whom his fathers did not know."

During the Revolution, in 1783, "the world for the first time heard an assembly of men, born and educated in civilization, and assuming the right to govern one of the finest of the European nations, uplift their united voice to deny the most solemn truth which man's soul receives, and renounce unanimously the belief and worship of a deity" (Sir Walter Scott, *The Life of Napoleon,* vol. 1, ch. 17, quoted in Madelin, *The French Revolution,* pages 269, 270). "France stands apart in the world's history as the single state which by the decree of her Legislative Assembly pronounced that there was no God. . . . Women as well as men danced and sang with joy in accepting the announcement" (*Blackwood's Magazine,* November, 1870).

Not only did France try to destroy the worship of God among her citizens, she also made divorce easier. One phrase in this prophecy could well relate to that: "Neither shall he regard . . . the desire of women" (verse 37), which theologian Thomas Newton declared could more properly be rendered: "the desire of wives." Other translations read: "nor care for the delight of women," Fenton; " 'the one whom women love,' " (Jerusalem Bible); " 'the god beloved of women,' " (NEB). Many interpreters emphasize that the phrase relates to the love of women, particularly conjugal love. In any case, divorce was established in Paris by decree on September 20, 1792, and carried still further by the Convention in 1794. Soon, according to Madelin, "women passed from hand to hand by a legal process" with the tragic result of a very steep rise in illegitimacy.

CHRISTIANITY ATTACKED BY ATHEISM

While homes were breaking up, churches were being desecrated. Church bells were melted and cast into cannon. Bibles were publicly burned, and the weekly day of worship was set aside. The Assembly by decree transformed even the famous Notre Dame Cathedral into the *Temple of Reason.* During the Reign of Terror, which lasted from 1792 until 1794, the Revolution reached its height, and both the church and the government were overthrown. The king and queen and many of the nobility of France were decapitated. An estimated fourteen thousand people were guillotined.

"Thus shall he do in the most strong holds with a strange god . . . and [he] *shall divide the land* for gain" (verse 39, emphasis supplied). Previous to the Revolution, the Roman Catholic Church and a few landlords owned two-thirds of the land of France. The landed estates were confiscated and sold at auction in small parcels; the sales provided much needed funds for the newly appointed government.

"When the restraints of God's law were cast aside, it was found that the laws of man were inadequate to hold in check the powerful tides of human passion. . . . Violence and lust held undisputed sway. . . .

"The cities of the kingdom were filled with scenes of horror. . . . And to add to the general misery, the nation became involved in a prolonged and devastating war with the great powers of Europe" (*The Great Controversy,* pages 282, 283).

The effort to capture the minds of men began in dead earnest about two hundred years ago with the new religion, so-called, of Rousseauism. Eugene Methvin, in his penetrating analysis *The Rise of Radicalism,* speaks of a quasi–Masonic secret order know as the Illuminati, "founded in 1776 by Adam Weishaupt, a professor from Ingalstadt and a renegade Jesuit. Weishaupt heartily hated the Jesuits and aimed to replace Christianity with a secular religion of reason" (page 121). Among the outstanding French leaders was Philippe Buonannoti, who "hailed the French Revolution as the dawning of heaven on earth." It proved to be anything but that, but the ideas inculcated at that time by these radical thinkers is the philosophy behind much of today's world unrest.

"The atheistical power that ruled in France under the Revolution and the Reign of Terror, did wage such a war against God and His holy word as the world had never witnessed. The worship of the deity was abolished by the National Assembly. Bibles were collected and publicly burned with every possible manifestation of scorn. The law of God was trampled underfoot. The institutions of the Bible were abolished. The weekly rest day was set aside, and in its stead every tenth day was devoted to reveling and blasphemy" (*The Great Controversy,* pages 273, 274).

SIX-POINTED PHILOSOPHY DISRUPTS FRANCE

The corruptive philosophy of Weishaupt and others had done its work in the nation, and the Revolution was the baleful fruit. The atheistic order aimed at nothing less than total world revolution and ultimately a single world government.

160

Nesta Webster, a British writer, sums up the teachings of the Illuminati in these six important points:

1. abolition of all ordered government
2. abolition of all monarchy
3. abolition of all private property and inheritance
4. abolition of all patriotism
5. abolition of the family (Marriage was regarded as outdated, and children became the responsibility of the state.)
6. abolition of all religion

Weishaupt adopted the name *Spartacus*, leader of an insurrection of slaves in ancient Rome. John Robison, in his book *Proofs of a Conspiracy Against the Religions and Governments of Europe*, published in 1798, declared that Weishaupt's real intention was to "abolish all religions, overthrow every government, and make the world a general plunder and wreck." Patriotism and loyalty were regarded as narrow-minded prejudices. These revolutionary ideas brought on the Reign of Terror, and "they have helped to light the fires of every revolution in the two hundred years since they were published [on May 1, 1776]" (Edward Hodnett, *The Cultivated Mind*, page 27).

The French Revolution was short lived. The seeds of anarchy, however, spread, ultimately finding fertile soil in Russia, where they developed slowly. A century later, in 1917, at the height of World War I, Russia was plunged into the Bolshevik Revolution, which embraced many of the principles of the French Revolution and resulted in an atheistic socialism that brought misery to its people and fear to the world for decades. How true is the statement in the book *Education* to which we referred earlier that "anarchy is seeking to sweep away all law, not only divine, but human." And this, we repeat, in combination with unsettling world conditions, is "tending to involve the whole world in a struggle similar to that which convulsed France" (page 228). The same writer says, "The enmity of Satan against good will be manifested more and more as he brings his forces into activity in his last work of rebellion; and every soul that is not fully surrendered to God, and kept by divine power, will form an alliance with Satan against heaven, and join in battle against the Ruler of the universe" (*Testimonies to Ministers*, page 465).

Unveiling Daniel and Revelation

At the dawning of the "time of the end," as we have seen, major political changes occurred: the imprisonment of the pope; the French Revolution; the appearance of a new and dominant personality—Napoleon, who said, "There will be no repose in Europe until it is under one head. . . . In five years I shall be master of the world." Describing Napoleon, Madame de Stael wrote, "This man really does possess the will to shift the world."

Verse 40 declares, "At the time of the end [1798] shall the king of the south push at him: and the king of the north shall come against him like a whirlwind, with chariots, and with horsemen, and with many ships." The king of the north and the king of the south have not been mentioned since verse 16, when we were viewing events occurring about 200 B.C., some two thousand years earlier.

The king of the south at that time was Egypt, and still is. While Rome ruled Egypt for a short time, that king was still Egypt. Not so with the king of the north. That territory changed hands several times. It was originally the Syrian power. But at "the time of the end" it was under Turkish rule. We might ask, Was there conflict between Egypt and France and between Turkey and France at "the time of the end," in 1798? There certainly was. A state of open hostility developed between France and Egypt. Napoleon was planning to invade Egypt at that time, but he declared he was coming only to chastise the Mamelukes for their robbing of certain French merchants. The Mamelukes were the governing class, and Napoleon sought to drive a wedge between them and the populace. Furthermore, he cherished hopes of subduing not only Egypt, but Syria, Persia, and India, even as far as the Ganges. These plans he placed before the Directory, and secured their authority for his campaign against Egypt.

He set sail from Toulon on May 19, 1798, with 27 large ships, many smaller vessels of war, and 300 transports. Counting the troops and the ships' crews, probably fifty thousand men were involved. On July 2 he took Alexandria. On the twenty-first he fought the Battle of the Pyramids. On July 25 he entered Cairo, the capital. Egypt, able to offer only weak resistance, suffered heavy losses of men and equipment. The words of the prophecy are significant: "The king of the south" shall "push at him"—a feeble resistance. But by contrast, "The king of the north shall come against him like a whirlwind, with chariots, and with horsemen, and with many ships" (verse 40). While this may have some future significance, it certainly had its fulfillment at the "time of the end," for on September 11, 1798, the Sultan of Turkey declared war on France. Thus the king of the south, Egypt, and the king of the north, which at that time was Turkey, both attacked France at the same time.

NAPOLEON'S FIRST RETREAT

Napoleon had crushed the armies of Egypt, and he attempted the same thing with the Turks in Syria. A strong body of Turks, however, had entrenched themselves at Jean d'Acre, and thousands of Muslims had gathered on the hills of Samaria. Just at that time Sir Sydney Smith arrived at Saint Jean d'Acre with a small fleet of English ships. His men, aided by Turkey, captured Napoleon's siege equipment.

The siege lasted some weeks, but Napoleon, seeing the situation was hopeless, sounded a call for retreat. On May 21, 1799, he began to retrace his steps toward the territory of the king of the south. But, as the prophecy declared, he was not through. This military genius had one ambition, to unite the world and make himself its supreme ruler.

The historian Guizot says of Napoleon, "In his secret thoughts, powerful and chimerical, he nursed the hope of pushing forward to Constantinople, seizing the city, and making himself master of Europe by attacking it from the eastern side. *It was to the conquest of the world* that he marched in advancing against Jaffa" (*Nations of the World,* "France," vol. 6, page 388, emphasis supplied).

Thiers, another French historian, says, "To penetrate into those countries of light and glory, where Alexander and Mahomet had conquered and founded empires, to make them ring with his name, and to have it sent back to France repeated by echoes of Asia, was for him a most ravishing prospect" (*The History of the French Revolution,* page 769).

It is unfortunate that in recent times there is a tendency on the part of some to minimize the importance of this period, especially Napoleon's campaigns. But the Napoleonic wars and the French

Revolution mark one of the great turning points of history. These events presaged a new era not only for Europe, but for the world.

When the armies of France, led by Napoleon, were defeated, Palestine once again became a small part of the sprawling Ottoman Empire and remained so for the next hundred years until General Allenby, in 1918, won his decisive victory on the age-old Palestinian battlefield of Megiddo. That hastened the end not only of World War I, but also of the Ottoman Empire. For his outstanding military leadership Allenby was given the title Earl of Meggido.

Since then the political face of the Middle East has changed tremendously. Europe, too, has undergone drastic changes. Between 1914 and 1918 four great empires collapsed—the Russian Empire under the czars; the German Empire under the kaisers; the Austrian Empire under the Hapsburgs; and the Ottoman Empire, under the sultans. Yes, we live today in a different world from that in which our grandfathers lived. But these changes were all foreseen by the prophet Daniel, who set forth clearly the conditions marking "the time of the end," one of the most imposing being the movement toward world government.

In identifying the power spoken of in the last verses of Daniel 11 it would appear wise for us to look for a larger power than the papacy. Here are twenty-one points of identity listed in the prophecy, not more than half of which could possibly relate to the papacy, but every one of which either has been, or could well be, fulfilled by a worldwide atheistic government:

1. This power manifests itself "at the time of the end," 1798.
2. It shall exalt "and magnify himself above every god."
3. It shall "prosper till the indignation be accomplished."
4. It shall "speak marvelous things against the God of gods."
5. It shall not "regard the God of his fathers."
6. It shall not regard "the desire of women."
7. It shall not "regard any god."
8. It shall "magnify himself above all."
9. It shall "honour the God of forces" ("munitions," margin).
10. It shall "honour with gold, and silver, and with precious stones."

11. It shall "cause them to rule over many."
12. It shall "divide the land for gain."
13. It shall "enter also into the glorious land."
14. The king of the south shall "push at him," and the king of the north shall "come against him."
15. It shall "stretch forth his hand also upon the countries."
16. It shall have power over the treasures of Egypt.
17. The "Libyans and the Ethiopians shall be at his steps."
18. "Tidings out of the east and out of the north shall trouble him."
19. "He shall go forth with great fury to destroy."
20. "He shall plant the tabernacles of his palace" in Jerusalem.
21. "He shall come to his end, and none shall help him."

Some interpreters apply these verses to antichrist, which they declare will appear *after* our Lord's return, that is, after the great resurrection. But Daniel 12 makes it clear that the willful king, or the antichrist, makes his attack on God's people *prior* to the standing up of Michael and the ushering in of the time of trouble, *before* our Lord's return. Just before that grand event Satan will make a desperate effort to delude the world. He will come "with all power and signs and lying wonders" (2 Thessalonians 2:9). "The last great delusion is soon to open before us. Antichrist is to perform his marvelous works in our sight" (*The Great Controversy,* page 593). A world church in collaboration with a world government could easily pave the way for this display of Satan's power.

THE RISE AND SPREAD OF A WORLD ATHEISTIC REVOLUTION

If such a union were to materialize, while it would include the papacy, yet it would be far more than a papal program; it would be man's final challenge to the living God. The history of God's faithful men in ancient Babylon might well be a miniature of God's ultimate victory over the world or modern Babylon. In Daniel, chapter 1, we see God's men standing firm in matters of diet. In Daniel 2 we see God's ability to foretell the future, triumphing over the knowledge of Babylon. In chapter 3 the worship of God proved victorious over the worship demanded by the king of Babylon. In chapter 4, as the king was sent out to eat grass, we see the rulership of God triumphing over the rulership of Babylon. In chapter 5, God rebukes Babylon's blasphemy, and the Persian conquerors take the city. In chapter 6 we see God triumphing over Daniel's persecutors.

Revelation 18 pictures the final collapse of all false religions, all worldly business and commerce, all shipping and finance under the judgments of God. Even "souls of men" (verse 13) are included in the list that makes up Babylon—the power that "reigneth over the kings of the earth" (Revelation 17:18). Chapters 17 and 18 of Revelation have a significant tie-in with Isaiah 2 and Micah 4, where a great peace movement is depicted, which ends in destruction when the Lord God "ariseth to shake terribly the earth" (Isaiah 2:19). It is important to note here the words in verse 3: "Come ye, and let us go up to the mountain of the LORD . . . for out of Zion shall go forth the law, and the word of the LORD from Jerusalem." While the idea is laudable, these are not the words of God, but the words of "many people." (Micah 4:2 says, "many nations.") Isaiah continues, "Thou hast forsaken thy people the house of Jacob, because they be replenished from the east, and are soothsayers [spiritualists]. . . . Their land is also full of horses . . [and] chariots [military equipment]" (verses 6, 7). "Their land is also full of idols; . . . therefore forgive them not" (verses 8, 9). God says, "Enter into the rock . . . for fear of the LORD, and for the glory of his majesty" (verse 10). Human plans for world peace and world religion will come to naught, for "the LORD alone shall be exalted in that day" (verse 17). The apostle Paul says, "When they shall say, Peace and safety; then sudden destruction cometh upon them, . . . and they shall not escape" (1 Thessalonians 5:3).

We cannot be dogmatic on certain details of these prophecies, for we are dealing with unfulfilled prophecy, and only after events transpire can we be certain. But the world seems to be shaping up for the final display of anti-God power. Jesus said, "I have told you before it come to pass, that, when it is come to pass, ye might believe" (John 14:29). Prophecy is given not to make us expert prognosticators, but rather, intelligent interpreters when the events occur.

The angel Gabriel, however, made it clear to Daniel that the power that *comes to his end* will be a power that has worldwide influence.

And his collapse will be the signal for our Lord's return. So we need to be alert and watching. The things we witness today throughout the world are surely the final movements of "the time of the end." We can know that the Lord is at hand. Jesus said, "Be ye also ready: for in such an hour as ye think not the Son of man cometh" (Matthew 24:44).

For decades, even centuries, men have envisioned a peaceful, united world. Any superman who could ensure the world of real and lasting peace would be hailed as the greatest deliverer of all time. Many Bible students predict the rise of such a world leader. They speak of him as the coming antichrist; they declare that he will accomplish many unbelievable things, as the Scripture declares, even calling down fire from heaven as did Elijah in the days of King Ahab. That such a personality will appear the Scriptures make abundantly clear. While he will appear as a man, he will be more than a man. He will be none other than Satan himself impersonating Christ. Stepping onto the world stage, he will deceive men and nations. In Revelation 16:14 we read that demon spirits will "go forth unto the kings of the earth and of the whole world, to gather them to the battle of that great day of God Almighty." To some extent this is happening now. Occultism in all its varied forms was never so popular as it is today. The Scripture says, "He gathered them together into a place called in the Hebrew tongue Armageddon" (verse 16).

Daniel also speaks of the rise of such a power, declaring that he "shall plant the tabernacles of his palace [" 'his royal pavilion,' " NEB] between the seas in the glorious holy mountain" (Daniel 11:45). But will his reign endure? On this Scripture is very definite. The angel said, "Yet he shall come to his end, and none shall help him. And at that time shall Michael stand up, the great prince which standeth for the children of thy people: and there shall be a time of trouble, such as never was since there was a nation even to that same time" (verse 45; 12:1).

God's people delivered

The "time of trouble" spoken of here will be short, but it will be a period of frightful distress—a different kind of trouble from anything ever before recorded. The medieval centuries, sometimes referred to as the Dark Ages, were tragic times for both Jews and Christians, but the coming time of trouble, which just precedes our Savior's return in glory, will exceed anything in history. Having finished His work of intercession, our great High Priest lays aside His mediatorial robes and clothes Himself in the garments of a conquering king. His destroying angels then pour out their bowls of wrath—the seven last plagues—upon the despisers of His grace. It will be a tragic time of judgment, but God's people will be protected in those awful days. "He shall give his angels charge over thee, to keep thee in all thy ways" (Psalm 91:11). "There shall no evil befall thee, neither shall any plague come nigh thy dwelling" (verse 10).

Many prophets have spoken of this coming time of turmoil. Jeremiah worried, "Alas! for that day is great, so that none is like it: it is even the time of Jacob's trouble; but he shall be saved out of it" (Jeremiah 30:7). Those last words are surely encouraging—"he shall be saved out of it." Daniel says, "At that time thy people shall be delivered, every one that shall be found written in the book" (Daniel 12:1). They are delivered, not because they belong to a certain group, but because their names are written in the book.

Gabriel came to tell Daniel what would happen to his people in the latter days. (See Daniel 10:14.) Daniel's people, of course, were the Jews, and vital things were to happen to Israel in the latter days. Some of these are happening right now. But the greatest thing that could happen to this once-scattered nation would be for the scales to fall from their eyes, and they, with clear spiritual insight, would turn to Jehovah in repentance, accepting "the great prince," Jesus of Nazareth, as their Messiah and prepare to meet Him when He returns in glory. The Scriptures do not indicate that the nation as a whole will do this, yet some of the greatest of the Hebrew prophets envisioned a tremendous turning back to God on the part of Daniel's "people," the Jews, just before the Savior appears. And among the multitudes who will accept salvation are more than natural born Jews, because all who turn to God in repentance and accept the grace of God become the children of God, whatever their racial background. "For," says the apostle Paul, "ye are all the children of

God by faith in Christ Jesus. . . . And if ye be Christ's, then are ye Abraham's seed, and heirs according to the promise" (Galatians 3:26, 29).

A hundred years before Daniel was born, Isaiah wrote about "the sons of the stranger, that join themselves to the LORD, to serve him, and to love the name of the LORD, to be his servants" (Isaiah 56:6). "Even unto them will I give . . . a name better than of sons and of daughters" (verse 5). "For mine house shall be called an house of prayer for all people" (verse 7). Paul speaks of "Israel after the flesh" (1 Corinthians 10:18). These are the natural sons of Abraham. But the apostle also speaks of the church made up of all nations as "the Israel of God" (Galatians 6:16). So, as already noted, Daniel's people include more than natural born Jews, for all who love the Lord and through faith accept salvation become "Abraham's seed, and heirs according to the promise" (Galatians 3:29).

Whether people are born Jews or members of another race, all are saved in exactly the same way. Through faith we all become part of spiritual Israel. Are you ready, dear friend, for that moment when "Michael [shall] stand up, the great prince which standeth for the children of thy people" (Daniel 12:1)? If you have not made that surrender, why not give your heart to Him now? Do not delay. He waits your decision. At this very moment you can pass from death to life. Accept Him as your Savior now, and be prepared for the "time of trouble" so soon to burst upon the world. Then it will be too late to make that surrender. "(Now is the accepted time; behold, now is the day of salvation)" (2 Corinthians 6:2).

When you make that choice, your name is written in the book of life, and if you are faithful, you will be protected during the awful days ahead. Soon our Lord will appear with all His holy angels, and together we will be caught up with all God's saints of all the ages to live with Him forever. May the Holy Spirit lead us all to make that decision now for His name's sake.

18. Is Earth Headed for World Government?

The end of the eighteenth century saw both the end and the beginning of many things. Not only did 1798 mark the end of the 1,260 years of papal dominance, as predicted in Daniel 7:25 and 12:7; it was also the portent of the industrial revolution and the scientific age, to which we shall refer more definitely in the next chapter.

It is difficult for us to picture the world as it was at the close of the eighteenth century. In 1797 the first cast iron plow was patented. Mechanized farming began to receive great impetus. Not only have our methods of work changed, but also our methods of war have changed unbelievably. To illustrate this, one need only recall that the nuclear age, marked by the dropping of atomic bombs on Japan at the close of World War II, took place less than seventy-five years ago. Now picture the nuclear weapons available to many nations today, with their capacity to destroy the world many times over. If we had nothing else to consider, the weapons of mass destruction that exist today would be enough to tell us that we have indeed reached the time of the end.

Gabriel's message to Daniel was given in order that God's people, godly Jews and Gentiles alike, might prepare themselves to stand in the day of final destruction. And among the messages of the angel none is more vital than the one found in Daniel 11:36 to the end of chapter 12. The angel spoke of a power that would arise in "the time of the end" (Daniel 11:40) which would wage an intensive war, not merely for the *bodies* of men, as in the days of slavery and labor camps, but for the *minds* of men; its weapons not military hardware but challenging ideas. The most bitter conflict is where human beings are hungry, longing for food and freedom, for education and the comforts of life. It is an ideological warfare waged in the name of humanity. Science and education are the watchwords of this new era. The fundamental conflict is not political but religious.

THE ANTI-GOD WAR OF TODAY

The technological world in which we live today has resulted in increasing efforts to push aside the Word of God as irrelevant and lacking credibility. The scriptural account of Creation is largely set aside, and the pseudo-scientific belief that human beings evolved from earlier forms of life is accepted as more reasonable. While evolution as we know it today is of fairly recent origin, it has its roots far back in history. The story of human beginnings has been a definite part of every ancient religion. But in the eighteenth century men of science probed deeper into both geology and biology, seeking a natural explanation of origins. Eventually they created a "ladder of life" with progressive stages stretching over millions of years. The more complex animals, including human beings, naturally belonged to the last stage. The Bible story of Creation was rejected and ridiculed, and in its place the Goddess of Reason was tacitly accepted.

"The time of the end" was marked, therefore, not only by the rise of military might and incredible technological advancement but also by sweeping changes in philosophy, science, and religion. Rationalism, claiming reason as a superior source of knowledge, laid aside what men called the "musty records of the past" as they sought for a new understanding of earth's origin. This resulted in the loss of faith. How relevant is our Lord's rhetorical question, "When the Son of man cometh, shall he find faith on the earth?" (Luke 18:8).

While atheism and infidelity have existed in the minds of certain philosophers throughout history, these philosophies are today being taught in the classrooms of high schools and colleges all over the world. In thousands of books and magazines, and by television programs, the theory of humanity's evolution, as opposed to the Bible account of Creation, is being presented as if it were a proved fact.

COMING WORLD GOVERNMENT

In addition to the challenges presented to Bible truth by evolution and rationalism, the prophecy points to a religious-political power that will assume an increasingly greater role in world affairs as the world draws ever nearer to the second advent of our Lord Jesus Christ. According to Bible prophecy, when the papacy has fully recovered

171

from the "deadly wound" (Revelation 13:3) inflicted by the state in 1798, she will play a vital role in the closing scenes of earth's history. Nor will she be alone, for John in the symbolic prophecy of Revelation 17 pictures a woman riding a scarlet-colored beast, and in her person she bears the "names of blasphemy" (Revelation 17:3). This symbolism is well understood by Bible students, for in prophecy a woman represents a church, and a beast symbolizes a political power. So in this prophetic picture we see a great political power being guided by a corrupt church. And in verse 14 we read, "These shall make war with the Lamb [Christ], and the Lamb shall overcome them: for he is the Lord of lords, and the King of kings: and they that are with him are called, and chosen, and faithful."

The next chapter of John's book unfolds the final collapse of a great religio-political colossus. (See Revelation 18:8–24.) These verses seem to be an enlargement on Daniel 11:45. How the books of Daniel and Revelation complement each other!

While dealing with unfulfilled prophecy we must be cautious. Yet it appears that politics, economics, and religion will ultimately combine to bring about the long-envisioned "world government." Doubtless many and varied influences will play a part in bringing such a program to fruition. Those leading the way to the long-dreamed-of world government have the apparent objective of international peace—a truly laudable aim. But the apostle says that at the very time when the world will be proclaiming "peace and safety," then "sudden destruction cometh upon them, . . . and they shall not escape" (1 Thessalonians 5:3). It is not that God does not desire peace among the nations, but until men's hearts are changed, there can be no lasting peace.

THE COMING OF THE INDISPENSABLE MAN

World government is not the answer to the world's dilemma. Increased military might is not the solution. Technology and human ingenuity is insufficient to meet our need, whether it be an energy crisis, a political crisis, a financial crisis, or a religious crisis. Only the coming of the Son of Man, the indispensable Man, the God-Man, can bring the peace for which all men and women hope and pray.

19. Righteous Shine as the Stars Forever

"At that time shall Michael stand up, the great prince which standeth for the children of thy people" (Daniel 12:1). These opening words of Daniel's last chapter are deeply significant. The previous nine verses picture events leading to the creation of a great world government. This masterful attempt of man to govern himself will be his final challenge to the living God.

In Revelation 16:13, 14 the prophet John speaks of the spirits of demons coming from three great sources—the dragon, the beast, and the false prophet. And the prophecy declares that these powers will gather the whole world "to the battle of that great day of God Almighty." The Scripture further states that they will be gathered together "into a place called in the Hebrew tongue Armageddon" (verse 16). When that happens, a mighty voice is heard from heaven announcing, "It is done!" Or "It is over!"

All is finished. Then the greatest demonstration of organization and power the world has ever known will collapse. For at that time God Himself will step in and take over the rulership of this runaway world. The prophecy declares, "He shall come to his end, and none shall help him" (Daniel 11:45). It is then that Michael stands up, "the great prince . . . and there shall be a time of trouble, such as never was since there was a nation" (Daniel 12:1).

WHO IS MICHAEL, THE GREAT PRINCE?

What does the standing up of Michael mean? Is this some intervention of one of heaven's highest angels on behalf of the Palestinian Jews? No! It is something far greater. Michael is not just one of heaven's highest angels; He is the Archangel whose mighty voice will call the dead to life again. In Jude 9 we read of Michael coming to raise the body of Moses, at which time the devil disputed His authority. But the Archangel Michael issued the divine command, "The Lord rebuke thee"!

Note three important words in this brief account: "Michael," "Lord," and "archangel." He who rebuked the devil and raised Moses from the dead is the One who will yet call to life and immortality all who have died in the blessed hope of the resurrection. Talking to Martha, Jesus said, "I am the resurrection, and the life: he that believeth in me, though he were dead, yet shall he live" (John 11:25). And at another time, "The hour is coming, in the which all that are in the graves shall hear his voice, and shall come forth" (John 5:28, 29).

The voice of the Archangel is the voice of the Life-Giver. His authoritative command will sound through all the world: "Awake and sing, ye that dwell in dust"; then "the earth shall cast out the dead" (Isaiah 26:19). At that time all who have died believing God's Word will toss aside their coverlet of dust and spring forth joyfully into eternal life.

The name *Michael* means "who is like God?" He is like God because He *is* God—One with the Father from all eternity. More than twenty times in the New Testament we read such statements as "Christ sitteth on the right hand of God" or "sat down on the right hand of God" (Colossians 3:1; Hebrews 10:12). At the throne of grace Christ has been officiating as our High Priest, our Intercessor, but someday soon His ministry of intercession will cease. No longer will He occupy the throne of grace, for mercy's door will have closed forever. It is then that He stands up to receive the kingdom and prepares to return to earth for His people.

THE GLORIOUS RETURN OF CHRIST

What wonderful pictures the prophets have given us of our Lord's return! When He comes, it will be in His own glory and in the glory of the Father and in the glory of the holy angels. Note these verses of Scripture: Luke 9:26; Matthew 25:31; 2 Thessalonians 1:7–10; Revelation 1:7.

"At that time thy people shall be delivered, every one that shall be found written in the book," said the angel (Daniel 12:1). They will be delivered not because they are Jews or Christians, not because they belong to a certain group or denomination, but because their names are written in the book—the book of life. It will be worth everything in that day to have our names in that book.

During that awful time of trouble there will be a partial resurrection. "Many of them that sleep in the dust of the earth shall awake, some to everlasting life, and some to shame and everlasting contempt" (Daniel 12:2). The resurrection spoken of here is not the general resurrection at the time our Lord is seen coming in the clouds of heaven, for then the righteous only are raised. Says the Scripture, "Blessed and holy is he that hath part in the first resurrection: on such the second death hath no power" (Revelation 20:6). "But the rest of the dead [the wicked dead] lived not again until the thousand years were finished" (verse 5). A short time before our Lord appears, there will be a special resurrection. This is emphasized in Revelation 1:7: "Behold, he cometh with clouds; and every eye shall see him," says John's prophecy, "and they also which pierced him." In Matthew's Gospel we read of a special resurrection when our Lord rose from the dead. (See Matthew 27:52.) So again there will be another special resurrection associated with His second advent. At that time those most prominent in their demand that Christ be crucified—those who gave sentence against Him in the judgment hall, crying, "Crucify Him," those who drove the nails through His hands and feet—will come forth from their graves to see Him coming in power and great glory.

When our Lord was arraigned before the Jewish court on trial for His life, the high priest demanded that Jesus tell him whether He was truly the Christ, the Son of God. With calm assurance the Savior answered, "Yes, I am," or "It is as you say," but He quickly added, "Nevertheless I say unto you, Hereafter shall ye see the Son of man sitting on the right hand of power, and coming in the clouds of heaven" (Matthew 26:64).

According to the words of Christ Himself, those who pierced Him, those who mocked and derided Him in His dying agonies, will be raised to witness the coming King of kings and Lord of lords returning in all His glory. And not only many wicked, but also many righteous will be raised, for the Scripture says, "some to everlasting life, and some to shame and everlasting contempt" (Daniel 12:2). Could there be anything more thrilling for those who have faithfully proclaimed God's last great message to the world than to come forth from their dusty beds to witness their Savior returning as conquering King accompanied by all the holy angels? Ellen G. White speaks of those who have died in the faith of the third angel's message as coming forth "to hear God's covenant of peace" (*The Great Controversy,* page 637).

AS THE STARS FOREVER

The promise in the next verse has a special meaning for us today. "And they that be wise [margin: teachers] shall shine as the brightness of the firmament; and they that turn many to righteousness as the stars for ever and ever" (verse 3). The stars have always attracted thoughtful minds, but in recent years we have learned much about these heavenly bodies. Kingdoms may rise and fall, empires go down to dust, but the stars in their stately orbits shine on from century to century. Some are so far away that it has taken a hundred million years for their light to reach us. The wise, said the angel—teachers of God's message of righteousness—will shine as those radiant orbs for all eternity.

Are you planning to be among them, dear friend? You can be, if you accept God's gift of righteousness. "Messiah the Prince" is still our ministering Intercessor in the heavenly sanctuary. Through His abundant grace all may become members of His family, and the promise is that we shall shine "as the stars for ever and ever."

Having finished his great prophecy, Gabriel now tells Daniel to "shut up the words, and seal the book, even to the time of the end" (verse 4), implying that many things the prophet did not understand would at that time be understood. Then Daniel overheard one asking the question, "How long shall it be till the end of these wonders?" And the answer came from the one clothed in linen, "It shall be for a time, times, and an half" (verses 6, 7). That, of course, is the same period mentioned in chapter 7, verse 25—the 1,260 prophetic days, or years, which began in A.D. 538 and ended in 1798. At that time many things not understandable in Daniel's day—nor could they be until the expiration of that period—would come into sharp focus. Even though the prophet himself said, "I heard, but I understood not" (verse 8), yet we who live in the time of the end can understand. How privileged we are!

WHAT ARE WE SEEING TODAY?

Jesus said, "Blessed are your eyes, for they see: and your ears, for they hear. For verily I say unto you, That many prophets and righteous men have desired to see those things which ye see, and have not seen them; and to hear those things which ye hear, and have not heard them" (Matthew 13:16, 17). "Blessed are your eyes, for they see!" If Christ were speaking in person to us now, He would be able to say the same thing: "Blessed are your eyes . . . and your ears."

This striking stanza from Bishop Arthur Coxe's "Hymn for the Times" (1842) might well have been penned this very decade:

We are living, we are dwelling
In a grand and awful time,
In an age on ages, telling—
To be living is sublime.
Hark! the waking up of nations,
Gog and Magog to the fray;
Hark! what soundeth? Is creation
Groaning for her latter day?

As the angel closed his message to Daniel, he said, "Knowledge shall be increased" (Daniel 12:4). The accuracy of this needs no emphasis. Think of the hundreds, the thousands, of things we use which were unknown and undreamed of at the beginning of the time of the end—nuclear power and space travel, for example. The increase of knowledge is not only in science, but also in biblical studies. In 1799, at the beginning of "the time of the end," the Rosetta Stone was unearthed by Napoleon's soldiers when stationed on the banks of the Nile. Deciphering that stone was a difficult task, but it gave scholars new tools to decipher other ancient artifacts. Numerous points of Bible history have been confirmed as a result—knowledge that has helped to confound the claims of the school of rationalism. Much more truth is understood today because of the increase of knowledge in both sacred and secular history.

DANIEL'S BOOK UNSEALED TO THE RIGHTEOUS

Daniel, still eager to understand, asked, "O my Lord, what shall be the end of these things?" Again the voice answered, "The words are closed up and sealed till the time of the end" (verses 8, 9), or " 'till the crisis at the close' " (Moffatt). While "none of the wicked shall understand," yet "the wise shall understand," said the angel (verse 10). And understanding, they become teachers of truth, preparing a people to endure in the great day of the Lord. At that time all nations will be convulsed, and the unprepared will flee in terror, calling for the mountains and rocks to bury them. They cannot endure that blazing vision of glory as they see Jesus riding forth in power, with all the holy angels, to deliver His people. Having defied the living God and given their allegiance to Satan, they will at last be compelled to witness the disintegration of their colossal world government.

In anticipation of that collapse, those who love God and His truth will, through the power of the Holy Spirit, "be purified, and made white, and tried [refined]" (verse 10). They will separate from every form of worldliness and idolatry and, accepting by His grace Christ's robe of righteousness, will abide "under the shadow of the Almighty" (Psalm 91:1) while the earth rocks to ruin. In the midst of the crashing skyscrapers and shaking mountains, they will sing to the glory of God: "Therefore will not we fear, though the earth be removed, and though the mountains be carried into the midst of the sea; though the waters thereof roar and be troubled. . . . The LORD of hosts is with us; the God of Jacob is our refuge" (Psalm 46:2, 3, 11).

Daniel's book closes with the mention of two prophetic periods— the 1,290 days and the 1,335 days. (See Daniel 12:11, 12.) The 1,290 days, or years, might well have begun with the alliance of church and state under King Clovis of France in 508. From that important event, the period then would reach to the time of the end, 1798. The 1,335 days, being an addition of 45 days, or years, could bring us to 1843, when the great Advent awakening reached its height.

Inasmuch as Gabriel was commissioned to make Daniel understand what would befall his people, the Jews, in the latter days, some have wondered if the 1,335 prophetic days, or years, might refer to the *Hegira,* or the Muslim era, which was exactly 1,335 lunar years. The *Hegira* began with the flight of Mohammed in A.D. 622 and would thus end in 1917, a short time before World War I ended and the Ottoman Empire collapsed. The last coins minted for the old Turkish government bear the date 1917, and on the reverse side in Arabic numerals, 1335!

THE MIDDLE EAST AWAKENS

The collapse of the Ottoman Empire, which for centuries had ruled that area of the world, not only gave new opportunity to the Jews as a nation but led to tremendous changes in the whole Middle East. Little did anyone realize how vast were the oil fields in that part of the world. Lands that for centuries existed in poverty suddenly became wealthy beyond computation. And riches have meant power to these peoples. Additional light will doubtless be shed on the 1,290 and 1,335 days, for "the path of the just is as the shining light, that shineth more and more unto the perfect day" (Proverbs 4:18). Till we get more light, we do well to keep alert and watch for God's providences.

The angel's last words to Daniel were, "Go thou thy way till the end be: for thou shalt rest, and stand in thy lot at the end of the days" (Daniel 12:13). Moffatt translates this as, " 'Go and wait for the end; you shall rest in the grave and then rise to enjoy your share at the end of the days.' "

Some might ask, "Where is that grave that entombs the remains of the great prophet?" Charles Boutflower says that by common consent Jews, Sabeans, and Mohammedans declare that the prophet's body lies close to the acropolis in Shushan, or Susa, near to the place where he received the great vision recorded in chapters 10–12. He further states that when Abu-Musa-Alashari invaded Persia in A.D. 640, it is reported that he sent word to the Khalif Omar that when he entered the castle he found a chamber under lock and key. On entering, he saw a stone coffin wrapped in gold brocade in which was the body of a man of great stature. Inquiring who this might be, he was told that the people of Iran, among whom he lived till the day of his death, called him Danyel Hakim, "Daniel the sage." When Omar heard the story, he ordered that the body in the coffin be reverently buried where the people of Shushan could no longer have access to it. Accordingly the stream which supplied the city with water—apparently a canal cut from the Ulai—was diverted, and a grave made in the dry channel, after which the waters were allowed to flow over the body of Daniel. (See Charles Boutflower, *In and Around the Book of Daniel,* pages 223, 224.)

Where the body of that great prophet actually lies is a matter of interest, but not of particular importance. He rests only till the great resurrection day, when the righteous dead will come forth immortal and glorified.

What a day of victory that will be when Christ, the great Conqueror, comes to claim His people! Accompanied by all the armies of heaven, He sweeps down the vaulted skies in the full panoply of His celestial greatness. Amid clouds of fire and pillars of smoke He descends in power and great glory in full view of all the people of the earth. Mountains melt. Hills skip like lambs, and the seas roll back in majesty as the voice of the Life-Giver, like peals of crashing thunder, summons the sleeping saints. What a sight to behold as these radiant ones, rising from their dusty beds, some even from the oceans, spring forth bearing the bloom of eternal youth!

Overcome and frenzied with fear, kings and slaves, mistresses and maids rush alike, seeking desperately for shelter from the blazing presence of Him whom they have despised. They shriek in terror, "The great day of his wrath is come; and who shall be able to stand?" (Revelation 6:17). Says the Scripture: "Our God shall come, and shall not keep silence: a fire shall devour before him, and it shall be very tempestuous round about him. He shall call to the heavens from above, and to the earth, that he may judge his people" (Psalm 50:3, 4).

Daniel will certainly be among those resurrected saints, for the last message of Gabriel to that man of God was both a promise and a triumph: "Thou shalt rest, and stand in thy lot at the end of the days," (Daniel 12:13). Or as the NEB puts it: " 'You shall arise to your destiny at the end of the age.' " Would that all of us, reader and author alike, might close our life record with such a ring of heavenly assurance. And each of us can, by the grace of God. Someday soon, if faithful, we will share with Daniel and the righteous of all the ages the eternal joys of the life to come. In the presence of Him who became the Son of man that He might make us the sons and daughters of God, we shall praise His holy name forever and ever. Amen.

Unveiling the Prophecies of Revelation

Jesus Christ, the Center of the Revelation

Every chapter of the book of Revelation contains its own revelation of Jesus Christ. Summarizing these thoughts, we see Him as

1. the all-sufficient Sacrifice and ministering Priest
2. the wonderful and sympathetic Reprover of the churches
3. the Creator who shares His throne with human beings
4. the Lamb slain from the foundation of the world
5. the One worthy of all adoration, honor, and praise
6. the Leader of the church that goes forth to conquer
7. the Lamb among the blood-washed multitude
8. the One who receives the prayers of the saints
9. the One who restrains the powers of evil
10. the Angel who announces that time shall be no longer
11. the One who receives from His Father the kingdoms of the world
12. the promised Child who conquered death and ascended to the throne
13. the Author of the Lamb's book of life, which contains the names of true worshipers
14. the Lamb of Mount Zion, sending His last message of mercy to the world
15. the Lamb receiving praise
16. the Lamb whose judgments destroy the apostate kingdom
17. the Lamb who calls His people from spiritual Babylon
18. the One who presides over the fall of Babylon
19. the descending King of kings and Lord of lords
20. the Angel who binds and destroys the devil
21. the Re-Creator who wipes away all tears
22. the Judge who brings final rewards to the righteous and wicked

20. The Book of Revelation

The Revelation of Jesus Christ, or the Apocalypse, is unique among the books of the Bible—unique in its form, its symbolism, and its meaning. It comes to us from God the Father and from Jesus, through whom alone any divine revelation can come to man. And He sent it to John through His angel messenger (see Revelation 1:1) who, according to Luke 1:19, is Gabriel.

Who wrote the Apocalypse?

Concerning the author's identity there need be little question. Four times he calls himself "John" and declares he has previously borne record of the Word of God. The fourth Gospel and three epistles bear his name. The first epistle opens with a declaration that the author is speaking of what his eyes have seen and his hands have handled of "the Word of life" (1 John 1:1). The opening sentence of the Gospel of John speaks of the "Word," or logos as being "with God." But more—"the Word was God" (John 1:1). Then later, "the Word was made flesh, and dwelt among us" (verse 14). Then near the close of this Gospel we read, "These are written, that ye might believe that Jesus is the Christ, the Son of God" (John 20:31).

Eusebius, the church historian, speaks of the author of Revelation as the "Elder John" who seems to have been well known in Ephesus, possibly being identified with the "Ephesian School," which developed in the latter part of the first century. The writer of the second and third epistles of John calls himself "the elder" (2 John 1; 3 John 1). There really is no reason to wonder whether John the elder and John the writer of the fourth Gospel are the same person as the writer of the Revelation.

While some may still doubt this authorship, it has been accepted from earliest times. What other John was there, of whom we have any knowledge, who had sufficient influence or authoritative standing in the early church to have addressed such a message to the churches?

Moreover, it is claimed that the author of the Apocalypse was the first person in church history to be known as *theologos,* "the theologian." The following statement by a scholar of a more than a century ago sums up the position, which seems even more certain today than when it was written:

> There is scarcely a book in the whole Bible whose genuineness and inspiration were more strongly attested on its first appearance than the Apocalypse. No doubts whatever seem to have been entertained on these points. Suffice it now to say, that Papias, Justin Martyr, Irenaeus, Melito,—that is, eminent teachers in the church, in the next age to that in which it was written—proclaim that its writer was St. John, the beloved disciple of Christ. Such was then the voice of the church (Chr. Wordsworth, *Lectures on the Apocalypse,* page 22. Quoted by J. A. Seiss in *The Apocalypse,* vol. 1, pages 30, 31).

According to tradition, John was the sole survivor of the original apostles, every one of the others having met a martyr's death. He was summoned to Rome to appear before Emperor Domitian, "the last of the twelve great Caesars," to be tried for his faith. So convincing was his defense that "his hearers were astonished at his wisdom and eloquence." They could not gainsay his testimony. The emperor, filled with rage, ordered that he be cast into a caldron of boiling oil. "But the Lord preserved the life of His faithful servant, even as He preserved the three Hebrews in the fiery furnace" (Ellen White, *The Acts of the Apostles,* pages 569, 570). Later, by decree of the emperor, he was banished to the Isle of Patmos to serve a life sentence.

It is generally believed that this was about A.D. 94–95. That would make John almost one hundred years old when these events occurred. Upon the death of Domitian, Nerva came to the throne, and the usual happened—the political prisoners were freed. It is believed that John then returned to Ephesus on the mainland. But while on Patmos, he received the vision contained in this unique book.

I have been privileged to visit this felon's isle, this jagged rock in the midst of the sea. What impressions I received! To be torn from home and kindred and abandoned to this inhospitable solitude, must have seemed to the apostle like being tethered with the leash of death. Yet his spot became a grandstand from which the poet-prophet viewed the whole panorama of human history. Though old in years, his eyes grew young as eternity burst into view. The rugged rocks and the surging seas seemed to echo the trumpet-voiced message he was commissioned to bear to the church. What though his hands were manacled and his feet in irons; his soul was nevertheless responsive to the Spirit. As the whirlpool of history was opened to him, he read its dark secrets, seeing and hearing things neither seen nor heard before. In the blaze of that burning vision life took on new meaning. The waves that crashed like thunder on the shore spoke of a power far greater than the mailed legions of Rome. Then, under the prophetic impulse, he dipped his pen in inspiration and wrote that deathless message which for centuries has been the great apocalyptic epic of all literature—the Revelation of Jesus Christ.

THE PURPOSE OF THE BOOK

The book is called "the Revelation of Jesus Christ," or "a Revelation *from* Jesus Christ" (Phillips), to show what will come to pass. But in another sense it is a revelation *about* Christ.

The *Old Testament* reveals Christ in prophecy; the *Gospels* reveal Him in His earthly life, ministry, sufferings, death, resurrection, and ascension; the *Acts* and the *Epistles* reveal the early triumphs of the church under the ministry of His Holy Spirit. In the *Revelation* Christ is pictured in glory at the right hand of God as the High Priest and Minister of the heavenly sanctuary. He is also pictured as the Supreme Judge before whom all nations must appear. The final scenes depict the Savior as King of kings and Lord of lords, reigning forever over the saints in Paradise restored. Thus the revelator performs the final unveiling ceremony that makes possible an unobstructed view of the Lamb of God. It is really a panorama of the glory of Christ. The book of Genesis tells the story of Creation, the fall of man, and Paradise lost. But the Revelation ushers in the scenes of Paradise restored.

Throughout the prophetic structure of the book, the focus is on Christ, who is the center of all prophecy—"the bright and morning star" (Revelation 22:16). "The prophecies of Daniel and Revelation should be carefully studied, and in connection with them, the words, 'Behold the Lamb of God which taketh away the sin of the world' " (Ellen White, *Gospel Workers,* page 148). The Son of God is mentioned by name, or by the pronoun denoting Him, more than one hundred forty times in the first three chapters of the book of Revelation. This emphasizes the fact that the central Person of the book is Jesus.

In the Gospel narrative, John says that the eternal God, "the Word," "was made flesh, and dwelt among us" (John 1:14). The Greek word translated "dwelt" is *skenoo,* more accurately rendered "tabernacled" or "encamped." The idea springs from a kindly Arab custom. One who wished to join a caravan was encouraged to pitch his tent beside the group and make his journey with them. This is a beautiful illustration of the Incarnation, for in flesh God was tabernacled with man. He stooped low to take our human nature, and thus He veiled His glory. Traveling with us over the rough side of life, He at last died for us on the cross to redeem us from death. The grave must take Him; but it could not hold Him. He shattered its power, ascended to His Father, and was "crowned with glory and honour" (Hebrews 2:9)—the glory which He had from all eternity. As He walked with men in the flesh that glory was veiled; but now, seated on the throne of the universe, He reigns in unveiled and unrivaled glory as coregent in the government of the universe. John, who knew His Lord so well in the flesh, now falls at His feet in breathless awe as he views Him in majesty (see Revelation 1:17), and so will we when this Revelation of Jesus Christ grips our souls. To know Him as our King, we must first know Him as "the Lamb of God, which taketh away the sin of the world" (John 1:29).

No American has etched his name deeper in history than Abraham Lincoln, who saved the Union and abolished slavery. A few years ago, a clever penman wrote the Emancipation Proclamation so deftly that to an onlooker standing just a few feet away it became a picture revealing every detail of Lincoln's rugged features. Closer inspection, however, showed that it was not a drawing but a copy of the declaration that freed the slaves. The penman had not only created a picture,

187

but through his art had also traced the philosophy that shaped the life of the great emancipator.

This unique book, the book of Revelation, unveils a greater Emancipator, who has freed not one race but all races of humanity. While the Apocalypse reveals things "which must shortly come to pass" (Revelation 1:1), it is primarily a revelation of Jesus Christ who died that we might live. When Lincoln died, his body was taken to his home city for burial. As the slow and silent procession made its way along hushed streets, the crowd was visibly moved to tears. A Negro mother, eager to help her little son to catch a better view, lifted him onto her shoulders and said through her tears, "Take a long look at him, honey; he died for you." As we turn the pages of the Apocalypse let us take a long look at Him who gave His all to emancipate us from death and the slavery of sin, knowing that through all the changing kaleidoscope of history He is working out His eternal purpose.

To whom was the Revelation written?

This Revelation might be said to have come in answer to the prayer of Paul. Writing to the church at Ephesus, he tells how he prayed that they might be given a revelation of Christ. (See Ephesians 1:15–18.) Thirty years later John received this Revelation, and the first church to which it was sent was Ephesus. It was written not for the world but for the church, for the servants of God. (See Revelation 1:1.) When God wrote on the palace wall of Belshazzar, the "wise men" could not read the writing. But Daniel interpreted the message. Those who walk with God can know His secret. "Surely the Lord GOD will do nothing, but he revealeth his secret unto his servants the prophets" (Amos 3:7).

The Second Advent and the keynote of the book

While this Revelation was particularly helpful for the persecuted saints in John's day, and has spoken to every age since, yet it has a special message for those living just before our Lord's return. (See Revelation 22:6, 7, 10.)

"Behold, he cometh with clouds," cries the apostle, "and every eye shall see him" (Revelation 1:7). No subject has a greater place in the

New Testament than has the second advent of Jesus. One verse in every twenty-five touches this theme. Perhaps no doctrine in the Christian message possesses more power than does this.

> Like a magnet, it lifts the heart of the believer out of the world, and out of his low self, and enables him to stand with Moses on the mount, and transfigures him with the rays of the blessed hope and promise which stream upon him in those sublime heights. It is the most animating and most sanctifying subject in the Bible (J. A. Seiss, *The Apocalypse,* vol. 1, page 35).

The Patmos seer closes the book with the exclamation, "Even so, come, Lord Jesus" (Revelation 22:20).

THE SEVEN APOCALYPTIC BEATITUDES

Like the Sermon on the Mount, the Revelation breathes the benediction of heaven. Note these beatitudes:

"Blessed is he that readeth, and they that hear" (Revelation 1:3).

"Blessed are the dead which die in the Lord" (Revelation 14:13).

"Blessed is he that watcheth, and keepeth his garments" (Revelation 16:15).

"Blessed are they which are called unto the marriage supper" (Revelation 19:9).

"Blessed and holy is he that hath part in the first resurrection" (Revelation 20:6).

"Blessed is he that keepeth the sayings of the prophecy of this book" (Revelation 22:7).

"Blessed are they that do his commandments ["those who wash their robes," RSV]" (Revelation 22:14).

TO WHOM WAS THE REVELATION SENT?

The seven churches mentioned in the Revelation were not the only churches in Asia, nor were they the most important. Their selection, however, is deeply significant. The cities where these churches existed lay along the imperial post road. This Roman highway was built about 133 B.C. It passed through Ephesus, Smyrna, Pergamos, Thyatira, Sardis, Philadelphia, and Laodicea, where it joined another main post highway. The number "seven" in the Revelation is very significant. There are seven churches, seven letters, seven stars, seven candlesticks, seven Spirits of God, seven lamps of fire, seven seals, seven trumpets, seven horns, seven eyes, seven thunders, seven heads, seven crowns, seven angels, seven vials, seven mountains, etc. The number "seven" as found throughout the Scriptures denotes completeness, universality, or perfection.

Not only the number "seven" but the *names* of the churches themselves are also significant. These seven letters to the seven churches contain a message for the Christian church through all the centuries from apostolic times until the setting up of Christ's kingdom.

> It is the opinion of very learned writers upon this book, that our Lord, by these seven churches, signifies all the churches of Christ to the end of the world; and by what he saith to them, designs to show what shall be the state of the churches in all ages, and what their duty is (Matthew Pool, *Annotations Upon the Holy Bible,* vol. 3, page 952).

> The seven churches represent seven phases or periods in the church's history, stretching from the time of the apostles to the coming again of Christ, the characteristics of which are set forth partly in the names of these churches, but more fully in the epistles addressed to them (J. A. Seiss, *The Apocalypse,* vol. 1, page 142).

> The epistles to the seven churches, besides describing what is undoubtedly historical, have so many allusions which are evidently figurative and mystical that there is the strongest reason for accepting the view . . . "that these seven churches should prophetically sample [show] us a sevenfold temper and constitution of the whole church according to the several ages thereof, answering the pattern of the churches named here" (A. J. Gordon, *Ecce Venit (Behold He Cometh),* pages 66, 67, note).

Some have attempted to declare the precise date when one period ended and another began, but as when traveling on a highway we pass from one city to another, the population becoming more dense or more sparse, making it difficult at times to know where one city really ends and another begins, so on this highway of the Christian Era, it is difficult to determine the exact date for the beginning and ending of any particular church period. Yet each period is marked by definite contrasts, enabling us to know when we are in the midst of a new era. This will be emphasized in the next chapter.

Savior, High Priest, and coming King

These letters to the seven churches not only forecast trends in church history, but they also set forth the varied aspects of the ministry of our Lord and form an appropriate setting for the message of the whole book.

> The seven descriptions all differ from one another; and, taken together, they make up the complete account given in Revelation 1 of *One like unto a* [sic] *son of man.* The Divine Author presents himself in a different aspect to each individual church; and the seven aspects make up his complete personal description, as the different churches make up the complete and universal church (W. M. Ramsay, *The Letters to the Seven Churches of Asia,* page 197).

The book opens with a picture of Christ's vicarious sacrifice and priestly ministry (see Revelation 1:5, 12, 13) and closes with the announcement of His certain return, at which time He will bring the reward of eternal life to those who have been faithful.

The Revelation is apocalyptic in its literary form, a form which views history as a unity culminating in the final establishment of the eternal kingdom of God. Victory comes at last to the saints of God through the redeeming Lamb, who was slain and yet lives. As we catch the echo of the ages, we cry with angels and redeemed humans: "Worthy is the Lamb that was slain" (Revelation 5:12).

THE GROUND OF SALVATION IS GRACE

The message of the book begins with a threefold salutation of grace, from the Father, the Holy Spirit, and the Son. (See Revelation 1:4, 5.) "The Father in the absoluteness of his unchanging nature and universal presence, the Spirit in all the completeness of his manifold energies and diversified operations, and the Son in the virtues of his blood-sealed testimony" (J. A. Seiss, *The Apocalypse*, vol. 1, page 47).

"Grace be unto you, and peace," writes John (verse 4). But it is a "peace" that is rooted in "grace." To what avail would it be to pass with pomp and power over the stage of time, only to sink at last into the darkness and sorrows of eternity? But if we would endure, our standing before God must be absolutely on the ground of grace, and not of works. This mighty truth of righteousness by faith in Christ alone is expressed in verses 5 and 6. The Lord "loved us," then He "washed us." After having washed us, He made us "kings and priests" or a "kingdom of priests" (R.V.). God did not wait until we were cleansed before He loved us, but because He loved us He cleansed us. It was while we were aliens, fleeing from His presence and actually His enemies, that "the Father sent the Son to be the Saviour of the world" (1 John 4:14). "Surely goodness and mercy shall follow me," cries David (Psalm 23:6). The Hebrew word, *radaph,* means "to pursue" or "to chase." Francis Thompson's poem "The Hound of Heaven" sets forth this thought in moving verse. God pursues the sinner constantly and for the one purpose that He might reclaim him and re-establish him as a king, sharing His throne with him.

DIVINE LOVE AN EXHAUSTLESS THEME

"Alpha and Omega," one of the symbolic names of Christ (see Revelation 1:8), is significant. As the alphabet provides an exhaustless medium of expression, so is Jesus and His love an exhaustless theme for contemplation. Eternity will be all too short to reveal the wonders of His love and power. In the book of Revelation our Savior is introduced to us under many different titles, each important and expressive. He is first introduced as Jesus Christ; and of all the names in the world, *Jesus* is the most beautiful. Dr. T. DeWitt Talmage, in moving eloquence, says of that name:

It stands for love, for patience, for kindness, for forbearance, for self-sacrifice, for magnanimity. It is aromatic with all odors and accordant with all harmonies. Sometimes I see that name, and the letters seem to be made out of tears, and then again they look like gleaming crowns. Sometimes they seem as though twisted out of the straw on which He lay, and then as though built out of the thrones on which His people shall reign. Sometimes I sound that word, "Jesus," and I hear coming through the two syllables the sigh of Gethsemane and the groan of Calvary; and again I sound it, and it is all a-ripple with gladness and a-ring with hosanna. . . . Let it drip from the harp's strings and thunder out in organ's diapason. Sound it often, sound it well, until every star shall seem to shine it, and every flower shall seem to breath it, and mountain and sea, and day and night, and earth and heaven acclaim in full chant: "Blessed be His glorious name forever; the name that is above every name" (*The Palestine Sermons of Rev. T. DeWitt Talmage*, page 184).

> Join all the glorious names of wisdom, love, and power
> That mortals ever knew, that angels ever bore;
> All are too mean to speak His worth
> Too mean to set my Saviour forth.
> —Isaac Watts

WALKING AMONG THE CHURCHES

In chapter 1, verse 20 of Revelation, Jesus is represented as holding the ministers of His church, symbolized by "the seven stars," in His right hand. It is a beautiful picture of His personal regard for His own. Then we see Him walking among the "candlesticks," or the churches. No matter what persecution the church has had to endure, the Lord has been with His suffering saints, upholding them, sharing their trials, and feeling every wound inflicted by their enemies.

If we would understand the message of this book, we must study it in relation to the transcendent Christ by whose power the massive tyranny of darkness was shattered and the future of the planet was forever changed. He who "brought life and immortality to light through the gospel" (2 Timothy 1:10) and who walks amid the churches, says to each and all, "He that hath an ear, let him hear what the Spirit saith unto the churches" (Revelation 2:7).

THE BOOK ROOTED IN THE OLD TESTAMENT

More than 270 direct quotations, or expressions couched in Old Testament language, are found in the Revelation. Rooted in this fertile soil, it is like a tree yielding the rich fruitage of the inspiration of the ages. Because the whole Bible is a manifestation of Christ, therefore this book, drawing its nurture from the prophets of old, could be nothing else but a revelation of Jesus Christ. While Patmos was regarded by Rome as a place of punishment, yet that barren island became to the apostle the door of hope and the setting for the most sublime communion with heaven. Then let us take our places at the side of the prophet, and by the enabling Spirit of God, let us catch the inspiration of these messages as we traverse the centuries and move on into the stupendous climax of human history. Let us witness this all-powerful King and Christ of God as He comes at last to vindicate His name, to strip the enemy of his power, to raise the dead, to be glorified in His saints, to destroy the author of evil, to renew this sin-cursed earth, to reward His suffering saints, and to reign forever as King of kings and Lord of lords.

21. The Seven Epistles of Christ to His Church

In Revelation 1:13 the Son of man is seen in the midst of the candlesticks, or the churches, sharing their experiences, understanding their needs. This has ever been a source of comfort, especially in times of persecution. In the following chapter, we will be studying the trials and the triumphs of the church. But whatever the experience through which the people of God are called to pass, they may be sure that the Lord is with them. His parting promise was, "Lo, I am with you alway, even unto the end of the world" (Matthew 28:20).

THE CONQUERING CHRIST IN THE MIDST OF HIS CHURCH

When the prophet John beheld in vision the glory of his Lord, His eyes were as flames of fire and His countenance shining as the sun. No wonder John fell at His feet as dead. (See Revelation 1:17.)

What a contrast from those days when Jesus tramped the dusty roads of Palestine! No longer is He despised and rejected of men; no longer is He clothed in the travel-stained garments of an itinerant teacher, but robed in royal attire befitting His office as King, He ministers before the throne. He is a Priest-King, to be sure, but nevertheless a King. In Genesis 14:18–20 and Hebrews 7:1–14, we read the story of Abraham's visit with Melchizedek, king of Salem. That Canaanite king who came forth and blessed the faithful patriarch is one of the many scriptural types of Christ. Just as Abraham offered his worship to God through the ministry of Melchizedek, the priest-king of Salem, so we today offer our worship to the eternal Father through out great High Priest who, as "King of Righteousness," officiates "after the order of Melchisedec" (Hebrews 6:20). It is important to notice that Christ is not a priest under the Aaronic order. Instead, He is of the royal order of Melchizedek. It is in glory and majesty that He ministers for us in heaven.

CHRIST, THE VICTOR OVER DEATH

When John in vision beheld Jesus in His glory, it overwhelmed him, and he "fell at his feet as dead." But the Lord said to him, "Fear not; . . . I am he that liveth, and was dead; and, behold, I am alive for evermore, Amen; and have the keys of hell and of death" (Revelation 1:17, 18). Precious promise indeed! What comfort those words must have brought to the people of God throughout the centuries!

Martyrs, millions of them, have gone to their graves sustained by the knowledge that Jesus, for whom they were giving their lives, had already conquered death, and in His nail-pierced hands is the key that will unlock every grave. Death can hold no terror for the one who really knows his Lord. Why should we fear? Our conquering Savior Himself declares, "All that are in the graves shall hear his voice, and shall come forth" (John 5:28, 29). Paul, in his great treatise on the resurrection, declares, "As in Adam all die, even so in Christ shall all be made alive." Then he refers to Hosea 13:14: "O death, where is thy sting? O grave, where is thy victory?" (1 Corinthians 15:22, 55). Death has no sting and the grave no victory since Jesus burst its cruel bands and unlocked the door of the tomb. So, with the apostle of old, let us say: "Thanks be to God, which giveth us the victory through our Lord Jesus Christ." "The last enemy that shall be destroyed is death" (verses 57, 26).

THE SEVEN EPISTLES OF CHRIST TO HIS CHURCH

Those messages to the churches were written for the people of God in every age. As we have already noticed, they cover the entire history of the New Testament church from the first advent of Christ to His return in glory. The imperial post road of Asia Minor, already referred to, became an impressive symbol of the great highway of time along which the church has traveled.

We will understand these letters better if we study them against the background of the cities to which they were first sent. Knowing something of the environment in which the members of those churches lived and labored gives new meaning to many expressions. Six outstanding features will be noted in each letter: (1) the meaning and significance of the name; (2) the characteristic of the city; (3) the commendation; (4) the reproof (in five of the letters); (5) the counsel; and (6) the promise to the overcomer.

196

The following diagram gives the sequence of the messages. We need to become familiar with their order:

First Advent _____ Second Advent

Ephesus / Smyrna / Pergamos / Thyatira / Sardis / Philadelphia / Laodicea

THE EPISTLE TO EPHESUS, REVELATION 2:1–7
Meaning and significance of the name. Ephesus means "desirable." The city itself was situated in a very desirable location geographically. So that period of church history when the apostles were living and could personally guide and counsel the leaders was indeed a desirable period.

Characteristic of the city. Ephesus has been called "the City of Change" because of the shifting character of the site on which the city was built. It could rightly represent the beginning of the Christian Era, for no period in history has witnessed more drastic changes in human thought. The revolutionary message Jesus brought challenged every system of thought. Nothing could impede the progress of Christianity. It was "born in a storm, nurtured in a cyclone, and swept the world like a tornado." And Ephesus, "the City of Change," symbolized that era.

Ephesus was built during the eleventh century B.C. It was beautifully situated. It could boast of one of the finest harbors in West Asia, but it was subject to great geographical changes, the result of earthquakes. The place of its once famous harbor is today a marsh and sandy beach, unapproachable by ships. The harbor was abandoned in the fourth century A.D.

Ephesus was a leading commercial city. By imperial edict it was made the gateway to the province of Asia and became the starting place of the land trade route.

The city was adorned with a number of beautiful temples. Here was the seat of the worship of Diana, or Artemis, of Ephesus, not to be confused with the virgin huntress, sister of Apollo in Greek mythology. This Ephesian deity was an equivalent of Astarte or Ashteroth, and was the center of orgiastic fertility rites of a highly immoral character. She was known as the "great mother" or "great mother of the gods." At the Council of Ephesus in A.D. 451 the title "Mother of

197

God" was applied to the Virgin Mary, an act which bears a strange odor in the setting of this pagan city.

The temple of Diana was originally built in 480 B.C. It was destroyed by fire on the night of Alexander's birth, 356 B.C. Alexander later offered to rebuild it at his own expense but was refused the honor. Donations were received from all over Asia Minor, and the rebuilding required 120 years. It was one of the seven wonders of the world, built of red, blue, yellow, and white marble. Gold was said to have been used even for mortar. Wealth was abundant, and there are records of gifts amounting to the equivalent of up to $850,000, which was an enormous sum for those days.

Ephesus was known as a "temple-keeper" for the emperor. (See Acts 19:35, margin.)

Commendation. Timothy was probably the pastor of the Ephesus church when John was writing. This church was commended for its unflagging zeal. It was a working church, toiling hard for God. Its members were loyal to the doctrines; they had tested their teachers. The Word of God was the standard of their faith. We could wish that every Christian church might require the same standard for its ministry. In many a church today, modernism or liberalism has eaten out the very heart of the Christian message.

The Nicolaitanes were a heretical group who believed that it was unnecessary to curb the desires of the flesh as required by the moral law. As Sir William Mitchel Ramsay points out, they joined the craft guilds and thus were required to pay worshipful homage to the emperor. They may have been the group in Ephesus referred to by Paul who burned their pagan books. (See Acts 19:19.) Nicolaitanes are mentioned also in the letter to the church at Pergamos.

Reproof. But all labor is dead unless inspired by love; and despite its zeal, Ephesus had lost its "first love," (Revelation 2:4), so Christ had to reprove His people. They had fallen from their place of high honor. The "mystery of iniquity" was already beginning its baneful work. (See 2 Thessalonians 2:3–7.) Nothing can replace true love. "The light of the whole life dies when love is done."

Counsel. Three words summarize the message: *Remember, repent,* and *return.* The Master is saying, "Remember your early joy, when true love filled your heart. Repent of your sin; realize your perilous condition. Return to your original state, or else I will have to remove you." Works do not produce love nor can they take the place of love. Works are only the evidence of love. The relationship of Christ to His church is that of a bridegroom to his bride. Loss of love in the home is a tragedy and usually ends in divorce court.

Promise. "To him that overcometh will I give to eat of the tree of life, which is in the midst of the paradise of God" (Revelation 2:7).

Certain trees were objects of worship by the pagans in Ephesus. That was true also in some parts of Greece. When the sacred olive tree on the Acropolis of Athens put forth a new shoot after the city had been burned by the Persians, it was hailed as an omen of the future safety of the state.

But here is a promise that reaches forward to the time when the overcomers will eat of the tree of life. When humans sinned, they forfeited their right to the tree of life and were driven from the garden of God. (See Genesis 3:22–24.) But if we will heed the voice of the Holy Spirit and by God's grace repent and overcome, we will eat of the tree of life when sorrow and sin are forever banished.

This is a wonderful promise of future bliss in the kingdom restored, but it must also be a present experience. Through the study of God's Word we become partakers of Christ—the source of all spiritual life. When we thus daily partake of Him who is the true Tree of Life, then paradise begins here and now. "The pure in heart" (Matthew 5:8) may see God now, but we still look forward to the time when, in His kingdom, we shall dwell with Him forevermore.

"Hear what the Spirit saith." Let us hear His loving message of rebuke. So many ears are stopped with doubt; so many voices lead astray. Let us, then, heed the counsel of the Lord and "hear what the Spirit saith unto the churches" (Revelation 2:7).

He speaks His message to every age, calling men and women, boys and girls, from selfishness and sin to righteousness and peace. Never did men look so eagerly for peace as they do today. War and tragedy, broken homes, broken hearts, and broken bodies have bowed the nations in grief, and from hearts everywhere comes the cry for peace. Let us hear His voice of love saying, "Come unto me, . . . and I will give you rest" (Matthew 11:28).

199

22. Christ's Epistles to Smyrna and Pergamos

Ephesus was the natural gateway to the province of Asia. The imperial post road began there and ran northward through Smyrna and Pergamos, east to Thyatira, then southeast through Sardis to Philadelphia and to Laodicea.

THE EPISTLE TO SMYRNA, REVELATION 2:8–11

Meaning and significance of the name. The name *Smyrna* means "sweet smelling" and is synonymous with myrrh. This church of Smyrna was to pass through bitter persecution, but her sufferings, instead of destroying her, would give forth to the world the rich perfume of heaven. The garments of our Lord are fragrant with the odor of myrrh and aloes and cassia. (See Psalm 45:8.) Myrrh symbolizes our Lord's suffering; aloes, the bitterness of sorrow; and cassia, the healing virtue of His sacrifice. For all who will open their hearts to Him, the promise is, "With his stripes we are healed" (Isaiah 53:5).

> The healing of His seamless dress
> Is by our beds of pain;
> We touch Him in life's throng and press,
> And we are whole again.
> —John Greenleaf Whittier

Characteristic of the city. Smyrna has been well called The City of Life. It is one of the oldest cities in the world and lies about forty miles north of Ephesus. Of all the seven, it is the only one existing as a strong city today; it is one of the largest cities in Asia Minor. At the time John was writing, it was a beautiful city and was frequently spoken of as The Ornament of Asia. It stood at an elevation of some six hundred feet. A small hill, Mount Pegus, arose from the center of the city; on its top was a shrine dedicated to the Greek goddess Nemesis. From a distance, the

200

city's skyline resembled a crown, and it was sometimes called The Crown of Ionia. No city has suffered more from sieges, massacres, earthquakes, fire, and plague, but still it lives. It is truly a city of life. It has a higher population of Christians than most Turkish cities today. It is significant that when Christ addresses the Christians of Smyrna, He speaks as one who "was dead, and is alive" (Revelation 2:8).

Commendation. Polycarp, one of the outstanding martyrs, is believed to have been the "angel," or minister, of this church at the time John was writing. According to Tertullian, Irenaeus, Eusebius, and Jerome, the apostle himself consecrated Polycarp bishop of Smyrna. The state required Polycarp to worship Caesar as god. His refusal cost him his life. He was burned at the stake on the hillside of Mount Pagus in A.D. 168. His martyrdom, as well as the bitter experiences through which the Smyrnean church was passing, could well symbolize that period of church history.

Christians throughout the empire were compelled during this time to meet in secret. This second period of church history extended from about the end of the first century to the time of Constantine or shortly thereafter, or from about A.D. 100 to 350. Christ had no word of censure for this church. He knew where the members of the church at Smyrna lived and how they had labored. Among them were some who called themselves Jews, but who were in reality of "the synagogue of Satan" (verse 9). These may have been descendants of Abraham by natural birth, but that was no guarantee of salvation. Paul says, "He is not a Jew, which is one outwardly; . . . But he is a Jew, which is one inwardly." "For they are not all Israel, which are of Israel: Neither, because they are the seed of Abraham, are they all children: . . . They which are the children of the flesh, these are not the children of God" (Romans 2:28, 29; 9:6–8). "If ye be Christ's, then are ye Abraham's seed, and heirs according to the promise" (Galatians 3:29). The real children of God are those who have been born again; that is, born of the Spirit. (See John 3:3–5.)

Counsel. The poverty and hardship of these people were all known to the Lord. But they were rich—rich in faith, in love, in service. (See 1 Timothy 6:18; James 2:5; Matthew 6:20.) It is possible to be a rich poor-man or a poor rich-man. True wealth is enrichment of character, not possession of goods or gold. "Fear none of those things which thou shalt suffer: behold, the devil shall cast some of you into prison, that ye may be tried" (Revelation 2:10). Trials come by divine permission, but God is not the author of temptation. "Let no man say when he is tempted, I am tempted of God" (James 1:13). Temptation comes from the devil, who continually opposes the people of God.

"Ye shall have tribulation ten days," Jesus said (Revelation 2:10). During the second and third centuries the Roman emperors tried to obliterate the church by persecution. They feared Christianity because it was making inroads into popular thought. They considered it a rival. A number of persecutions were instigated, ten in all, but Diocletian's persecution was the worst. This lasted ten years, from A.D. 303 to 313, or until Constantine came to the throne. If we reckon this as prophetic time, where a day represents a literal year (see Numbers 14:34; Ezekiel 4:6), then the "ten days" of persecution was truly fulfilled.

"Be thou faithful unto death," says God (Revelation 2:10). What inspiration this text has brought to the persecuted people of God through the centuries! With these words on their lips, millions have gone to their death. God may not always see fit to remove the trial, but He pledges Himself to sustain us in it and promises the reward of eternal life.

Promise. "I will give thee a crown of life" (verse 10). The crown of royalty can be worn for but a few years. But the crown of life endures forever. In the athletic contests so common in Smyrna, garlands adorned the victor's brow. Such honor, however, was short lived. But here is a promise of *everlasting* glory and honor. It may cost us our lives to be faithful, but death for the Christian is but a brief interlude when we rest from our labors. "When the chief Shepherd shall appear, ye shall receive a crown of glory that fadeth not away" (1 Peter 5:4). And he "shall not be hurt of the second death" (Revelation 2:11). When the wicked man dies, he finds another death awaiting him— the "second death," or the death of judgment. (See Revelation 20:6.) But when the overcomer falls asleep in Jesus, he knows he will be raised not for judgment but for eternal life with Christ. Praise God for the certain hope of the gospel!

THE EPISTLE TO PERGAMOS, REVELATION 2:12–17

Meaning and significance of the name. The name *Pergamos* means "height" or "elevation." The city stood on an elevation of one thousand feet and was built by the Aeolian Greeks about 1150 B.C. The elevation was a natural defense, and the city considered itself impregnable. Kings sometimes deposited their treasure there for safekeeping. Lysimachus placed his fortune of ten million dollars in this city.

Characteristic of the city. It was a "royal city." It was made the capital of the province of Asia when Attalus III, the last of the Attalid kings, bequeathed his kingdom to Rome in 133 B.C. The proconsuls who ruled there were vested with the symbol of authority: the broad, double-edged sword. The supreme court of the province was also located in Pergamos. Life or death awaited the prisoners who came to this court. The One who addresses this church is "he which hath the sharp sword with two edges" (Revelation 2:12). In the final judgment He will pronounce sentence on every soul. (See 2 Corinthians 5:10.) But He knows the conditions under which humans live, and His judgment will be just. He takes note of where men were born. (See Psalm 87:4–6.)

Pergamos was the headquarters of Satan's religion. Christ said to this church, "I know thy works, and where thou dwellest, even where Satan's seat is" (Revelation 2:13). When the Persians overthrew Babylon, they gave the inhabitants of the city their freedom. But the Babylonian priests later led a revolt and were driven from the city. "The defeated Chaldeans fled to Asia Minor, and fixed their central college at Pergamos, and took the palladium of Babylon, the cubic stone, with them. Here, independent of state control, they carried on the rites of their religion" (William B. Barker, *Lares and Penates,* pages 232, 233). Pergamos, therefore, became the "seat" of the satanic system of the Babylonian "mysteries."

This counterfeit religion was built on the claim that it made a bridge between heaven and earth. The ruling monarch became the head of the system. He had many titles, one of which, "Pontifex Maximus," is significant. *Pont* means "a bridge"; *factio,* "I make"; and *maximus,* "greatest." Put together, it simply means "the greatest bridge builder." In Genesis 11:1–5 we have the story of the ancient Babel builders. They wanted to have a tower whose top might reach to heaven, or "be in the heavens," as other translators read this passage. This occurred shortly after the great Flood in the days of Noah. Tremendous physical changes took place in our world at that time. In Genesis 8:22 we read of "cold and heat." These changes of temperature, so real in our lives today, seem to have been unknown before the Deluge. They are not mentioned in the Genesis record of the times prior to that catastrophe.

The atmosphere as well as the surface of the earth is vastly different from what it was in antediluvian days, and we can well imagine that those who were preserved in the ark and were therefore able to compare the world after the Flood with the world as it was before the Flood were well aware of the changes and contrasts. The inhabitants of that time were not ignorant of the world in which they lived. But what caused the Flood? That was the question in their minds. And would there be another flood? God had assured Noah and his family that the world would never again be destroyed by a flood, but these scientific and religious philosophers were not content with the divine promise. They wanted to build a tower—an observatory—high enough to reach above the dense atmosphere and thus enable them through so-called scientific investigation to discover a natural cause for the Flood and possibly assure themselves that nothing like that could ever happen again. The whole movement was apostate and grew out of unbelief of God's promise. The mystery cult of Babylon sprang from this, and in one form or another this apostate religion has plagued the people of God ever since.

Pergamos was for some time the headquarters of this mystery cult. But when the king of Pergamos bequeathed his kingdom to the Romans, this whole cult was transferred to Rome, which has since been the headquarters of this false system. The "title," the "keys," and the "vestments" have all been absorbed into apostate Christianity. Pergamos thus became a link between ancient Babylon and Rome. It seemed natural for the deification of the emperors to begin in this city.

Pergamos was a city of temples, the most important of which was the Temple of Zeus. This temple was dedicated to Aesculapius, "the serpent god" or "the god of healing" or "the man-instructing serpent," who gave man knowledge of good and evil. A living serpent was always kept in the Temple of Zeus as an object of worship. A famous school of medicine was also located there, the emblem of which was the serpent or the caduceus twined around a pole. This has come down to us today as the emblem of the medical profession. The city was a great educational center. Its library of two hundred thousand books rivaled the Egyptian library at Alexandria. When Egypt refused to supply the people of Pergamos with papyrus for the manufacture of paper, they prepared a new kind of writing material from carefully treated skins. This new writing material was called "parchment"—in German, *Pergament.*

Commendation. "Thou holdest fast my name, and hast not denied my faith" (Revelation 2:13). Even in Pergamos, the center of state religion and the very throne of Satan, God had a faithful people. Antipas is mentioned as having been martyred in Pergamos. Tradition tells us he was slowly baked in a brass bull that was heated until it was red hot. "Antipas" might well be a symbolic name representing all the martyrs of that period. Some have seen in this name the symbol of a movement to withstand the development of a hierarchy: *Anti,* meaning "against;" *papas,* meaning "father" or "pope." Whatever may have been the significance of the name *Antipas,* the church of Pergamos itself was commended for courage. And it took real courage to withstand the popular trend when apostate Christianity was being made the state religion and sat, as it were, on the throne of the Roman world.

Reproof. How quickly apostasy works! The Nicolaitane heresy, condemned by Christ in the letter to Ephesus, has developed from "deeds" on the part of a few (see Revelation 2:6) to become a "doctrine" within the church (see verse 15). Commenting on this heresy, Ramsay says:

> This school of thought and conduct played an important part in the church of the first century. . . . It was evidently an attempt to effect a reasonable compromise with the established usages of Greco-Roman society and to retain as many as possible of those usages in the Christian system of life. It

affected most of all the cultured and well-to-do classes in the church, those who had most temptation to retain all that they could of the established social order and custom of the Greco-Roman world, and who by their more elaborate education had been trained to take a somewhat artificial view of life and to reconcile contradictory principles in practical conduct through subtle philosophical reasoning. . . . It is highly probable that the Nicolaitanes either already had, or soon would have, reached the conclusion that they might justifiably comply with the current test of loyalty, and burn a little incense in honor of the emperor. . . . Their teaching was earthly, sensual, devilish (W. M. Ramsay, *The Letters to the Seven Churches of Asia,* pages 298–301).

It is compared to the subtle plan of Balaam, whose compromise led Israel into sin and vice.

Counsel and promise. "To him that overcometh will I give to eat of the hidden manna, and will give him a white stone, and in the stone a new name written, which no man knoweth saving he that receiveth it" (verse 17). A pot of manna was placed in the sacred ark of the sanctuary erected by Moses. This was known as "the hidden manna" (see Hebrews 9:3, 4), and was a type of Christ. (See John 6:26–63.) Only as we feed on Him, "the living Bread," can we grow into His likeness.

The "white stone" also was significant. Judges in the courts of that day used white and black stones in making their decisions: white for acquittal, black for condemnation. Also, when slaves were freed, they were given white stones on which their names, sometimes new names, were inscribed. These stones were called *tessera.* They were badges of friendship, and they entitled the holders to special privileges. If a gladiator won fifteen victories in combat, he was given a white stone, symbol of freedom and honor.

As overcomers in Christ, we are set free from the shackles of sin to become members of the family of God, and are given a new name. "If the Son therefore shall make you free, ye shall be free indeed" (John 8:36). Possessing this "new name" (Isaiah 62:2), we are made "heirs of God, and joint-heirs with Christ." "What shall we then say to these things? If God be for us, who can be against us?" (Romans 8:17, 31). Not only does the Christian need a new name, but he must also feed on "the hidden manna" of God's Word. Jeremiah says, "Thy words were found, and I did eat them; and thy word was unto me the joy and rejoicing of mine heart" (Jeremiah 15:16). That is the experience of all who feed upon the precious Word of God. Our trouble is we get so busy that we fail to take our portion of heavenly manna each day. God's ancient people were commanded to gather fresh manna every morning. Then we read, "When the sun waxed hot, it melted (Exodus 16:21). If they failed to gather it early, they had none for that day. Let us determine that we will gather our portion before the day's duties begin.

> O child of God! Awake and see the radiant dawn of day,
> The rising sun bids thee arise to meditate and pray.
> Arise and breathe the redolence of fragrant, dew-kissed flowers,
> And gather morning manna in the early morning hours.
>
> All nature is responsive to God's summons to arise,
> Ten thousand happy voices raise a chorus to the skies.
> The busy bee is searching for his honey from the flowers;
> Thus search for "hidden manna" in the early morning hours.
>
> There's a sweetness in the lily—in the Rose of Sharon, too.
> The Bible's leaves are petals—you must search them through and
>   through,
> If you hunger for this nectar, you will search in every flower,
> And you'll find the manna sweeter in the early morning hour.
>
> —Adlai A. Esteb

23. Christ's Epistles to Thyatira and Sardis

Traveling along the imperial Roman road, we come to the fourth city, Thyatira. As we have noticed in earlier chapters, this highway symbolizes the experience of the Christian church from the days of the apostles to the time when Christ returns in glory.

The sequence of these seven letters, as well as the particular messages themselves, is significant, for, taken together, the letters give a perfect picture of the church as seen through the eyes of her Lord. Christianity, which began in the fervor of the apostolic faith, suffered a severe lapse in the Middle Ages. This was foreseen by Paul, Peter, and John, each of whom, like the Lord Jesus Himself, warned the church of her peril. In Paul's letter to the Thessalonians he said, "That day [the day of our Lord's appearing] shall not come, except there come a falling away first." And further, "The mystery of iniquity doth already work" (2 Thessalonians 2:3, 7). The spirit of apostasy was already at work in his day, but the full fruitage was yet to appear. The "falling away" that was to take place would permit "that man of sin" to "be revealed" who "opposeth and exalteth himself above all that is called God, or that is worshipped; so that he as God sitteth in the temple of God, shewing himself that he is God" (verses 3, 4). Or as James Moffatt translates it, "with the proclamation that he himself is God." Before the end of time, however, the church of God was to be brought back to the pure apostolic faith and fully clothed in the righteousness of Christ and filled with the zeal and fervor of her original faith. Those who await the return of Jesus will have a pure faith and "be like him" (1 John 3:2).

THE EPISTLE TO THYATIRA, REVELATION 2:18–28

Meaning and significance of the name. The name *Thyatira* means "sacrifice of contrition" and fittingly represents that period in church history when through apostasy simple faith was exchanged, or sacrificed, for outward works and penances. Salvation cannot be bought or earned; it is the gift of God. It comes to us by grace and grace alone. But in the fourth period of church history men turned from the simple gospel of Christ and in its place built up an elaborate ritual and a man-made priesthood. It was a sad day when professing Christianity exchanged contrition of heart for dead works; when the simple faith of Jesus was replaced by the elaborate ritual of the mass.

Characteristic of the city. The city itself gave the impression of weakness made strong. It was built by Seleucus, one of Alexander's generals, in 280 B.C. and was first a cavalry outpost. "It came into existence to be a garrison city. . . . But no city has been given by nature less of the look or strength of a fortress than Thyatira. . . . It possesses no proper acropolis, and the whole impression which the situation gives is of weakness, subjection, and dependence. . . .The history of Thyatira is a blank" (W. M. Ramsay, *The Letters to the Seven Churches of Asia,* pages 318, 319, 323).

There being no natural fortifications in that area, it was necessary to strengthen the northern defenses, so this city came into being. In later years it became a manufacturing city. Its leading industries were the manufacture of brass and bronze instruments. It was a place of foundries. It was also famed for the dyeing of cloth, especially red and purple. Lydia, whom Paul met at Philippi, was evidently a representative of one of those industries. (See Acts 16:14.) Tradition has it that it was she who carried the Christian message to Thyatira.

A great temple built in honor of Apollo, the sun god, had a commanding place in the city. In this temple was an altar dedicated to a female deity.

Some Bible students believe that at the time John wrote this letter there was a woman in the church who posed as a prophetess and dominated the church, and that he referred to her as Jezebel (Revelation 2:20).

Commendation. The One who addresses this church has eyes like flaming fire and feet like glowing bronze. (See verses 8–29.) This language would have particular appeal in a city of foundries. It is as "the Son of God" that he speaks (verse 18). This is the only place in all the book of Revelation where this title is used. During the Middle Ages the place of the Son of God was usurped by the son of perdition; the

Man of Sorrows was replaced by the man of sin. As "the Son of God," Christ addresses this church.

Thyatira symbolizes the longest of the church periods—about one thousand years. Beginning with the sixth century, it lasts until the seventeenth century. B. Holzhauser, a Roman Catholic writer, says, "Thyatira is the middle church of the seven, and consequently stands as the symbol of the church of the Middle Ages" (*The Apocalypse*, page 158).

The believers, however, are commended for their works, especially the last works. " 'I know . . . that of late you have toiled harder than you did at first' " (verse 19, Weymouth). A change came at the end of the Thyatira period when the great Reformation arose. Such men as Luther, Knox, Calvin, Zwingli, and scores of others came to lead the people back to God.

Reproof. This is the longest of the seven letters, and it contains the most definite denunciations. The reference to Jezebel is particularly significant (see verse 20). Jezebel was a princess of Phoenicia. But when Ahab, king of Israel, married her, she set herself to introduce sun worship into Israel, and she succeeded. Almost the whole nation went into idolatry.

Then came Elijah the prophet, who was called of God to denounce the apostasy of Israel. His word locked the heavens, and he walked away with the key. The land suffered drought and famine. Three and a half years later Elijah led the people back to the true God. He destroyed the 850 prophets and priests of Baal. Jezebel and her wicked family were later destroyed by Jehu, the reformer.

This marriage of Ahab to Jezebel, and the subsequent apostasy of Israel, was a type of the time when paganism would come into the church and the head of the church become the head of the state. Sun worship, the foundation of pagan worship, came with all its trappings into the Christian church and is still perpetuated among certain groups. Red and purple were pronounced in the cloth trade of Thyatira, and these colors became a vital part of the attire of the apostate church (See Revelation 17:4.)

In A.D. 538 Emperor Justinian made effective a decree establishing the bishop of Rome as "the corrector of heretics," thus giving him temporal and ecclesiastical authority over all the churches. For three and a half prophetic years, or 1,260 literal years (A.D. 538–1798), this power was vested in the bishop of Rome. The Napoleonic wars stripped the Roman Church of her temporal power, but in recent decades she has been rapidly regaining her prestige. During the long centuries the church was suffering from a spiritual drought. God gave her opportunity to repent. The Reformation of the sixteenth century was God's appeal to His people, but "she repented not" (Revelation 2:21). That is, those symbolized by Jezebel refused to heed God's pleas. The Counter-Reformation was launched in opposition to the Protestant Reformation; thus the minds of many were blinded to God's real message for that time.

Counsel. "Hold fast till I come" (see verse 25) is the call of Christ to the church of this period. This is the first reference in these apocalyptic letters to the approaching Second Advent. This great doctrine has been largely set aside by the teachings of such men as Augustine, whose interpretation of Scripture undermined the basic truth of the resurrection. Those Scriptures which so emphatically teach the resurrection of the body at the return of Christ were interpreted as applying to the resurrection of dead souls to spiritual life. Moreover, the promise of the establishment of the City of God, the New Jerusalem, on the renewed earth was declared to predict the establishment of the church as the ruling power among the nations, making the Second Advent of little importance.

Promise. To the overcomer, Christ promised "power" or "authority" over the nations (verse 26); a heartening promise, indeed, in the face of the persecution of those days. The martyrs were looked upon as powerless and insignificant, and so they were by comparison with the pomp and power of the Holy Roman Empire. But the promise is that they will yet reign with Christ in His coming kingdom and will then have "power over the nations" (verse 26).

But there was another promise: "I will give him the morning Star" (verse 28). As the daystar, or morning star, appears in a dark hour of the night, so Christ, "the day star" (2 Peter 1:19), or "the bright and morning star" (Revelation 22:16), promises to appear in the hour of our greatest trial. At the time the church was passing through her darkest hour of apostasy, the Spirit of Christ inspired God-fearing men like Wycliffe, Huss, and others, who led the people back to the Word of God. They were heralds of the coming day of Reformation. In fact, Wycliffe is sometimes called the "Morning Star of the Reformation."

THE EPISTLE TO SARDIS, REVELATION 3:1–6

Meaning and significance of the name. The name *Sardis* means "that which remains" or "the escape of the remnant." Actually there was little real faith remaining after the centuries of apostasy and persecution. But a remnant escaped, as it were, and started out on a career of fresh spiritual life. But the new life which had begun with such promise soon became enfeebled and was ready to die.

Characteristic of the city. It is significant that W. M. Ramsay speaks of Sardis as "The City of Death." In every way, it was a contrast with Smyrna, "The City of Life." Ramsay's comment is significant: "Smyrna was dead, and yet lived. Sardis lived, and yet was dead" (*The Letters to the Seven Churches of Asia,* page 375). "The letter to the Sardian church breathes the spirit of death, of appearance without reality, promise without performance, outward show of strength betrayed by want of watchfulness and careless confidence" (ibid., page 44).

The city of Sardis grew into power about 1150 B.C. Built upon a crumbling rock, it stood at an elevation of fifteen hundred feet. It later became the capital of the kingdom of Lydia, one of the richest kingdoms of the ancient world. Coined money is believed to have originated there.

The almost perpendicular walls of the elevation on which this city stood made it appear impregnable. There was only one entrance into the city, and this could easily be guarded. Because of overconfidence, however, during the reign of Croesus the city of Sardis was captured by Cyrus, 549 B.C. One of Cyrus's soldiers scaled the rock on a dark night when the guards were not watching. Entering the city, he opened the gates to the Persians. The same thing was repeated in the days of Antiochus the Great, 213 B.C.

"The sudden ruin of that great empire and the wealthiest king of all the world was an event of that character which most impressed the

Greek mind, emphasizing a moral lesson by a great national disaster. A little carelessness was shown; a watchman was wanting at the necessary point, or a sentinel slept at his post for an hour, and the greatest power on the earth was hurled to destruction. The great king trusted to Sardis, and Sardis failed him at the critical moment" (ibid., page 377).

The surrounding country was a favorite haunt for thieves. The city had little or no influence in the Roman period. Its glory was all in the past. Dana describes it as a typical example of broken-down aristocracy. And that is the impression any student gets who visits this site today. As I wandered over its grass-grown streets, I said, "Can it be that this was the great capital of Lydia, the headquarters of Croesus?" How short lived is human greatness! Here were tombs of forgotten monarchs and temple ruins of dead religions. As I watched the sun rise over the gaping wall, a feeling of desolation crept over me. Mighty pillars of marble jutted up into the sky, casting strange shadows over what had been the banquet hall of royalty. A few goats were the only inhabitants of a city that at one time had been the envy of Cyrus the Great. Sardis, the city that once was alive but now is dead.

Commendation. There seemed to be little indeed to commend. When John wrote in A.D. 95, Sardis was living mostly on its past reputation. The few things that were alive seemed ready to die. The outward activity of the believers at Sardis was not backed up by an inner spirituality. What they had received and heard they had not remembered and held. Yet there were a few even in Sardis who had not defiled their garments.

Reproof. "Thou hast a name that thou livest, and art dead" (Revelation 3:1). Like the city itself, the Sardis church had begun with great promise, but its pretensions were unjustified. No church and no individual Christian can live upon a past reputation, no matter how wonderful it may have been.

Counsel. "Be watchful, . . . and repent" (verses 2, 3). How impressive are these words in the light of the city's history! A Christian dare not be overconfident. "Let him that thinketh he standeth take heed lest he fall" (1 Corinthians 10:12).

"With every conceivable artifice and device he [Satan] is seeking to take souls captive. Unless we are constantly on guard we shall fall an easy prey to his unnumbered deceptions. . . . Many today are asleep, as were the disciples. They are not watching and praying lest they enter into temptation. Let us read and study those portions of God's word that have special reference to these last days, pointing out the dangers that will threaten God's people" (Ellen G. White, *Testimonies for the Church,* vol. 8, pages 100, 101).

Applying this message to the post–Reformation period, it fits exactly. Those who led out in the Reformation were men of vigor and consecration, but their followers, thinking that the battles had been won, settle down to organized religion. Great movements begun by men like Luther and Knox became mere state religions, supported by the public treasury. Self-sufficient and satisfied with past attainments, these people failed to sense the need of the great heathen world. Matthew Arnolds's descriptive verse gives a true picture:

Its form stood still without a breach,
When life and warmth were fled,
And still it spoke its wonted speech
But every word was dead.

Forms are all right, providing they are filled with power; but too often forms become mere formality and dead works. "Hold fast, and repent," pleads the Lord. "If therefore thou shalt not watch, I will come on thee as a thief" (Revelation 3:3). When Christ returns in glory, He will come as a thief in the night. The world, and even many professed Christians, will be unprepared for that glorious event. It will come as an overwhelming surprise to millions.

But God had not forsaken His people, even in the Sardis period. Some of the greatest events of history were happening at that time. Cromwell's revolution in England overthrew the false idea of "the divine right of kings." At the same time, the American colonies were being established, and these became the foundation of a new nation and a new civilization. New opportunities were thus opening before the church.

Promise. To the faithful remnant in Sardis, God said, "They shall walk with me in white" (verse 4). White is the symbol of purity and righteousness. (See Revelation 19:8; Zechariah 3:3–5.) The white toga in Rome symbolized triumph and joy, and was worn by candidates for high office. Black, a symbol of mourning or defeat, was worn by slaves and captives.

One of the most beautiful promises in God's Word is found in Revelation 3:5: "I will not blot out his name out of the book of life, but I will confess his name before my Father, and before his angels." How wonderful to know that even if our names are blotted from the record books of man and for the sake of the gospel we are disowned by friends and family, yet in heaven our High Priest claims us as His own and confesses our name before His Father! Honor and security are ours, and we can look confidently into the future, knowing that soon our Lord will come and receive us unto Himself. In that great day this will be the command that goes forth: "Open ye the gates, that the righteous nation which keepeth the truth may enter in" (Isaiah 26:2).

24. Christ's Epistles to Philadelphia and Laodicea

Philadelphia means "brotherly love." The city derived its name from Attalus II, whose loyalty to his brother Eumenes won for him the epithet Philadelphus. The city was founded about 150 B.C.

Characteristic of the city. W. M. Ramsay calls Philadelphia a "missionary city," giving the word a little different meaning, perhaps, from what we usually think of as "missionary" today. He says, "The intention of its founder was to make it a center of the Greco-Asiatic civilization and a means of spreading the Greek language and manners in the eastern parts of Lydia and in Phrygia. It was a missionary city from the beginning, founded to promote a certain unity of spirit, customs, and loyalty within the realm, the apostle of Hellenism in an Oriental land. It was a successful teacher. Before A.D. 19 the Lydian tongue had ceased to be spoken in Lydia, and Greek was the only language in the country" (*The Letters to the Seven Churches of Asia,* pages 391, 392).

Philadelphia was located at the entrance to the beautiful valley of Hermus, and was, as it were, the key or gateway to this fertile area. The message of Christ, therefore, had special significance (see Revelation 3:7, 8). Because of its magnificence, Philadelphia was sometimes referred to as "Little Athens." But it was subject to frequent earthquakes, and the populace lived always in the dread of disaster. It was almost totally destroyed in A.D. 17. Most of its citizens fled from the city, and many never returned. Others lived for weeks and months in tents and temporary dwellings. Amid the wreckage stood a lone column; it was still standing in the eighteenth century. The citizens rebuilt the city, however, with Tiberius Caesar donating quite a large sum of money from his personal treasury. In his honor the people renamed the city Neo-Caesarus. In fact, the city has changed its name several times. Under the reign of Caracalla it was called Neokorus, and later changed the name to Flavia. Today, its Turkish name is Alaşehir, meaning The Red City or The City of God. Its present population is about fifteen thousand. Few, if any, Christians live in the city today.

THE EPISTLE TO PHILADELPHIA, REVELATION 3:7–13

Commendation. As in His message to Smyrna, Christ commends the believers in Philadelphia for meeting the approval of the Holy One. By contrast, how different was His message to Sardis! People of that church had a name that they were living but were spiritually dead! But the Philadelphian church had kept His Word and had not denied His name.

Reproof. It is significant that Christ gave no reproof to this church. Its name was a beautiful symbol of the affection that characterized the believers.

Counsel. Philadelphia represents that period in church history which was ushered in by the evangelical preaching of the Wesleys, Whitefield, Jonathan Edwards, and a multitude of others. "The world is my parish," declared John Wesley, whose message of "free grace" challenged the Calvinistic theology of "election." This evangelical movement became the prelude to the era of modern missions that came with the dawn of the eighteenth century. To the church of this period the Lord said significantly, "I have set before thee an open door" (verse 8). Providence opened the door to missionary endeavor in practically every land of earth. "A great door and effectual is opened unto me," said Paul (1 Corinthians 16:9).

Two great political revolutions, one in America, 1776, the other in France, 1789, affected tremendously the thinking of the world. Then suddenly the world began to open up for the gospel. William Carey went to India in 1793; Robert Morrison to China in 1807; Robert Moffatt to Africa in 1817; followed by David Livingstone in 1841. The British and Foreign Bible Society began its work in 1804, and the American Bible Society came into being in 1816. The Sunday School movement also began around this time.

These were the beginnings of a great missionary program that was to carry "the everlasting gospel" to "every nation, and kindred, and tongue, and people" (Revelation 14:6). The Philadelphia period culminated in the great Second Advent awakening of the nineteenth century. Through the study of Daniel and the Revelation, and the interpretation of Christ's own prophecy, a profound conviction came to Christendom that the return of Christ was at hand. The remarkable dark day of May 19, 1780, and the phenomenal falling of the stars in 1833 were recognized as a direct fulfillment of prophecy and as omens of the Savior's imminent appearing. A new impetus was given to the study of prophecy. The prophetic periods of the 1,260 days, as relating to the antichrist, and the 2,300 days, which related to the message of the judgment, received particular attention. Prophetic conferences convened, and these gave impetus to one of the greatest eras of preaching since the days of the apostles. Side by side with the revival in the study of the prophecies came an advance in scientific investigation. This was followed by an era of invention, and the world seemed suddenly to leap forward, first on wheels, then on wings. New methods of transportation and communication came into being to make possible the carrying of the gospel to all the world in this generation.

The word *Philadelphia* means "brotherly love," and the Philadelphian period was characterized by just such an experience among God's people. "Love for the Elder Brother always leads to love for the other brothers. This was the love that was lost during the Ephesian period. . . . Its return to the church will bring a repetition of Pentecostal power" (Taylor G. Bunch, *The Seven Epistles of Christ*, page 198). God's work will close in the power of His Spirit, which is the power of divine love. And when the gospel has gone to all the world, the end will come (see Matthew 24:14), and our Lord will appear in glory (see Matthew 25:31). To the church in Philadelphia came the message: "Behold, I come quickly: hold that fast which thou hast, that no man take [or cheat thee of] thy crown" (Revelation 3:11). It is as if God said, "Let no man or business or property or ambition or anxiety deprive you of your crown." (See Colossians 2:18.)

Promise. The keynote of the Revelation is the Second Advent, and in this epistle Christ promises that the faithful who endure will be kept in the hour of universal trial that shall come upon the whole world. (See Revelation 3:10.) But more: Those who ridiculed His faithful ones and disowned them will at last come to recognize the truth of the message that caused their separation, and they will know that God loves those whom they despised. (See verse 9.)

Mention has already been made of the pillar, or column, that withstood the devastating earthquake in A.D. 17 and remained through the centuries like a sentinel amid the ruins. It could well symbolize the overcomer. Christ promises to make those who overcome "a pillar" in the temple of God and to write upon them His "new name" (verse 12). We bear the name of God who owns us and the name of the New Jerusalem, our destination.

Some years ago when the political relationships between Hungary and Romania were strained and all nationals of either country residing in the other were compelled to return to their homeland, a little girl, four years old, who had been staying with relatives, was to be returned on the train to her home in Hungary. No one, however, was permitted to accompany her; she had to travel alone. But how could she? Well, love always finds a way. Her relatives labeled her and put her in the baggage car. Her picture, showing the label, both back and front, appeared in the London papers. She traveled with the baggage, crossed the border between the countries, and arrived in safety at her destination. Her mother met her. Imagine the eager anticipation of that mother and the joy of the little one as the train pulled into the home station! Just so, our Lord awaits our homecoming. We may not always have a first class seat; we may even have to travel, as it were, with the baggage. But what does it matter? We are on our way home! We are labeled for the New Jerusalem! Christ's name is inscribed on our hearts. We are members of the family of God.

THE EPISTLE TO LAODICEA, REVELATION 3:14–22

Meaning and significance of the name. The name *Laodicea* means "judging of the people." This city was built by Antiochus II, 261–246 B.C., and was named in honor of his wife, Laodice, reference to whom is found in Daniel 11:6. This is the last of the seven churches, and significantly it covers that period of church history when our heavenly High Priest will be carrying out His ministry of judgment just prior to His return in glory. The name might also be interpreted "a just people" or "a justified people." Only as our Advocate represents us at the throne of grace can we be justified. We are justified by His grace (see Romans 3:24), by His blood (see Romans 5:9), and by faith (see Romans 5:1). Grace is the source; blood is the means; faith is the method by which we appropriate it. We show it by works (see James 2:22, 24). Good works can never produce justification, but justification is revealed by good works.

Characteristic of the city. Laodicea could well be called City of Compromise. "There is no city whose spirit and nature are more difficult to describe than Laodicea. There are no extremes, and hardly any very strongly marked features. But in this even balance lies its peculiar character. Those were the qualities that contributed to make it essentially the successful trading city, the city of bankers and finance, which could adapt itself to the needs and wishes of others, ever pliable and accommodating, full of the spirit of compromise" (W. M. Ramsay, *The Letters to the Seven Churches of Asia,* pages 422, 423).

Situated about fifty miles from Philadelphia and about six miles from Colossae, it stood at the junction of two important roads. It was a city of wealth, with large markets, a large banking exchange, and large manufacturing interests. A rich farming district surrounded Laodicea. Valuable wool was produced in the valley, soft in texture, glossy black in color, but tinged, as it were, with violet. Black garments were worn almost exclusively by the Laodiceans as evidence of their wealth. This wool is no longer produced.

Laodicea was one of the leading health resorts in the Greco-Roman Empire. Lukewarm baths and mineral springs attracted many visitors from Europe and Asia. An important school of medicine was situated in the temple of Karu, one of some two hundred temples in the ancient world dedicated to Aesculapius, the Greek god of medicine, or a counterfeit messiah. Connected with this school was an industry for the manufacture of a special eye medicine, collyrium. It was made from the famous Phrygian stone. W. M. Ramsay says, "This Phrygian powder came through Laodicea into general use among the Greeks" (ibid., page 419). Because of their wealth, the citizens were proud, arrogant, and self-satisfied. The city itself was well ordered and successful, but those very features made it self-sufficient.

Paul evidently wrote an epistle to Laodicea (see Colossians 4:13, 16), but his letter has been lost and is not now a part of the New Testament. Some scholars believe that this mention of a letter might refer to Paul's letter to the Ephesians, for it was to be read in all the churches. However, it probably refers to a letter specifically written to the Laodiceans, for, according to our records, Paul never visited this church in person.

An important church council, known as the Council of Laodicea, was later held in this city. This council convened about the middle of the fourth century with thirty-two bishops in attendance, and one of the special items on the agenda concerned the canon of Scripture, or the cataloguing of the books of the Bible. It is interesting to note that this particular council seems to have omitted the entire book of Revelation from the canon. But the extant records of this council are challenged by scholarship.

We have now arrived at the terminal point of our journey, having traveled from Ephesus to Laodicea. This is Christ's last message to the churches, and He speaks as "the Amen" and "the faithful and true witness." He has the right to speak at the close of human history, for He was also "the beginning" in the original creation (Revelation 3:14). Weymouth's translation (third edition) reads, " 'The Beginning and Lord of God's Creation.' " He was the One who "spake, and it was done; he commanded, and it stood fast" (Psalm 33:9). As the "Word" or "Logos" (Greek), He was with God, and He was God. Christ was not part of the creation, for He was the Creator. (See John 1:1–3; Colossians 1:13–16; Ephesians 3:9; Hebrews 1:1–3; 1 Corinthians 8:6.)

Not only is He the Author of the original creation, He is also "the author and finisher of our faith" (Hebrews 12:2). As such, He speaks to a Christianized generation, cultured and educated, but skeptical and self-complacent, having lost its God in the theories of "science falsely so called" (1 Timothy 6:20). The evolutionary philosophy, studied from any angle, must be recognized as an attack on the veracity of God's Word. Its one great aim seems to be to destroy faith in the Creator. If man has been growing gradually better and never had a fall through sin, then he does not need a Savior. Evolution and true Christianity can never be harmonized. They begin at two different points; they travel in two different directions; and they end at terminals as wide apart as the poles. This will be developed in the comments on Revelation chapter 7.

Commendation. There was nothing to commend in Laodicea, for this church had imbibed the proud spirit of the world around it, and its people were in spiritual jeopardy. This called forth the Lord's clear rebuke. "Thou art lukewarm," He says (Revelation 3:16).

Reproof. Christ sees this last church as miserable and poor and blind and naked; yet interestingly, they possessed all the essentials that go to make an impressive appearance. They are orthodox, to be sure, but orthodoxy of itself is insufficient; it is dead. One can be sound in theology, yet sound asleep. It is impossible to be an earnest, glowing Christian without the fire of the faith of Jesus. The lukewarm baths of Laodicea, neither cold nor hot, were a tragic symbol of professing Christians just prior to the return of Christ. He does not charge them with being hypocrites, for a hypocrite is an imposter or a pretender; he knows better. But here is a church of which the Lord says, thou "knowest not" (verse 17). They possess all the outward evidence of cultural attainment, yet they are actually wretched and miserable and poor and blind and naked. "Increased with goods," (verse 17), they are wealthy as measured by the world's standards, possessing beautiful church buildings, wonderful institutions, and centers of learning, yet lacking the very essentials of Christian experience. When worldliness eats its way into our hearts, it destroys our passion for souls. All too many of us are comfortable and self-satisfied, yet we know not our real condition; we are inoculated with just enough Christianity to make us immune to the genuine thing. Could anything be more tragic? And this condition prevails at the very time when our Lord is about to return.

Counsel. But despite all this, the Savior has not forsaken His people. He says, "Buy of me gold tried in the fire" (verse 18; cf. Job 23:10), and "white raiment, that thou mayest be clothed" (verse 18; cf. Isaiah 61:10; Revelation 19:8). Christ's parable of the man who lacked a wedding garment (see Matthew 22) is a true picture of this last church. "Anoint thine eyes with eyesalve, that thou mayest see," says the Lord (verse 18; cf. Ephesians 1:18; John 16:13). When we cease to trust ourselves and recognize our poverty, when we see for the riches of heaven, only then can we be ready for His appearing. We are blind, but not incurably blind. We need to be healed, but look! The Great Physician waits to help us. We need to be clothed, and He is waiting to cover us with His own robe of righteousness. No garment woven on the looms of earth can meet our need. The black garments of the Laodiceans, which to them were evidences of their superiority, were in reality an evidence of their spiritual poverty. In the Greco-Roman world, black was generally considered as a symbol of subjection. In medieval times, groups in certain countries were compelled to wear black to show their subjection. But white is a symbol of purity and victory. God wants us to be *pure,* that we may be *victorious.* He appeals to us in tenderness and love, saying, "I counsel thee."

"When the soul surrenders itself to Christ, a new power takes possession of the new heart. A change is wrought which man can never accomplish for himself. It is a supernatural work, bringing a supernatural element into human nature. The soul that has yielded to Christ becomes His own fortress, which He holds in a revolted world, and He intends that no authority shall be known in it but His own. A soul thus kept in possession by the heavenly agencies is impregnable to the assaults of Satan" (Ellen White, *The Desire of Ages,* pages 323, 324).

The righteousness by which we are justified is imputed; that is, we had no part in it whatsoever. It comes wholly from God. But the righteousness by which we are sanctified is imparted; that is, it is worked out in our lives by the power of the Holy Spirit. "The first is our title to heaven; the second is our fitness for heaven" (Ellen White, *The Review and Herald,* June 4, 1895).

Promise. The Lord rebukes those whom He loves, but if we refuse His rebuke, then we must be separated from Him. It is not sufficient to accept His pardon—we must accept His provision. At the door of every heart He stands and knocks, and knocks again. He appeals to us to let Him in. Not only does He knock, but He calls to us: "If any man hear my voice . . ." (Revelation 3:20). It is not the person inside that is taking the initiative, but the Lord, who is outside, stands there pressing against the door, pleading for entrance. He had come from the throne of heaven that He might dine with the sons of men. And it makes no difference who we are or what is our condition. "If any man . . . open the door," He says, "I will come in to him, and will sup with him, and he with me" (verse 20). Salvation is always a personal matter. As individuals, we must heed His voice and let Him in. Not only will He sup with us; He will share His throne with us. This is surely the most profound promise in the Bible.

It is a beautiful picture and reveals the intimate fellowship the believer may have with his risen Lord. The act of dining together creates a bond of fellowship between two persons. This is particularly true in the Orient. Sharing a meal is a symbol of friendship, the host furnishing not only the meal, but greater still, the freedom of his home. As we open our heart's door to Christ, we thereby invite Him to share our innermost lives.

O Jesus! Thou art standing
Outside the fast closed door,
In lowly patience waiting
To pass the threshold o'er.
We bear the name of Christians,
Thy name and sign we bear;
Oh, shame, thrice shame upon us!
To keep Thee standing there.

O Jesus! Thou art knocking;
And lo! that hand is scarred,
And thorns Thy brow encircle,
And tears Thy face have marred.
O love that passeth knowledge,
So patiently to wait!
O sin that hath no equal,
So fast to bar the gate!

O Jesus! Thou art pleading
In accents meek and low—
"I died for you, My children,
And will ye treat Me so?"
O Lord, with shame and sorrow
We open now the door.
Dear Savior, enter, enter,
And leave us nevermore!
—William W. How

In concluding the study of these seven epistles of Christ to His church, we should note the scope of His promises to the overcomer. Sin brought Adam not only the loss of life but also the loss of his Eden home. But greater still, it robbed him of the companionship of God. The opening chapters of Genesis tell us the story of man's failure and loss through sin. The closing chapters of Revelation tell of man's victory and full restoration through Christ. Everything lost through sin will be restored through grace. Note these contrasts in Genesis and Revelation:

SIN	GRACE
Sin deprived us of the tree of life (Gen. 3:22, 23).	Grace restores tree of life (Rev. 2:7).
Sin put us under death sentence (Gen. 2:17).	Grace gives victory over second death (Rev. 2:11).
Sin sent us out to earn our bread (Gen. 3:19).	Grace provides hidden manna (Rev. 2:17).
Sin stole our dominion (Gen. 3:24).	Grace promises power over nations (Rev. 2:26).
Sin left us naked (Gen. 3:7).	Grace clothes us in white raiment (Rev. 3:5).
Sin drove us from God's presence (Gen. 3:23).	Grace pledges we go out no more (Rev. 3:12).
Sin returned us to dust (Gen. 3:19).	Grace places us on throne of God (Rev. 3:21).

Marvelous heritage for sinners saved by grace! When the seventh trumpet sounds and the kingdoms of this world become the kingdom of our Lord, that settles forever the question of the ownership of this world. On Calvary Jesus defeated the devil and reconciled the world to God. But this will be the signal for the expulsion of Satan, the great deceiver and usurper. The rightful ownership of Christ will have been fully determined in the great judgment scenes of heaven. This we will study in succeeding chapters. Wisdom, worthiness, wealth, and worship belong to Him! "He that hath an ear, let him hear what the Spirit saith unto the churches" (Revelation 3:22).

25. The Vision of the Throne, the Lamb, and the Sealed Book

Now begins the real pageant of the Apocalypse. What has been presented hitherto has been but an introduction. The whole objective of these prophecies is to reveal the justice of God and to show how His character will be vindicated before the universe. Our comprehension of these themes will be greatly aided if we permit ourselves to think of John as being carried forward to the time when the judgment of God begins. Chapter 4 opens with the invitation for him to "come up hither" that he might behold things which "must be hereafter" (verse 1). In vision he enters the sanctuary of God, and from the throne room of the Eternal he witnesses the portrayal of the great judgment scenes, when the cases of all are decided. These events in the moving drama of redemption fill him with awe. Paul says God "hath appointed a day, in the which he will judge the world in righteousness by that man whom he hath ordained" (Acts 17:31). And again: "For we must all appear before the judgment seat of Christ" (2 Corinthians 5:10).

A DOOR OPENED IN HEAVEN

The earthly sanctuary built by Moses contained two apartments. These were called the Holy Place and the Most Holy Place. No one entered the Most Holy Place except the high priest, and then only once a year, on the Day of Atonement. Throughout all their history, the Hebrews have understood the Day of Atonement to prefigure the day of judgment when the cases of all will be decided. The earthly sanctuary was a type of the heavenly (see Hebrews 9), and in vision John saw "a door . . . opened in heaven" (Revelation 4:1)—not *into* heaven, but *in* heaven. It was the opening of an inner door in the heavenly sanctuary. He was taken in vision to behold the solemn scenes of the judgment when the High Priest performs His closing work of ministry.

A voice spoke and said, "Come up hither, and I will shew thee things which must be hereafter" (verse 1). The prophet responds, and the first thing he sees is a throne. There is a striking similarity between John's description in Revelation 4 and Daniel's description in Daniel 7:9–14. Both prophets were looking at the same scene. Each pictures "the thrones" or "seats" set in order around the central throne, and both Daniel and John attempt to describe the One occupying that throne. Daniel says His "garment was white as snow" (Daniel 7:9). John says He was "like a jasper" (Revelation 4:3), or more accurately, "like a diamond." Daniel says, "A fiery stream issued and came forth from before him" (Daniel 7:10). John says He was like "a sardine stone" (Revelation 4:3) or the sardius, a brilliant red stone. The dazzling white of the jasper, or diamond, would well represent His holiness, while the fiery stream, or the blood red of the sardius, could symbolize His righteousness. Says Ellen White:

> The sanctuary in heaven is the very center of Christ's work in behalf of men. It concerns every soul living upon the earth. It opens to view the plan of redemption, bringing us down to the very close of time and revealing the triumphant issue of the contest between righteousness and sin. It is of the utmost importance that all should thoroughly investigate these subjects and be able to give an answer to everyone that asketh them a reason of the hope that is in them.
>
> The intercession of Christ in man's behalf in the sanctuary above is as essential to the plan of salvation as was His death upon the cross" (*The Great Controversy,* pages 488, 489).

The throne itself was like "an emerald" (verse 3). Green, being the living color, well expresses the mercy of God, while the "rainbow round about the throne" (verse 3) is a beautiful symbol of hope. When the rainbow first appeared, it was a sign of God's everlasting covenant of peace. (See Genesis 9.) But there could be no rainbow without the shower; it is the mingling of the sunshine and the shower that produces it. So the rainbow-encircled throne is where God's mercy and His justice meet and mingle. At the throne of grace "mercy and truth are met together; righteousness and peace have kissed each other"

(Psalm 85:10). The throne John and Daniel described is not the "throne of . . . glory" (Matthew 25:31; Revelation 20:11). No, it is "the throne of grace" (Hebrews 4:16), where you and I can come for mercy and pardon from sin.

But the greatest comfort and the first guarantee of victory is the fact that God is on His throne. He has not abdicated in favor of any other power. No earthly dictatorship can overthrow the Occupant of that throne.

The word translated "seat" is the Greek word *thronos,* from which we get our English word "throne." These seats were seats of honor, or thrones, on which the twenty-four elders were sitting. Daniel says the thrones were "cast down" or "placed" (Daniel 7:9). The custom in those days, when an assize was to be held, was for one to throw down, or place, cushions on which the dignitaries would lean during the court session. These elders, like the priests of ancient Israel, were clothed in white raiment, a symbol of "the righteousness of saints" (Revelation 19:8). Ministering as they do in the Melchizedek order, they are therefore crowned as king-priests.

But who are these elders? From whence did they come? They themselves declare they were redeemed from the earth. (See Revelation 5:9.) They are, therefore, sinners saved by grace. A priest had to be chosen from among his brethren. (See Hebrews 2:17.) These men, being priests, were the chosen representatives from every race and nation of the world. When Christ arose from the grave, "many bodies of the saints which slept arose, and came out of the graves" (Matthew 27:52, 53). Then "when he ascended up on high, he led a multitude of captives" (Ephesians 4:8, margin). It was in this sense that He became "the firstborn among many brethren" (Romans 8:29). When He was installed as our High Priest, He was anointed with the oil of gladness above His fellows. (See Hebrews 1:9.) Those "fellows" were not angels; they were men. They were His "brethren" who arose with Him from the grave. They were the antitypical wave-sheaf offering, as it were, and became the antitype of the ceremonial in the Mosaic ritual. (See Leviticus 23:15.) Christ is our First Fruits (see 1 Corinthians 15:20), and He arose on the very day of the first-fruit offering. Jesus died on the fourteenth day of Nisan, the first month of the Jewish calendar, and He arose on the sixteenth day, exactly fulfilling the type.

Twenty-four priests appear with Christ in His priestly ministry. This, too, is a fulfillment of the type. In the temple service there were twenty-four courses of the Levitical priesthood. (See 1 Chronicles 24:13–19; 2 Chronicles 8:14.)

THE SEVEN LAMPS OF FIRE

These lamps are declared to be the "seven Spirits of God," (Revelation 4:5), seven being the figure of completeness or perfection. This is a beautiful picture of the Holy Spirit searching constantly throughout the whole world for those whose hearts are perfect toward Him. (See 2 Chronicles 16:9; Proverbs 15:3.)

THE LIVING CREATURES ABOUT THE THRONE, REVELATION 4:4

The "four beasts" or "living creatures" (verse 6), as other translators render the Greek word *zoon,* seem to be more intimately connected with the throne than are even the twenty-four elders. The symbolism of a lion, a calf, a man, and a flying eagle is particularly significant. Similar imagery is found also in the first chapter of Ezekiel. These four creatures, doubtless, denote strength, perseverance, intelligence, and swiftness. Commentators for centuries have linked these symbols with the four aspects of our Savior as emphasized particularly in the four Gospels. Matthew writes on the kingly side of our Lord, emphasizing the King and His kingdom. This is well symbolized by the lion, the majestic king of beasts. Mark deals largely with the Savior as the servant of man, the ox symbolizing service. Luke, the physician, reveals Jesus' human aspect as the Son of man, hence the face of a man. John emphasizes His deity—Christ the eternal Word—who created all things. This phase of our Lord is symbolized by the flying eagle.

Though the account of the organization of the tribes of Israel in the wilderness as given in Numbers 2 does not so state, nonbiblical records indicate that these symbols were used as follows: The tribes grouped around Judah were under the lion standard; those standing near Ephraim, under the ox; those around Reuben, under the standard of a man; and those around Dan, under the flying eagle.

The scene that is about to open is one of the great climaxes in the apocalyptic story. The tremendous sweep of events here introduced leaves one awestruck with wonder as he tries to catch the true significance.

THE BOOK WITH THE BINDING SEALS

The One who occupies the throne has a book in His hand, sealed with seven seals. Whatever this book is, it concerns the redemption of human beings, for as soon as it is taken from the hand of the Occupant of the throne, a paean of praise breaks forth as the elders cry in rapturous exaltation, "Worthy is the Lamb that was slain" "and hast redeemed us to God by thy blood" (Revelation 5:12, 9). Yes, it has everything to do with our redemption. And that is why the study of this book is so important.

While redemption has its roots in the past, its full realization lies in the future. The price of our redemption was paid when our Lord shed His precious blood on Calvary's cross. But not until He comes the second time in power and glory is redemption complete. This world, so long under the sway of the powers of evil, is to be repossessed and given back to the people of God. "Blessed are the meek," said Jesus, "for they shall inherit the earth" (Matthew 5:5). That inheritance is still future. Looking forward to that hour of victory, He told us to be ready and outlined many signs which locate the time of His appearing. "When these things begin to come to pass," He said, "then look up, and lift up your heads; for your redemption draweth nigh" (Luke 21:28).

The apostle Paul spoke about the inheritance as a future hope. The gift of the Holy Spirit is the earnest, or pledge, of that inheritance, which is "the redemption of the purchased possession" (Ephesians 1:14). While the inheritance is pledged, yet it has to be repossessed from its usurper and made ready for its eternal citizens. That cannot be accomplished until after the judgment.

Under the ancient laws and customs of the Hebrews it was impossible to alienate estates beyond a certain time. If one found it necessary through misfortune to dispose of his land, the new ownership continued only until the year of jubilee, when each property automatically came back to its original owner or his heirs. In fact, an owner or heir did not even have to wait until the jubilee, providing he could establish legal claim to the property and could pay the redemption price.

At the time of forfeiture of the property a legal document was executed in duplicate, specifying the terms, so that the proper authorities would have a basis for adjudicating a redemption before the year of jubilee.

"For the manner of writing the contract, he who was to buy the ground wrote two instruments [documents]; the one to be sealed with his own signet, the other he showed unclosed to the witnesses, that they might subscribe and bear witness of that which was written. This, the witness did subscribe upon the back of the enclosed instrument" (*Weemse on the Judicial Law of Moses,* chapter 30. Quoted by J. A. Seiss in *The Apocalypse,* vol. 1, page 273).

The one who had possession of an alienated, or forfeited, property thus was always liable for the return of it, according to the terms of the agreement. But the repossession, or redemption, could be negotiated only by a *goel,* the nearest of kin. The story of Ruth involves such a transaction; however, in that instance the nearest of kin deferred to Boaz, who was next of kin. In Jeremiah 32 there is an account of a redemption of property involving the sealed and unsealed books of purchase, and the witnesses.

Now let us catch the significance of this heavenly scene. When Adam sinned, he forfeited all rights to this world. And the inheritance passed not only out of his hands but out of the hands of all his posterity. Satan claimed this world, and for all these thousands of years strangers and intruders have overrun and debased it. Yet all the while those title deeds have been awaiting the time when the Redeemer, or the *Goel,* would take that sealed book and repossess the lost inheritance.

Before the enemy and his seed can be evicted and the rightful heirs reinstated, there must be a thorough investigation of all the rights and claims. This calls for the opening of the books in heaven. These must be searched before pronouncement can be made. Before our Lord returns in power and glory to receive His church, every case will have been decided, for He brings His rewards with Him, to give to "every man according as his work shall be" (Revelation 22:12). Before He comes as King, He terminates His work as Priest as He pronounces eternal sentence on the whole human race in these words: "He that is unjust, let him be unjust still: and he which is filthy, let him be filthy still: and he that is righteous, let him be righteous still: and he that is holy, let him be holy still" (verse 11).

In every judgment there are three phases: (1) the investigation of the evidence, (2) the decision and pronouncement of sentence, and (3) the execution of the sentence. In the great assize in heaven these same three phases are evident. The execution of the sentence is not the whole judgment. Before that can be carried into effect there must be the pronouncement of the sentence. Before that there must be an examination, or investigation, of every case. This takes place not because God needs the evidence, for He is God and knows all things, but that the whole universe may know the justice of the sentence and God's name may be vindicated.

The apostle Paul says, "For we must all appear before the judgment seat of Christ" (2 Corinthians 5:10). He furthermore declares that Christ shall judge the secrets of men. (See Romans 2:16.) And again: God "hath appointed a day, in the which he will judge the world in righteousness by that man whom he hath ordained." And the appointment of the ordained Man is assured by the fact that "he hath raised him from the dead" (Acts 17:31). This Man, who can be no other than Christ Himself, declares, "The Father judgeth no man, but hath committed all judgment unto the Son." "And hath given him authority to execute judgment also, because he is the Son of man" (John 5:22, 27).

These words of Jesus emphasize two of the phases of the judgment, namely, that which brings into review the record of every life, and second, that which follows when the sentence of judgment is carried into effect. Note these strong statements by Ellen White:

Christ has been made our Judge. The Father is not the Judge. The angels are not. He who took humanity upon Himself, and in this world lived a perfect life, is to judge us. He only can be our Judge. Will you remember this, brethren? Will you remember it, ministers? Will you remember it, fathers and mothers? Christ took humanity that He might be our Judge (*Testimonies for the Church,* vol. 9, page 185).

He who has given the light, He who has followed the soul with tenderest entreaty, seeking to win it from sin to holiness, is in one its advocate and judge. . . . It is He who has encountered the deceiver, and who through all the ages has been seeking to wrest the captives from his grasp, who will pass judgment upon every soul (*The Desire of Ages,* page 210).

Christ Himself will decide who are worthy to dwell with the family of heaven. He will judge every man according to his words and his works (*Christ's Object Lessons,* page 74).

The Ancient of Days is God the Father. . . . It is He, the source of all being, and the fountain of all law, that is to *preside* in the judgment. . . . Attended by heavenly angels, our great High Priest enters the holy of holies, and there appears in the presence of God, to engage in the last acts of His ministration in behalf of man,—to *perform* the work of investigative judgment (*The Great Controversy,* pages 479, 480, emphasis supplied).

Why is Christ our appointed Judge? We quote His own words: "Because he is the Son of man" (John 5:27).

Because He has tasted the very dregs of human affliction and temptation, and understands the frailties and sins of men; because in our behalf He has victoriously withstood the temptations of Satan, and will deal justly and tenderly with the souls that His own blood has been poured out to save,—because of this, the Son of man is appointed to execute the judgment (*The Desire of Ages,* page 210).

God designed that the Prince of sufferers in humanity should be judge of the whole world. He who came from the heavenly courts to save man from eternal death; . . . He who submitted to be arraigned before an earthly tribunal, and who suffered the ignominious death of the cross,—He alone is to pronounce the sentence of reward or punishment. . . .

Both saints and sinners will recognize in Him who was crucified the Judge of all living (*The Review and Herald*, November 22, 1898).

To Jesus the Son of man is committed all judgment. From His decision there is no appeal. . . . He will pronounce judgment, rendering to every man according to his works (*Manuscript 42*, 1901).

Among ancient Israel's annual feasts, two were particularly important: the Passover and the Day of Atonement. The first came in the spring; the second in the autumn. These represented vital phases in the work of Christ. Paul says, "Christ our Passover is sacrificed for us" (1 Corinthians 5:7). He rose from the tomb to become our High Priest in heaven, where He ministers the virtues of His sacrifice, making effective by His Spirit *in* us what He did *for* us on the cross. That ministry reaches its climax in a work of judgment. This was prefigured by the services of the great Day of Atonement. Coming just at the time of harvest, it typified the great pre-Advent judgment in heaven just before our Lord comes to reap the harvest of the earth. We are now living in the antitypical day of atonement when our Lord climaxes His intercessory ministry in heaven.

With these thoughts as a background, let us visualize the scene in heaven as it is outlined in Revelation chapters 4 and 5.

The Ancient of Days, seated upon the rainbow-encircled throne, is presiding over that mighty assembly. The majesty of that scene is beyond words. Close to the great throne are four living ones, and around them are the four and twenty elders, occupying seats or lesser thrones. In the hand of the Almighty is a book. It is written on the inside and also on "the backside" (Revelation 5:1), or the outside. A mighty angel steps forward and challenges the universe. "Who is worthy to open the book," he cries, "and to loose the seals thereof?" (verse 2).

In the light of what we have already noticed concerning lost inheritances, such an announcement has tremendous significance, for the destiny of this lost world seems to hang in the balance. All heaven is silent. Will no one reach forth and take the book? The suspense is awful. John's tender heart is moved to tears. He weeps, but not because he is impatient to see inside the book. His tears are not those of disappointed curiosity. This disciplined and saintly soldier of the cross knows the significance of that sealed book. If no one is found worthy to open the book and to break its binding seals, then all the promises of the prophets, all the hopes of the suffering people of God, all the messages of apostles and evangelists, have been in vain. If no *goel* appears, then the purchased possession must go by default. The sons of the lost race can never inhabit the earth. The thought is overwhelming.

Then one of the elders comes and speaks to the prophet. He says, "Weep not: behold, the Lion of the tribe of Juda, . . . hath prevailed to open the book, and to loose the seven seals" (verse 5). Drying his eyes, he looks, and lo! in the midst of the throne area is a Lamb, but not in unblemished beauty and innocence; it is as if in the very act of being slain. The Lamb reaches forth and takes the book from the hand of Him who sits upon the throne. As He does, a thrill of joy sweeps through the whole universe, and the heavenly host bursts forth into praise. There stands the *Goel*. A Redeemer has been found; the redemption of the purchased possession is assured.

As the Lamb steps forth to lift the title deeds of the alienated inheritance, the prophet notices some prominent features. He is a Lamb, but at the same time He is a Lion-Lamb. Thus the sacrificial virtue is prominent. But He has seven horns. These denote His strength. His eyes emphasize intelligence and wisdom. Seven being the number of perfection, He is therefore the symbol of perfect strength and perfect wisdom. Twenty-eight times in this book He is called the Lamb. But the symbols in this scene link with other prophetic utterances.

Habakkuk describes Him as having "horns coming out of his hand," or "bright beams out of his side" (Habakkuk 3:4). He was wounded in His feet that He might atone for sins of walking; He was wounded in His hands that He might atone for sins of actions; He was wounded in His head that He might atone for sins of thought; and in His side that He might atone for sins of unholy affection.

His hands alone are worthy to break the binding seals of that book. The destiny of men and nations is in the nail-pierced hands of the Lamb that was slain. Moreover, every revelation we get of God comes to us through the Man of the cross. All we know of the future comes to us through Him who loved us and gave Himself for us.

> The Jewish leaders made their choice. Their decision [to reject Christ] was registered in the book which John saw in the hand of Him that sat upon the throne, the book which no man could open. In all its vindictiveness this decision will appear before them in the day when this book is unsealed by the Lion of the tribe of Judah (Ellen White, *Christ's Object Lessons,* page 294).

THE NEW SONG BEFORE THE THRONE, REVELATION 5:9–13

As the Lamb takes the book, the living ones and the elders in adoration and praise raise the anthem, "Worthy is the Lamb that was slain" (Revelation 5:12). In Revelation 4:8–11 a similar song was heard, but it was praise to Him who, as Creator of all things, is seated upon the throne. But in chapter 5 we hear the same group of heavenly beings singing "a new song" (verse 9). It, too, is a song of praise, but it is addressed especially to the Lamb as He lifts the book from the hand of the Almighty. They sense what this means. The centuries of sorrow are about to come to an end, for He who has paid the purchase price—the heavenly *Goel*—is now entering upon the final phase of His mediation for lost men and women; the judgment is about to begin.

"Worthy is the Lamb that was slain," "and hast redeemed us to God by thy blood" (verses 12, 9), is the anthem that bursts from redeemed lips. But something else arrests our attention—the four and twenty elders are seen with golden bowls full of incense "which are the prayers of saints" (verse 8). Why this reference here to prayers? Could it be that the great prayer of all the saints of all ages is about to be answered? Since Adam fell, the cry of centuries has been, "Thy kingdom come." Persecuted prophets, suffering saints, and martyrs without number have prayed and longed for this day. Through all the long and tragic night of sin, when men and women sealed their testimony in the blood, a great chorus of prayer has come up before God. Not one prayer has been lost. All have been carefully treasured, as it were, in these golden bowls.

"The revenue of glory has been accumulating for this closing work of the third angel's message. The prayers that have been accumulating for the fulfillment of the promise, the descent of the Holy Spirit, not one has been lost. Each prayer has been accumulating ready to overflow all over the world" (Ellen White, *Letter 96A,* 1899).

While the elders lead the song of praise, it does not stop there; its theme is caught by the innumerable company of angels. Then it sweeps out into the periphery of God's mighty creation. Far off in the depths of space the prophet hears the same sound of praise. Wider and wider it spreads until it reaches every creature in God's mighty creation, in earth, and on and on through the limitless expanse of the universe, until it reaches the proportions of epic song. The whole universe is exclaiming in one rapturous song, "Blessing, and honour, and glory, and power, be unto him that sitteth upon the throne, and unto the Lamb for ever and ever" (verse 13).

"We shall reign on the earth" (verse 10), sing the elders in triumph. They are not on the earth now, nor will they always be in heaven. The earth is their home, and if faithful, we with them shall reign on the earth made new. This is prefigured in the marvelous setting of this great assembly. What majesty! What glory is there! Daniel, describing this, says, "His throne was like the fiery flame, and his wheels as burning fire. A fiery stream issued and came forth from before him: thousand thousands ministered unto him, and ten thousand times ten thousand stood before him: the judgment was set, and the books were opened" (Daniel 7:9, 10).

But the prophet John, guided by the Spirit of God, describes the scene in greater detail. The old apostle is invited to join the company of the angelic host. He takes his place beside the living ones and the elders, and from that place of vantage he begins to watch as each event moves forward in a mighty panorama. This great scene is without parallel in all the Scriptures. It is the opening of the judgment, culminating in the Second Advent.

As we close this first of the thrilling scenes of the Revelation, let us with the triumphant saints unite our voices in thanksgiving to God for the hope that is ours, that throughout eternal ages it will be our privilege to sing of the Lamb and His sacrifice. Our constant song will be of Him who, having conquered death, has redeemed us to God by His blood. But if we would join in that eternal anthem of praise in the hereafter, we must catch the echo of it now, as we cry with angels and redeemed men—

"WORTHY IS THE LAMB THAT WAS SLAIN."

26. The Apocalyptic Horsemen

Probably no symbolic prophecy has received more comment than has this dramatic prophecy of the horsemen. As far back as the third century A.D., persecuted Christians were drawing much comfort and inspiration from this chapter. It was impossible, however, for this book to be fully understood until the unfolding of events. Nevertheless, Victorinus, who was martyred in A.D. 303 under the Diocletian persecutions, wrote a complete commentary on Revelation. This commentary still exists, and the fundamental principle of repetition which he emphasizes is vital. The prophecies of the Revelation are not successive; they are repetitive. That is, they double back, covering the same periods of time. For example, the seven seals and the seven trumpets cover the same period as do the seven churches. Naturally, there were many things that Victorinus could not know in his day, for the events portrayed had not taken place.

Another important principle in prophetic interpretation, and one that was emphasized by our Lord, is that only when prophecy is meeting its fulfillment can it be fully understood. Three times Jesus said this in the upper room: "And now I have told you before it come to pass, that, when it is come to pass, ye might believe" (John 14:29; 13:19; 16:4). The purpose of prophecy is not to make us experts in prognostication, but rather to make us humble in the presence of God, realizing that only He knows the end from the beginning. It is both interesting and inspiring to note in the study of church history that when a prophecy was being fulfilled, there were always some who recognized it. In fact, nothing is more rewarding in such study than the discovery that whenever God's great clock indicated the time had arrived when some important prophecy was about to be fulfilled, His messengers were there, ready at the risk of their lives, if need be, to herald that message. Unfulfilled prophecy, however, has ever been a fruitful field for speculation, and all too often those who are unwise and frequently uninformed have ventured into this realm. When their prognostications have not come to pass, the enemies of God's Word have found cause to ridicule and denounce the whole field of prophetic interpretation. This prophecy that we are about to study has suffered much from wild and extravagant interpretations. But it is one of the most enlightening and comforting of all the prophecies in the Word of God. Revelation 6 should be studied in the setting of chapters 4 and 5. Only then can we catch its true significance.

Let us visualize John standing in the midst of the angels and the elders and witnessing the procedure of the greatest tribunal ever held. The cases of all professed children of God are being weighed. Each is being studied in the light of the environment in which he lived. So in that great heavenly court is made to appear the history of the ages. The books are opened, and with them another book is opened, which is the book of life. The judgment is mentioned more than a thousand times in Scripture, but it is left to Daniel and John to bring us the setting.

Says the prophet Daniel, "The judgment was set, and the books were opened" (Daniel 7:10). The revelator, describing the same scene, adds, "Another book was opened, which is the book of life: and the dead were judged out of those things which were written in the books, according to their works" (Revelation 20:12). (It is significant that these two expressions are associated with the same scene. That book of life is opened again at the end of the millennium, as is revealed in Revelation 20:12.)

The book of life contains the names of all who have ever entered the service of God. Jesus bade His disciples, "Rejoice, because your names are written in heaven" (Luke 10:20). Paul speaks of his faithful fellow workers, "whose names are in the book of life" (Philippians 4:3). Daniel, looking down to "a time of trouble, such as never was," declares that God's people shall be delivered, "every one that shall be found written in the book" (Daniel 12:1). And the revelator says that those only shall enter the City of God whose names "are written in the Lamb's book of life" (Revelation 21:27).

"A book of remembrance" is written before God, in which are recorded the good deeds of "them that feared the Lord, and that thought upon his name." Their words of faith, their acts of love, are registered in heaven. Nehemiah refers to this when he says, "Remember me, O my God, . . . and wipe not out my good deeds that I have done for the house of my God." In the book of God's remembrance every deed of righteousness is immortalized. There every temptation resisted, every evil overcome, every word of tender pity expressed, is faithfully chronicled. And every act of sacrifice, every suffering and sorrow endured for Christ's sake, is recorded. Says the psalmist, "Thou tellest my wanderings: put thou my tears in thy bottle: are they not in thy book?" (Ellen White, *The Great Controversy*, pages 480, 481).

How comforting it is to know that when our cases come up in review before God, our joys, our sorrows, our environment, the conditions under which each child of God has lived, will be taken into account. All is known to Him. "Shall not the Judge of all the earth do right?" asked Abraham (Genesis 18:25). The psalmist expresses it even more emphatically when he says, "The LORD shall count, when he writeth up the people, that this man was born there" (Psalm 87:4–6).

When our High Priest, the heavenly *Goel,* the Lion of the tribe of Judah and the Lamb of God, breaks the seals and opens the books, the panorama of the ages is unfolded before the great tribunal. Let us then reverently take our places beside the astonished prophet and watch as the Lamb of God unrolls the scroll.

THE OPENING OF THE SEALS

As each seal opens, one of the "living creatures," or "living ones," cries with a voice like thunder, "Come" (Revelation 6:1, 3, etc.). The words "and see" are omitted from many of the ancient manuscripts. Actually it is more a command directed to the contents of the seal than it is an invitation for the prophet to observe. Each particular period of church history is compressed into one great symbol, and, obedient to the authoritative command, the symbolic horses in a moving panorama gallop forth with their riders.

First seal—a white horse, symbol of purity and victory. The rider is crowned, and, bearing a bow, He goes forth conquering and to conquer, a beautiful symbol of the triumphs of the gospel in the first century of the Christian dispensation. It fulfills such prophecies as Habakkuk 3:8, 9: "Thou didst ride upon thine horses and thy chariots of salvation? Thy bow was made quite naked." And Psalm 64:7–9: "But God shall shoot at them with an arrow; suddenly shall they be wounded. . . . And all men shall fear, and shall declare the work of God; for they shall wisely consider of his doing."

Whatever spiritual lessons we may gather from this prophecy, the historic interpretation since as far back as the third century has been that these symbols picture in graphic language the decline of the spiritual life of the church.

Victorinus, that early commentator to whom we have already referred, interprets the going forth of the white horse under the first seal as the victories of the gospel over paganism in the first century.

> "After the Lord ascended into heaven and opened all things, He sent the Holy Spirit, whose words the preachers sent forth as arrows reaching the human heart, that they might overcome unbelief. . . . Therefore the white horse is the word of preaching with the Holy Spirit sent into the world" (*Victorinus's Commentary,* quoted by L. E. Froom, *Prophetic Faith of Our Fathers,* vol. 1, page 339).

In Psalm 45:5 we learn that the wounds inflicted by the arrows of the archer are emblematical of the conquests of Messiah. "The symbol of a spiritual or heavenly warrior . . . denotes the host of the Lord, i.e., His church militant, shining with its primitive purity and going forth in a career of victory" (William Cuninghame, *A Dissertation on the Seals and Trumpets of the Apocalypse,* fourth edition, page 4).

In Edward Gibbon's *History of the Decline and Fall of the Roman Empire,* chapter 15, paragraph 54, we read, "The progress of Christianity was not confined to the Roman Empire," but "the new religion, within a century after the death of its divine Author, had already visited every part of the globe." As to numbers, the same historian declared that the Christian congregation in the city of Rome numbered not less than fifty thousand, and that of Antioch one hundred thousand, or one-fifth of the population. The Christian population within the empire alone was estimated at five million. Paul, writing to the church in Rome, said: "I thank my God . . . that your faith is spoken of throughout the whole world" (Romans 1:8). And to the Colossians he wrote that the gospel of which he was a minister was being "preached to every creature which is under heaven" (Colossians 1:23).

Second seal—a red horse, symbol of war and bloodshed. The contrast in color is significant. The "mystery of iniquity" was already beginning to work. The church was "falling away." (See 2 Thessalonians 2:2–7.) Paul's predictions were being rapidly fulfilled. (See Acts 20:28–30.)

> The fiery color of the second horse . . . and of the dreadful weapon with which he was armed, indicate to us, that, after the first and purest age of Christianity, the spirit of love and peace should recede from the visible church, and be succeeded by a spirit of discord, or dissension and controversy, a fierce and fiery zeal, instigating Christians to destroy one another. The ecclesiastical history of the fourth and fifth centuries, sufficiently evinces, that such a change did take place (William Cuninghame, *A Dissertation on the Seals and Trumpets of the Apocalypse,* fourth edition, page 5).

> The enmity of the Christians towards each other surpassed the fury of savage beasts against man; and Gregory of Nazianzen most pathetically laments that the kingdom of heaven was converted by discord into the image of chaos, of a nocturnal tempest, and of hell itself (Edward Gibbon, *History of the Decline and Fall of the Roman Empire,* chapter 21, paragraph 40).

"The fruit of righteousness is sown in peace of them that make peace" (James 3:18). But in the period denoted by the red horse, peace was taken from the earth. This corresponds with the church of Smyrna, the period of pagan persecution. How tragic that the body of believers, so pure in their faith and so filled with love for each other, should, within a century and a half, have become so contaminated by worldly ambition and competition that their condition could be symbolized by this fiery red horse! How sin and self blunt our spiritual senses!

Third seal—a black horse, symbol of subjection. The work of corruption truly progresses fast. How the church has fallen from her high estate! Beginning in purity and power, the church became corrupted and is now in subjection to the powers of darkness. Commercialism replaces her piety. Black, the symbol of evil, error, defeat, and moral and spiritual darkness, has replaced the purity with which she began her conquests.

As the stream of Christianity flowed farther from its fountain, it became more and more corrupt, and as the centuries advanced, superstition advanced with them; and . . . tales of purgatory, and pious frauds, and the worship of saints, relics, and images, took the place of pure and simple Christianity: till at length, the Book of God being laid aside for legendary tales, and "the traditions of men," all these corruptions were collected into a regular system of superstition and oppression (J. D. Woodhouse, *The Apocalypse,* page 146).

An enormous train of different superstitions were gradually substituted in the place of true religion and genuine piety. This odious revolution was owing to a variety of causes. . . . A preposterous desire of imitating the pagan rites, and of blending them with the Christian worship, and that idle propensity which the generality of mankind have toward a gaudy and ostentatious religion, all contributed to establish the reign of superstition upon the ruins of Christianity (J. L. Mosheim, *Institutes of Ecclesiastical History,* bk. 2, cent. 4, pt. 2, ch. 3).

Gibbon ironically declares that paganism disappeared only to emerge again in the church. Christianity conquered Rome, but Rome also conquered Christianity. Superstition abounded, and ceremonies multiplied.

Quantities of dust and earth, brought from Palestine and other places remarkable for their supposed sanctity, were handed about as the most wonderful remedies against the violence of wicked spirits and were sold and bought everywhere at enormous prices. The public processions and supplications by which the pagans endeavored to appease their gods were now adopted into the Christian worship and celebrated in many places with great pomp and magnificence (ibid.).

THE BALANCES, OR THE YOKE, IN THE RIDER'S HAND

The balances denoted that religion and civil power would be united in the person who would administer the executive power in the government, and that he would claim the judicial authority both in church and state. This was true among the Roman emperors from the days of Constantine until the reign of Justinian, when he gave the same judicial power to the bishop of Rome (William Miller, *Evidence From Scripture and History of the Second Coming of Christ,* page 176).

THE WHEAT AND BARLEY

A spiritual dearth marked the experience of the church during these centuries. A measure *(choenix)* of wheat was less than a quart. This was considered a scanty allowance for a soldier. In ordinary times, a penny would buy twenty-four measures of barley, but here only three—the amount allotted to a slave. Barley was eaten only by the poorest. It was considered a much cheaper grade of food than wheat.

A denarius [penny] was the ordinary wages for a full day's labor. And when a *choenix* of wheat costs a *denarius,* it is as much as a man can do to earn the bread he himself consumes, leaving nothing for his family or for his other wants. . . . The arrival of things at such a pass, accordingly argues a severity of hard times, distress, and want, almost beyond the power of imagination to depict (J. A. Seiss, *The Apocalypse,* vol.1, pages 333, 334).

During this period of spiritual famine, a cheaper grade of spiritual food was being offered to the people, and they could receive only the smallest amount of the Word of God. Tradition and the teachings of the Catholic fathers were being taught rather than the pure doctrines of Christ. This corrupted religion was being sold or bartered as a commodity. But pure religion cannot be purchased either by pence or penance. The Lord's invitation is, "Come ye, buy, and eat; yea, come, buy wine and milk without money and without price" (Isaiah 55:1). The foundations for the whole system of apostate Christianity were laid during this period.

Fourth seal—a pale horse, symbol of death. When a plant is shut away from the sun, it loses its color; it turns pale green. So, the church having departed from the apostolic faith, it was scarcely possible for the rays of the Sun of Righteousness to penetrate the spiritual darkness of those days. Those who should have been the ministers of life became actually the ministers of death. Controlled by the instigator of death, the devil (see Hebrews 2:14), these ministers of death slew men and women by hunger, sword, and the beasts of the earth.

> The pale livid green color of this horse is emblematical of a state of things even more dreadful than that of the preceding seal. The character of his rider corresponds with this idea; his name is called Death, the king of terrors. He is followed by Hell. . . . The whole assemblage of figures constitutes an hieroglyphical representation of the most horrible and terrific nature, and points out to us a period when the rulers of the visible church should seem to lose the character of men, and to assume that of malignant demons and savage beasts, and of Death himself; and should extirpate, by fire and sword, all who dared to prefer death to the sacrifice of a good conscience. This seal evidently represents the state of the church during those ages, when the flames of persecution were kindled by the papal power (William Cuninghame, *A Dissertation on the Seals and Trumpets of the Apocalypse,* page 10).

Millions were martyred for their faith during these dark centuries. J. A. Wylie stated it well when he said, "The noon of the papacy was the midnight of the world" (*The History of Protestantism,* vol. 1, page 16).

H. G. Wells described the papacy as an attempt at world dominion through religion. What Alexander, Caesar, and others had tried to do, but failed, this politico-religious power seemed determined to accomplish. The persecutions of this power are found in other prophecies: Daniel 7:21, 25; 11:33; Matthew 24:21, 22; Revelation 13:7; 12:6, 14; 17:6. During this period, the "two witnesses" had to do their work clothed in sackcloth. (See Revelation 11:1–3.) But God has a record of every suffering saint, and the martyrs will have a special place of honor in the coming kingdom of glory. (See Revelation 7:13–17; 20:4.)

Fifth seal—souls under the altar. As the prophet witnessed the unfolding of events, he heard voices from under the altar crying for justice. In the Mosaic sanctuary there were two altars—the altar of incense inside, and the altar of burnt offerings outside, in the court. The sacrifices were offered outside the sanctuary, the blood being poured out at the base of the altar of burnt offering. When the fifth seal was opened, John saw the martyrs of Jesus "under the altar" (Revelation 6:9), or "at the foot of the altar" (Weymouth). Their blood had been shed in the cause of Christ, and came up, as it were, in a chorus crying, "How long, O Lord, how long?" (See verse 10.)

No more dramatic picture could be given of the Reformation, which burst upon the world with a call to return to "the Bible and the Bible only" as the textbook of belief. It was a cry to God for spiritual power, and like the blood of Abel, which cried unto God for vengeance (see Genesis 4:10), there rose a great appeal for vindication of the truth for which the martyrs had died. "The souls are represented under the altar, just as victims slain upon it would pour out their blood beneath it, and fall by its side" (Uriah Smith, *The Prophecies of Daniel and the Revelation,* page 433). Albert Barnes, the noted Presbyterian commentator, tells us, "We are not to suppose that this literally occurred, and that John actually saw the souls of the martyrs beneath the altars—for the whole representation is symbolical" (*Notes on the New Testament,* vol. 9, [Book of Revelation], page 171).

John was beholding the unfolding of the panorama of the ages. This was another cycle of history.

The white robes are a symbol of the righteousness of Christ. (See Revelation 19:8.) Those who come out of great tribulation receive white robes. (See Revelation 7:13, 14.) They include a multitude that no man can number. (See verse 9.) Only overcomers are clothed in white raiment. (See Revelation 3:5.) This is the wedding garment (see Matthew 22:11, 12) of which Christ spoke in the parable. In the great judgment scene in heaven, when individual cases come before God for review, each is considered in the light of heredity, opportunity, and environment. (See Psalm 87:6; Luke 10:10–12.) And rewards will be given to each according to his faith and works under the environment in which he lived.

When Sir Samuel Morland, sent by Cromwell to investigate the papal massacre of the Waldenses, returned from the Piedmont Alps with the tragic story, the blind poet John Milton, secretary of state under Cromwell, expressed the revulsion of the civilized world in his immortal sonnet:

> Avenge, O Lord, Thy slaughtered saints, whose bones
> Lie scattered on the Alpine mountains cold;
> Even them who kept Thy truth so pure of old,
> When all our fathers worshiped stocks and stones,
> Forget not: in Thy book record their groans
> Who were Thy sheep, and in their ancient fold
> Slain by the bloody Piedmontese, that rolled
> Mother with infant down the rocks. Their moans
> The vales redoubled to the hills, and they
> To heaven their martyred blood and ashes sow
> O'er all the Italian fields, where still doth sway
> The triple tyrant; that from these may grow
> A hundredfold, who, having learnt Thy way,
> Early may fly the Babylonian woe.

Sixth seal—signs of the Lord's imminent return. As the sixth seal opens, it is self-evident that the language changes from symbolic to literal. The Old Testament writers and Christ Himself spoke many times of great signs in the physical universe, in the sun, the moon, the stars, and the earth. These would be special indications of the imminence of our Lord's return. The fact that generations of men lived through these events makes it necessary that they come in review before God.

A GREAT EARTHQUAKE

The sixth seal opens with great convulsions of the earth. One of the most extensively felt earthquakes ever recorded occurred November 1, 1755. It is sometimes called the Lisbon earthquake because the greater part of that city was destroyed, with the loss of between sixty thousand and ninety thousand lives. The sea rose to fifty feet above its ordinary level.

248

The great earthquake of [November 1,] 1755, extended over a tract of at least four millions of square miles. . . . It pervaded the greater portion of the continents of Europe, Africa, and America; but its extreme violence was exercised on the southwestern part of the former. . . .

In Africa, this earthquake was felt almost as severely as it had been in Europe. . . . It is probable . . . that all Africa was shaken. . . . At the north, it extended to Norway and Sweden; Germany, Holland, France, Great Britain, and Ireland were all more or less agitated by the same great and terrible commotion of the elements (Robert Sears, *Wonders of the World,* pages 50, 58).

Earthquakes are a sign of our Lord's near return. Devastating quakes have occurred in recent times which have taken a frightful toll of lives: San Francisco, Jamaica, China, Japan, Mexico, Turkey, etc.

THE SUN BLACK; THE MOON AS BLOOD

A few years after the great convulsion of 1755, other signs began to occur in the sun, the moon, and the stars.

Almost, if not altogether alone, as the most mysterious and as yet unexplained phenomenon of its kind, in nature's diversified range of events, . . . stands the dark day of May 19th, 1780,—a most unaccountable darkening of the whole visible heavens and atmosphere in New England (R. M. Devens, *Our First Century,* pages 89, 90).

"The dark day in Northern America was one of those wonderful phenomena of nature which will always be read of with interest, but which philosophy is at a loss to explain" (Sir William Herschel, quoted by R. M. Devens in *Our First Century,* page 90).

"The darkness of the following evening was probably as gross as ever has been observed since the Almighty fiat gave birth to light. . . . I could not help conceiving at the time, that if every luminous body in the universe had been shrouded in impenetrable shade, or struck out of existence, the darkness could not have been more complete. A sheet of white paper held within a few inches of the eyes, was equally invisible with the blackest velvet" (Samuel Tenny of Exeter, New Hampshire, quoted by Uriah Smith in *The Prophecies of Daniel and the Revelation*, page 445).

That the darkness was not caused by an eclipse is manifest by the various positions of the planets of our system at that time; for the moon was more than one hundred fifty degrees from the sun all that day (Dr. Samuel Stearns, *Independent Chronicle*, Boston, June 22, 1780).

The next night the moon appeared blood-red. The exact cause has never been settled. Forest fires seem to offer a paltry explanation, especially in the light of scientific statements that the cause is unknown.

THE FALLING STARS

On the night of November 12–13, 1833, a tempest of falling stars broke over the earth. North America bore the brunt of the pelting. From the Gulf of Mexico to Halifax, until daylight with some difficulty put an end to the display, the sky was scored in every direction with shining tracks and illuminated with majestic fireballs (Agnes M. Clerke, *History of Astronomy in the Nineteenth Century*, page 328).

Probably the most remarkable of all the meteoric showers that have ever occurred was that of the Leonids on [the night following] November 12, 1833. The number at some stations was estimated as high as 200,000 an hour for five or six hours (C. A. Young, *Manual of Astronomy*, page 469).

Another great display of falling stars occurred in the Old World in 1866. While this did not meet the prophetic description so accurately, it was undoubtedly another sign of the Savior's near return.

There were times when it seemed as if a mighty wind had caught the old stars, loosed them from their holding, and swept them across the firmament. . . . A most startling and most awful phenomenon. . . . But science, which dispels so many terrors and proves so many appearances, illusions, and nothing more, does not do so in this instance (*London Times,* November 15 [Thursday], 1866).

The dark day and the falling stars were remarkable signs for that generation. But other things are happening in this generation. A few decades ago science hurled humanity into the atomic age. Human beings have plunged into space. Do these amazing facts have any meaning for us? The Lord's coming will be preceded by signs in heaven and earth.

THE HEAVEN DEPARTED AS A SCROLL

This cannot refer to the celestial heavens, but rather to the atmospheric heavens. The atmosphere, or firmament, is also called "heaven." (See Genesis 1:8.) At the second coming of Christ the atmosphere will pass away, and the mountains and islands will disappear. (See Revelation 6:14; 16:18–20.) Those who have spurned His grace will flee for cover, crying, "Who shall be able to stand?" (Revelation 6:17). Only those whose lives have been sanctified by the truth will stand. (See Ephesians 6:11–17.) They will not fear. (See Psalm 46.) It is significant to realize that our generation finds itself just between verses 13 and 14 of Revelation chapter 6. The signs in the heavens have been fulfilled, and we can look confidently for the coming of our Lord. But the great question is, Who shall be able to stand?

Seventh seal—silence in heaven. The opening of the seventh seal is found in Revelation 8:1—chapter 7 being really a parenthetical chapter. This chapter we will study later. When Jesus returns for His people, every angel in glory will accompany Him. (See Matthew 25:31.) Those heavenly beings whose voices are heard in continual praise will descend with their Commander to bring back the ransomed of the Lord. No wonder heaven is silent, the dwelling place of God hushed because of their absence; the earth is a scene of both victory and tragedy. The righteous and the wicked are then separated. Those who have rejected the grace of God will be unable to withstand the glory that accompanies the Savior when he returns to earth, and they will be destroyed by the brightness of His coming. (See 2 Thessalonians 2:8.) Those whose hearts are perfect toward Him will be changed in a moment (see 1 Corinthians 15:51, 52), and then caught up to meet the Lord in the air (see 1 Thessalonians 4:16, 17). This mighty host is "the righteous nation which keepeth the truth" (Isaiah 26:2), the redeemed of all ages. They ascend together to the City of God. Will you be among them?

This vibrant hymn was written many years ago, but it paints a vivid picture of the power and glory of our Lord's return. The author, an Irish minister, had one passion—to preach Christ and His saving grace. He presented truth with such conviction that the pulpits of the land were later closed to him. Yet the crowds flocked to fields and factories to hear his message. This is one of 765 hymns that he wrote:

> Look, ye saints, the sight is glorious,
>   See the Man of sorrows now;
> From the fight returned victorious,
>   Ev'ry knee to Him shall bow;
> Crown Him, crown Him, crown Him, crown Him,
>   Crowns become the victor's brow.
>
> Sinners in derision crowned Him,
>   Mocking thus the Savior's claim;
> Saints and angels crowd around Him,
>   Own His title, praise His name;
> Crown Him, crown Him, crown Him, crown Him,
>   Spread abroad the victor's fame.
>
> Hark! those bursts of acclamation;
>   Hark! those loud triumphant chords;
> Jesus takes the highest station;
>   Oh, what joy the sight affords!
> Crown Him, crown Him, crown Him, crown Him,
>   King of kings, the Lord of lords.
>   —Thomas Kelly (1769–1854)

27. The Sealed Number and the Innumerable Company

This prophecy is parenthetical. It fits into the picture as describing events that take place between verses 13 and 14 of Revelation chapter 6 just before our Lord returns in glory. When the wicked, those who have rejected salvation, see the cataclysmic events brought to view under the sixth seal, they cry in anguish of soul: "Who shall be able to stand?" (Revelation 6:17). But *some* will stand. These will be the righteous who have prepared themselves to meet the Lord. In confidence they look up into the radiant heavens filled with the angelic host and in praise exclaim, "Lo, this is our God; we have waited for him, and he will save us" (Isaiah 25:9). This is the climax of the ages. And those who live to witness our Savior's glorious appearing will need a special preparation of heart and life.

Angels holding the four winds, Revelation 7:1. Here is a picture of divine interposition. As the judgments of God are about to fall, the Lord reveals that a restraining hand is over the affairs of men. But for this, civilization would destroy itself.

"The four winds" denote the four points of the compass. (See Jeremiah 49:36.) Wind symbolizes war or strife and commotion. (See Daniel 7:2; Jeremiah 25:31–34; 51:1, 2, 11.) The powers of evil, however, are not permitted to do their deadly work until God's people have been sealed for His kingdom. A seal stands for ownership and protection. At the very time all the world is turning away from God, there are faithful ones on whom the Lord can place His seal.

The angel ascending from the east, having the seal. The word *angel,* used symbolically in the Revelation, means "messenger" or "message." This angel, or message, carries the seal of the living God. Some translations of Revelation 7:2 read, "ascending from the sun rising." This is a more true translation. It appears that the *manner,* rather than the *locality,* is emphasized. As the sun arises with its rays at first oblique and comparatively powerless, but increases in strength and glory until it reaches its zenith, so the work of this angel, or message, moves onward with ever increasing influence until its work closes in strength and power, the whole earth being "lightened with his glory" (Revelation 18:1).

In vision the prophet watches the panorama. He sees angels of God holding in check the forces of destruction. At the same time wicked angels are stirring up strife among the nations of the whole world, leading them on to "the battle of that great day of God Almighty" (Revelation 16:14). However, not until God's work is finished in the earth are these powers of darkness permitted full scope.

THE SEALING

"This action of sealing with the seal or signet of God, is equivalent to a declaration that they who are so sealed appertain to God and are distinguished as such from others who do not thus belong to Him, and are assured by Him of His protection against all evil" (Christian Wordsworth, Lectures on the Apocalypse. Quoted by J. A. Seiss in *The Apocalypse,* vol. 1, pages 423, 424).

Paul says, "The foundation of God standeth sure, having this seal, The Lord knoweth them that are his" (2 Timothy 2:19). God is building a noble castle, or a spiritual house, and His people are the living stones that form that house, each stone bearing the seal of His ownership. (See 1 Peter 2:5.) Among the ruins of the ancient city of Babylon are bricks stamped with the name of the builder, King Nebuchadnezzar. So we, by the grace of God, are stones in the house of God, and we bear His name or the mark of His ownership. "This sealing secures the safety of the sealed ones as the judgment of the great day goes over the nations" (J. A. Seiss, *The Apocalypse,* page 424).

A seal is used to render valid or authentic any enactments or laws that a person or power may promulgate. Frequent instances of its use occur in the Scriptures. In 1 Kings 21:8 we read that Jezebel "wrote letters in Ahab's name, and sealed them with his seal." These letters then had all the authority of King Ahab. Again, in Esther 3:12: "In the name of King Ahasuerus was it written, and sealed with the king's ring." So also in Esther 8:8:

"The writing which is written in the king's name, and sealed with the king's ring, may no man reverse" (Uriah Smith, *The Prophecies of Daniel and the Revelation,* page 455).

Through the prophet Isaiah the Lord says: "Seal the law among my disciples" (Isaiah 8:16). When a law is placed on the statute books of the land, it is made valid by the seal of the ruler. And it is God's law that is sealed in the hearts and minds of His people. God's law was written in Christ's heart (see Psalm 40:8), and one of the blessings of the new covenant is, "I will put my laws into their mind, and write them in their hearts" (Hebrews 8:10). Only as God's law is in the heart can one be victorious over sin, which is "the transgression of the law" (1 John 3:4). The Holy Spirit is the power by which we "are sealed unto the day of redemption" (Ephesians 4:30).

Someone tells the story of an old soldier of the czar who was having a bullet removed from his chest. As the surgeon probed about in an effort to find it (there were no X-rays or anesthetics in those days), the patient spoke up and said, "Dig a little deeper, doctor, and there you'll find the image of the emperor." Do our hearts reflect as truly the image of our Master?

A ruler's seal must of necessity contain three things: (1) his name, (2) his office, and (3) the territory over which he has jurisdiction. Thus we should be able to find in God's law His *name,* His *office,* and the *territory* over which He rules. All are found in one commandment only—the fourth. Five of the Ten Commandments mention the Lord, but four of the five do not identify Him. Only the fourth (see Exodus 20:8–11) reveals His identity and His relationship to us as Creator. Note this statement from the fourth commandment: "In six days the LORD made heaven and earth, the sea, and all that in them is" (verse 11). Here God declares Himself as (1) the *Lord*—Jehovah or the eternally existing One, (2) the *Creator*—He made, (3) the *universe*—His territory, heaven and earth, and the sea. As Creator, He has authority to command His creatures, and the fourth commandment, which requires us to "remember the sabbath day, to keep it holy" (verse 8), is the only commandment that emphasizes God as the Creator. No wonder the enemy of God and man attacks this commandment particularly! It is the one commandment of all the ten that men and women are prone to forget. Moreover, this Sabbath commandment is attacked from inside the church as well as from outside it.

Through all the ages the enemy of God has tried to turn the minds of men away from the Creator, but in our generation his attack is more subtle. Through the evolutionary theory, millions have been led to disbelieve the whole story of Creation. In so doing, they are actually rejecting God as both Creator and Redeemer, for only creative power can redeem us. It was the Creator Himself who became man that He might redeem us by His blood. Only as He creates in us a clean heart and renews in us a right spirit (see Psalm 51:10) can we be citizens of His kingdom. But this is as definitely a work of creation as when He spoke worlds into existence. God's special message for this time, the message of the everlasting gospel which announces that the hour of His judgment is come, also calls men and women to "worship him that made heaven, and earth, and the sea, and the fountains of waters" (Revelation 14:7). This is a call to full obedience, and in the hearts of those who heed God's call He writes His law in which is His seal or His name. The wicked, by contrast, have the name or the mark of the beast, written either in their foreheads (symbol of the mind) or in their hands (symbol of service). (See Revelation 13:16.) But the seal of God, or the "Father's name," is found only in the foreheads of the sealed ones. (See Revelation 14:1; 22:4.) It is not received in the hand, because the hand is a symbol of service or works. Works can never be a qualification for the reception of that seal. We are made perfect by grace alone.

TWO GREAT WORLD MOVEMENTS

With the dawn of the nineteenth century two great movements arose: (1) worldwide missionary propaganda (see Revelation 14:6, 7; Matthew 24:14), and (2) worldwide atheistic propaganda (see 2 Peter 3:3–6). The two movements are diametrically opposed. The gospel of Christ is the basis of the first; the evolutionary theory is the basis of the second. The theory of evolution is not new. It was taught more than two thousand years ago. It became the foundation of Greek philosophy, although it was not universally believed. Today, however, it has invaded every field of education and human thought. It claims to explain life and the universe from star dust to the mind of man. Education today is permeated with this "philosophy and vain deceit"—this "science falsely so called" (Colossians 2:8; 1 Timothy 6:20). In speculating on the age of the rocks, many have lost sight of the Rock of Ages.

It is far more than an educational problem, however; it is a challenge to religion. Modern philosophy has tremendously affected the physical, mental, and spiritual outlook of humankind.

EVOLUTION NOT CONFIRMED BY SCIENTIFIC EVIDENCE

Geology does not confirm the evolutionary theory. Even Herbert Spencer, the apostle of this philosophy, declares: "It cannot be concluded with any certainty that formations in which similar organic remains are found were of contemporaneous origin. Nor can it be safely concluded that strata containing different organic remains are of different ages" (quoted from his famous essay "Illogical Geology" in *Illustrations of Universal Progress,* page 340).

Jesus said, "When the Son of man cometh, shall he find faith on the earth?" (Luke 18:8). He will have a faithful, obedient people awaiting His return. John saw these servants of God being gathered out of every nation, kindred, tongue, and people and exclaimed with joy, "Here is the patience of the saints: here are they that keep the commandments of God, and the faith of Jesus" (Revelation 14:12). To have the faith of Jesus means to have His abiding presence in our day-by-day living. Here is a people saved by the grace of Jesus, living by the faith of Jesus, and victorious through the power of Jesus.

THE SEALED COMPANY

The redeemed of the Lord are an innumerable company, but among them is a special group designated as "the 144,000." (See Revelation 7:4.) This number is significant. Twelve is God's kingdom number. In ancient Israel there were twelve tribes, twelve rods, twelve stones gathered from Jordan, twelve precious stones in the high priest's breastplate, etc. In the New Testament there are twelve apostles. Their names are engraved on the twelve foundations of the wall of the New Jerusalem. The names of the twelve tribes are engraved on the twelve gates of the city. This number twelve is mentioned seven times in the Revelation. The circumference of the city is twelve thousand furlongs.

Now 144,000 is the square of twelve, multiplied by a thousand. This company is mentioned again in Revelation 14:1. In these chapters are found many metaphorical passages, and we may lose the beauty in this symbol by insisting on making this a literal number. The number signifies completeness. E. W. Bullinger declares, "This number is found in all that has to do with rule. The sun which 'rules' the day, and the moon and the stars which 'govern' the night, do so by their passage through the twelve signs of the zodiac, which completes the great circle of the heavens of 360 (12 × 30) degrees or divisions, and thus govern the year" (*Number in Scripture,* page 252).

WHO ARE THE SEALED ONES?

The word *Israel* means "God ruled" and designates an overcomer. (See Psalm 73:1.) Jacob received the name "Israel" after he had wrestled with the angel. God said, "As a prince hast thou power with God and with men, and hast prevailed" (Genesis 32:28). Only those who have overcome are the true Israel of God. (See Romans 2:28, 29; 9:6; Galatians 3:29; 6:15, 16.)

These tribes from which the 144,000 come cannot be the literal tribes of Jacob, because two of the original tribes—Ephraim and Dan—are not even named. Both were leaders in idolatry. The tribe of Ephraim was proud and haughty, while Dan was "a serpent by the way, an adder in the path, that biteth the horse heels, so that his rider shall fall backward" (Genesis 49:17). Pride, criticism, and idolatry will have no place in the kingdom of God.

Those only who are victorious over sin receive the seal of God. (See Revelation 7:2–4.) They are victorious over the beast and his image. (See Revelation 15:2.) They are the first fruits, first in quality, among the redeemed. (See Revelation 14:3, 4.) They stand with the Lamb on heavenly Mount Zion. (See verse 1.) They sing a song no one else can learn. (See verse 3.) They have no guile and are without fault before the throne. (See verse 5.) They follow the Lamb whithersoever He goes. (See verse 4.)

THE INNUMERABLE COMPANY, REVELATION 7:9–17

The expression "after this" (Revelation 7:9) applies naturally to a scene following the sealing of the special company. The prophet saw "a great multitude, which no man could number," gathered from "all nations." While this seems to indicate a different group from the 144,000, yet they may well be included in the great multitude, for this innumerable company "came out of great tribulation" (verse 14). Daniel speaks of "a time of trouble, such as never was" (Daniel 12:1) during which God's people will be preserved. That time of trouble will burst upon the unready world as Christ finishes His work of intercession and judgment.

> When He [Christ] leaves the sanctuary, darkness covers the inhabitants of the earth. In that fearful time the righteous must live in the sight of a holy God without an intercessor. The restraint which has been upon the wicked is removed, and Satan has entire control of the finally impenitent. God's long-suffering has ended. The world has rejected His mercy, despised His love, and trampled upon His law. The wicked have passed the boundary of their probation; the Spirit of God, persistently resisted, has been at last withdrawn. Unsheltered by divine grace, they have no protection from the wicked one. Satan will then plunge the inhabitants of the earth into one great, final trouble. As the angels of God cease to hold in check the fierce winds of human passion, all the elements of strife will be let loose. The whole world will be involved in ruin more terrible than that which came upon Jerusalem of old (Ellen White, *The Great Controversy,* page 614).

"They shall hunger no more" (Revelation 7:16). Evidently these have passed through the seven last plagues and have known what it is to be hungry and thirsty and to have the discomfort of the sun when it scorches the wicked. (See Revelation 16:8.) But through all these plagues and convulsions of nature they have been protected. Now they are beyond the need of protection, and, wearing the robes of victors, "they . . . follow the Lamb whithersoever he goeth" (Revelation 14:4; 7:17).

When God's work of salvation is complete, what a wonderful testimony it will bear to His love and grace! Even now, scattered among all people, there are those who are endeavoring to serve God. They are living up to all the light they have, and although they are amid darkness, the Lord knows them, and in the great crisis just ahead they will stand firmly for the living God and His truth.

> Among earth's inhabitants, scattered in every land, there are those who have not bowed the knee to Baal. Like the stars of heaven, which appear only at night, these faithful ones will shine forth when darkness covers the earth and gross darkness the people. In heathen Africa, in the Catholic lands of Europe and of South America, in China, in India, in the islands of the sea, and in all the dark corners of the earth, God has in reserve a firmament of chosen ones that will yet shine forth amidst the darkness, revealing clearly to an apostate world the transforming power of obedience to His law. . . . The darker the night, the more brilliantly will they shine.
>
> What strange work Elijah would have done in numbering Israel at the time when God's judgments were falling upon the backsliding people! He could count only one on the Lord's side. . . . The word of the Lord surprised him, "Yet I have left me seven thousand in Israel, all the knees which have not bowed unto Baal" (Ellen White, *Prophets and Kings*, pages 188, 189).

Elijah was worried about the spiritual conditions of his day. It seemed that he was the only one left who was serving Jehovah. But God declared that things were seven thousand times better than he thought. God has many of His children scattered around the world. They are found in all the churches and even outside the churches. His sealing message is speeding to every land, gathering those whose hearts are perfect toward Him. Clad in white robes and arrayed in the righteousness of Christ, they stand at last a victorious host, saved by divine grace. Of them we read, "They shall hunger no more, neither thirst any more. . . . For the Lamb which is in the midst of the throne shall feed them, and shall lead them unto living fountains of waters: and God shall wipe away all tears from their eyes" (Revelation 7:16, 17).

Everyone of us can be among that group. The call is wide as the world. "Whosever will" may come (Revelation 22:17).

28. History's Pageant of Conquest and Defeat

Having witnessed some of the fast-moving scenes connected with the climax of history, the prophet suddenly breaks off and speaks of a strange and awesome silence. It is like a hush before a storm, or a tension before great armies are launched in battle. What means this silence? And what about the angel who offers incense upon the golden altar before the throne? In the priestly services of ancient Israel we find the answers.

Could we be transported back to the Mosaic sanctuary we would see the daily sacrifice carried out by the priests. Every day one of them took fire from the altar and, filling a censer, burned the incense. As the fragrance permeated the camp it was in reality a call to prayer. But on one particular day of the year—the great Day of Atonement—the work was performed by the high priest alone. While he was offering the incense upon the altar, the congregation outside the sanctuary was engaged in solemn, soul-searching prayer. The high priest then would fill a censer, and after offering "much incense," he would solemnly enter the Most Holy Place and, pausing before the sacred ark in which rested the Ten Commandments, he would sprinkle the mercy seat seven times with blood in a ceremonial cleansing. On this important day, Moses said, the whole congregation and the sanctuary itself must "be clean from all your sins before the Lord" (Leviticus 16:30).

The Day of Atonement was also known as the day of expiation or judgment, for on that day all the confessed sins of Israel were ceremonially removed. To complete the day's services, the scapegoat, defiled by those sins and acting as a vehicle for their removal, was led out into the wilderness. Several outstanding students and Bible commentators have noted the similarity of expression in this ancient service and the description here in Revelation 8:1–5. To mention just one, Sir Isaac Newton says that these events do not belong in the days when John wrote but are a prophecy relating to the very closing days of human history. With this we heartily agree, for the services of the Mosaic ritual were but a foreshadowing of a greater service carried on by Christ, our antitypical High Priest, in a greater sanctuary, not on earth, but in heaven.

In ancient Israel the religious year began in the ceremonial Passover Feast and the offering of the wave sheaf, and the Feast of First Fruits, or Pentecost. These typified our Lord's death, His resurrection, and the outpouring of the Holy Spirit. In the autumn came the Feast of Trumpets, the Day of Atonement, the Feast of Tabernacles, and, every fifty years, the jubilee. These foreshadowed events connected with the climaxing of our Lord's high-priestly ministry and His return in glory. The Day of Atonement in ancient Israel was of particular significance, for it represented the pre-Advent judgment when the cases of all human beings will be settled for eternity.

From the study of related prophecies we are confident that we are now living in the antitypical day of atonement, or day of judgment. The attitude of God's ancient people as they searched their souls and confessed their sins should be the attitude of His people today. If the typical Day of Atonement, or judgment, was important to them, how much more is the antitypical day of judgment for us? So long as the high priest was performing his work of intercession in the sanctuary of old, the opportunity of getting right with God was theirs. But when the high priest came out of the sanctuary it was too late to make confession. Those refusing to confess were banished from the congregation.

We learn much from that typology, for Jesus Christ, our heavenly High Priest, is still making intercession for us in the heavenly sanctuary. How wonderful to know He can be touched with the feelings of our infirmities. He is neither deaf nor indifferent. Our prayers come up before Him as sweet incense, and He delights to take our poor praises and petitions and mingle them with His spotless righteousness that they may be acceptable at the throne of grace.

No matter what the conditions in our world—war, calamity, or spiritual declension—the child of God can still have fellowship with Him in prayer. The great pre-Advent judgment where our Lord is both Advocate and Judge is now in session. But soon it will close, and just as ancient Israel's priest came out of the earthly sanctuary on the typical Day of Atonement, or day of expiation, so will our great High Priest during this antitypical day of atonement conclude His work of ministry. Then, summoning every angel in glory, He will descend the flaming skies as King of kings and Lord of lords. All these great truths are implied in John's description in the first five verses of chapter 8.

They actually belong to the preceding prophecy. The division of the Bible into chapters and verses was to help the reader in locating Scripture references and was the work of later scholars. The divisions are, therefore, not part of the inspired writing, and sometimes they come in unfortunate places. This is one of them, for it is self-evident that these opening verses belong to the preceding chapter.

Now we come to the great prophecy of the seven trumpets, one of the most arresting portions of God's Word. It unfolds history from the military aspect, revealing the great international movements which so definitely affected the church and her witness for Christ. Like other prophecies, it climaxes in the coming of our Lord in glory, for with the seventh and last trumpet blast the world and its affairs are brought to an end. (See Revelation 11:15.) This prophecy established the Advent message.

The empire of Rome was ruling when this great panorama was opened to the apostle John. The rule of Rome was autocratic and at times brutally cruel and unjust, yet strangely enough, the Christians of that time were praying for her continuance, for they understood from the writings of both Daniel and Paul that the collapse of the empire would mark the time for the appearance of the dreaded antichrist. But Rome was so corrupt that it was impossible for her to continue. Like the empires that preceded her, she at last fell and found herself on the rubbish heap of history. Any nation that defies God and corrupts her people is doomed. Rome's subsequent division was clearly prophesied by Daniel. The prophetic symbols of the seven trumpets show how the empire broke up.

SIGNIFICANCE OF THE FIRST TRUMPET, REVELATION 8:7

Anciently, the trumpet was used to summon great gatherings as in Israel (see Leviticus 23:24) or to herald the approach of disaster or war. So the prophecy of the seven trumpets unfolds seven great warnings;

the first four telling of the collapse of *Western Rome;* the next two, the overthrow of *Eastern Rome;* and the seventh, the last, revealing the collapse of *all human government,* when the kingdom of eternal peace will be ushered in.

The first great judgment that fell on Western Rome came from Alaric, a man who had been an officer in the Roman army. He united the powerful Germanic peoples and led the first invasion of Rome. The death of Theodosius, the Roman emperor, occurred in January, A.D. 395, and before the end of the winter the Goths, under Alaric, were in arms. After several years of ravaging the eastern empire, they crossed the Danube and came like a hailstorm from the Alps, thus answering the apocalyptic description. The city of Rome fell to this plundering invader in A.D. 410. The blast of this first trumpet, which shook the empire to its foundation, was represented by "hail" and "fire" and "blood," a dramatic description of the terrible slaughter that followed the invasion by the Goths. For six days the armies of Alaric pillaged the palaces, carrying off gold and silver plate, furniture, and priceless statuary. After pillaging the city, he went down to southern Italy and was later buried, with much of his treasure, in the bottom of a river. The slaves who buried him were all slain, so the place of that burial remains a secret.

THE SECOND TRUMPET SOUNDS, REVELATION 8:8, 9

This second trumpet describes a maritime war. It was as if "a great mountain burning with fire was cast into the sea" (verse 8). The Vandals invaded Rome from Africa through the Mediterranean. Their ambitious leader possessed no scruples. Once in the waters of the Mediterranean, Genseric set his heart on Rome. In the year 455 he sailed into the mouth of the Tiber, pillaged the city, and took thousands of citizens prisoner, including the empress and her two daughters. *Vandalism* is a word in our vocabulary today, and it comes to us with all these implications. The fleet of Rome, thirteen hundred ships, far outnumbered the fleet of the invader. Therefore the Romans entered the battle with some assurance of victory. But this clever admiral of the Vandals, under cover of darkness, towed some ships loaded with combustibles among the ships of the Roman fleet, setting fire to them. That night saw more than eleven hundred ships destroyed. How accurate and descriptive is the divine record!

THE THIRD TRUMPET SOUNDS, REVELATION 8:10, 11

The next invasion was by the Huns. The star that burned like a lamp is universally taken to be Attila, their leader. He did not attack Rome itself, but his devastations helped in the overthrow of the empire. Attila was a fearless, muscular pagan. His men scarified their faces to add terror to their appearance. Each man rode one horse and led three. The star, called "Wormwood" (verse 11), denotes the bitter consequences of Attila's attacks. The whole breadth of Europe, from the Volga to the Danube, was invaded, occupied, and desolated by the hordes of Attila, who called himself The Scourge of God. Rushing like a blazing meteor, this bold and crafty leader boasted that the grass would never grow where his horse's feet had trod. In addition to his devastation, he compelled Rome to pay a large indemnity. The word *Hun* to this day is a synonym for plunder and destruction. The mighty fabric of Rome was shaken, and she was already in a state of collapse, but still greater calamity was yet to befall the corrupt empire.

Lest we wonder why such devastation was permitted, the prophet tells us that "the rest of the men which were not killed by these plagues yet repented not of the works of their hands, . . . neither repented they of their murders, nor of their sorceries, nor of their fornication, nor of their thefts" (Revelation 9:20, 21).

THE FOURTH TRUMPET SOUNDS, REVELATION 8:12

When the fourth angel sounded, the sun, moon, and stars were smitten. One puppet emperor after another arose, until at last a mere boy, Romulus Augustulus, was given the Roman purple. In the year 476, Odoacer, the chief of a barbarian remnant of Attila, declared that the name and office of the Roman emperor of the West should be abolished. The senate bowed in submission, and so Romulus Agustulus, the last of the Roman rulers, was dethroned. Thus, the "sun" of the empire had set. The "moon" and "stars"—the consuls and the senate—lingered a little longer, but before another half century had passed, these, too, were extinguished. Barbarian warfare was terrible, but the overthrow of Rome was but the harvest of is own sowing. It declined as it had arisen—by conquest. It was the coming of a vacant night, spoken of by historians as the Dark Ages.

Western Rome had collapsed. "Woe, woe, woe," cried the angel (verse 13), because the next three trumpets were yet to be sounded.

THE FIFTH TRUMPET SOUNDS, REVELATION 9:1–11

Eastern Rome is the focal point of interest under the fifth and sixth trumpets. No more descriptive prophecy can be found in all the Bible. The blast of the fifth trumpet was fulfilled in the rise and progress of the Arabs. Arabia has been called "the pit of the abyss," because of its deserts and empty areas. It was here that Mohammedanism arose and spread like "a smoke" (Revelation 9:2). This false and fanatical faith threatened at one time to obscure the light of the gospel. The Saracenic invasion could be described in no better language than is used here. Like a horde of locusts out of the smoke, Mohammedanism swept on. The "star" (verse 1) to whom the key was given well describes the prophet Mohammed. But, although fanatical, they were not plunderers like the conquerors of Western Rome.

When the Arabian tribes gathered for the conquest of Syria, A.D. 632, Mohammed's uncle, Abu Bekr, who succeeded the prophet after his death, gave this following order, which fits the Bible prophecy exactly:

> When you fight the battles of the Lord, acquit yourselves like men, without turning your backs; but let not your victory be stained with the blood of women or children. Destroy no palm trees, nor burn any fields of corn. Cut down no fruit trees, nor do any mischief to cattle, only such as you kill to eat. [See Revelation 9:4.] When you make any covenant or article, stand to it, and be as good as your word. As you go on, you will find some religious persons who live retired in monasteries and propose to themselves to serve God that way: let them alone, and neither kill them nor destroy their monasteries: and you will find another sort of people, that belong to the

synagogue of Satan, who have shaven crowns; be sure you cleave their skulls, and give them no quarter till they either turn Mahommetans or pay tribute (Edward Gibbon, *The History of the Decline and Fall of the Roman Empire,* ch. 51, par. 10).

Note the accurate description of these conquerors in Revelation 9:7–9. "Their faces were as the faces of men." (They wore beards.) "They had hair as the hair of women." (Their hair was long.) They had "crowns like gold." (These stately warriors wore a brilliant headdress or turban.) "Their teeth were as the teeth of lions." (They were fearless fighters.) "The shapes of the locusts were like unto horses prepared unto battle." (The Arabian horse is still a synonym of quality among equestrians, while skill in horsemanship is an Arabian art.) How accurate is God's Word! They would "hurt men five months" (verse 10). For hundreds of years, the Mohammedan and Tatar tribes were divided into bands under separate leaders with little or no organization. Near the close of the thirteenth century, Othman founded a government, which ever since has been known as the Ottoman Empire. This grew until it extended over all the principal Mohammedan tribes, consolidating them into one monarchy.

"They had a king over them, . . . whose name in the Hebrew tongue is Abaddon, but in the Greek tongue hath his name Apollyon" (verse 11). These two names denote the character of the people. *Abaddon* means "the destroyer," and *Apollyon,* "one that exterminates." The five months is an important prophetic period that establishes prophetic chronology in a marvelous way. Recognizing the well-proved principle in prophetic chronology that a day represents a year, we have the following: Five months of 30 days each would mean 5 × 30, or 150 days. But reckoning a "day for a year" (Numbers 14:34; Ezekiel 4:6), this period of 150 prophetic days become 150 literal years during which the Ottoman Empire would hurt and destroy men. The historian Edward Gibbon says, "It was on the twenty-seventh of July, in the year twelve hundred and ninety-nine of the Christian Era, that Othman first invaded the territory of Nicomedia; and the singular accuracy of the dates seems to disclose some foresight of the rapid and destructive growth of the monster" (*The History of the Decline and Fall of the Roman Empire,* ch. 64, par. 14). Starting from this date, we count 150 years, and this brings us to A.D. 1449. During these 150 years the Ottoman Empire engaged in almost continual warfare against the Greek Empire. The Ottomans did not conquer the Greeks until 1499, when the last of the Greek emperors, Constantine, took the throne, but only after seeking permission of the sultan of the Ottoman Empire!—a striking fulfillment of prophecy that they should hurt men for 5 months, or 150 years. Their increased power, now, would enable them "to slay" (Revelation 9:15) under the next trumpet, which they did until their decline.

THE SIXTH TRUMPET SOUNDS, REVELATION 9:12–21

This particular portion of the Revelation became a subject of intense study during the great Advent awakening of 1830–1844. The accuracy and drama of its fulfillment led to the conversion of more than one thousand infidels. When the sixth trumpet sounded, John declared that four angels were loosed which were bound to the great river Euphrates. (See verse 4.) This expression, scholars have believed, refers to the four leading sultanies, *Aleppo, Iconium, Damascus,* and *Baghdad,* which comprised the Ottoman Empire. They were situated in the region of the Euphrates River. They were to be loosed for a specific period: an hour, a day, a month, and a year. Before making this remarkable calculation, let us notice verse 17: "And thus I saw the horses in the vision, and them that sat on them, having breastplates of fire, and of jacinth, and brimstone: and the heads of the horses were as the heads of lions; and out of their mouths issued fire and smoke and brimstone." Could language more accurately describe the Turkish horsemen as they rode to battle clad in uniforms of red and blue and yellow?—"fire," "jacinth," (or hyacinth), and "brimstone."

It was the Ottoman Turk who largely introduced firearms into warfare. These old-time cavalrymen fired their muskets from their hips as they rode along, and to the prophet it would appear as if smoke were issuing from the horses' mouths. The stories of conquests by the Turks have filled many volumes. Rising like a mighty tide, these fanatical followers of Mohammed spread from country to country, threatening to submerge all Europe. But this phenomenal rise has been eclipsed only by the speed of their decline. The Turk lost his possessions slice by slice, until, in 1838, trouble broke out between the sultan and Mehemet Ali, pasha of Egypt. Foreign intervention, however, for a time prevented war. But peace was not to last long, for the following year, when hostilities again broke out, the sultan's army was entirely cut up and destroyed, while his fleet was captured and taken to Egypt.

It appeared certain that Constantinople would became an Egyptian possession. Helpless and hopeless, the sultan appealed to Europe for help. A conference was called in London among England, Russia, Austria, and Prussia, with Effendi Bey Likgis as mediator for the Ottoman power. An ultimatum was drawn up to be presented to Egypt in the year 1840. Now notice this prophet's measurement—"a day, and a month, and a year" (verse 15). This was the period given to this power. As already mentioned, the five-month period associated with the previous trumpet commenced in 1299, according to Gibbon, and ended in 1449. Still calculating a day for a year and recognizing that a prophetic month is thirty days, let us make this further calculation: One day equals 1 year; 1 month equals 30 years; 1 year equals 360 years. This totals 391 years. Reckoning from the summer of 1449, the 391 years will bring us to the summer of 1840. As already mentioned, it was on July 27, 1299, that Othman invaded Nicomedia. This began the previous measurement of 150 years. Now let us add the last fraction of the measurement—the "one hour." An hour is one-twenty-fourth part of a day. This fractional part of a year is fifteen days. Adding fifteen days brings us to August 11, the day the fog lifted allowing the ships to enter the harbor.

It is significant that, following the London conference already referred to, the sultan dispatched Rifat Bey as plenipotentiary to Alexandria to communicate the ultimatum to the pasha. At the same time the great powers pledged themselves to be ready to take any steps they might deem necessary in the event of further hostilities. It is recorded that on the very day, August 11, the ultimatum reached Alexandria. How accurate is the finger of prophetic time! But where was the sultan's independence? Gone! As a sick man, he virtually collapsed into the friendly arms of the great powers of Europe, and from that day until 1917, when the last of the sultans fled in terror from his capital, the Turk was styled The Sick Man of the East.

This remarkable fulfillment of prophecy had a tremendous effect upon the public mind at the time. The evidence was inescapable. Two years prior to this time, Josiah Litch of Philadelphia published his interpretation of this prophecy, in which he took the unqualified position that the Ottoman Empire would fall in August 1840. It seemed a bold thing to do, especially in the face of a growing infidelity and rationalism. His statement is arresting:

> But when will this power be overthrown? According to the calculations already made that the five months ended 1449, the hour, fifteen days; the day, one year; the month, thirty years; and the year, three hundred and sixty years; in all—three hundred and ninety-one years and fifteen days, will end in A.D. 1840, sometime in the month of August (Josiah Litch, *The Probability of the Second Coming of Christ About A.D. 1843*, page 157).

A short time before the event, Litch even went so far as to declare it would be the eleventh day of August. His views on the Ottoman question were noted in public journals, and various infidel clubs discussed his views, ridiculing the man for having the audacity to make such a claim. He was a deep student of both history and prophecy and became a fearless champion of the cause of Christ, declaring that the future would vindicate the veracity of God's Word. It did! When the news of the collapse of the sultan's empire was flashed to the unbelieving world, it was startling. Moreover, some of the very ones who had ridiculed now renounced their rationalism. Within a few months, it is reported Litch "received letters from more than one thousand prominent infidels, some of them leaders of infidel clubs, in which they stated they had given up the battle against the Bible and had accepted it as God's revelation to man." Some expressed themselves in such words as these: "We have said that expositors of prophecy quote from the musty pages of history to substantiate their claims of prophetic fulfillments, but in this case we have the living facts before our eyes."

These two prophetic periods, the 150 years and the 391 years, connected with the fifth and sixth trumpets, are differently applied, but always they are associated with this same Mohammedan power. From the time the prophet Mohammed began his public preaching in A.D. 612, to the founding of the city of Baghdad by Al-Mansur in A.D. 762, is 150 years. This city, made famous in English literature by the *Arabian Nights,* was called Dar es Salaam, "house of peace," or "city of peace," and it marks the termination of the spread of the Arabian Empire.

And it is also significant that from 1453, which marks the fall of Constantinople, the collapse of the Byzantine Empire, and the establishment of the Ottomans, until the hour of God's judgment began in 1844, is exactly 391 years.

"The second woe is past," declared the voice in heaven, "and, behold, the third woe cometh quickly" (Revelation 11:14). Between the end of the sixth and the sounding of the seventh trumpet, a great movement was to arise through which God is to carry the message of the everlasting gospel to all the world. This will be explained in the next chapter, on Revelation 10.

THE SEVENTH TRUMPET SOUNDS, REVELATION 11:15

With the sounding of the seventh trumpet the mystery of God is finished and "the kingdoms of this world are become the kingdoms of our Lord, and of his Christ; and he shall reign for ever and ever" (verse 15). O long-expected day of glory! O welcome voice that declares the mystery of God finished and ushers in the eternal reign of righteousness! Saints, apostles, patriarchs, and martyrs have all alike been looking for the dawning of that day. It cannot be far distant, for with the closing of the sixth trumpet, or the second woe, the seventh trumpet, or the "third woe cometh quickly" (verse 14). It will be a day of deliverance to the people of God.

When the elders, seated on their thrones, hear the sound of voices in heaven declaring that the kingdoms of this world are given over to Christ, they fall on their faces in worship, saying, "We give thee thanks, O Lord God Almighty, . . . because thou hast taken to thee thy great power" (verse 17). It is the time "that thou shouldest give reward unto thy servants the prophets," they exclaim, "and to the saints, and them that fear thy name, small and great" (verse 18). It is also a time of terrible judgment upon the despisers of His grace when God will "destroy them which destroy [or "corrupt," margin] the earth" (verse 18). "The nations were angry," declare the elders. How true! We see the results of their anger in the blood-soaked cities where ghastly ruins mark the awful march of war. The words of Jesus as recorded in Luke 21:26 are certainly true today: "Men's hearts failing them for fear, and for looking after those things which are coming on the earth."

But this mighty panorama shows us where we are; we are almost home. The very things we see are but the omens of the coming day of triumph. The work of the gospel will soon be finished. Some day not distant, the last sermon will be preached, the last invitation given, and then it will be too late to accept salvation. The saddest words in all the Bible are these: "The harvest is past, the summer is ended, and we are not saved" (Jeremiah 8:20).

But as Christians we need not fear the tragedies of our time. If the peace of God that passeth all understanding fills our hearts and we are walking with our Lord in sacrifice and service, then we can confidently look for His appearing, knowing we shall be received of Him when He appears in glory. With John the revelator we can say with confidence, "Even so, come, Lord Jesus" (Revelation 22:20).

29. The Angel With the Open Book

Like chapter 7, this prophecy also is parenthetical. It falls between the sixth trumpet of chapters 8 and 9 and the seventh trumpet of chapter 11:15. It gives another picture of God's last message to the world before the second coming of Christ. When the seventh angel sounds, "the kingdoms of this world are become the kingdoms of our Lord" (Revelation 11:15). But he is restrained from blowing his trumpet until the sealing work is accomplished. This work is pictured in Revelation 7:1–3.

THE MIGHTY ANGEL

Six times in the Revelation a heaven-sent message is symbolized by an angel. But the description of this angel is more glorious than the others. "His face was as it were the sun" (Revelation 10:1). The similarity to the description of Christ in 1:13–16 leads many to believe that this angel must be Christ. When transfigured before the disciples, "his face did shine as the sun" (Matthew 17:2). He is called "the messenger of the covenant" (Malachi 3:1) and "the Angel which redeemed me" (Genesis 48:16).

THE RAINBOW AND THE CLOUD

A rainbow, or, more accurately, *the* rainbow (see Revelation 4:3), glows about His head, a token of His covenant of love. The "cloud" is also a token of Deity. Clouds and glory covered Him at Sinai. "Clouds [are] his chariots" (Psalm 104:3).

This mighty Angel's standing on both the land and the sea indicates that the message He brings is for all the world. Thus in prophetic pictures John gives us the beginning of a world movement.

THE OPEN BOOK

The language suggests that the little book had not always been open. The message symbolized by this angel unsealed the book to permit the study of its message. What book could it be? There seems only one answer, for as far as is recorded the only part of Scripture closed, or sealed, was a portion of the book of Daniel. The prophet was told definitely to "shut up the words, and seal the book, even to the time of the end" (Daniel 12:4, 9). Since it was closed up only *till* the time of the end, it naturally follows that *at* the time of the end it would be opened.

> It was not given him [Daniel] to understand all that God had revealed of the divine purpose. "Shut up the words, and seal the book," he was directed concerning his prophetic writings; these were to be sealed "even to the time of the end." "Go thy way, Daniel," the angel once more directed the faithful messenger of Jehovah; "for the words are closed up and sealed till the time of the end. . . . Go thou thy way till the end be: for thou shalt rest, and stand in thy lot at the end of the days."
>
> As we near the close of this world's history, the prophecies recorded by Daniel demand our special attention, as they relate to the very time in which we are living. With them should be linked the teachings of the last book of the New Testament Scriptures. Satan has led many to believe that the prophetic portions of the writings of Daniel and of John the revelator cannot be understood. But the promise is plain that special blessing will accompany the study of these prophecies. "The wise shall understand," was spoken of the visions of Daniel that were to be unsealed in the latter days (Ellen White, *Prophets and Kings,* pages, 547, 548).

Daniel had asked, "How long shall it be to the end of these wonders?" (verse 6). The angel, in giving the answer, spoke about the scattering of the holy people. That seemed strange to him, and he says, "I heard, but I understood not" (verses 7, 8). It was not possible, when Daniel wrote, for him to understand, because certain events must occur first. But at "the time of the end," he was assured, some would understand. (See verses 8–10.)

THE TIME OF THE END OF DANIEL'S PROPHECY

The prophetic expression "the time of the end" (verse 9) is not the end of time. It refers to the end of the 1,260-year period of papal supremacy which lasted from A.D. 538 to 1798. And, true to the prediction, when the prophetic period of 1,260 years terminated, students of Bible prophecy in many lands began simultaneously, and without any collusion, to concentrate on the study of the 2,300-day prophecy in Daniel 8 and 9. (See *The Prophetic Faith of Our Fathers,* by L. E. Froom, vol. 3, pages 263–277.)

The prophecy of these chapters concerns two periods of time, that is, the 70 weeks and the 2,300 days. Jewish scholars since before the time of Christ were interpreting the 70-week prophecy. John the Baptist, Israel's greatest reformer, came with a definite message relating to time. He applied these Messianic prophecies to Christ, declaring that "the Lamb of God, which taketh away the sin of the world," (John 1:29) was none other than Jesus. John's forceful interpretations of prophecy made him the herald of the Messiah. Jesus said, "There hath not arisen a greater than John" (Matthew 11:11).

CALCULATING THE 70 WEEKS OF DANIEL

When Jesus began to preach, He declared: "The time is fulfilled" (Mark 1:15). The fulfillment of the 70-week prophecy revealed conclusively that Jesus was indeed the Messiah. He was "cut off" (Daniel 9:26) exactly in the midst of the last prophetic week. He was to "confirm the covenant with many for 1 week [7 years]: and in the midst of the week [after 3 1/2 years] he shall cause the sacrifice and oblation to cease" (verse 27). By His death, our Lord brought to an end the whole sacrificial service of the Old Testament. The 70-week prophecy began with the decree to rebuild Jerusalem. (See verse 25.) This decree was issued in 457 B.C. (See Ezra 7:11–26.) This date, disputed by some, has been confirmed by sound scientific proofs. (See *The Chronology of Ezra 7,* by S. H. Horn and L. H. Woods.)

Sixty-nine of those prophetic weeks, or 483 literal years, will bring us down to the Messiah. The decree for rebuilding Jerusalem having gone forth in 457 B.C., it is easy to determine when the period of 69 weeks, or 483 years, would terminate. In calculating B.C. dates, we must subtract. So, 483 years from the date 457 B.C. will bring us actually to A.D. 27. Jesus was indeed baptized in A.D. 27, and in that year He began His ministry. His message, like that of John, was: "The time is fulfilled, and the kingdom of God is at hand: repent ye, and believe the gospel" (Mark 1:15). Just 3 1/2 years later, or A.D. 31, "the midst of the week," Jesus was crucified.

There were still 3 1/2 years left of that last prophetic week. What do we find? The church in Jerusalem preached the gospel of Christ unhindered for 3 1/2 years. Then in A.D. 34, Stephen, the first Christian martyr, met his death. At that time there was a great persecution against the church that was at Jerusalem, and its members were all scattered abroad. The believers then began to give the gospel in earnest to the Gentiles. Saul of Tarsus was converted that year, A.D. 34, and he became the great missionary to the Gentile world. This prophecy of the 70 weeks proves beyond question the messiahship of Jesus.

It is interesting to note in passing that Jewish teachers and rabbis have for centuries been forbidden to teach and interpret this prophecy.

> In 1656, a dispute occurred in Poland between some distinguished Jewish rabbis and the Catholics respecting the seventy weeks. The rabbis were so hard pushed by the argument that proved Jesus to be the Messiah, the time of His sufferings being at the end of the seventy weeks, that they broke up the discussion. The rabbis then held a meeting and pronounced a curse upon any Jew who should attempt to ascertain the chronology of the prophetic period. Their anathema was this: "May his bones and his memory rot who shall attempt to number the seventy weeks" (*The Midnight Cry*, August 10, 1843).

These events concerning the sacrifice of Christ and the establishment of the church, however, not only terminated the 70-week prophecy, they also sealed up the vision of the 2,300 days of Daniel 8:14 and 9:24. The purpose of this 70-week, or 490-year, prophecy was to establish and clarify the vision of the 2,300 days that Daniel did not understand. (See Daniel 8:27; 9:23.) The time for the commencement of the 70 weeks, or 490 years, is the same as for the 2,300 days or years. Both periods began in the "seventh year of Artaxerxes the king" (Ezra 7:7), or 457 B.C. The 490 years were a period "determined," "shortened," or "cut off" from the longer period of 2,300 years. (See Daniel 9:24.) Subtracting 490 from 2,300 leaves a remainder of 1,810 years. Now add this remainder, 1,810, to the date A.D. 34, which is the terminal date for the 490 years, and you are brought to the significant date 1844. What happened then? This was the year when our great High Priest, Jesus Christ, the *Goel*, or Redeemer, of the lost inheritance, lifted the fast-closed title deeds, opened the books, and began the closing phase of His ministry. Those marvelous events of Revelation chapter 5 were fulfilled at the termination of the 2,300 years, or in 1844. While almost every Bible writer deals with the judgment and its effects, yet Daniel is the only prophet who locates the actual time when this work began.

THE PROPHECY UNSEALED

So long as his prophecy was sealed and that portion of his book closed, men were unable to fully understand or interpret the message of the judgment. But with the overthrow of papal domination in 1798, men began to study this prophecy of the 2,300 days, or years, with a keen desire to understand it. Daniel's prophecy declared that the people of God *would* understand it; and they did. The unfolding of this great prophecy led multiplied thousands to the conviction that the coming of the Lord was very near, and thousands began to proclaim the message of the soon returning Savior. The great religious awakening of the nineteenth century resulted from this intensive study. Nothing since apostolic days has caused a greater interest in spiritual things, except for the Reformation of the sixteenth century.

"TAKE IT [THE LITTLE BOOK], AND EAT IT UP" (REVELATION 10:9)

Basing their conclusions on the prophecy of the 2,300 days, hundreds of preachers in Europe, America, and many other lands predicted the literal return of Christ in or about the year 1844. Among these preachers were many leaders of the Congregationalists, Methodists,

Baptists, Presbyterians, Episcopalians, etc. It was a heart-stirring message and appealed to the most spiritual of the congregations. They eagerly devoured the message. Like Jeremiah of old, they could say, "Thy words were found, and I did eat them; and thy word was unto me the joy and rejoicing of mine heart" (Jeremiah 15:16).

The angel with uplifted hand in the attitude of an oath was startling. He said that "there should be time no longer" (Revelation 10:6). Prophetic time had reached its end. No chronological prophecy would extend beyond that time. And actually those who were interpreting the 2,300-year prophecy were declaring that *time would be no longer.* They fully expected the Lord to come in 1844 or near that time. The central theme of their message was the imminent return of Christ. The announcement of the angel in Revelation 10, however, was not concerning the end of *literal* time, but rather the end of *prophetic* time. The year 1844 marks the termination of the 2,300-day prophecy, since which time the world has been living in what might be called "borrowed time." *There is no chronological prophecy in the Bible that extends beyond 1844.*

"It shall be in thy mouth sweet as honey" (Revelation 10:9)

The announcement of our Lord's near return in glory was received with great enthusiasm. Multitudes of the most devout Christians, especially in America and Europe, were thrilled by the message, and, like the prophet John, they took the book and ate it up. Like the prophet Ezekiel, they ate the roll, then went and proclaimed the message. (See Ezekiel 3:1.) This perfectly describes the experience of earnest believers at that time. Joy filled their hearts. But they were doomed to disappointment. When the time arrived, and Jesus did not appear, it was a crushing blow to their faith. What had been as sweet as honey now became as bitter as gall. "It shall make thy belly bitter," said the angel (Revelation 10:9).

The disciples of Christ passed through a similar experience. Could anything have been more tragic than the death of Jesus, for men who had given up their all, believing He was the Christ? When they took the form of their loved Lord from the cross, they buried their hopes with His body in Joseph's new tomb. But their work was not finished.

In fact, it had hardly begun. It was after their great disappointment that the apostles did their greatest work. On the evening after the Resurrection, we read that the Lord "opened . . . their understanding, that they might understand the Scriptures" (Luke 24:45). Disappointments are often His appointments, and, like the disappointment of the apostles eighteen centuries before, this great disappointment of 1844 proved to be a blessing in disguise. A greater message was yet to be given to the world. True, some renounced their faith and turned from the Word of God, but that very disappointment drove others to a deeper study of the Bible.

"THOU MUST PROPHESY AGAIN BEFORE MANY PEOPLES" (REVELATION 10:11)

Thrilling as was the message that swept through the churches prior to 1844, it was not the final message of God. New light was to break upon the path of the searchers of God's Word. A greater message, embracing prophecies not even thought about, was to come into focus as the result of that study. And that message in its fullness was to be given to the whole world to prepare a people to stand in the day of God. The command to John to "prophesy again before many peoples, and nations, and tongues, and kings" (verse 11), was prophetic of the church, which, following the Great Disappointment, was to hasten to the earth's far ends with a message for all, kings and peasants alike.

"RISE, AND MEASURE THE TEMPLE" (REVELATION 11:1)

Again the command comes to John and is prophetic of the renewed study of the prophecies on the part of those earnest searchers for truth. The prophet's attitude and response to these mighty unfoldings has been, and is again, emblematic of the attitude of the true church of God when these events became history. The discouraged worshipers after the passing of the date 1844 were to arise and shine, for new light had come, and the glory of the Lord was to be upon them. (See Isaiah 60:1.) And that light was a mightier message that would illumine the whole world with its glory. (See Revelation 18:1.) It would shine forth in its brilliance in the darkest hour of human history. (See Isaiah 60:2.)

Since 1844, God's last message, greater in scope and power, has been hastening on to the earth's far ends. The "everlasting gospel" (Revelation 14:6) is being proclaimed in the setting of the judgment-hour message, and it is being preached in nearly every language on earth.

"THE MYSTERY OF GOD SHOULD BE FINISHED" (REVELATION 10:7)

The mystery of God is the gospel of Jesus Christ. (See Ephesians 6:19.) It is embodied in His person and His work. Paul speaks of it as "the mystery of his will" (Ephesians 1:9). "Great is the mystery of godliness," he exclaims (1 Timothy 3:16). The purpose of the gospel is to take out a people for His name. (See Acts 15:14.) And they are being hastily gathered from every nation under heaven. (See Revelation 14:6.)

God's last message that gathers out the people who are to stand in the final days of earth's history is a message that embraces *every truth of every reformation of every age.* Here is God's true plan for the union of the churches. If men would come together with open minds determined to know the will of God and a readiness to obey His Word, then His message of truth would unite us all, for it centers truly in a crucified, risen, ministering, and soon-coming Savior.

30. Measuring the Worshipers and the Power of the Two Witnesses

This chapter is really a consummation of the prophecy of chapter 10. After the prophet had eaten "the little book," which seemed sweet at first, but which later became bitter, he was told to prophesy again before many peoples and even before kings. (See Revelation 10:11.)

Then said the angel, "Rise, and measure the temple of God, and the altar, and them that worship therein" (Revelation 11:1). The temple here mentioned cannot be the church, for the expression "them that worship therein" must refer to the worshipers. Neither could it refer to the temple of Jerusalem, for that temple was destroyed years before the Revelation was written, and it has never been rebuilt. (John received this vision about A.D. 96, and the Jewish temple was destroyed by Titus in A.D. 70. In any case, the whole Mosaic service was only "a shadow of good things to come" [Hebrews 10:1] and had met its fulfillment in Christ, His sacrifice, and His priesthood in the heavenly sanctuary.) But at the time this prophecy was applied (1844), the eyes of the worshipers were especially directed to the ministry of Jesus as our great High Priest in heaven, in "the true tabernacle, which the Lord pitched, and not man" (Hebrews 8:2).

INTERNATIONAL EVENTS GIVE NEW IMPETUS TO STUDY OF PROPHECY

When Pope Pius VI was taken prisoner by General Berthier of France in 1798 and dominance of the church had come to its end, that shook Europe. But when this was followed in 1840 by the virtual collapse of the Ottoman Empire, it shook the world. Both these events had been clearly foreseen by students of prophecy. The first date, 1798, marked the termination of Daniel's prophecy of the "time, times, and an half" (Daniel 12:7), or the 1,260 days, or years, of Revelation 12:6, during which the apostate church would exercise her power. And as has already been emphasized, the second date, 1840, marked the termination of the prophetic periods of the "five months" and also the "hour, and a day, and a month, and a year" (Revelation 9:5, 15) that were given to the Ottoman power. The exactitude of these prophecies and their fulfillments gave new impetus to the whole study of prophecy, and this came at a time when atheism was eating at the very vitals of Christianity.

What John was about to witness, and what he recorded for us, is the battle between the Bible and atheism. This battle reached a climax in the French Revolution. Terrible as that was, it was but a skirmish in comparison with the battle to be waged on a worldwide scale just before the return of Christ. The happenings of that awful revolution have been repeated during recent decades among such groups as the "society of the godless." This prophecy therefore has a particular meaning for earth's last generation.

THE TWO WITNESSES

There has been much speculation as to the identity of these witnesses. Some try to make them literal, even going so far as to name them, declaring they will be as Moses and Elijah. But the whole language is figurative. Revelation 11:4 says, "These are the two olive trees, and the two candlesticks standing before the God of the earth." In Zechariah 4:11–14, the two olive trees represent the Word of God, and God's Word is indeed a light. In Psalm 119:105, 130 David said, "Thy word is a lamp unto my feet," and "The entrance of thy words giveth light." But the Scriptures are more than a light; they also bear witness, or testify, of God's grace. Jesus declared that the Old Testament Scriptures "testify [or bear witness] of me" (John 5:39). In Matthew 24:14 we read, "This gospel of the kingdom shall be preached in all the world for a witness unto all nations."

The clearest explanation of this prophecy is that the witnesses are the Old and New Testaments. They do indeed testify of Christ. "They are they which testify of me," Jesus said (John 5:39).

The two witnesses represent the Scriptures of the Old and the New Testament. Both are important testimonies to the origin and perpetuity of the law of God. Both are witnesses also to the plan of salvation. The types, sacrifices, and prophecies of the Old Testament point forward to a Saviour to come. The Gospels and Epistles of the New Testament tell of a Saviour who has come in the exact manner foretold by type and prophecy (Ellen White, *The Great Controversy*, page 267).

But the prophecy declares that the witnesses were to be clothed in sackcloth, the symbol of mourning. The Old and New Testaments were practically silenced, first by the apostasy within the church and later by the attacks of infidelity and rationalism. But each "witness" gave the same testimony, i.e., that for 1,260 years the apostasy would vaunt itself, but at the end of the days these Scriptures would speak with new power. References from both the Old and New Testaments covering this 1,260-year period will be found in the next chapter.

THE WITNESSES POSSESS POWER

In Revelation chapter 11, verses 5 and 6 we are told that those who hurt these witnesses will themselves be killed and will be smitten with the plagues and judgments of God, for these witnesses have power over nature to shut heaven and turn the waters into blood. Moses warned Israel that if they turned away from God, He would "shut up the heaven, that there be no rain" (Deuteronomy 11:17). They did turn from God, and Elijah the prophet was raised up to bring the nation back to God. He commanded that there be no rain, and it did not rain for three and a half years. (See James 5:17; 1 Kings 17 and 18.) It is significant that three and a half years measures 1,260 days, or 1,260 years in prophecy. (A prophetic year is 360 prophetic days, or literal years, so that three and a half prophetic years equals 1,260 literal years.)

When Pharaoh said to Moses, "Who is the LORD, that I should obey his voice?" he challenged the very God of heaven (Exodus 5:2). Forthwith the rivers of Egypt were turned into blood. That same power resides in the New Testament, for one of the seven last plagues will be the turning of the water into blood. (See Revelation 16:4.)

283

MODERN MILITANT ATHEISM IS BORN

The same defiant attitude seen in the ruler of ancient Egypt arose again during the French Revolution, when for the first time in more than two thousand years, a nation in her capacity as a kingdom made war on the Monarchy of heaven. By the legislature of France, the two witnesses, the Old and New Testaments, were figuratively slain in the streets. In 1793 the French assembly passed a decree suppressing the Bible. On November 11 of that year a "Grand Festival" was held in the leading church of Paris in honor of "Reason and Truth," while the authorities attending this burlesque carried out an insulting ceremony. Paris, the center of nationalism, did indeed become a spiritual Sodom, for licentiousness seemed one of its chief characteristics. The city also became a spiritual Egypt, as militant atheism hurled insults at the God of heaven. Such mottoes as "Crush the Wretch" (meaning Christ) were carried through the streets that ran with blood. But this was not to last. Godless revelers may make merry for a time, but when men have done their worst the Almighty can always add a closing chapter. And He always does.

THE SLAIN WITNESSES RESURRECTED

The prophet declared that after three and a half prophetic days, or years, the witnesses would come to life again, and, standing on their feet, would cause great fear to fall upon all men. Though the French assembly had passed a decree suppressing the Bible, three years later a decree giving toleration to the Scriptures was passed by the same assembly. The resolution, however, lay on the table for six months, after which it was taken up and passed without a dissenting vote. This was exactly three and a half years after it had been enacted. How accurate is God's prophetic Word!

> The church and the Bible had been slain in France from November, 1793, till June, 1797. The *three years* and a *half* were expended, and the Bible, so long and so sternly repressed before, was placed in honor, and was openly the book of free Protestantism! (George Croly, *The Apocalypse of St. John,* page 183).

284

Measuring the Worshipers and the Power of the Two Witnesses

THE BIBLE EXALTED

The prophecy says, "And they [the two witnesses] ascended up to heaven in a cloud; and their enemies beheld them" (Revelation 11:12). The Scriptures, so vigorously suppressed by the godless, were to be exalted in the eyes of all nations. It is significant that in 1804, almost immediately following the French Revolution, the British and Foreign Bible Society was organized. At that time the Scriptures were translated into very few languages. Today the Word of God can be read in about eleven hundred different languages. It is estimated that nine-tenths of the people living on earth can hear the Bible, or portions of it, in their own tongue.

Militant atheism, however, did not end with the setting up of the French Republic. The forces of the godless, so dominant in the revolution, spread north and east to find a fertile soil. Even more destitute and downtrodden than the French peasants during the reign of the last kings of France was the great nation of the far north and east. Religion to them was something that symbolized make-believe and oppression. Is it any wonder that when that country was plunged into political revolution in 1917, a vital part of that uprising was an attack upon religion? It took about a century for the seeds of revolution in France to reach its full fruitage in Russia. Weishaupt of Germany, in 1776, laid the foundation of a false philosophy which, in one form or another, has since spread around the world.

MEASURE THE ALTAR AND THE WORSHIPERS, REVELATION 11:1

While the powers of atheism and apostate Christianity are preparing for their last assault on the church, God is sending His last warning message to every "nation, and kindred, and tongue, and people" (Revelation 14:6). Truth, which for centuries has been repressed and submerged by apostate teachers and blatant unbelief, is now shining with new radiance from the Word of God. Special attention has been given to the study of the ministry of Jesus, our great Advocate and Judge. Since He has been appointed by the Father to pass judgment on every soul, it is important that every nation on earth realize that "the hour of his judgment is come" (verse 7), so that men of every

285

language and tribe may prepare to meet their God. The attitude of our worship is the measure of our spiritual power. "The second woe is past; and, behold, the third woe cometh quickly" (Revelation 11:14).

The greatest issues of all time are before us. We are on the very borders of the eternal world. How essential, then, that we be found worshiping God in spirit and in truth! The last great battle is soon to be fought—the battle between the forces of light and darkness, truth and error. When the "third woe" comes, it will be forever too late to make our peace with God. "The worldwide dissemination of the same teaching that led to the French Revolution—all tend to involve the whole world in a struggle similar to that which convulsed France" (Ellen White, *Education,* page 228). The only answer to an apostate, atheistic world is a church on fire for God.

31. The Conflict of the Church

This is one of the most illuminating and comprehensive chapters in the book of Revelation. Gazing in wonder as the whole panorama moves forward, the prophet says, "And there appeared a great wonder in heaven" (Revelation 12:1). Through the aid of divine imagery he is swept back to witness the very inception of sin, when Lucifer challenged the throne of Deity; then on to Satan's final conflict with Christ's loyal witnesses just prior to His return.

The activities of the prince of evil against the government of God and His people are presented in this panorama. It is a drama of four acts:

1. the origin of sin and the beginning of the controversy in heaven
2. the attack on Christ when He lived among men
3. the persecution of the church in the subsequent centuries
4. the final war on the remnant people of God

We are halfway through the book of Revelation. The chapters that follow give remarkable details in the final struggle between the forces of good and evil. The final victory of the church, the overthrow of Satan and his hosts, the complete establishment of God's kingdom upon earth—these themes climax the Revelation.

A WOMAN CLOTHED WITH THE SUN

The gloriously arrayed woman, with the sun as her garments, the moon as her footstool, and twelve stars for a crown, is in some ways the most attractive of all the prophetic symbols. A woman in prophecy represents a church. The pure, true church of God is represented by a virtuous woman. (See Jeremiah 6:2; Isaiah 54:5, 6; Hosea 2:19, 20; John 3:29; 2 Corinthians 11:2; Revelation 19:7, 8.) The apostate, corrupt church is represented by a lewd woman. (See Revelation 17:1–5; Jeremiah 3:1, 8; Ezekiel 16:26–29; Isaiah 50:1.)

Christ has only one body, His church, and this has existed in all ages. Ancient Israel, while being led by Moses, was spoken of as "the church in the wilderness" (Acts 7:38). There has ever been only *one* chosen people, *one* family of the Lord, *one* vineyard, *one* bride, *one* New Jerusalem. The gates of that glorious city bear the names of the twelve tribes of Israel, while the foundations carry the names of the twelve apostles. The whole Bible has but *one* story—the story of the conflict between Christ and His enemy; between the Seed of the woman and the dragon.

> There has really been but one church upon earth, existing through all times and under all economies. And so we have here, as the symbol of it, this one glorious woman, in whom all its highest excellences and chief characteristics are summed up from the beginning even unto the great consummation (J. A. Seiss, *The Apocalypse,* vol. 2, page 277).

> We regard the woman as the symbol of God's religious system on earth from the beginning of His testimony until the consummation (Davis, *The Vision of Patmos,* page 178).

As Eve was created from the side of Adam during his deep sleep (see Genesis 2:21, 22), so Christ, the Second Adam, brought His bride, the church, into existence through His death and resurrection. Only as we become members of His body, of His flesh, and of His bones, are we part of the true church. (See Ephesians 5:30.)

The true church of Jesus Christ has ever been clothed with the "Sun of righteousness" (Malachi 4:2). Jesus Christ is also the "light of the world" (John 8:12; 9:5). Only those who walk in harmony with God's Word can be called the children of light. (See Luke 16:8; Ephesians 5:8; 1 Thessalonians 5:5–8.)

THE MOON UNDER HER FEET

The moon has no light of its own; it merely reflects the glory of the sun. So it is also with the church. We have no light of ourselves, but merely reflect the glory of Christ, the "Sun of Righteousness."

This was beautifully revealed in the ancient Hebrew sanctuary service, which was only "a shadow of good things to come" (Hebrews 10:1). Just as coming events cast their shadows before, so the cross of Christ cast a long shadow. It reached from Eden to Calvary.

The church is here revealed as standing on the moon, not in disdain of the Old Testament gospels of Moses and the prophets, but using them rather as a foundation. The everlasting gospel has the same message for all ages. The method of teaching salvation may differ, but men and women have always been, and can now be saved from sin by only one way, and that is by the grace of God.

We must not confuse this with the moon goddess of pagan religions. Neither the sun, nor the moon, nor even the woman are objects of worship, but merely symbols. The woman, or the church, is standing on the moon. In Psalm 89:34–37 the Lord declares that His covenant and His Word are as faithful and unaltered as the moon. The church was established upon the Word of God.

Upon her head a crown of twelve stars

The crown is a symbol of royalty. The church is called "a royal priesthood" (1 Peter 2:9). As we have noted before, twelve is God's kingdom number. There were twelve tribes in the Old Testament church and twelve apostles in the New Testament church. There are twelve foundations in the New Jerusalem and twelve gates to the city. There will also be twelve thrones in the church triumphant. (See Matthew 19:27, 28; Luke 22:28–30.)

She brought forth a man child

In Genesis 3:15 we find the first promise of the coming Redeemer. Eve seems to have thought that Cain was the promised One. Spurrel's translation of Genesis 4:1 reads, "I have obtained the man Jehovah." But instead of being the giver of life, Cain became the taker of life. Through all the centuries the devout children of God were looking for the coming Savior. "But when the fulness of the time was come, God sent forth his Son" (Galatians 4:4). And, true to the prophetic word, He came as a helpless babe.

The great red dragon

The dragon is clearly stated to be the devil. (See verse 9.) But in his attack upon God's people he has always worked through earthly persecuting powers, such as ancient Egypt and pagan Rome, both of which are represented in Scripture by this same symbol. (See Ezekiel 29:2–4.) "The pagan Romans used the image of a dragon on their standards, as well as the eagle. These dragon standards were red. 'The purple standard of the dragon' " (Ammianus Marcellinus, *History of the Roman Empire,* bk. 16, ch. 12).

This prophecy unmasks the monster and reveals the real power that has hidden behind such earthly kingdoms as Babylon, Tyre, and Rome. In Isaiah 14 and Ezekiel 28 is found the same power. From Eden to the end of time the slimy trail of the serpent appears. He poisoned the stream of life at the fountainhead, and his deception of the woman was actually an attack upon God. As the enemy of both Christ and His church he is mentioned thirteen times in Revelation.

The dragon waiting to devour the Child

God's promise made to Eve in Eden was cherished by His people. But they waited long for the coming of the promised "Seed"—Christ. (See Galatians 3:16.) The devil also waited, and at every turn he endeavored to thwart the plan of heaven to save the world. Many times he almost succeeded. Before the Flood all flesh was "corrupt," "but Noah found grace in the eyes of the LORD" (Genesis 6:8).

Then, as the promise of the Seed was narrowed at various times, such as to the tribe of Judah and to the family of David, there we find the enemy concentrating his forces. In the days of the Persians a decree was passed by the dictator monarch that the Jews as a nation were to be exterminated; but in spite of all the devil's plots and schemes, the plan of God was fulfilled. The New Testament opens with these triumphant words: "The book of the generation of Jesus Christ, the son of David, the son of Abraham" (Matthew 1:1). The Child was born in spite of the overwhelming opposition of the united powers of evil.

When Jesus was born, the dragon was there to attack Him. Escape came by fleeing to Egypt. In the wilderness the dragon leaped to the attack, only to be defeated by the Word of God. Then all the black passions of hate were let loose at Golgotha. Betrayed and crucified, the world's Redeemer was at last buried in a rock-hewn tomb. How evil triumphed! But only for a few hours. By His death and resurrection, Christ raided the realm of demonism and shattered the forces of darkness.

HER CHILD WAS CAUGHT UP UNTO GOD AND TO HIS THRONE

He arose for our justification, and as King of righteousness He now ministers at the throne of grace. (See Hebrews 4:14; 8:1; 10:12.) Who can bring any accusation against the elect of God? As we are justified in Christ and vindicated by His power, nothing now can separate us from the love of God which is in Christ Jesus. (See Romans 8:33, 34.)

How marvelous all this must have appeared to John! His own persecution, the early martyrdom of his brother James, the execution of Peter and Paul, he could now understand as he watched this unfolding panorama. Then, so that he could comprehend the full significance of the drama of sin and salvation, the curtain was rolled back, and the past as well as the future was opened to his view.

THERE WAS WAR IN HEAVEN

War did not begin on earth; it began in heaven. And the history of sin is long and ugly. Sin is a mystery for whose presence no excuse can be found. It did not originate on earth, but began in heaven when Lucifer instigated rebellion among the angels. As leader of the heavenly host, he challenged the rulership of God. (See Isaiah 14:12–15.) He was "perfect in beauty" and perfect in character "till iniquity was found in [him]" (Ezekiel 28:12, 15). Although the most honored of all the angelic host, he became jealous of the Creator, and, coveting His throne, began to sow discord among the angels, thus causing rebellion. "God permitted him [Satan] to demonstrate the nature of his claims, to show the working out of his proposed changes in the divine law. His own work must condemn him. . . . The whole universe must see the deceiver unmasked" (Ellen White, *Patriarchs and Prophets,* page 42).

MICHAEL AND HIS ANGELS FOUGHT AGAINST THE DRAGON

Peter speaks of "the angels that sinned" (2 Peter 2:4). Some of the angelic host joined Lucifer in his attack against God. These "angels which kept not their first estate, but left their own habitation," God will bring to judgment (Jude 6). John pictures the dragon as deceiving a "third part of the stars of heaven" (Revelation 12:4). They joined the forces of rebellion. It was a tragic day when the serpent won the allegiance of Adam and Eve, for this newly created earth then became the battleground of contending forces led by two great generals, Michael and the dragon. Until the death of Christ, Satan was the legal representative of this world. Although he had usurped the kingdom, he was always man's accuser. (See Job 1:6, 9–11.) The conflict between good and evil, therefore, has a far wider range than this visible earth. But sin will come to its end on this planet. (See Ezekiel 18:18, 19.)

THE ACCUSER OF OUR BRETHREN IS CAST DOWN

This mighty spiritual combat reached a new climax when Christ hung upon the cross. All heaven

watched the battle between light and darkness as it waxed stronger. And as Christ in his expiring agony upon the cross cried out, "It is finished," a shout of triumph rang through every world, and through heaven itself. The great contest that had been so long in progress in this world was now decided, and Christ was conqueror. His death had answered the question whether the Father and the Son had sufficient love for man to exercise self-denial and a spirit of sacrifice. Satan had revealed his true character as a liar and a murderer. It was seen that the very same spirit with which he had ruled the children of men who were under his power, he would have manifested if permitted to control the intelligences of heaven. With one voice the loyal universe united in extolling the divine administration (Ellen White, *Patriarchs and Prophets,* pages 69, 70).

When Christ arose from the grave, He then became the rightful representative of this world. His death reconciled the world to God, and the accuser, the devil, has no more claim to it. No wonder a shout was heard in heaven! Moreover, the inhabitants of heaven speak of the devil as "the accuser of *our* brethren" (Revelation 12:10, emphasis supplied). The elders knew something of his power, for they, too, had met him in mortal combat. The accuser and deceiver was finally cast down from his place of usurpation, and Christ, the Second Adam, became our Representative. (See verses 10, 12.)

Woe to the inhabitants of the earth!

And now is revealed the underlying cause of the great struggles of the church. The devil, knowing he has lost the battle against God, and recognizing that his time is short, is now concentrating all his power upon the followers of Christ. The prophet was shown this enemy of God and man persecuting the woman—the church. Up until the time of Christ's death Satan was eager to get other worlds to join him in rebellion. But now he is defeated. So he transfers all his energy to combating the church. To escape the attacks of the enemy, she flees to the place God has prepared for her, where she is nourished for 1,260 prophetic days, or literal years. This period is mentioned seven times in Daniel and in the Revelation: (1) Daniel 7:25; (2) Daniel 12:7; (3) Revelation 11:2; (4) Revelation 11:3; (5) Revelation 12:6; (6) Revelation 12:14; (7) Revelation 13:5. It began, as we have seen, with the decree of Justinian in A.D. 538 and ended with the overthrow of papal dominion in 1798. Secluded places, such as the Piedmont valleys and the Alpine mountain fastnesses, even the friendly land of young America, all became havens of refuge for the persecuted people of God.

The serpent cast out of his mouth water

Water in prophecy represents people. (See Revelation 17:15.) During the papal supremacy, many different peoples were used in an endeavor to destroy the true, faithful people of God. History's pages are stained with the blood of bitter persecutions and ruthless massacres. But all failed to destroy God's people. On the contrary, as one early church leader put it, "the blood of the martyrs is the seed of the church."

Heaven rejoices in the victory of the saints over the dragon's power. "They overcame him by the blood of the Lamb, and by the word of their testimony" (Revelation 12:11). But the prophet watches as another and more subtle attempt is made to destroy the church. The enemy casts out of his mouth a flood to carry the woman away. Truly a flood of false teachers steeped in evolution and human philosophy has arisen to oppose the truth of God. This is especially so since the end of the 1,260 years. The water was coming from the *mouth* of the serpent. What he failed to accomplish by armies and persecution, he seeks to attain by an army of false educators. Lying propaganda and "science falsely so called" (1 Timothy 6:20) will reach their climax in the final battle against truth.

THE EARTH OPENED HER MOUTH

To meet this new attack, "the earth opened her mouth" (Revelation 12:16). Through the centuries the earth helped the woman by providing a refuge for the persecuted people of God. But this new attack coming from the mouth of the serpent has been overcome in another way. As the new science of archaeology came into being, evidence from the buried cities of the past began to be piled up confirming the accuracy of the Bible records. Marvelous discoveries in the fields of archaeology, history, and geology have all substantiated and vindicated the Word of God. The Rosetta Stone, discovered in 1799, became the key to the past. It enabled scholars to learn the ancient Egyptian languages, thus opening the whole story of the ancients. Thousands of discoveries have been made in substantiation of biblical history. The earth has indeed opened her mouth, and the very stones are crying out in the ears of this skeptical age, "Thy word is truth" (John 17:17).

THE DRAGON WAS WROTH AND WENT TO MAKE WAR WITH THE REMNANT

Satan's final and greatest attempt will be made on the very last church, called in this chapter "the remnant of her seed" (Revelation 12:17). These loyal ones, obedient to "the commandments of God" and having "the testimony of Jesus" (verse 17), stand as faithful witnesses.

From the very beginning of the great controversy in heaven, it has been Satan's purpose to overthrow the law of God. It was to accomplish this that he entered upon his rebellion against the Creator; and though he was cast out of heaven, he has continued the same warfare upon the earth.

. . . The last great conflict between truth and error is but the final struggle of the long-standing controversy concerning the law of God (Ellen White, *The Great Controversy*, page 582).

In every great crisis of history God has had faithful servants whose allegiance to Him was more precious to them than life. The prophet Isaiah, writing at a time when truth was being compromised, spoke of those who were loyal to God as His "remnant." (See Isaiah 37:32; Zephaniah 3:12, 13; Micah 4:7.)

In the last great crisis of the ages, God will have a loyal "remnant" who by His grace will stand for truth and righteousness. John describes them as those that "keep the commandments of God, and have the testimony of Jesus," which the angel declared "is the spirit of prophecy" (Revelation 12:17; 19:10). Through His Word and the counsels of His Spirit, God is even now preparing that remnant to stand "in the evil day" when principalities and powers and "the rulers of the darkness of this world" will make their last attack upon the church (Ephesians 6:12, 14; see also 2 Thessalonians 2:9–13).

It is through this remnant that God is giving His last message of mercy to the world and revealing at the same time the machinations of the "man of sin" (2 Thessalonians 2:3) whose counterfeit system of salvation has obscured the glorious gospel of Christ and His saving grace. The church that is "waiting for the coming of our Lord" will "come behind in no gift," says the apostle Paul (1 Corinthians 1:7). God has His servants in every land of earth. These He is gathering by the power of the everlasting gospel as it is heralded to "every nation, and kindred, and tongue, and people" (Revelation 14:6). This is clearly expressed in the following quotation:

Among earth's inhabitants, scattered in every land, there are those who have not bowed the knee to Baal. Like the stars of heaven, which appear only at night, these faithful ones will shine forth when darkness covers the earth and gross darkness the people. In heathen Africa, in the Catholic lands of Europe and of South America, in China, in India, in the islands of the sea, and in all the dark corners of the earth, God has in reserve a firmament of chosen ones that will yet shine forth amidst the darkness, revealing clearly to an apostate world the transforming power of obedience to His law (Ellen White, *Prophets and Kings,* pages 188, 189).

32. The Beast From the Sea and the Man With the Mystic Number 666

How quickly the scenes change in this apocalyptic portrayal! John still watches enraptured as the drama of the ages unfolds. As the prophet now scans the restless sea, suddenly before his startled gaze there arises from the water a hideous wild beast. As we have seen when we examined the book of Daniel, that prophet also, in vision, saw beasts arise as symbols of powerful earthly kingdoms. (See Daniel 7.)

It was the dragon power, Rome, that gave the beast of Revelation 13 its seat (Greek: *thronos*) and great authority. John tells us that this beast power would utter blasphemy against God. (See Revelation 13:1, 5.) Domitian, who banished John to Patmos, issued state papers under the blasphemous title of "Emperor Domitian, Our Lord and Our God." It was this pagan power that gave the beast its authority. Let us take our places beside John and view these tremendous scenes in the great revelation of redemption as he saw them opened in heaven.

THE BEAST WITH SEVEN HEADS AND TEN HORNS

Some, because of the similarity of language in John's and Daniel's descriptions, claim that John was only borrowing from Daniel. Actually, Daniel was looking forward into history that was yet to come. He saw a succession of powers arising. First there was the lion kingdom (Babylon), then the bear (Persia), then the leopard (Greece), then the ten-horned beast (Rome). All these characteristics are embodied in this beast of Revelation 13. It is, therefore, a composite symbol of the kingdoms of this world over which Satan has exercised his dominion.

John, who was living six hundred years later than Daniel, viewed those same powers, but from a different perspective. He was looking both *backward* and *forward*. Though Rome was the ruling power, nevertheless so much of Greek civilization was preserved in the empire that we speak of it as the "Greco-Roman" culture. The prophetic symbol combines the ten-horned head of Rome with the leopard body of Greece. But the beast also embodies features of the former kingdoms of Persia and Babylon, for it had the feet of the bear (Persia) and the mouth of the lion (Babylon). Both Daniel and John emphasized the ten horns—the subsequent divisions of Rome.

THE DRAGON GIVES THE BEAST HIS POWER, SEAT, AND AUTHORITY

The dragon—"the Devil, and Satan" (Revelation 12:9)—always works through earthly kingdoms and institutions. Ancient Egypt was likened to the dragon. (See Ezekiel 29:3.) But the application in Revelation 12 is definitely to pagan Rome, the power that sought to destroy the Child Jesus as soon as He was born. Pagan Rome collapsed later and was replaced by Christianized Rome, or the papacy. The ancient city of Rome became the capital and center of authority for this new and growing power. In A.D. 330 Constantine left Rome to build Constantinople, the new capital. This might be called the beginning of the breakup of the empire. Constantinople later became the capital of Eastern Rome.

Many writers reveal the way the transference from pagan Rome to papal Rome was made. Eusebius in his *Life of Constantine* declares, "In order to render Christianity more attractive to the Gentiles, the priests adopted the exterior vestments and ornaments used in the pagan cult."

Pope Gregory, instructing Augustine, is credited with saying, "Destroy the idols, never the temples. Sprinkle them with holy water, place in them relics, and let the nations worship in the places they are accustomed to." Cardinal Baronius is said to have made the statement, "The Holy Church was permitted to appropriate the rites and ceremonies used by the pagans in their idolatrous cult since she [the church] expiated them by her consecration." These are indicative of the attitude of the Roman Church at that time. Compromise was its constant characteristic, while truth was tragically sacrificed on the altars of form and liturgy.

PONTIFEX MAXIMUS

Constantine, foreseeing the ultimate triumph of Christianity, became its champion. As emperor, he was already invested with the power and honors of paganism. These he did not renounce, but instead brought them over into Christianity. He therefore became the bridge uniting paganism with Christianity. Half a century later, A.D. 375, the Christian emperor Gratian refused the pagan vestments and the pagan title "Pontifex Maximus." But the bishop of Rome, seeing an opportunity to exalt his dignity, assumed the title and vestments of Pontifex Maximus.

In an earlier chapter, we noted that *pontifex* comes from two Latin words, *pons* (nominative) or *pontis* (genitive), meaning "bridge," and *factio,* meaning "I make" or *factor,* meaning "maker." *Maximus* means "the greatest." Putting these meanings together, we get "The Greatest Bridge Builder," or "Bridge Collector," as a toll collector. This was the historic title of the high priest of paganism. These titles and vestments perpetuated paganism in the church, but always under the disguise of Christianity. A former Roman Catholic bishop, who was a professor of church history in one of the main theological seminaries in Rome, pointed out that one reason for acceptance of the title was that a toll could be demanded of all who entered the city of Rome. It is claimed that this toll collection continued until the year 1870.

666—THE NUMBER OF THE BEAST

This mystic number represented a system, rather than an individual man. The dragon, or the serpent (paganism), gave the beast "his power, and his seat [or throne], and great authority" (Revelation 13:2).

Paganism is largely a religion of nature worship, the sun and the moon being prominent deities. The sun is often the male deity, and the moon is the female deity. In ancient mythology the serpent was universally the symbol of the sun. Sun worship and serpent worship began side by side, the *sun* being hailed as the source of all *physical* life, and the *serpent* as the source of all *spiritual* life.

The serpent, however, was certainly *not* the source of spiritual life, for the Bible declares that the serpent was the deceiver of humankind and so robbed human beings of spiritual life. Aesculapius, ancient god of medicine, was often represented by a serpent entwining itself around a dead tree trunk, symbol of the restorer of life.

The ancients claimed that God works by mathematics. Their religion was a conglomeration of religion, astrology, alchemy, physical and mental science, and mathematics. Ancient astrology divided the starry heavens into thirty-six constellations. These were represented by different amulets called *Sigilla Solis,* or the sun seal. These amulets were worn by pagan priests, and they contained all the numbers from one to thirty-six. By these figures they claimed to be able to foretell future events. These amulets were usually made of gold, yellow being the sun color. While being carried, these amulets were wrapped in yellow silk, as it was thought that the bearer would thus receive beneficent powers believed to emanate from the jewel.

One such amulet reveals the veneration the ancients had for the sun-god. On the front side is a depiction of the god of the sun standing on a lion. This indicates the sun's position in the constellation Leo (the lion) during the hot days of August. On the back is inscribed the word *nachyel,* meaning "intelligence of the sun." And the numerals one through thirty-six are arranged in squares in such a way that adding the numbers of any column, either horizontally or vertically, as well as the two diagonal columns crossing the square, the total is the same—111. The sum of the six columns, computed either horizontally or vertically is, therefore, 6×111—or 666.

After the empire of Babylon fell, the whole system of Egyptian and Babylonian mythology was transferred to Pergamos in Asia Minor. Later, it was brought over to the city of Rome. No wonder the Lord, writing to the church in Pergamos, said, "I know thy works, and where thou dwellest, even where Satan's seat is" (Revelation 2:13).

The corrupting system of idolatry through which the church departed from the faith is called by Paul "the mystery of iniquity" (2 Thessalonians 2:7) and by John, "MYSTERY, BABYLON THE GREAT" (Revelation 17:5). Already working in the days of the apostles, the full revelation of this apostasy was yet to be revealed. The Babylonian mysteries, always shrouded in secrecy, have from the most ancient times challenged God's truth. Paul speaks of "the unfruitful works of darkness," declaring that "it is a shame even to speak of those things which are done of them in secret" (Ephesians 5:11, 12).

The Beast From the Sea and the Man With the Mystic Number 666

When the Son of God was nailed to a cross it seemed as if evil had triumphed. But our Lord "endured the cross, despising the shame" (Hebrews 12:2), the cross being the symbol of this shameful cult.

This mystery-god mentioned by Plutarch as "the hidden god" (*De Iside et Osiride,* vol. 2, page 354) and by others as "the hidden system" was worshiped under the name *Saturn,* which means "to lie hidden." In the Chaldaic or Aramaic it is spelled S-T-U-R. Chambers, in his *Book of Days,* speaks of "the festival of St. Satur, the martyr." This "hidden system" of shame and apostasy invaded the church in the early centuries and has left its trail of corruption on every succeeding generation. The true God is not hidden; He is revealed in Jesus Christ.

Now let us note the significance of the letters S-T-U-R:

S -	200	"The Hidden God" of Babylonia
T -	60	(Aramaic language)
U -	400	
R -	6	
	666	

When this system was established in Rome, "City of the Seven Hills," Italy became the land of the mystery cults and was known for centuries as Saturnian Land, of the Land of Mystery. Saturn was also identical with Janus, the Grand Mediator and Opener and Shutter. And the high priests of paganism were invested with the keys of Janus and Cybele.

CHRISTIANITY CHALLENGES PAGANISM

When the Christian church began, the simplicity of the apostolic message was a strange contrast from the elaborate system of pagan mysteries. That a sinner could come directly into the presence of God and find salvation without the mediation of a whole system of priests and incantations seemed almost too good to be true. That simple message produced a purity of life. Men were different. They acted differently; there was a joy and peace which could not be gainsaid. Paul spoke of "the mystery of godliness" (1 Timothy 3:16) that embraced the Incarnation of our Lord, His blameless life, His ascension, and His ministry at the throne of Deity. What a contrast with the "mystery of iniquity" (2 Thessalonians 2:7)! Apart from the gospel of Christ, men could not have victory over sin. The Christian message was a call out of the darkness of the whole system of pagan mysteries. "Have no fellowship with the unfruitful works of darkness," wrote Paul, "for it is a shame even to speak of those things which are done of them in secret" (Ephesians 5:11, 12). And that was all too tragically true. The secret mysteries were often a cloak for debasing immorality.

The apostles, foreseeing that the pagan system would corrupt the simplicity of the gospel, warned the leaders of the churches. But little by little, despite their warnings, the church suffered "a falling away" (2 Thessalonians 2:3), and paganism became completely established in the apostate church. That branch of Christianity, at least, became not "the daughter of Zion," as God's ancient church was called, but instead, "the daughter of paganism," with headquarters in Rome. All the vestments of paganism became a part of the so-called Christian system. For example, the "keys of St. Peter" found on the papal coat of arms and worn by the pope, the head of the system, are not the keys of St. Peter, but are the modern counterpart of the pagan keys of Janus and Cybele. Many of the church festivals are pagan, as for example, the festival of St. Satur, the martyr, held on the twenty-ninth day of March. One of the prayers in the litany of the mass is, "God hidden, and my Saviour have mercy upon us" (W. McGavin, *The Protestant*, vol. 2, page 79). Saturn was the "hidden god" of paganism. No wonder God calls the system "MYSTERY, BABYLON THE GREAT" (Revelation 17:5).

Regarding the beast John saw, both the name and the number of his name are significant to the student of the Revelation, yet only by the wisdom of God can we know the apostate one designated. Therefore, we seek the guidance of our God as we unfold this divine secret. Accepting God's challenge to discover the significance of this number, 666, we would be as those searching for the hidden things of God, rather than as children playing with a conundrum. The dignity of the Apocalypse, while demanding our sober search, also demands a diligence that is rarely revealed in commentaries and books written on the Revelation. This mystic number was given the prophet John by the Holy Spirit, its secret to be revealed to those only who possess the wisdom of God. Many names have been suggested through the centuries, some too ridiculous to merit comment. This had led some to bypass the issue as if it deserved no further thought. But God says, "Let him that hath understanding [not the wisdom of the serpent, but the wisdom of God] count the number" (Revelation 13:18). As obedient servants, we have sought "the wisdom that is from above" (James 3:17), and our discoveries have led to some tremendous conclusions.

By decree, the sacred language of the Roman Church has been for centuries, not Greek or Hebrew, but Latin. When the pope speaks *ex cathedra,* he speaks in Latin. Until relatively recently the mass was always said in Latin. The ancient Greek word for "the Latin-speaking man" is *Lateinos,* which from very early times has been recognized as the name denoted in Revelation 13:18.

L	-	30		H	-	0
A	-	1		Ē	-	8
T	-	300	"Latin-speaking man"			"The Latin Kingdom"
E	-	5	or Latin Church	L	-	30 (Greek language)
I	-	10	(Greek language)	A	-	1
N	-	50		T	-	300
O	-	70		I	-	10
S	-	200		N	-	50
		666		Ē	-	8
				B	-	2
				A	-	1
				S	-	200
				I	-	10
				L	-	30
				E	-	5
				I	-	10
				A	-	1
						666

The computation appearing in the second column is significant. The Greek for "the Latin Kingdom" is HĒ LATINĒ BASILEIA, which also numbers 666. E. B. Elliott, in his *Horae Apocalypticae,* says, "But that which alone completely answers to every requirement of the sacred enigma, and which I, therefore fully believe to be the one intended by the Spirit is Irenaeus's solution, LATEINOS" (fourth edition, vol. 3, page 233). The letter "E" is usually omitted in the more modern spelling of the word, but such authorities as Irenaeus, Hippolytus, Andreas, and others spell it as set forth here. This title has also the same numerical significance in the Greek.

As previously mentioned, Italy was for a long time known as the Land of Mystery or Saturnian Land. When the Italian branch of the Christian church pushed its way into the ascendancy and sought control of the church universal or the Catholic Church, it became the *Roman* Catholic Church or the church of Italy. And it is significant that this name in Greek—ITALIKA EKKLĒSIA—the "Italian Church" also counts up to 666.

I	-	10	E	-	5	"Italian Church"
T	-	300	K	-	20	
A	-	1	K	-	20	
L	-	30	L	-	30	
I	-	10	Ē	-	8	(Greek language)
K	-	20	S	-	200	
A	-	1	I	-	10	
		372	A	-	1	
					294	

The head of the apostate church came into possession of a temporal kingdom when Pepin conferred upon Pope Stephen II the first grant of the Papal States in A.D. 755. The Roman pontiff then became a temporal sovereign and remained such for eleven centuries. But he was deprived of these states in 1870 when Italy was united by Garibaldi during the reign of King Victor Emmanuel II.

The pope, however, remained in the Vatican as a self-styled "prisoner" until February 11, 1929, when Mussolini restored to the supreme pontiff a fragment of the former domains, giving him about 180 acres. That restoration made him a "king" again, and the number of his kingdom is 666. Greek scholars have tested the names of some 400 other kingdoms, not one of which amounts in its number to the precise value of this mystic number—666.

PAPAL ADMISSIONS

But 666 is also the number *of a man*—the representative of the power. (See Revelation 13:18.) The Roman Catholic Bible, the Douay Version, contains a special footnote on Revelation 13:18 that reads, "The numeral letters of his name shall make up this number." There are many names and titles assumed by the Roman pontiff, but one of the most significant is VICARIUS FILII DEI, meaning the "Vicar of the Son of God." This title is incorporated in the canon law of the Roman Catholic Church. "Beatus Petrus in terris vicarius filii Dei videtur esse constitutus" (*Decretum Gratiani,* prima pars., dist. 96).

"The title *Vicarius Filii Dei* . . . is very common as the title for the Pope" (Dr. J. Quaston, S.T.D., professor of ancient history and Christian archaeology, School of Sacred Theology, Catholic University of America, Washington, D.C., March 5, 1943). This title was confirmed by a church council, according to Binius, a Roman Catholic dignitary of Cologne. (See *Sacrosancta Concilia,* vol. 1, pages 1539–1541.)

"The title of the Pope of Rome is Vicarius Filii Dei, and if you take the letters of his title which represent Latin numerals (printed large) and add them together, they come to 666" (*Our Sunday Visitor,* November 15, 1914).

It is to no purpose merely to multiply names and count the numerals. While many names have been seized upon through the centuries in an effort to interpret this prophecy, yet too often it has meant little more than idle speculation. We repeat, the challenge is not to the mathematician as such, nor to the philosopher with his worldly wisdom, but to the servant of God who earnestly seeks for "the wisdom that is from above" (James 3:17).

The title below is particularly significant as the climax to our investigation. Note its computation:

V	-	5	F	-	0	"Vicarius Filii Dei"
I	-	1	I	-	1	One of the pope's official
C	-	100	L	-	50	titles (Latin language).
A	-	0	I	-	1	
R	-	0	I	-	1	
I	-	1				
U	-	5	D	-	500	
S	-	0	E	-	0	
			I	-	1	
					666	

It is surely significant that through all the changing centuries from ancient Babylon to modern Babylon, the power that has corrupted the truth of God is branded with the number 666! When Babylon is mentioned in God's Word, the number six is strangely prominent. Nebuchadnezzar's image of gold, for example, was sixty cubits high and six cubits wide. And there were six different musical instruments in his "band" when the loyal Hebrews refused to worship that symbol of Babylonian greatness. (See Daniel 3.) In Daniel chapter 4, the "tree" that represented Babylonian power is mentioned just six times. Belshazzar met his doom while praising the gods of "gold," "silver," "brass," "iron," "wood," and "stone"—six in all. (See Daniel 5:4.) In the Revelation the name Babylon occurs just six times. In Lucifer's defiance of God, the personal pronoun "I" or "my" is used six times. (See Isaiah 14:13, 14.) Also in the story of the building of the Tower of Babel, or Babylon, the personal pronoun "us" or "we" is used just six times.

Anciently the Jews believed there was "a doom upon the number six even when it stood alone. Triple it, . . . you obtain three mysterious sixes following one another, 666, and we have represented a potency of evil than which there can be none greater, a direfulness of fate than which there can be none worse" (William Milligan, *The Expositor's Bible,* vol. 6, page 890).

The Beast From the Sea and the Man With the Mystic Number 666

To the Jew, six was the number of unrest or the number of man, who was created on the sixth day; seven was the number of perfection, and eight is the number of victory. If a number was tripled, it indicated the eternity of the thing symbolized, for example, 666 meant *eternal unrest; 777, eternal perfection;* 888, *eternal victory.* (See *The Antichrist 666,* pages 137–146.)

The fact that the papal number is identical with the sacred number of the ancient sun-god is significant. Against this system of deception, God has spoken in no uncertain language. He calls it "Babylon," or "confusion." And His message today is, "Come out of her, my people" (Revelation 18:4). His true church will be victorious. They will stand on the sea of glass, singing the song of Moses and the Lamb, the song of victory "over the beast, and over his image, and over his mark, and over the number of his name" (Revelation 15:2). Through a greater name, the name of Jesus, they have conquered sin, for "there is none other name under heaven given among men, whereby we must be saved" (Acts 4:12). God hath "given him [Jesus] a name which is above every name: that at the name of Jesus every knee should bow" (Philippians 2:9, 10). All hail the power of Jesus' name!

33. The Collapse of Intolerance and the Rise of America

When paganism invaded the church, it brought with it not only its vestments and mysteries but also its spirit of intolerance. When man ceases to rule by love, he resorts to force.

The church loses her mission in the world. When the early church began to lose her "first love," she also lost her vision. When she entered politics, she fell from her high spiritual estate. Instead of continuing as a mighty missionary movement concerned only with carrying the good news of a free salvation to all men everywhere, she began to build herself into a great financial institution with the avowed objective of ruling the nations. Then instead of looking forward to the return of Christ, accompanied by His angels with power and great glory, as the consummation of her hopes, this apostate church began to teach that her mission in the world was to establish herself as the political leader of the world, and through a so-called spiritual rulership usher in the kingdom of God on the earth. This concept of the church and her work was a complete reversal of the apostolic message. Augustine's book *The City of God* interpreted Revelation 20 to mean that the church would rule the nations.

THE CHURCH BECOMES AN ESTABLISHED INSTITUTION

In the days of the apostles the church made tremendous spiritual conquests. She truly "went forth conquering, and to conquer" (Revelation 6:2). But a change came. Paul spoke of that coming change as the "falling away" (2 Thessalonians 2:3). This apostasy, he said, would give rise to "that man of sin" who, while exalting himself above all that is called God, and sitting as a ruler in the temple of God, and even claiming to be God, would, in the guise of Christianity, corrupt the truth and oppose any who differed with him. (See 2 Thessalonians 2:3, 4.)

THE BEAST ARISES FROM THE SEA

The decline of spiritual power within the established church was not sudden. Church history traces the tragic steps that finally placed civil and religious authority in one hand. Power-hungry popes boasting the title "God's vicegerent on earth" usurped the prerogatives of Deity. Purporting to be the successors of Peter, they claimed authority, not over the church alone, but over the entire world. For example, Pope Innocent III (ruled 1198–1216) wrote that "as the sun and moon are placed in the firmament, the greater as the light of day and the lesser of the night, so there are two powers on earth, the greater the pontifical and the lesser the royal." Making and unmaking kings was the pastime of pontiffs. Trampling on the rights of conscience, these medieval rulers dominated princes, states, and parliaments, compelling submission through the most horrible engine of tyranny, the Inquisition. Plotting and scheming to gain more power, this dominating church continued to "wear out the saints of the most High" and attempted to change God's law (Daniel 7:25). And this was to continue for forty-two months.

This prophetic period John has already introduced five times and in three different ways, while Daniel speaks of it twice. One method of expression used by both John and Daniel is "a time, and times, and half a time" (Revelation 12:14; Daniel 7:25; 12:7). A "time" was a Hebrew way of expressing a year. (See Daniel 4:16; 11:13, margin.) The calculation is clear and convincing:

1 "time" equals 1 year or	360 days
2 "times" equals 2 years or	720 days
½ "time" equals ½ year or	<u>180 days</u>
Total	1,260 days

The expression "forty and two months" is arresting. A prophetic month consists of thirty days. So forty-two months multiplied by thirty would give us 1,260 days. Biblical authorities agree that in prophecy a day represents a year. Commencing with the decree of Justinian in A.D. 538, this extended to 1798. Two and a half centuries before this significant date, Europe was being rocked by revolution—a revolution of ideas stemming largely from the Protestant Reformation. Nation after nation severed its allegiance to ecclesiastical authority.

Bible prophecy foretold not only the rise of the papacy but also her downfall. This power that pretended to speak for Christ was actually speaking against Him. Every Reformer without exception spoke of this apostate church as "antichrist." Now the word *anti* means "against" and "rivalry" or "supplanting." The papacy fulfills both ideas, as the leaders of the sixteenth century Reformation so ably set forth. But the arrogant and blasphemous power was nearing the end of her allotted period of dominance, and political events were shaping up for her collapse. Napoleon, one of the most powerful figures of history, began with rapid strides to change the face of Europe. And it was during the Napoleonic wars that the papal head of this beast conglomerate (see Revelation 13) was "as it were wounded to death" (Revelation 13:3). "He that leadeth into captivity shall go into captivity: he that killeth with the sword must be killed with the sword" (verse 10). In 1798 General Berthier, by no means a strong general, took Pope Pius VI prisoner. The pope was exiled until his death a year later; during this time there was no ruling pope. With what remarkable precision the prophetic period of 1,260 years was completely fulfilled!

John, however, not only foretold her wounding and her captivity but also declared that her deadly wound would be healed. Then, he said, "all the world wondered after the beast" (verse 3)—a truly remarkable prediction. When Italy was united under Garibaldi's revolution (1866–1870), the church was stripped of even her lands, leaving the pope a virtual prisoner in the Vatican. Fifty-nine years later, on February 11, 1929, the famous concordat signed by Mussolini and Cardinal Gaspari restored a part of those lands, since which time the pope has been a king again among the sovereigns of earth. The official church reporter, describing this history-making event, said, "We are now witnessing the signing of this document. As the ink flows from these pens *it is healing the wound* of fifty-nine years" (emphasis supplied).

The Collapse of Intolerance and the Rise of America

Even the most casual observer is compelled to recognize the rapid growth and international prestige and power of the Roman Catholic Church. She is today exercising a greater influence on world affairs than at any time in her long and checkered history. And more and more is her influence being felt in the United States.

ANOTHER BEAST COMES UP OUT OF THE EARTH

At the time the ten-horned beast received its deadly wound (1798) another power was seen to arise. (See Revelation 13:11–17.) The first beast was from the "sea"; the second came up from the "earth." The sea represents "peoples, and multitudes, and nations, and tongues" (Revelation 17:15), a true picture of Europe, where the papal beast arose. The *earth* must represent, not a crowded country of diverse nations, but a sparsely populated and isolated area. And where was there such a place? Certainly not in Europe or Asia. True to the prophecy, something tremendous was happening across the Atlantic. A century and a half before this time, colonies had begun to spring up in America. By 1776 these colonies had bound themselves together and were waging their Revolutionary War, severing themselves from Europe. Thus the foundation was laid for a completely new nation.

Following the war the American Constitution was framed and ratified, going into effect in 1789. The same year the French Revolution broke out, causing an upheaval not only in France but throughout Europe. This brought an end to the Holy Roman Empire. The downfall of the first beast from the sea marked the rise of the beast from the earth. And it came up in a land far removed from the "peoples, and multitudes, and nations, and tongues" of the Old World. John Wesley, interpreting this prophecy about 1760, said, "He is not yet come, though he cannot be far off. For he is to appear at the end of the forty-two months of the first beast" (*Explanatory Notes Upon the New Testament,* 17th ed., page 704). The Greek word *anabainō* means to come up quietly, unobtrusively, but quickly, as a springing vegetable. And that is how America arose. One historian says, "Like a silent seed we grew into an empire."

TWO HORNS LIKE A LAMB

Horns denote power, as we have already observed, the ten horns of the wild beast from the sea representing the ten divisions of ancient Rome. This new beast has not ten, but two, horns, lamblike, innocent, even Christian in appearance. How representative of the two great cornerstones of the American republic—civil and religious liberty, or republicanism and Protestantism. Those founding fathers of the new nation wanted "a country without a king, and a church without a pope." And their ideals were embodied in the American Constitution, which, declared Gladstone, one of the greatest prime ministers of Great Britain, is "the most wonderful work ever struck off at a given time by the brain and purpose of man."

That constitution, which so definitely separates church and state, was the fruit of a long struggle for liberty and also of an intensive study of great minds. Its greatness lies in this: It protects the divine right of man against the so-called right of kings and dictators, and it permits Congress to establish a court, but not a religion; to suppress an insurrection, but not a newspaper; to close a port, but not her citizens' mouths; to regulate commerce, but not a church; to take a vacation, but not her citizens' property. It stands as a buffer between freedom and despotism. It is a stumbling block in the path of ambitious and designing men who would destroy true liberty. It protects the weak against the strong, the minority against the majority. It upholds the sovereignty of the individual.

At the time of the Declaration of Independence, the population of the American colonies was not more than three million. Today it has reached almost one hundred times that number—or almost three hundred million. In 1776 the land area of the states was only 500,000 square miles; today it is 3,537,438 square miles. America indeed came up at the right *time* and in the right *way,* and she has done the *very things* prophecy stated would be her history. But no statesman, even fifty years ago, would have dared to predict the international role the United States is playing today. "Isolation" and "noninterference" seem outmoded phrases in her foreign policy as she has assumed an unprecedented role in world affairs.

The Collapse of Intolerance and the Rise of America

HE SPEAKS AS A DRAGON

The illustrious history of the United States would seem to make impossible the rise of intolerance. But God's Word declares that this country, which has been the very cradle of liberty, will yet speak with the voice of a dictator, exercising "all the power of the first beast" and compelling men "to worship the first beast, whose deadly wound was healed" (Revelation 13:12). How slow we are to learn the lessons of history.

Edwin Burke, speaking before the British House of Commons in 1784, declared, "People never give up their liberties but under some delusion." Benjamin Franklin said, "Those who would give up essential liberty to purchase a little temporary safety, deserve neither liberty nor safety." Daniel Webster emphasizes the same truth by declaring, "God grants liberty only to those who love it, and are always ready to guard and defend it." All too many in lands where liberty prevails seem to take freedom for granted, forgetting the price paid in sacrifice and blood.

LIBERTY ENDANGERED

The very freedom of the United States makes it possible for organizations that are alien to freedom to undermine the principles of liberty. Some who reside in America do not share the principles that have characterized this country from its beginning. In the political climate of today, personal liberties can become fragile as the United States and the many other countries around the world try to protect themselves against those who would destroy them. As a result, many are urging that government be made stronger and that personal liberties may need to be curtailed. Therein lies the danger. When government becomes the master instead of the servant, personal freedoms can disappear quickly. Liberties are safeguarded by citizens, not by politics. The future freedom of America depends upon every citizen being aware of the real issues at stake. When there is so much fog in the political atmosphere, it is easy to be misunderstood, and to be concerned is to run the risk of being looked upon as an alarmist. But the issues of the future are too vital to remain silent.

They are slaves who fear to speak
For the fallen and the weak;
They are slaves who will not choose
Hatred, scoffing, and abuse,
Rather than in silence shrink
From the truth they needs must think;
They are slaves who dare not be
In the right with two or three.
　　　　　　　—James Russell Lowell

While liberty is often the most costly possession, it is also the most fragile, and "eternal vigilance" is its price. Liberty is the very heart of the gospel. "The truth shall make you free," declared Jesus (John 8:32), and His freedom is not license but liberty. False liberty is a man's freedom to do what he likes, but true liberty is a man's freedom to do what he ought. "Where the Spirit of the Lord is, there is liberty," declares the apostle Paul (2 Corinthians 3:17).

EFFORTS TO AMEND THE CONSTITUTION

Even before the dawn of the twentieth century, such organizations as the National Reform Association, the International Reform Federation, and the Lord's Day Alliance were working tirelessly to insert changes into the American Constitution which, although appearing harmless, could completely destroy freedom. Notice these statements of objectives from an official source at that time:

> To secure such an amendment to the Constitution of the United States as will . . . indicate that this is a Christian nation, and place all the Christian laws, institutions, and usages of our government on an undeniably legal basis in the fundamental law of the land (David McAllister, *The National Reform Movement, . . . A Manual of Christian Civil Government,* "Article II of Constitution," 1898 ed., pages 15, 16).

We cordially, gladly recognize the fact that in South American Republics, and in France and other European countries, the Roman Catholics are the recognized advocates of national Christianity, and stand opposed to all the proposals of secularism. . . . Whenever they are willing to cooperate in resisting the progress of political atheism, we will gladly join hands with them in a World's Conference for the Promotion of National Christianity,—which ought to be held at no distant day—many countries could be represented only by Roman Catholics (*Christian Statesman* [the official organ of the National Reform Association], December 11, 1884, page 2).

We quote these to show that the determination to have changes made in the Constitution is not new. The rapid growth of Roman Catholic influence in this country makes the situation more alarming.

On September 7, 1947, Pope Pius XII declared that " 'the time for reflection and planning is past' in religious and moral fields and the 'time for action' has arrived." He said that "the battle in religious and moral fields hinged on five points: Religious culture, the sanctifying of Sunday, the saving of the Christian family, social justice, and loyalty and truthfulness in dealings" (*Evening Star,* Washington, D.C., September 8, 1947).

With the 1961 decision of the Supreme Court of the United States declaring state Sunday-closing laws to be constitutional, a long step was taken toward the sanctifying of Sunday. Protestants have for many years sought Sunday enforcement deliberately as religious legislation and indirectly as welfare legislation. As Catholics have added their voice, there as been a joining of forces between Protestants and Catholics to bring about a more favorable legal environment for Sunday observance and more stringent state laws to achieve this objective—with the ultimate aim of a national Sunday law.

No one should be denied the right to worship God according to the dictates of his own conscience, but the history of the papacy where she has gained control should lead all thoughtful citizens to view with real concern the present trend. Such groups are aware of the danger of these demanded changes, as is evidence in such statements as this:

> If Congress shall declare the first day of the week holy, it will not convince the Jew nor the Sabbatarian. It will dissatisfy both, and consequently, convert neither. . . . If a solemn act of legislation shall, in one point, define the law of God, or point out to the citizen one religious duty, it may, with equal propriety, proceed to define every part of divine revelation, and enforce every religious obligation, even to the forms and ceremonies of worship, the endowment of the church, and the support of the clergy. . . .
>
> The framers of the Constitution recognized the eternal principle that man's relation with his God is above human legislation, and his rights of conscience inalienable (*Sunday Mail,* U.S. House Reports, vol. 2, no. 271, pages 1–4).

GROWTH OF CATHOLICISM

At the beginning of the twentieth century, Roman Catholicism in North America was regarded as a mission project supported by gifts from outside the nation. That is no longer the case, and according to some estimates, more money flows into Rome from the United States than from all other sources. History has a way of repeating itself, and old controversies can come to life again at a mere pretext. That which has safeguarded the liberties of the people of the United States has been the determination to keep forever separate church and state. And American Catholics generally have recognized the wisdom of this. As stated by Oscar Halecki, "The Vatican knows well that the separation of church and state in the United States actually assists Roman Catholicism" (Oscar Halecki and James F. Murray, Jr., *Eugenio Pacelli: Pope of Peace,* [New York: Creative Age Press, 1951]. Quoted in the *Catholic*

Digest 15:7 [May, 1951] article, "Pius XII and the U.S.A.," by Oscar Halecki).

In an address in July 1953, at the New York University Center, John B. Sherrin, C.S.P., editor of the *Catholic World,* said, "It is not true, . . . that the Holy See condemned the proposition that 'the Church must be separated from the State and the State from the Church.' What was condemned, he said, was a separation of Church and State as the ideal relationship, 'not the proposition that the Church may be separated from the State.' " (*Religious News Service,* July 14, 1953.)

This reasoning is clear in its implications, however. Events today are moving rapidly, and Catholicism and Protestantism are agreeing on an increasing number of social issues and joining forces to achieve common religious objectives.

AN IMAGE TO THE BEAST

An image is not the exact thing, but something so near to the original that it looks or acts the same. With the United States stretching her hands across the sea to clasp hands with the restored papacy, the world scarcely need be surprised to see the union completed. The wound of 1798 is rapidly being healed, and even the scar is disappearing. Her future role will be tremendous.

THAT NO MAN MAY BUY OR SELL

This graphic chapter of the Revelation closes with a picture of a worldwide boycott. In an endeavor to unify religious thought and establish peace among the nations, this two-horned beast power, America, will yet lead out in programs of religious confederation that will result in loss of liberty. Those only who identify themselves with the beast and receive his mark will be permitted to buy and sell. Contrary to all her history, America will join forces with the revived power of Rome and, contrary to all expectations, will find herself actually in the role of a religious oppressor.

Vatican Council II (1962–1965) was a most significant and far reaching event. Pope John was fired with a desire to see a new Pentecost. He therefore set out to adapt the church's whole life to the revolutionary changes taking place in science, economics, and politics—to make it more Catholic and less Roman. He began by calling Protestants "separated brethren" rather than "heretics." The aim of this laudable attitude is Christian unity. This is exactly what prophecy indicates.

DEVILS WORKING MIRACLES

The modern intrusion of demon power into Western culture is one of the most significant fulfillments of this amazing prophecy. At the very time that America was beginning to influence world thought, modern spiritism made its appearance. Since then it has swept around the world and can count its adherents by millions. Many branches of occult science have arisen in recent decades. While these are not actually new, for they have always been a vital part of heathen religions, yet they are now invading the West with new powers of deception. Miracles are being wrought, not by the power of God, but by demonism.

Spiritism, with its attendant table tipping and rappings, had its modern origin in 1848 at the home of the Fox sisters in Rochester, New York. It began in this crude form, but is has since then developed into more or less of a science. At least it is claiming the attention of many leading scientists. God declares it a deceiver by which earth's last generation will be led away from the saving truth of the gospel of Christ. Fire will even be brought down from heaven to compel the attention of the multitudes. (See Revelation 13:13.) But the issue will reach a real climax when a coalition is made between spiritism, Catholicism, and apostate Protestantism. This will culminate in the forced worship of the beast and the reception of his mark. The identity of this mark will be discussed in the next chapter. These events will lead to the setting up of the image of the beast. And occultism in various ways, but especially through spiritualism, will play a major role in the final worldwide deception. This movement will draw together every form of religious culture with the avowed objective of building a world government headed by a world church. And persecution has historically followed on the heels of a uniting of church and state.

The Collapse of Intolerance and the Rise of America

THE TORCH OF LIBERTY

A family had been seeing the sights of New York for the first time. They had visited many places, among them the famous Statue of Liberty. After an exciting day, the little girl found it difficult to get to sleep. "Why don't you go to sleep, honey?" asked the father.

She replied, "Daddy, I'm thinking about that lady with the lamp out there in the dark. She's all alone. Don't you think we should be helping Miss Liberty to hold up the lamp?"

To help hold up the torch of liberty is the duty, not only of one family, but of every true Christian throughout America and the world.

34. God's Final Appeal to Mankind

The significance of this chapter—Revelation 14—will be missed unless we view it in relation to chapters 12 and 13. In vision, John has been watching the preparations for the final battle between two great opposing powers. The enemy of all righteousness is marshalling his strength against God's loyal remnant. Even America, the champion of freedom, will forget her history. With such a combination of evil, and all the world acclaiming the greatness of the beast and his image, how can true Christianity possibly survive?

THE VICTORIOUS COMPANY ON MOUNT ZION WITH THE LAMB

With dramatic instinct, the prophet quickly shifts the scene. We gaze not upon oppressing powers of earth, but on the victorious company standing with the Lamb on Mount Zion. What a contrast! The "Father's name," not the mark of the beast, is "written in their foreheads" (Revelation 14:1). They are a special group, the same group we noticed in chapter 7. In the setting of that prophecy this group was still on the earth surrounded by their enemies, but ready to be sealed with the seal of the living God. They are gathered from all nations. In chapter 14, the same company is seen with Christ.

THEY SING A NEW SONG

As John watches, he is enthralled by the sound of singing. It is like the rolling of many waters or the voice of a great multitude. Forty-six times in the Apocalypse voices are heard, and they are almost all voices of victory. This is not only a song of victory; it is a song of experience. Only those who have passed through the time of trouble, who have stood firmly for God's truth when all the world wondered after the beast, and who have witnessed the awful effects of the seven last plagues, will be able to join in this particular song. It is a *new* song, for it records a *new* experience. It is majestic and sublime, yet sweet and tender—the most lovely song in heaven or earth, like "harpers harping with their harps" (verse 2). Those only who have experienced full salvation from sin can learn it.

NOT DEFILED WITH WOMEN

Those constituting this special company are undefiled in life and doctrine. A woman in prophecy denotes a church. In Revelation 17:5 we have the picture of an impure woman with her daughters, all of whom have partaken of the same unholy nature. The woman is called "MYSTERY, BABYLON THE GREAT." This is the apostate church that reigns over the kings of the earth. (See verse 18.) While this has had its application through the centuries, yet its special fulfillment is just before Christ returns. But the 144,000 are not defiled with these women, or these apostate churches. They have a pure faith not defiled by false teachings; it is "the faith of Jesus" (Revelation 14:12).

THEY ARE VIRGINS

The church that will be waiting for the Master's return is described in the parable of the ten virgins. (See Matthew 25:1–13.) They are virgins because they have a pure faith. They keep the commandments of God and the faith of Jesus. (See Revelation 14:12.) The "lamps" in the hands of the waiting virgins are a symbol of the Word of God, which David declared was a lamp unto his feet. (See Psalm 119:105.) It is not sufficient to have the lamp; we also need the oil—a deep Christian experience that comes through the indwelling Spirit of God.

FIRST FRUITS TO GOD AND TO THE LAMB

The expression "first fruits" refers to quality. Of all those redeemed from the earth, these are the first in quality. They have been purchased away from men. They have been separated from the sinful habits and conversation of the world. (See 1 Corinthians 6:20.) They have not been deluded by the deceptions of the devil. (See 2 Thessalonians 2:9–11.)

In his letter to the church, John said that when Jesus shall appear, we shall be like Him. (See 1 John 3:3.) To be like the Master is the highest spiritual attainment.

Those who come from the grave at the second coming of Christ will be raised in a state of perfection by the creative power of God. Those who will be living to witness Jesus' coming will have grown into perfection by the grace and power of the indwelling Spirit. This, too, is a manifestation of creative power.

THEY ARE WITHOUT FAULT

"In their mouth was found no guile" (Revelation 14:5). Here is God's description of the victorious remnant awaiting their Master's return. James says, "If any man offend not in word, the same is a perfect man" (James 3:2). Zephaniah, describing the remnant church, says that they "shall not do iniquity, nor speak lies; neither shall a deceitful tongue be found in their mouth" (Zephaniah 3:13).

THESE FOLLOW THE LAMB

The highest honor God can ever grant is reserved for this special company. "These are they which follow the Lamb whithersoever he goeth" (Revelation 14:4). Accompanying their loved Commander throughout the vast universe, they become a special trophy of grace. Having lived through earth's most tragic hour when the deceptions of the devil have been the greatest, they have nevertheless been victorious. What a wonderful reward for their faith! What is the secret of their victory when everything is set against them? The answer is found in the three angels' messages brought to view in the next few verses.

THE ANGEL HAVING THE EVERLASTING GOSPEL

Symbolizing a message or a messenger, this first angel represents a worldwide message; not some new message, but rather the message of the old, the everlasting, gospel. God has always had but one gospel, sometimes called "the gospel of God," "the gospel of grace," the gospel of Jesus Christ," "the gospel of the kingdom," etc. These different expressions merely emphasize different phases of the same glorious gospel of good news. It was proclaimed to Adam before he was driven from Eden. Noah, too, was "a preacher of righteousness" (2 Peter 2:5). He proclaimed salvation from sin because he "found grace in the eyes of the LORD" (Genesis 6:8). Faithful Abraham taught the same glorious gospel (see Galatians 3:8), and Moses esteemed "the reproach of Christ greater riches than the treasures in Egypt" (Hebrews 11:26). These all looked *forward* to the Redeemer, whereas we who are living on this side of the cross of Christ look *backward.* But men of every age are saved from sin by the same grace and the same Savior. Paul speaks of God's "eternal purpose" (Ephesians 3:11), but it was made known to men in the setting they could understand. In each particular age some special emphasis has been given to some particular phase of the gospel. In this last generation the great burden of the gospel is to herald the imminent return of our Lord and to prepare a special people to meet Him. It is therefore in the setting of the judgment hour that the everlasting gospel is being proclaimed today. It comes with special warning to all them that "dwell" or "sit" on the earth, those who are at ease and settled.

THE FIRST ANGEL'S MESSAGE: GOD'S JUDGMENT HOUR IS COME

From his vantage point in the heavenly sanctuary John envisions dramatic happenings. Three angels are sent forth from God's headquarters as recruiting officers. They are bidden to hurry with special messages to every nation, kindred, tongue, and people. They are to enlist recruits for God. Not all in the world have made their decision to be wholly for God or for Satan. "Multitudes in the valley of decision" (Joel 3:14) is another prophet's description. In the very hour of God's judgment millions hear the messages, and a great multitude rally to the call of the Captain of their salvation and join the ranks of God's people.

Judgment is intrinsic to the gospel of Christ, for only in the judgment will the righteousness of God be revealed and His character vindicated. And in that count the names of overcomers only are retained in the Lamb's book of life. (See Revelation 3:5; Daniel 12:1.) When Paul preached, he looked forward to the judgment. "He reasoned of righteousness, temperance, and judgment *to come*" (Acts 24:25, emphasis supplied). But the last message of mercy that goes to the world declares that the hour of God's judgment *is* come. (See Revelation 14:7). This is the truth for this generation. The hour of God's judgment has already struck.

This judgment announcement is a call to worship the Creator. At the time the beast and his image are claiming the worship of the nation, God calls men to worship Him who made heaven and earth. Like the Romans to whom Paul wrote, men today are worshiping "the creature more than the Creator" (Romans 1:25). Education and human philosophy have robbed men of the concept of a personal God. The Creator has been lost in His creation. To worship the Creator fully, we must also recognize the sign of His creative power, and that sign is the Sabbath. "For in six days the LORD made heaven and earth, . . . and rested the seventh day: wherefore the LORD blessed the sabbath day, and hallowed it" (Exodus 20:11).

"God's *blessing* and *sanctifying* the day meant that He separated it from a common to a religious use, to be a perpetual memorial or sign that all who thus observe it would show themselves to be the worshipers of that God who made the world in six days and rested on the seventh" (*Binney's Theological Compend,* pages 169, 170.)

"The importance of the Sabbath as a memorial of creation is that it keeps ever present the true reason why worship is due to God"—because He is the Creator, and we are His creatures. "The Sabbath, therefore lies at the very foundation of divine worship; for it teaches this great truth in the most impressive manner, and no other institution does this. The true ground of divine worship, not of that on the seventh day merely, but of all worship, is found in the distinction between the Creator and His creatures. This great fact can never become obsolete, and must never be forgotten" (J. N. Andrews, *History of the Sabbath,* chapter 27). It was to keep this truth ever before the minds of men, that God instituted the Sabbath in Eden; and so long as the fact that He is our Creator continues to be a reason why we should worship Him, so long the Sabbath will continue as its sign and memorial. Had the Sabbath been universally kept, man's thoughts and affections would have been led to the Creator as the object of reverence and worship, and there would never have been an idolator, an atheist, or an infidel. The keeping of the Sabbath is a sign of

324

loyalty to the true God, "Him that made heaven and earth, and the sea, and the fountains of waters." It follows that the message which commands men to worship God and keep His commandments, will especially call upon them to keep the fourth commandment (Ellen White, *The Great Controversy*, pages 437, 438).

THE SECOND ANGEL'S MESSAGE—BABYLON IS FALLEN

This is the first time the word *Babylon* occurs in the book of Revelation, and as we have already noticed, it is used just six times. We have observed that the number six is prominent in the mystery worship of ancient Babylon. This ancient city had its origin when men willfully and knowingly turned from the grace of God and sought salvation by their own works. Nimrod's building of the city of Babylon culminated in the apostasy of the Tower of Babel.

"Let us make us a name," they said (Genesis 11:4). Reference has already been made to this deliberate and organized apostasy. This whole project was in defiance of God's promise that He would never again destroy the world by a flood. The name by which they would have desired to be remembered was *Bab-ril,* meaning "gate of God," but God sent confusion to them, and they never finished their project. God called the place "Babel" or "Babylon," which means confusion. Their tower, which was to be a monument to their pride, became a memorial to their folly.

From that day to this, Babylon has symbolized apostasy, arrogance, confusion, and a man-made salvation. Two ancient cities, Jerusalem and Babylon, are set in contrast in the Scriptures—Salem, meaning "peace," and Babel, meaning "confusion." One city (Jerusalem) became the center of God's earthly kingdom; the other (Babylon) became the center of Satan's earthly kingdom. In the New Testament, and especially in the Revelation, these cities represent two spiritual kingdoms.

Part of God's threefold message today is, "Babylon is fallen, . . . because she made all nations drink" (Revelation 14:8). Many professing Christians, like the ancient Babel builders, have turned from the everlasting gospel to follow their own devisings, with the theory of evolution replacing the Bible account of Creation. It is being heralded today, not only in the halls of learning, but even from the pulpits. The effect of this modern evolutionary theory upon Christian belief is tremendous. Faith is being subtly undermined. Professor Randall of Columbia University stated, "Today it seems that the great Hebrew-Christian moral tradition, the most ancient part of our heritage, is crumbling to pieces before our very eyes. . . . The man who trusts a physical science to describe the world finds no conceivable place into which to fit a deity" (*Current History,* June, 1929, pages 359–361). James Gilkey states the truth about liberal Christianity thus: "Liberal Protestants have abandoned belief in the verbal infallibility of the Bible" (*A Faith to Affirm,* page 3). To emphasize this, he quotes from recent speeches of certain modernist leaders, who seem to delight in expressing blatant unbelief of the cardinal doctrines of true Christianity. One preacher said, "We believe that Jesus was a human being, . . . that He was born in the normal way. . . . To us Jesus' death is, in essence, no different from the death of other heroes" (ibid., pages 9, 10).

Summing it up, Gilkey says:

Today the ancient belief that Jesus will reappear in the sky, inaugurate a dramatic world judgment, . . . has dwindled from a universally accepted and enormously influential Christian conviction to the esoteric doctrine of a minority. Once a modern man accepts what historians tell him about the age of the universe and once he accepts what scientists tell him about the nature of the evolutionary process, he cannot believe that there will ever be any such spectacular wind-up of the world's affairs as the one which the early Christians believed would presently take place (ibid., page 24).

The nations and even many churches are drunk with the intoxicating wine of Babylon. As the ancient Babylonians, "mad upon their idols" (Jeremiah 50:38), defied God and were overthrown (see Daniel 5), so also will modern Babylon meet her doom. Ancient Babylon could have been healed, but she refused the truth of God. (See Jeremiah 51:9.) Like that ancient city, modern Babylon is also rejecting the divine counsel. Having despised the Word of God, she has actually "become the habitation of devils, and the hold of every foul spirit" (Revelation 18:2).

Every unholy doctrine found in ancient Babylon—spiritism, sun worship, astrology, etc., with all their accompanying evils—can be found in modern Babylon. Because she is doomed, God is calling His people to separate from her. "Come out of her, my people, that ye be not partakers of her sins" (verse 4). "Come out from among them, and be ye separate, saith the Lord, . . . and I will receive you" (2 Corinthians 6:17).

THE THIRD ANGEL'S MESSAGE—A WARNING AGAINST FALSE WORSHIP

"If any man worship the beast and his image, and receive his mark in his forehead, or in his hand, the same shall drink of the wine of the wrath of God, which is poured out without mixture" (Revelation 14:9, 10). No other message in all the Bible is as solemn as this, and it comes with particular meaning in view of the worldwide apostasy and boycott prophesied in Revelation 13:16, 17, when universal allegiance to the apostate power will be enforced.

THE MARK OF THE BEAST

Whatever the mark of the beast is, it must be something clear and definite. God's unmingled wrath would not be reserved as a punishment for an unknown offense. Furthermore, the mark of the beast must be in contradistinction to the "seal" or mark of God. His seal, the sign of His creative power, as we have already noted, is God's rest day, or the true Sabbath. It follows that the seal or mark of this universal apostasy would be man's rest day, or the false day of worship.

When the church began to fall away from the apostolic faith, she gradually accepted pagan practices. False teachings took the place of truth. Among other things, she took a false day of worship. In the *Catholic World*, March 1894, page 809, we read, "She took the pagan Sunday and made it the Christian Sunday. . . . And thus the pagan Sunday, dedicated to Balder, became the Christian Sunday, sacred to Jesus."

"The Christian Sabbath is therefore to this day the acknowledged offspring of the Catholic Church, as Spouse of the Holy Ghost, without a word of remonstrance from the Protestant world" (*The Catholic Mirror,* September 23, 1893).

The late Cardinal Gibbons of Baltimore says in his book *The Faith of Our Fathers,* "You may read the Bible from Genesis to Revelation, and you will not find a single line authorizing the sanctification of Sunday. The Scriptures enforce the religious observance of Saturday, a day which we never sanctify" (Seventy-sixth edition, page 86).

In a letter written October 8, 1901, Mr. C. F. Thomas, chancellor to Cardinal Gibbons, said that "it was the Catholic Church that authorized and sanctioned the change in the Lord's Day from the seventh day of the week with the first. She did it very early in her life."

In a Catholic work, *An Abridgment of the Christian Doctrine,* by Rev. Henry Tuberville, D.D., we read on page 58,

Q. How prove you that the church hath power to command feasts and holydays?

A. By the very act of changing the Sabbath into Sunday.

From another Roman Catholic work we read,

Q. Have you any other way of proving that the church has power to institute festivals of precept?

A. Had she not such power, she could not have . . . substituted the observance of Sunday the first day of the week, for the observance of Saturday the seventh day, a change for which there is no Scriptural authority (Stephen Keenan, *A Doctrinal Catechism,* page 174).

The earliest recognition of the observance of Sunday as a legal duty is a constitution of Constantine in A.D. 321, enacting that all courts of justice, inhabitants of towns, and workshops were to be at rest on Sunday (venerabili die solis), with an exception in favor of those engaged in agricultural labor (*The Encyclopaedia Britannica,* eleventh edition, article, "Sunday").

The mark of apostasy is thus clearly identified. The third angel warns against receiving this mark. But we do not know all that is to be known on this, nor can we know, until the unfolding of events. "The light we have received upon the third angel's message is the true light. The mark of the beast is exactly what it has been proclaimed to be. Not all in regard to this matter is yet understood, nor will it be understood until the unrolling of the scroll" (Ellen White, *Testimonies for the Church*, vol. 6, page 17).

Before the Savior appears in glory, every soul will have made his choice either to obey or to disobey the Lord. Great issues are before the church. International law will require universal allegiance to the false power of Rome. But those who heed such a law will dishonor God and break His command. It is then that men receive the mark of the beast. *Not until the issues are clearly set forth and all the world has heard God's message will men receive the mark of the beast.* (See Ellen White, *The Great Controversy*, page 449.) God has His loyal witnesses in every church. They love His Word and are living up to all the light they have received.

> No one has yet received the mark of the beast. . . . There are true Christians in every church, not excepting the Roman Catholic communion. None are condemned until they have had the light and have seen the obligation of the fourth commandment. But when the decree shall go forth enforcing the counterfeit Sabbath, and the loud cry of the third angel shall warn men against the worship of the beast and his image, the line will be clearly drawn between the false and the true. Then those who still continue in transgression will receive the mark of the beast (Ellen White, *Evangelism*, pages 234, 235).

Before our Lord returns, every individual will be compelled to make his choice. Those who refuse to obey the powers of earth and will at all costs keep the faith of Jesus will be ostracized from society. Even as Daniel refused to compromise his faith and accepted the death decree rather than deny his God and was miraculously delivered from the power of the lions, so it will be in this last crisis with those who stand true to heaven's commands. It is then that those who willfully and knowingly choose to obey this apostate power and receive the mark of the beast "shall drink of the wine of the wrath of God" (Revelation 14:10).

THE PATIENCE OF THE SAINTS

This word *patience* is also translated "steadfastness." It will be a patient and steadfast people that will be waiting for the coming of the Lord. (See Hebrews 10:36, 37.) They will also be an obedient people " 'who carefully keep His commandments and the faith of Jesus!' " (Revelation 14:12, Weymouth).

The church of the Reformation was commended for her patience and faith. And her obedience will be particularly conspicuous. In worshiping the Creator, she keeps holy the Sabbath day, recognizing it as a sign of God's sanctifying power. (See Ezekiel 20:12.) Those who accept this final message of God to the world are themselves a sign of God's power to convert and re-create. (See Isaiah 8:18; Zechariah 3:8, margin.)

God's remnant people are known in different countries by various names descriptive of their Christian experience. In Fiji the natives early called them "the clean church"; in Liberia, "the people of the washing of hearts"; in other places, "the walking Ten Commandments"; "the Second Advent people"; and "the people of love." Jesus said, "By this shall all men know that ye are my disciples, if ye have love one to another" (John 13:35). And Paul says that Christ "loved the church, and gave himself for it; that he might sanctify and cleanse it with the washing of water by the word, that he might present it to himself a glorious church, not having spot, or wrinkle, or any such thing; but that it should be holy and without blemish" (Ephesians 5:25–27).

35. The Triumph of the Church and the Seven Last Plagues

As the prophet John watched the unfolding panorama, he saw that prior to the return of Jesus the whole world will have heard God's final warning and appeal. He saw the everlasting gospel going "to every nation, and kindred, and tongue, and people" (Revelation 14:6). Being proclaimed in the setting of the three angels' messages, it becomes a power in the earth.

A GREAT WORLDWIDE DELUSION

The greatest deception of all time is yet to be staged, and this will take place just before the appearing of our Lord, when "Satan with all power and signs and lying wonders" (2 Thessalonians 2:9) deceives the whole world. Those who fail to heed God's message will be ensnared by this delusion, and they will actually believe a lie, or "the lie" (R.V.). (See verse 11.)

Jesus spoke of this delusion, saying that the whole world would be caught in the snare. (See Luke 21:35.) The deception would be so great that if possible even the very elect would be deceived. (See Matthew 24:24.) But they will not be deceived. Because they love the truth and have fortified themselves by the Word of God, they will be able to withstand the delusion. (See Ephesians 6:10–17.) The devil is even now spreading a veil over the nations. (See Isaiah 25:7.) He is putting "a bridle in the jaws of the people, causing them to err" (Isaiah 30:28), and men are making lies their refuge. (See Isaiah 28:17.)

"Satan himself is transformed into an angel of light" (2 Corinthians 11:14). It is the spirits of devils that go forth to the kings of the earth and to the whole world to fasten them in deception and urge them on to unite with Satan in his last struggle against the government of heaven. By these agencies, rulers and subjects alike will be deceived.

As the crowning act in the great drama of deception, Satan himself will personate Christ. The church has long professed to look to the Saviour's advent as the consummation of her hopes. Now the great deceiver will make it appear that Christ has come. In different parts of the earth, Satan will manifest himself among men as a majestic being of dazzling brightness, resembling the description of the Son of God given by John in the Revelation. The glory that surrounds him is unsurpassed by anything that mortal eyes have yet beheld. The shout of triumph rings out upon the air, "Christ has come! Christ has come!" The people prostrate themselves in adoration before him, while he lifts up his hands, and pronounces a blessing upon them, as Christ blessed His disciples when He was upon the earth. His voice is soft and subdued, yet full of melody. In gentle, compassionate tones he presents some of the same gracious, heavenly truths which the Saviour uttered; he heals the diseases of the people. . . . This is the strong, almost overmastering delusion. . . .

But the people of God will not be misled. The teachings of this false Christ are not in accordance with the Scriptures. His blessing is pronounced upon the worshipers of the beast and his image, the very class upon whom the Bible declares that God's unmingled wrath shall be poured out. . . .

Only those who have been diligent students of the Scriptures, and who have received the love of the truth, *will be shielded from the powerful delusion that takes the world captive* (Ellen White, *The Great Controversy,* pages 624, 625, emphasis supplied).

These victorious ones will, by the grace of Christ, be keeping "the commandments of God, and the faith of Jesus" (Revelation 14:12).

The wine of God's wrath

God's last message climaxes with the tremendous announcement that those who refuse to accept salvation will ultimately drink of the wine of the wrath of God, unmixed with mercy. (See Revelation 14:9–11.) The word *torment* (verse 11) is an unfortunate translation and is not sustained by the original. The Greek word *basanismos* properly means to examine by the use of the *basanos*, a species of stone from Lydia that was applied to metals, as it was thought to indicate any alloy that might be mixed with them. Gold left a yellow streak on this touchstone. Today we test gold by acid or fire. In Matthew 14:24 the word *basanidzomenon,* from the verb *basanidzo,* which comes from the above noun, *basanos,* is translated "tossed," where it describes a ship tossed or "tested" by the waves. In Revelation 14:11, the word *torment* really means to "test" or "prove by trial."

One important thought, often overlooked by certain interpreters, is the fact that this testing takes place, not in some far away place of torture or purgatory, but "in the presence of the holy angels, and in the presence of the Lamb" (verse 10). Paul says, "The fire shall try [prove] every man's work of what sort it is" (1 Corinthians 3:13). And all, righteous and wicked alike, will go through the same test, and before the whole fallen universe will be revealed those who are really God's people and those who are not. Isaiah asks, "Who among us shall dwell with the devouring fire? who among us shall dwell with everlasting burnings?" (Isaiah 33:14). Then is revealed the fact that some will stand the test, but those only who are righteous and upright before God. (See verse 15.)

Just as the three Hebrew worthies were preserved in the burning fiery furnace, so will the righteous stand at last in the presence of a holy God whom the Scripture speaks of as "a consuming fire" (Hebrews 12:29).

THE RETURN OF CHRIST—THE CLIMAX OF THE AGES

A most beautiful description of our Savior's second advent is found in Revelation 14:14. Surrounded by a cloud of angels, His brow adorned with a golden crown, and carrying a sharp sickle, He comes to reap the harvest of the earth. Jesus, in His parable of the wheat and tares (see Matthew 13:24–30, 37–43), emphasized this reaping and declared that the good seed represented the children of the kingdom.

Another harvest is brought to view in Revelation 14:18—the harvest of the ripened grapes. Two vines have been growing in the earth, one of heavenly origin, the other of the earth, earthy. Jesus said, "I am the true vine" and "ye are the branches" (John 15:1, 5). The Scriptures speak of evil being destroyed "root" and "branch" (Malachi 4:1). The devil and his followers comprise this other vine. When at last the angels of God gather the ripe clusters of the grapes of wrath and cast them into the wine press of God's judgment, terrible indeed will be the vintage. (See Psalm 75:8.)

A SEA OF GLASS MINGLED WITH FIRE

In contrast with the scene of destruction in the closing verses of chapter 14, the next scene that opens to the view of this prophet is one of victory. Those who have witnessed the brilliant spectacle of a tropic sunset at sea have caught a faint idea of the glory the prophet here attempts to describe. As the great sun sinks like a ball of blazing fire, the ocean itself seems to break forth into flames of glory; the waves, touched with crimson, transform the whole scene into a mingling of flood and flame. So was the scene that opened to the Patmos prophet. The scene of glory became more real as he thought of it in retrospect. Picture him returning to his place of rest after a convict's hard day. Suddenly he catches a glimpse of sunset glory over the Mediterranean. It becomes to him a beautiful symbol of that great day of realities when the toil of earth is ended and all disappointments are past and the saints stand at last in the presence of their God. Then, lifting his eyes from the scenes on earth to a scene more wondrous, his thoughts make more glorious the "sea of glass mingled with fire" (Revelation 15:2) on which the redeemed stand at last victorious. Then he catches the sound of singing. It is the song of victory. The saints are home at last. Insignificant indeed are the trials of earth in comparison with that scene of splendor!

THE SONG OF MOSES AND THE LAMB

What marvelous contrasts are found in this book! Apocalyptic writings follow this pattern. Scenes of victory and glory are set over in vivid contrast with the scenes of defeat and desolation. John caught the echo of this mighty anthem as it bursts from the lips of those who, by grace, have conquered the power of the enemy. They sing the song of Moses and the Lamb. It is the song of Moses because it voices the praise of those who, like ancient Israel at the Red Sea, have been miraculously delivered from impending destruction. But it is also the song of the Lamb because it speaks of the triumph of God's people over death and the grave. It will be a song of experience, and only those who have passed through the experience will be able to join in that paean of praise. The angels will not be able to sing that song, but poor lost sinners redeemed by grace will tell the story in an anthem never heard before.

> But when I sing redemption's story,
>   They will fold their wings,
> For angels never felt the joys
>   That our salvation brings.
>   —Johnson Oatman, Jr.

Wonderful is the music we sometimes hear on earth, but nothing can compare with this tremendous chorus as this redeemed company sweep their harps of gold, and, pitching their celestial song a note higher, change from the minor key of sorrow into the major key of everlasting joy. And the wonder of it all is that, we, too, can be among them. "Who shall not fear thee, O Lord, and glorify thy name?" (verse 4).

THE SEVEN ANGELS WITH THE VIALS

The closing verses of chapter 15 unfold one of the most arresting scenes in the whole book. When the seven angels go forth with the vials of wrath, the Scripture says that until their work was finished "no man was able to enter into the temple" (verse 8). Before the judgments of God break upon a guilty world, the gospel message of invitation will have been heard by every soul on earth; man's opportunity for salvation will have passed, and the door of mercy will have been closed forever.

Some commentators try to make this prophecy of the plagues run parallel with the seals and the trumpets. That really cannot be, for the plagues are poured out upon those who have received the mark of the beast, and that mark will not be received until just before Christ appears in glory. These judgments fall *after* Christ has finished His ministry on behalf of sinners. Furthermore, the Scripture declares that theses plagues shall "come in one day, death, and mourning, and famine" (Revelation 18:8). We have already mentioned that a day in prophecy is a year, and it is evident that this could not possibly be a literal day of twenty-four hours, for no famine could result in so short a time no matter how bad the conditions. Moreover, the Scripture indicates that some of the same men who suffer under the first plague also suffer under the other plagues. It is therefore evident that these judgments fall on the same generation and will last through a prophetic day or a literal year.

THE DESCRIPTION OF THE PLAGUES

A number of the prophets have described the effect of these judgments, Isaiah and Joel particularly. Joel 1:17–20 says: "The seed is rotten under their clods, . . . the corn is withered. . . . The flocks of sheep are made desolate. . . . The rivers of waters are dried up, and the fire hath devoured the pastures." While this doubtless had a spiritual application in the days in which Joel was writing, yet it was "the day of the Lord" that he was describing. (See Joel 1:15; 2:1.)

The first plague is a grievous sore which falls upon those who have the mark of the beast. (See Revelation 16:2.) Before this first angel pours out his vial, the whole human race will have divided itself into two classes—those who are sealed with the seal of the living God, and those who have the mark of the beast. To the one class who are under the protecting wings of the Almighty, the promise is, "Thou shalt not be afraid for the . . . pestilence that walketh in darkness. . . . A thousand shall fall at thy side, and ten thousand at thy right hand; but it shall not come nigh thee. . . . Neither shall any plague come nigh thy dwelling" (Psalm 91:5–10).

The second and third plagues fall upon the waters, turning the sea and the water supplies of the nations into a putrefaction resembling the blood of a dead man. When the ocean becomes a place of death, the inhabitants of every country in the world will be affected. But God's people need not fear. Some of the most beautiful promises in God's Word reveal His plan to protect His chosen ones during those awful days. Here is one:

336

When the poor and needy seek water, and there is none, and their tongue faileth for thirst, I the LORD will hear them, I the God of Israel will not forsake them. I will open rivers in high places, and fountains in the midst of the valleys: I will make the wilderness a pool of water, and the dry land springs of water (Isaiah 41:17, 18).

And again:

He shall dwell on high: his place of defence shall be the munitions of rocks: bread shall be given him; his waters shall be sure (Isaiah 33:16).

The fourth plague is poured out on the sun, which is given power to scorch men with heat. Their only response is to blaspheme the Almighty. They cannot repent because repentance is the work of the Holy Spirit. But before the plagues fall, the Spirit of God will have been withdrawn from this earth.

The fifth vial is poured out on the seat, or throne, of the beast, plunging the kingdom of error into dense darkness. There is a similarity between these plagues and the plagues that fell on Egypt. Those, however, were judgments on one small country, while these seven last plagues affect the whole world and men of every nation. When Egypt was dark, there was light in dwellings of Israel.

When the sixth angel poured out his vial, the prophet John says he beheld "three unclean spirits like frogs come out of the mouth of the dragon, and out of the mouth of the beast, and out of the mouth of the false prophet" (Revelation 16:13). In ancient Egypt the frog was an object of veneration, and three black frogs were a symbol of their pagan and spirit deities. The introduction of this symbol of the frog into this prophecy is arresting. As is well known, this little creature hibernates, that is, it disappears for a time, only to return and disturb us with its croaking. So paganism and spiritism disappeared, as it were, for a time, at least in the Western world, but these are reappearing under many disguises. Pagan thinking has entered our educational classrooms. It has even claimed many pulpits. In the final scenes of earth's history, paganism and spiritism under the cloak of religion are to exercise tremendous influence.

These unclean spirits come from the *mouths* of the dragon, the beast, and the false prophet. The power of lying propaganda has been amply demonstrated in recent decades in our world, but it will reach its maximum extent under the sixth plague, when the spirits of demons will gather the nations of the whole world for "the battle of that great day of God Almighty" (verse 14). Protestant churches whose founders went to the stake for their faith

> will be foremost in stretching their hands across the gulf to grasp the hand of Spiritualism; they will reach over the abyss to clasp hands with the Roman power; and under the influence of this threefold union, this country will follow in the steps of Rome in trampling on the rights of conscience.
>
> As Spiritualism more closely imitates the nominal Christianity of the day, it has greater power to deceive and ensnare. Satan himself is converted, after the modern order of things. He will appear in the character of an angel of light. Through the agency of Spiritualism, miracles will be wrought, the sick will be healed, and many undeniable wonders will be performed. And as the spirits will profess faith in the Bible, and manifest respect for the institutions of the church, their work will be accepted as a manifestation of divine power (Ellen White, *The Great Controversy*, page 588).

Through the combined influence of spiritism, Roman Catholicism, and apostate Protestantism, the world will be led, not to peace, but to war. And that war will be against God Himself. Revelation 16:16 says that the nations are gathered together "into a place called in the Hebrew tongue Armageddon."

Through the centuries many ideas have been expressed concerning Armageddon. Unfulfilled prophecy has always been a fertile field for human speculation. Palestine may well be the storm center of a worldwide conflict, but the battle of the day of God

Almighty will not be confined to any one land in particular. The issues are much larger than many have imagined. It is not *geographical location* that the Lord is emphasizing as much as a revelation of *the issues at stake.* The Holy Land will be involved, because *every* land of earth will be a scene for this last great struggle. "The kings of the earth and of the whole world" (verse 14) will be involved. It would be physically impossible to gather all the armies of the world on one battlefield. The word *battle* in this verse is translated from the Greek word *polemos,* which is often translated "war" rather than "battle." It may be either a single encounter or a series of engagements. In this death struggle between the combined powers of darkness and hate and the legions of light and love, the whole world will be the battlefield, and so terrible will be the slaughter of that day that "they shall not be lamented, neither gathered, nor buried" (Jeremiah 25:33).

> Soon, very soon, will be fought the last great battle between good and evil. The earth is to be the battlefield—the scene of the final contest and the final victory. Here, where for so long Satan has led men against God, rebellion is to be forever suppressed (Ellen White, *The Review and Herald,* May 13, 1902, page 9).

> The battle of Armageddon is soon to be fought. He on whose vesture is written the name, King of kings, and Lord of lords, is soon to lead forth the armies of heaven (Ellen White, *Testimonies for the Church,* vol. 6, page 406).

This battle is between heaven and earth, Christ and Satan.

Describing the tremendous scope of this conflict, John says, "These shall make war with the Lamb, and the Lamb shall overcome them: for he is Lord of lords, and King of kings" (Revelation 17:14). Again, he says, "And I saw the beast, and the kings of the earth, and their armies, gathered together to make war against him . . . and against his army" (Revelation 19:19). The phrase "make war" occurs sixteen times in the New Testament; nine times in the Revelation.

Who but the most spiritually blind could fail to see the shaping of events that will lead to the final battle which ends the misrule of men and ushers in the long-expected kingdom of peace?

> The real issue at stake in Armageddon will not be so much material and international as spiritual. It will actually be a struggle between the devil and wicked nations on the one side and God and His people on the other (W. W. Branson, *Drama of the Ages,* page 533).

So tremendous will be that conflagration that were it not for the fact that God sends down His mighty ones to protect His people, they would be wiped off the earth. "In the midst of the time of trouble that is coming, . . . God's chosen people will stand unmoved. Satan and his host cannot destroy them, for angels that excel in strength will protect them" (Ellen White, *Testimonies for the Church,* vol. 9, page 17). Describing this coming conflict, the prophet Joel says, "Thither cause thy mighty ones to come down, O LORD" (Joel 3:11). The battle of the great day of God Almighty will cease, not by the conquest of one nation over another nation or one group of nations over another group of nations, but by the sudden appearing of Jesus Christ as He comes in power and great glory. The wicked will then flee in terror.

When the seventh angel pours out his vial, a voice from heaven is heard to say, "It is done." Then follow lightnings, thunderings, and a great earthquake, the like of which has never been "since men were upon the earth" (Revelation 16:17, 18).

Great Babylon, the symbol of an apostate world, now receives her full judgment. Islands flee away, and the mountains are not found; hailstones weighing fifty to one hundred pounds fall from heaven. This plague comes from God and not from men. The Lord said to Job, "Hast thou entered into the treasures of the snow? or hast thou seen the treasures of the hail, which I have reserved against the time of trouble, against the day of battle and war?" (Job 38:22, 23). Isaiah spoke of "the overflowing scourge" (Isaiah 28:15) that will pass through the land and destroy those who have made lies their refuge. Daniel speaks of it as the "time of trouble, such as never was." Then he adds, "Thy people shall be delivered, every one that shall be found written in the book"—the book of life (Daniel 12:1).

Before the coming of this day of destruction, God sends an invitation to all to gather together and seek Him. Those who heed His message will be sheltered from these plagues (see Zephaniah 2:1–3), for "the LORD will be the hope of his people" (Joel 3:16). Psalms 46 and 91 are both moving descriptions of this time of earthly calamity. But God's people will be protected "under his wings" (Psalm 91:4). In the midst of all the conflagration, the resurrection will take place. "Amid the reeling of the earth, the flash of lightning, and the roar of thunder, the voice of the Son of God calls forth the sleeping saints" (Ellen White, *The Great Controversy*, page 644). This will be the overwhelming evidence of God's supreme power over His enemies. When the sleeping saints are raised to immortality and the living saints are caught up to meet Him in the air, the wicked who have refused salvation will flee in terror, only to be destroyed "with the brightness of his coming" (2 Thessalonians 2:8). What a scene of victory and tragedy—victory for the saints; tragedy for the sinners! May God help us to be ready.

36. The Judgment of the Scarlet Woman

Revelation 17 is to many an enigma. But like a combination lock, if we know the right combination, it is no longer an enigma. Having beheld the outpouring of God's judgments in the seven last plagues, and the climax of history in the tremendous convulsions of nature, when mountains and islands disappear and the works of man are destroyed, the Patmos prophet now sees a more intimate view of the power that intoxicates the nations and defies the God of heaven.

With dramatic instinct the prophet paints his word pictures. A woman sits upon a scarlet beast. "On her forehead was a name with a secret meaning" (Revelation 17:5, NEB). She is decked in royal purple and shameless scarlet; her title: "MYSTERY, BABYLON THE GREAT, THE MOTHER OF HARLOTS AND ABOMINATIONS OF THE EARTH" (verse 5).

THE IDENTITY OF THE WOMAN

This language is impressive; yet we must ask, Who is this woman called Mystery, Babylon the Great? There can be no doubt as to her identity. As we have already noticed, a woman in prophecy represents a church. The woman in chapter 12 is a beautiful symbol of the true church of Jesus Christ, but this woman in chapter 17, corrupt in character and deceptive in nature, contrasts in every way with that virtuous woman. God likened His people to "a comely and delicate woman" (Jeremiah 6:2), or to a woman "dwelling at home" (margin). But this woman is not dwelling at home. Instead she is courting kings and living in illicit relationship with the world. She is not attired in "fine linen," which "is the righteousness of saints" (Revelation 19:8), but is lavishly adorned in purple and scarlet, and decked with gold and costly gems. John saw her also drunken with the blood of the saints and of the martyrs of Jesus. He was viewing this apostate church subsequent to the centuries of persecution. She was holding in her hand a cup "full of abominations" (Revelation 17:4). In Scripture the words *abomination, lie, graven image,* and *false god* are all used synonymously. (See 1 Kings 11:7, 2, 3; Isaiah 44:15, 19, 20.) This is not the cup of salvation for which David of old prayed (see Psalm 116:13) but is full of false gods and lying abominations, such as the counterfeit doctrines of false priesthood that claims power to forgive sins and decide cases. St. Alphonsus de Liguori, writing under the imprimatur of papal authorities, says:

> The priest has the power of the keys, or the power of delivering sinners from hell, of making them worthy of paradise, and of changing them from the slaves of Satan into the children of God. And God himself is obligated to abide by the judgment of his priests, and either not to pardon or to pardon (*Dignity and Duties of the Priest,* edited by Rev. Eugene Grimm, 1927, page 27).

> When St. Michael comes to a dying Christian who invokes his aid, the holy archangel can chase away the devils, but he cannot free his clients from their chains till a priest comes to absolve him (ibid.).

Incredible blasphemy! But millions of sincere souls believe it and order their lives accordingly.

And the woman had "a golden cup in her hand" (Revelation 17:4). One of the most vital doctrines in this apostate church is the daily sacrifice of the mass. The wafer in the golden monstrance, they claim, is the living Christ. Sacred as is the doctrine of transubstantiation to the devout Roman Catholic, it surely is idolatry to say that this piece of bread is actually the Creator of heaven and earth. Since the infliction of the "deadly wound" (Revelation 13:3) in 1798, the papacy has fought her way back to prestige and power. Perhaps nothing has contributed more to her recovery than have the International Eucharistic Congresses held throughout the world, in which the elevation of the "Eucharistic Christ" is the dominant point of the whole proceedings.

THE CHURCH FALLS FROM HER PURE FAITH

In the study of the seven churches and the seven seals, we saw how corruption came into the church in the early centuries. Her purity was lost as soon as she courted the favor of the world. Then little by little she became corrupt. Even before the days of Dante in the twelfth century, literary thinkers and true theologians were consistently applying this prophecy to the Church of Rome. In his *Divine Comedy*, Dante made a forthright indictment of the established church of his day. Ignaz Döllinger declares of this masterpiece that it was "the boldest, most unsparing, most incisive, denunciatory song that has ever been composed."

> Your avarice
> O'ercasts the world with mourning, underfoot
> Treading the good, and raising bad men up,
> Of shepherds like to you, the Evangelist
> Was ware, when her, who sits upon the waves,
> With kings in filthy whoredom he beheld,
> She who with seven heads towered at her birth,
> And from ten horns her proof of glory drew. . . .
> Of gold and silver ye have made your god. . . .
> Ah, Constantine! to how much ill gave birth,
> Not thy conversion, but that plenteous dower,
> Which the first wealthy Father gained from thee.
> —Canto 19

Space and time forbid quoting from many others who wrote during those centuries. The application of this prophecy to the Roman Church is practically universal. Of course, those earlier writers, like Dante, were actually members of the established Church of Rome, and this was hundreds of years before the rise of Protestantism.

The beast on which the woman sits, like the other beasts of prophecy, represents the civil or political power. Upheld by the power of the state, this woman, symbol of the apostate church, is seen guiding and controlling the nations. She does it for her own ends. Students of history recognize in this the pattern of Roman Catholicism during the past fifteen hundred years, at least whenever and wherever she has been strong enough to gain that control.

On the occasion of the jubilee of Pope Leo XII, a medal was struck bearing on the one side his image, and on the other side a symbol of the Church of Rome. On this medal we see a woman holding in her left hand a cross and in her right, a cup, with this legend around her: *Sedet super universum* ("the whole world is her seat"). This unwitting fulfillment of prophecy is only one of many that could be mentioned. The apostasy and the antichrist, which the apostle Paul foretold would arise and be found sitting in the temple of God, claiming to be God (2 Thessalonians 2:3, 4), is not something to arise in the future—it is in the world today.

SIGNIFICANCE OF HER NAME

She had a name written, "MYSTERY, BABYLON THE GREAT" (Revelation 17:5). When the mystery cults of ancient Babylon came into the church, the foundations for the mystery of iniquity were laid. The mysteries took the form of religion only a short time after the Flood and were a definite attempt to destroy the knowledge of the true God from the minds of men.

Nimrod, "a mighty hunter before the LORD" (Genesis 10:9), began the kingdom of Babylon, and legend has it that upon his death his depraved and licentious queen, eager to hold her influence over the people, instituted certain rites in which she was worshiped as Rhea, the great "Mother" of the gods. This Chaldean queen is a fitting prototype of this woman in the Apocalypse on whose forehead is the name, "MYSTERY, BABYLON THE GREAT, THE MOTHER OF HARLOTS AND ABOMINATIONS OF THE EARTH" (Revelation 17:5). When John saw her she was drunk. But her debauchery was at an end; she was awaiting her judgment. He was astonished, and well he might be. The angel, unfolding to him the mystery of it all, said: "The woman which thou sawest is that great city, which reigneth over the kings of the earth" (verse 18).

Nine times in the Revelation we find the expression the "great city" as applied to this apostate system. The woman represents ecclesiastical power; the beast, political power. In this symbol we find the complete union of the church and state, and all "whose names are not written in the book of life" (Revelation 13:8) are amazed as they witness the rise and influence of this tremendous religio-political power described as "the beast that was, and is not, and yet is" (Revelation 17:8).

THE POWER THAT FELL AND ROSE AGAIN

Having received state recognition at the time when Justinian's decree became effective in A.D. 538, this apostate power in Rome began her dominance, which was to last 1,260 years. During those centuries she practically controlled the political scene in Europe, crowning kings and excommunicating even royal "heretics." But she received a deadly wound in the Napoleonic Wars, and the pope himself was taken prisoner. This occurred August 9, 1798. Some Bible interpreters see in this event a particular fulfillment of this rather difficult portion of the prophecy. The power that "was," they say, ceased to control, and another period of her existence was unfolded, comparatively described as the "is not" period. She had gone into captivity (see Revelation 13:10), and many writers of this time fully believed that the papacy could never rise again. A number of books were published by secular historians emphasizing that belief. But John was shown that she would ascend again and become a world power.

It is never wise to be dogmatic when studying unfulfilled prophecies. A biblical principle is clear; Jesus said, "I have told you *before* it come to pass, that, *when it is come to pass,* ye might believe" (John 14:29, emphasis supplied). The unfolding of events are even now clarifying many of these difficult passages.

During the last century, the Church of Rome has been regaining her political influence until today she is strong once more. In 1854 the papal dogma of the Immaculate Conception was pronounced. In 1870 she enunciated the dogma of papal infallibility. In 1929 the pope received recognition as a sovereign ruler. In 1951 she set forth the dogma of the Assumption of the Virgin Mary. But greater things are yet to come, for "all the world" will wonder "after the beast" (Revelation 13:3). Thus some Bible interpreters hold that it could be said that the beast, or the political power of the papacy, *was* from 538 to 1798; that it *was not* from 1798 to 1929; and that now it *yet is*. Her power will be even greater before our Savior returns. Her pride will mount up to heaven.

As we have noticed in earlier chapters, when John received this vision, he was witnessing scenes in heaven when "the judgment was set, and the books were opened" (Daniel 7:10). Thus, in vision, he was brought forward to our own time, and as the scroll of prophecy and history unrolled before him, he was instructed to write what he was seeing. While these messages have been studied with profit and inspiration throughout the centuries, they have their special application to earth's last generation. Through the study of His Word, the Lord by His Spirit is preparing a people to stand through the final days of deception and be ready for the appearing of our Lord. The prophet was, therefore, witnessing events of our own day.

THE BEAST WITH SEVEN HEADS

At the time this prophecy had its special application, five of the seven heads of the beast were "fallen." While it might not be wise to be dogmatic on the specific identity of these heads, yet it is significant that there are seven different and distinct powers introduced into Scripture by prophetic symbols. These are clearly indicated: (1) Babylon (the lion, Daniel 7:4); (2) Persia (the bear, verse 5); (3) Grecia (the leopard, verse 6); (4) pagan Rome (the ten-horned beast, verse 7); (5) papal, or ecclesiastical Rome (the seven-headed beast of Revelation 13), also the horn that spoke great words and blasphemies (Daniel 7:8; Revelation 13:2, 5); (6) republicanism or democracy (the two-horned beast, Revelation 13:11); and (7) the last great confederacy of evil (the scarlet beast, Revelation 17:3). The "great red dragon" (Revelation 12:3) cannot be a symbol of any one specific power, for while it represents Rome's attack on the infant Jesus, later verses in the chapter show its warfare against God's last people. In reality, it covers the whole period occupied by all these beast powers, for behind every political attack upon the people of God is the dragon, or prince of evil. Even ancient Egypt was spoken of as the dragon. But the apocalyptic prophecies of Daniel and the Revelation which unfold the reign of the great Gentile powers begin with the overthrow of the throne of Judah, which occurred under the reign of Nebuchadnezzar, king of Babylon, thus clearing the way for Gentile rule in the world. Jesus spoke of "the times of the Gentiles" (Luke 21:24). The Gentile "times" are terminating now.

Through all the centuries the dragon, or the devil, was *waiting for the Child to be born.* He was therefore in existence *before* the Christian Era, but *he will make his most severe attack upon the remnant* or the last true church. This dragon power is a symbol of more than pagan Rome. As we have already emphasized, John was brought forward in vision and was witnessing the events of the judgment. At the time that great scene opened in heaven (1844), the papacy was at a low ebb. Only a few years earlier she had received her deadly wound. At the time this prophecy of Revelation 17 had its special application, five of these great powers had fallen. These were Babylon, Persia, Greece, pagan Rome, and papal Rome—the deadly wound having been inflicted upon the papacy in 1798.

Now the prophet, watching, says that "one is," that is, it was existent after 1798. The Revolutionary War in America overthrew the "divine right" of kings, but it also overthrew the divine right of majorities. Prelates and popes have had no place in this growing nation. Democracy had its real opportunity in America, and, as we have already noticed, she arose at the time the papacy went down. Yet, startling as it may seem, this prophecy reveals that these great principles of liberty will ultimately be abandoned and that what was free Protestant America will actually become an ally of Rome and "make an image to the beast" which had the "wound by a sword, and did live" (Revelation 13:14). We would be blind if we failed to see that this very thing is taking place before our eyes today. The foundation is being laid for the papacy's sudden rise to complete worldwide dominance. But the angel declared, "When he cometh, he must continue a short space" (Revelation 17:10). Never again will this power dominate the centuries as she did before. Her power will be great, but for a short time.

HORNS WITHOUT CROWNS

A significant difference between the leopard beast of Revelation 12 and the scarlet colored beast of Revelation 17 should be emphasized. Each beast has ten horns, but while the horns on the leopard had ten crowns, no crowns are mentioned in the description of the scarlet beast. This last beast, as we have noticed, is descriptive of a period in history when crowns and monarchies are, to a large extent, out of fashion. The ten horns, the angel said, represent ten kings, yet these are uncrowned kings. They possess kingly power, however, and might better be called dictators.

During World War I, four great empires passed away—the German, the Russian, the Austrian, and the Ottoman. These great powers collapsed, and they are no longer empires. Many other monarchies have also passed away in the aftermath of that war. It is said that between August and December of 1914, more than two hundred royalties and petty royalties had abdicated. With the disappearance of the kings, it became the fashion in government to establish republics, and these arose in many countries. However, it takes more than a mere change of governmental structure to bring liberty. History reveals that if power is placed in the hands of men whose love of power is greater than their love of people, then "sovereign demos," or the rule of the people, can be as cruel a tyrant as any autocrat that ever occupied a throne.

THESE HAVE ONE MIND

Now the prophet learns that these so-called kings "have one mind, and shall give their power and strength unto the beast" (verse 13). That is, they surrender their power to the beast, an evidence of their confidence in this restored kingdom. But this great new confederacy of political and ecclesiastical power is short lived. They reign "as kings one hour with the beast" (verse 12). Some interpret the expression "one hour" as an actual measurement of time, an hour being one twenty-fourth part of a day; and one twenty-fourth of a prophetic day or a literal year would be fifteen days. Others, however, claim it is an expression of an indefinite period. In any case, it is indeed a short space of time, but sufficient for this resuscitated power to make her blasphemous and arrogant claim, when she says, "I sit a queen, and am no widow" (Revelation 18:7). To make the sin the greater, this confederacy of evil passes sentence of death upon anyone who refuses to render her homage. All who do identify themselves with her will receive the mark of the beast. (See Revelation 13:16.)

This revived power of the papacy actually constitutes another head, and when, for a brief time, the beast and the false prophet unite their powers, they will then constitute another head, i.e., even "the eighth." But this eighth head "is of the seven" (Revelation 17:11).

She says she is "no widow" (Revelation 18:7). She was widowed when she was stripped of her temporal power in 1798, but before the end of time she will be completely reinstated, and all "peoples, and multitudes, and nations, and tongues" will pay her homage (Revelation 17:15). The kings of the earth will be committing spiritual fornication with her. That is, they will be in unholy alliance with her. (See Revelation 18:3.) This will be the greatest union of church and state the world has ever known.

Babylon denounced

To prepare His people for that tremendous crisis, God is sending His last message of mercy. The whole world will be illumined with the glory of that message (see Revelation 18:1), which declares that Babylon, or the fallen church, has "become the habitation of devils, and hold of every foul spirit, and a cage of every unclean and hateful bird" (Revelation 18:2). A dove is the emblem of the Holy Spirit, but the emblems of Babylon are unclean and hateful birds, scavengers who feed on carrion. By her sorceries she deceived the nations (see verse 23), and now, drunk with her wine, they are living in unholy alliance with her while the merchants are being made rich by her commerce. Babylon is not one church. In Revelation 17:5 she is called "THE MOTHER OF HARLOTS." She has daughters, other churches, and these partake of the same unholy nature and are found drinking her wine and teaching her doctrines that are not in harmony with the Bible.

COME OUT OF HER, MY PEOPLE
This is God's call today:

> Notwithstanding the spiritual darkness and alienation from God that exists in the churches which constitute Babylon, the great body of Christ's true followers are still to be found in their communion. There are many of these who have never seen the special truths for this time. Not a few are dissatisfied with their present condition and are longing for clearer light. They look in vain for the image of Christ in the churches with which they are connected. As these bodies depart further and further from the truth, and ally themselves more closely with the world, the difference between the two classes will widen, and it will finally result in separation. The time will come when those who love God supremely can no longer remain in connection with such as are "lovers of pleasures more than lovers of God; having a form of godliness, but denying the power thereof."
>
> Revelation 18 points to the time when, as the result of rejecting the threefold warning of Revelation 14:6-12, the church will have fully reached the condition foretold by the second angel, and the people of God still in Babylon will be called upon to separate from her communion. This message is the last that will ever be given to the world; and it will accomplish its work. When those that "believed not the truth, but had pleasure in unrighteousness," shall be left to receive strong delusion and to believe a lie, then the light of truth will shine upon all whose hearts are open to receive it, and all the children of the Lord that remain in Babylon will heed the call, "Come out of her, My people" (Ellen White, *The Great Controversy*, page 390; see also pages 604–608).

God's judgments are about to fall in the seven last plagues, and all who refuse to separate from Babylon and her sins will suffer destruction with her. "Flee out of the midst of Babylon" was God's message to Israel when ancient Babylon was about to fall (Jeremiah 51:6). As we have noticed, these plagues "come in one day" (Revelation 18:8). This is a prophetic day, or a literal year. When those who have put their confidence in this great world power witness the complete collapse of the whole political, economic, religious, financial, and educational confederacy, they stand aghast, crying, "Alas, alas that great city Babylon, that mighty city! for in one hour is thy judgment come" (verse 10). Four times in the book of Revelation we find the expression "one hour." It is for just one hour that the powers of the world reign with her (see Revelation 17:12); in "one hour" her judgment comes (Revelation 18:10); in "one hour" her riches come to naught (verse 17); in "one hour" she is made desolate (verse 19).

Like the ancient Babel builders, whose efforts to build a tower whose top would reach up to heaven were thwarted, and who were scattered by a divine hand, so this modern Babylonian structure, whose "sins have reached unto heaven" (verse 5), will also collapse. The merchants that have been made rich by her abundance will ultimately turn upon her and destroy her. (See Revelation 17:16.) Shipmasters and dealers in precious stones, farmers and traders, sculptors and manufacturers, all will bewail her burning. (See Revelation 18:9–17.) Having put their confidence in her, they see their hopes collapse as they witness her destruction.

Six times over in verses 21–23 we read that she will be no more at all. Her music, her industry, her finance, her commerce will be no more at all. Her destruction will be complete, and God charges her with the blood "of all that were slain upon the earth" (verse 24)—a tremendous picture of the final scenes that will usher in the coming kingdom of glory! When the whole confederacy of evil declares war on God and His people, the promise is that "the Lamb shall overcome them: . . . and they that are with Him are called, and chosen, and faithful" (Revelation 17:14). God has *called* us by His grace. He has *chosen* us to be a holy people; it remains for us to be *faithful*. Entrance to the kingdom is not promised to the successful, but to the faithful. "Well done, thou good and faithful servant" (Matthew 25:21).

To God's faithful servants comes the command, "Arise, shine; for thy light is come, and the glory of the Lord is risen upon thee. For behold, the darkness shall cover the earth, and gross darkness the people: but the Lord shall arise upon thee, and his glory shall be seen upon thee" (Isaiah 60:1, 2).

During the loud cry, the church, aided by the providential interpositions of her exalted Lord, will diffuse the knowledge of salvation so abundantly that light will be communicated to every city and town. The earth will be filled with the knowledge of salvation. So abundantly will the renewing Spirit of God have crowned with success the intensely active agencies, that the light of present truth will be seen flashing everywhere (Ellen White, *Evangelism*, page 694).

37. The Triumph of the Church and the Two Great Suppers

"The marriage of the Lamb is come"! (Revelation 19:7). What a theme for the song of a multitude! And John hears them uttering their praises. It is truly the shout of triumph. The great system of evil and deception is overthrown. The great, boastful Babylon is now a desolation, and the saints are about to enter into their final reward. From the throne there peals forth a command, summoning the servants of God and all that fear Him, both great and small, to voice their praise. That chorus is like the sound of "many waters" and like "the voice of mighty thunderings." They cry, in triumph, "Alleluia: for the Lord God omnipotent reigneth. Let us be glad and rejoice, and give honor to him: for the marriage of the Lamb is come, and his wife hath made herself ready" (Revelation 19:6, 7).

Eastern marriage customs. This burst of jubilation is one of the most sublime passages of all Scripture. But to understand it better, we must see it in the setting of a marriage according to the ancient customs of the East.

First there was the *betrothal,* considered much more binding than the "engagements" of our Western custom. Then came payment of the *wedding dowry,* an important part of the contract.

After this came a period of personal preparation on the part of the bride while the bridegroom was preparing the home.

The *marriage* was not conducted in a church, with a ceremony such as we are accustomed to, but was a simple ceremony when the bridegroom gave public recognition of his claim to the bride. This was done by throwing his cloak around her shoulder as the procession moved along the highway where the wedding feast was to be held.

The wedding feast, or the *marriage supper,* was a spectacular event lasting at times for days and even weeks. The father of the bridegroom provided this feast, and it was usually held at the father's home. This was an occasion for honoring his son, and, in the case of a royal wed-

354

ding, the king would often bequeath a city or a whole province to the young couple as a token of affection and honor. This gift was usually made just prior to the wedding. Now let us make the application.

WHO IS THE BRIDE?

In Revelation 21:9, 10 the bride is clearly defined as the Holy City, New Jerusalem. But in other Scriptures, the church is called "the bride." Even in the Revelation itself, the bride is mentioned as being arrayed "in fine linen, clean and white," and this is called "the righteousness of saints" (Revelation 19:8)—a figure hardly applicable to a merely material city. Is there any contradiction here?

Decidedly not. The city is the bride, but a city without inhabitants is only a group of buildings and streets. It is the people who occupy those buildings that make the city what it is. And the New Jerusalem, with its jasper walls and golden streets, all radiant with the glory of God, is to be filled with the righteous of all ages. Moreover, the Holy City is not spoken of as the bride in the Revelation until the saints are already occupying it. Paul calls the heavenly Jerusalem "the mother of us all" (Galatians 4:26). Thus he likens the church to the children of the bride. Our Lord does the same when He speaks of His people as "the children of the bridechamber" (Mark 2:19). In His parables He likens the church to the guests (see Matthew 22:11), and on another occasion to "ten virgins," or the maids of honor (Matthew 25:1). These different illustrations are used to teach important lessons. This is not a contradiction. It rather opens up new vistas of divine revelation. We need them all in order to get the full picture.

From the beginning of human history, God has been seeking subjects for His kingdom. When Adam sinned, the kingdoms of this world were claimed by Satan, man's seducer. But in "the fullness of the time" (Galatians 4:4), God Himself came in the person of His Son "to seek and to save that which was lost" (Luke 19:10), and by the sacrifice of His own life the Son purchased back the lost possession. He is the Redeemer, or the heavenly *Goel,* as we noticed in chapter 6. And we must never forget that "God was in Christ, reconciling the world unto Himself" (2 Corinthians 5:19).

355

Anticipating the time when the kingdom would again be restored to the lost race, God has, through all the centuries, been calling men to forsake their sins and come into fellowship with Him. In the Scriptures the relationship between God and His people has often been illustrated by the bridegroom and the bride. (See Isaiah 54:5; 62:5; Jeremiah 2:32; 6:2; Hosea 2:19, 20; Matthew 9:15; John 3:29; 2 Corinthians 11:2; Ephesians 5:32.) The most beautiful illustration of this revelation of God's love for His people, however, is found in the story of Abraham's sending his servant to seek a bride for his son, Isaac. (See Genesis 24.)

When God called the nation of Israel, He spoke of it as a betrothal. "I will betroth thee unto me in righteousness," He said (Hosea 2:19). Some separate these Scriptures, endeavoring to apply them either to Israel as a nation or to the church as separate from Israel, depending upon the viewpoint of the particular interpreter. God has ever had only one church—made up of all nations and gathered out of every generation of men. In Acts 7:38 we read of "the church in the wilderness." This church was definitely composed of those whom Moses led out of Egypt. They were part of the true church of God, which has existed ever since the days of Adam. For this bride, or the church, the heavenly Bridegroom paid a dowry far above the price of gold and rubies. This dowry was His own blood, which He freely gave.

> From heaven He came and sought her
>   To be His holy bride;
> With His own blood He bought her,
>   And for her life He died.
>   —Samuel J. Stone.

After His sacrifice came the *interval of separation* when He went back to His Father's house, during which time the bride was to make herself ready. She was to "be arrayed in fine linen, clean and white: for the fine linen is the righteousness of saints" (Revelation 19:8, see also chapter 7:13).

While the bride is making herself ready, the Bridegroom is preparing a place for her. "I go to prepare a place for you," He said. "And if I go and prepare a place for you, I will come again, and receive you unto myself" (John 14:2, 3). O blessed reception when we are called to His side!

In Christ we have been chosen from eternity. (See Ephesians 1:4; 2 Timothy 1:9.) Throughout the Old Testament dispensation the *wedding* has been announced. When the Son of God assumed our flesh, the *betrothal* took place. When He sacrificed Himself on Calvary, the *dowry* was paid. Since He ascended, *the bride has been preparing herself* and *the Bridegroom has been preparing her home*—the New Jerusalem. Soon *He will come and call her* to occupy the place He has prepared.

Before He leaves the courts of glory, after having finished His intercession, He comes before the Father, the Ancient of Days, and there is "given him dominion, and glory, and a kingdom, that all people, nations, and languages, should serve him" (Daniel 7:13, 14). Then the announcement is made, "Let us be glad and rejoice, and give honor to him: for the marriage of the Lamb is come, and his wife hath made herself ready" (Revelation 19:7).

If we think of the Holy City as the bride, then we know that city is ready. But it remains for the inhabitants of that city to be ready, for soon the Bridegroom will ride forth in all the authority of heaven as He comes a Conqueror to claim His own. The apostle, describing that scene, says, "I saw heaven opened, and behold a white horse; and He that sat upon him was called Faithful and True, and in righteousness he doth judge and make war" (verse 11, see also verse 14). Note the thrilling description of the coming King contained in verses 12 and 13—His eyes like flames of fire, His head adorned with many crowns, His blood-red vesture and challenging title, "King of kings, and Lord of lords"! No wonder the ungodly are startled and the unprepared inhabitants of earth flee to the rocks and mountains, begging to be buried "from the face of him that sitteth on the throne, and from the wrath of the Lamb" (Revelation 6:16)!

In contrast with this is the waiting bride—the church. The promise is, "Blessed are they which are called unto the marriage supper of the Lamb" (Revelation 19:9). When the Bridegroom comes, He catches up His people and leads them back to the kingdom of His

Father, where they will partake of the marriage supper. Looking forward to that time, Jesus said, Ye shall "eat and drink at my table in my kingdom" (Luke 22:30). Again, "I will not drink henceforth of this fruit of the vine, until that day when I drink it new with you in my Father's kingdom" (Matthew 26:29).

WHEN DOES THE WEDDING TAKE PLACE?

When Jesus has finished His intercessory ministry, He then comes before "the Ancient of Days" to receive the kingdom and dominion for which He died. (See Daniel 7:13.) This is actually the marriage of the Bridegroom—the Lamb—and occurs before He returns to earth for His saints. His waiting saints, those caught up to meet Him, are then taken to the marriage supper of the Lamb in the Father's house. (See Revelation 19:7–9.) Jesus said, "Let your loins be girded about, and your lights burning; and ye yourselves like unto men that wait for their lord, when he will return from the wedding" (Luke 12:35, 36. See also *Early Writings,* pages 55, 251, 280; *The Great Controversy,* pages 426–428).

Those waiting saints are the bride for whom He comes. The kingdom and the subjects of the kingdom are all one. As guests they go in to the wedding feast; as the bride they share the wedding gift, which is bestowed by the Father as a token of His affection when "the kingdom and dominion, and the greatness of the kingdom under the whole heaven, shall be given to the people of the saints of the most High." "And the time came that the saints possessed the kingdom" (Daniel 7:27, 22). Marvelous possession! Hasten on, great day of God!

THE SECOND SUPPER

The closing verses of chapter 19 bring to view another supper. This is not the marriage supper of joy and victory, which will be celebrated when the righteous gather in the Father's presence, but it is the tragic supper of the birds of prey who come to feed on the flesh of kings and captains, those who, having rejected the invitation to the wedding feast of the Lamb, are destroyed by the brightness of the appearing of our Lord. The days in which we live are days of preparation. While the people of God are preparing themselves to meet their Lord in peace, the nations of earth are preparing themselves for war and bloodshed. Here is the call that goes to the nations: "Prepare war, wake up the mighty men, let all the men of war draw near" (Joel 3:9). The slogan of our day seems to be: "Talk peace, but prepare for war." Surely the harvest is ripening.

A SAFE HIDING PLACE

Soon the beast and the false prophet, the two great systems of deception, are to be finally cast into the consuming fires of God (see Revelation 19:20), and the wicked, so long boastful and defiant, will then be destroyed "with the brightness of His coming" (2 Thessalonians 2:8).

Frenzied with fear, the wicked, as they see the Lord coming in majesty and power, hasten to "the clefts of the rocks, and into the tops of the ragged rocks, for fear of the Lord, and for the glory of His majesty, when he ariseth to shake terribly the earth" (Isaiah 2:21). Lordly palaces and so-called fireproof buildings will burn like pitch. The only thing that will stand in that day will be a godly character. It was character and Christian experience that the foolish virgins lacked in the Master's parable. (See Matthew 25:1–8.) God says, "I will cause the arrogancy of the proud to cease, and will lay low the haughtiness of the terrible. I will make a man more precious than fine gold; even a man than the golden wedge of Ophir" (Isaiah 13:11, 12). Precious promise!

From the throne of God a voice was heard saying, "Praise our God, all his servants" (Revelation 19:5). The word *thronos,* translated as "throne," or "seat," occurs fifty times in this book, referring thirty-seven times to the throne of God and thirteen times to the throne of Satan. Thus we have a battle between thrones and the kingdoms they represent. At God's throne His character is vindicated and the purpose of sin exposed. When the great judgment closes, two announcements peal forth from the throne. First, "It is done!" (Revelation 16:7), and then, "Behold, I come quickly!" (Revelation 22:7). John sees this mighty King descending in majesty, His brow adorned with many diadems, for Christ is King of a sevenfold kingdom: "King of the Jews"—racial; King of Israel—national; "King of Righteous-ness"—spiritual; "King of the ages"—historical; "King of saints"—ecclesiastical; "King of heaven"—celestial; "King of glory"—supernal. All these are united in the title "King of kings" (Revelation 19:16).

When David overthrew the king Ammon, he took his crown. It is told that when the Prince of Wales defeated King John of Bohemia in the Battle of Crécy, he brought back King John's crown in which there were three ostrich plumes; ever since then the emblem of the Prince of Wales has been three feathers under which are the words, *ich dien,* "I serve." When Jesus conquered death and the author of sin, He wrested from him his claim to kingship. And so He descends as King of kings and Lord of lords. He died that He might make us citizens of His kingdom.

38. The Millennium and Christ's Final Victory Over Sin

The history of this little planet, Earth, is the story of a bitter conflict between two opposing forces—the kingdom of light and truth led by Christ and His angels, and the kingdom of darkness and error led by the devil and his angels.

Angels are not human beings who have departed this life. They never lived on this earth. They are a higher order of creatures than mankind. They existed long before this earth was created. As God's messengers and representatives, they have the oversight of divine plans throughout the mighty universe. Like all intelligent beings, at the time they were created they were given the power of choice. Their loyalty to God was not something forced upon them, for God wants His creatures to serve Him through love rather than through fear or force.

WAR IN HEAVEN

Previous studies have revealed that, back in the cycle of the ages, rebellion broke out among the angels and one-third of these heavenly beings proved disloyal to God. "And there was war in heaven: Michael and his angels fought against the dragon; and the dragon fought and his angels, and prevailed not; neither was their place found any more in heaven. And the great Dragon was cast out, that old serpent, called the Devil and Satan, which deceiveth the whole world: he was cast out into the earth, and his angels were cast out with him" (Revelation 12:7–9). That war that began in heaven has continued through the ages. When our first parents proved disloyal to their Creator and yielded allegiance to Satan, they thus became the servants of sin and allies of the enemy of God. By subtle strategy the devil had conquered humanity, and, as a usurper, he claimed this world as his kingdom.

THE EARTH A BATTLEFIELD

This transplanted the scene of the controversy, and the earth became the battlefield of the conflict. It was to bring this little world back into harmony with the universe and to save mankind from the dominion of Satan, that the Son of God left His home in heaven, came to Earth, lived a sinless life, suffered indignities at the hand of degenerate humanity, and died a vicarious death. He did all this to give every human being on Earth an opportunity of breaking from the power of Satan and of becoming, by God's grace, a member of the family of heaven. All who believe on Him are made sons and daughters of God, and every angel in glory becomes a messenger of God sent forth to help us. (See Hebrews 1:14.)

SIN TO BE DESTROYED

But the time is coming when the instigator of sin, the devil, together with all his angels and his followers, will be destroyed. Sin will then be eradicated from the universe. This will take place at *the end* of the thousand years, or the millennium. At *the beginning* of the millennium the devil will be arrested and imprisoned. "And I saw an angel come down from heaven, having the key of the bottomless pit and a great chain in his hand. And he laid hold on the dragon, that old serpent, which is the Devil, and Satan, and bound him a thousand years" (Revelation 20:1, 2). This occurs when Christ returns as "KING OF KINGS AND LORD OF LORDS" (Revelation 19:16). The devil is actually a supernatural terrorist, and, the time having drawn near for his death sentence, he is now arrested and bound awaiting his execution.

The chain that binds him cannot be literal, for a spirit being could not be held by a physical chain. It is rather a chain of circumstances, each link forged by an event over which the devil and his angels have no power. Let us notice these events, bearing in mind that many more Scriptural references could be given for each point.

OUR LORD'S RETURN—LITERAL, VISIBLE, AND PERSONAL

"Our God shall come, and shall not keep silence," said David (Psalm 50:3). Jesus said, "I will come again" (John 14:3). "And they shall see the Son of man coming in the clouds of heaven with power and great glory" (Matthew 24:30). Paul said, "The Lord himself shall descend from heaven with a shout, with the voice of the archangel, and with the trump of God" (1 Thessalonians 4:16). John said, "Every eye shall see him" (Revelation 1:7).

RIGHTEOUS DEAD RAISED TO LIFE

Jesus declared, "All that are in the graves shall hear his [Jesus'] voice, and shall come forth; they that have done good, unto the resurrection of life" (John 5:28, 29). Paul declared, "As in Adam all die, even so in Christ shall all be made alive. . . . They that are Christ's at his coming" (1 Corinthians 15:22, 23). "For the trumpet shall sound, and the dead shall be raised incorruptible" (verse 52).

GREAT EARTHQUAKES; CITIES BROKEN DOWN; EARTH BECOMES A WILDERNESS

When Jesus returns, the earth will be convulsed. The prophets are a united voice as they emphasize this fact. "And there was a great earthquake, such as was not since men were upon the earth, so mighty an earthquake, and so great" (Revelation 16:18). "The earth is utterly broken down, . . . the earth is moved exceedingly. The earth shall reel to and fro like a drunkard. . . . The Lord shall punish the host of the high ones that are on high, and the kings of the earth upon the earth" (Isaiah 24:19–21). "I beheld, and, lo, the fruitful place was a wilderness, and all the cities thereof were broken down at the presence of the Lord" (Jeremiah 4:16). "I beheld the earth, and, lo, it was without form and void" (verse 23).

THE LIVING RIGHTEOUS TRANSLATED

Paul declares, "We which are alive and remain shall be caught up . . . in the clouds, to meet the Lord in the air: and so shall we ever be with the Lord" (1 Thessalonians 4:17). Jesus said, "He that believeth in me, though he were dead, yet shall he live: and whosoever liveth [or "is living"] and believeth in me shall never die" (John 11:25, 26). Like Enoch and Elijah, neither of whom died but were taken up from this world alive into heaven, so will the righteous who are alive when Jesus comes be caught up to meet him without ever experiencing death.

THE LIVING WICKED SLAIN BY THE BRIGHTNESS OF HIS GLORY

When Jesus appears in glory, the sight will be tremendous. The apostle declares, "The Lord Jesus shall be revealed from heaven with his mighty angels, in flaming fire taking vengeance on them that know not God" (2 Thessalonians 1:7, 8). "Then shall that wicked be revealed, whom the Lord shall consume with the spirit of his mouth, and shall destroy with the brightness of his coming" (2 Thessalonians 2:8).

Those tremendous events will bring an anticlimax to all that the devil has been claiming through the ages. He has made all kinds of promises to humans—promises he cannot make good. He told Jesus that he would give Him all the kingdoms of this world and the glory of them if only He would bow down and worship him. (See Luke 4:5, 6.) Satan never could have fulfilled that promise, for this world was not his to give. True, he claimed it, and had Christ not defeated the enemy, this world would really then have become the kingdom of Satan and his hosts. But, thanks be to God, our Lord won the victory over sin and Satan, and when He returns He will take possession of the kingdoms of this world, which He won by His sinless life and vicarious death, and then the works of sinful man will all be destroyed. "The towers shall fall, and every wall shall fall to the ground" (Ezekiel 38:20, margin). Every "high tower" and every "fenced wall" and "all the ships" and "the idols" will be destroyed when the Lord arises to "shake terribly the earth" (See Isaiah 2:12–21.) In that great day the earth, with all its boasted grandeur, its lovely palaces, and its earthquake-proof buildings, will be reduced to ruin and rubble.

THE BOTTOMLESS PIT

The Greek word *abussos* is the word from which we get our English word *abyss*. It is translated "deep" in Romans 10:7 and is applied to the grave. The Greek translation of Genesis 1:2 uses this same word in the description of the earth before creation: "The earth was without form, and void; and darkness was upon the face of the deep [*abussos*]." Almost the same language is employed by the prophet Jeremiah when he says, "I beheld the earth, and, lo, it was without form, and void; and the heavens, and they had no light" (Jeremiah 4:23). It is evident that this follows the coming of the Lord in glory, for verse 26 says, "All the cities thereof were broken down at the presence of the Lord." The story, however, is not finished. "For thus hath the Lord said, The whole land shall be desolate; yet will I not make a full end" (verse 27). The works of sinful man must be eradicated before God can remake the world. So we read, "Behold, the Lord maketh the earth empty, and maketh it waste, and turneth it upside down [margin: "and perverteth the face thereof"]. . . . The land shall be utterly emptied, and utterly spoiled: for the Lord hath spoken this word" (Isaiah 24:1–3).

Then he says, "The inhabitants of the earth are burned, and few men left" (verse 6). These will be the despisers of the grace of God who have walked in the "broad" way of destruction. They will be burned or destroyed by the brightness of Christ's coming. Those who are left are the ones who have accepted salvation and have walked in the "narrow" way that leads to life. (See Matthew 7:13, 14.) On this desolate earth the devil will be bound. Satan was once the leader of the angelic hosts of heaven. (See Ezekiel 28:14–19.) Through his sin he lost his high position. He was cast out and has been sinking lower and lower. When Christ returns to take the faithful to Himself, the devil and his angels will be confined to this planet and for a thousand years will be forced to wander up and down the dark wilderness of broken cities and chaos to behold the tragic result of sin.

WHERE ARE THE RIGHTEOUS?

Jesus said, "Then shall the righteous shine forth as the sun in the kingdom of their Father" (Matthew 13:43). When our Lord returns, all the righteous, both the resurrected dead and the translated living, are "caught up" to be with Him, and they accompany Christ and His angels back to heaven. During the thousand years, the millennium, they will be in heaven judging the world; that is, they will be studying the records of heaven. "Do ye not know that the saints shall judge the world?" asks the apostle Paul. He further says, "We shall judge angels" (1 Corinthians 6:2, 3). John says, "I saw thrones, and they sat upon them, and judgment was given unto them: . . . and they lived and reigned with Christ a thousand years" (Revelation 20:4; see also Psalm 149:5–9).

The wicked dead are not raised at Christ's second coming, for they "lived not again until the thousand years were finished" (Revelation 20:5). All the wicked who are living when Jesus appears will be slain by His glory. (See 2 Thessalonians 2:8.) Therefore there will be no human inhabitants remaining on the earth; it will indeed be "desolate."

SATAN LOOSED

The devil will be in confinement during the thousand years. He deceives "the nations no more, till the thousand years should be fulfilled: and after that he must be loosed a little season" (Revelation 20:3). "And when the thousand years are expired, Satan shall be loosed out of his prison" (verse 7). He was bound by circumstances; therefore the reversal of those conditions will release him, and he "shall go out to deceive the nations, . . . to gather them together to battle" (verse 8). The second resurrection, which is a resurrection to judgment, occurs at the end of the millennium. (See verse 5.)

THE RESURRECTION OF THE WICKED

John, in vision, witnessed this tremendous resurrection. He says, "And the sea gave up the dead which were in it; and death and hell [the grave] delivered up the dead which were in them." "And the dead were judged out of those things which were written in the books, according to their works" (verses 13, 12). Speaking of this resurrection, Jesus said, "The hour is coming, in the which all that are in the graves shall hear his [Jesus'] voice, and shall come forth; . . . they that have done evil, unto the resurrection of damnation" or judgment (John 5:28, 29). "The rest of the dead," that is, those who were not raised with the righteous in the first resurrection at the coming of Jesus, "lived not again until the thousand years were finished" (Revelation 20:5). After they are raised, the devil goes forth to deceive them. (See verse 8.) Although resurrected by the power of God, they are nevertheless still enemies of God, and Satan, as their great leader, will persuade them that this is their opportunity to establish their eternal kingdom on the earth.

THE HOLY CITY DESCENDS

Then the prophet says, "And I John saw the Holy City, New Jerusalem, coming down from God out of heaven, prepared as a bride adorned for her husband" (Revelation 21:2). Beholding this mighty city descending in all its radiant glory, its jasper walls and golden streets beyond anything mortal eyes have ever beheld; then seeing it settle down on the site of the old Jerusalem—this startles the hosts of the wicked, and in consternation they flee from the scene. (See Zechariah 14:5, 6.) But Satan then deceives them into thinking they can take the city by force. And John says, "They went up on the breadth of the earth, and compassed the camp of the saints about, and the beloved city" (Revelation 20:9).

Coming near to the city, the wicked will be able to gaze through its transparent walls of jasper. To their astonishment they will recognize some in that city whom they have despised. But these are inside the city and saved, while they themselves are outside the city and lost.

Before the execution of their sentence of judgment, the whole drama of sin and salvation will pass in review before them. Above that glorious city the Lord Himself will appear, and as scene after scene comes before them in panorama, they see the plan of God to save this lost world. What John was privileged to behold as he stood in the throne room of the Eternal to receive the Revelation of Jesus Christ, all will be enabled to see with undimmed vision.

> Now Christ again appears to the view of His enemies. Far above the city, upon a foundation of burnished gold, is a throne, high and lifted up. Upon this throne sits the Son of God, and around Him are the subjects of His kingdom. . . .
>
> Nearest the throne are those who were once zealous in the cause of Satan, but who, plucked as brands from the burning, have followed their Saviour with deep, intense devotion (Ellen White, *The Great Controversy*, page 665).

Then the realization of their eternal loss sweeps over the wicked, and a mighty wail bursts from their lips as they see, too late, that they can never share in the kingdom of God. They can never be saved, for the day of salvation will have ended prior to the second advent of Jesus at the beginning of the thousand years. Like Esau, their repentance will come too late. Jesus said, "There shall be weeping and gnashing of teeth, when ye shall see Abraham, and Isaac, and Jacob, and all the prophets, in the kingdom of God, and you yourselves thrust out" (Luke 13:28). The saddest words that will ever be uttered are these: "The harvest is past, the summer is ended, and we are not saved" (Jeremiah 8:20).

THE FINAL DESTRUCTION OF SIN

The tragic story of sin comes to an end as the wicked are destroyed root and branch. "Fire came down from God out of heaven and devoured them," John says (Revelation 20:9). It is in mercy that the devil and his hosts are destroyed, for "sin, when it is finished, bringeth forth death" (James 1:15). "And the devil that deceived them was cast into the lake of fire and brimstone, where the beast and the false prophet are, and shall be tormented [or tested] day and night forever and ever" (Revelation 20:10). While this destruction is eternal in its effect, yet the process of destruction will be, as it were, but "a moment." "The wicked shall perish: . . . they shall consume; into smoke shall they consume away" (Psalm 37:20). When the cities of Sodom and Gomorrah were destroyed, they suffered "the vengeance of eternal fire" (Jude 7). In Lamentations 4:6 we read that Sodom "was overthrown as in a moment." It is everlasting *punishment,* a result, not everlasting *punishing,* a process. "For, behold, the day cometh, that shall burn as an oven; and all the proud, yea, and all that do wickedly, shall be stubble: and the day that cometh shall burn them up, saith the Lord of hosts, that it shall leave them neither root nor branch" (Malachi 4:1). David said, "For yet a little while, and the wicked shall not be: yea, thou shalt diligently consider his place, and it shall not be" (Psalm 37:10).

The great controversy is ended. Sin and sinners are no more. The entire universe is clean. One pulse of harmony and gladness beats throughout the vast creation. From Him who

368

created all, flow life and light and gladness, throughout the realms of illimitable space. From the minutest atom to the greatest world, all things, animate and inanimate, in their unshadowed beauty and perfect joy, declare that God is love (Ellen White, *The Great Controversy,* page 678).

The conflict is over. Tribulation and strife are at an end. Songs of victory fill all heaven as the ransomed ones take up the joyful strain, Worthy, worthy is the Lamb that was slain, and lives again, a triumphant conqueror (Ellen White, *The Acts of the Apostles,* page 602).

After the destruction of sin and sinners, Christ, the Conqueror of sin and the Creator of the universe, re-creates this earth, which becomes the eternal home of the redeemed. "Sorrow and sighing shall flee away" (Isaiah 35:10).

39. The New Earth, Home of the Saved

"And I saw a new heaven and a new earth: for the first heaven and the first earth were passed away; and there was no more sea" (Revelation 21:1). At last the controversy is ended; the battle won. This blood-stained planet where sorrow, pain, and tears have held sway has been transformed into a place of joy and peace. Sin and sinners are no more. The universe is clean, and God's character is vindicated. How precious are the promises of God! "We, according to his promise, look for new heavens and a new earth, wherein dwelleth righteousness" (2 Peter 3:13). "For, behold, I create new heavens and a new earth: and the former shall not be remembered, nor come into mind" (Isaiah 65:17). Even the memory of sin will be blotted out.

THE THREE WORLDS

Peter speaks of three worlds: "the world that then was" (the world before the Flood), "the heavens and the earth, which are now" (the present world), and the "new heavens and a new earth" (the world to come). (See 2 Peter 3:6, 7, 13.) Jesus said, "Blessed are the meek: for they shall inherit the earth" (Matthew 5:5). The meek, those who have wrought righteousness, are the ones that shall inherit the earth. But it will not be as it is today, sin-cursed and sorrow-smitten; it will be a world of radiant glory.

> In the place where sin abounded, God grace much more abounds. The earth itself, the very field that Satan claims as his, is to be not only ransomed but exalted. Our little world, under the curse of sin the one dark blot in His glorious creation, will be honored above all other worlds in the universe of God (Ellen White, *The Desire of Ages,* page 26).

Ever since man sinned, this world has been the battleground of the forces of good and evil. The meek have actually possessed little of it. But a change is coming, when the meek shall inherit the earth. They do not have to buy it nor fight for it; it is an inheritance, redeemed for them forever. "The time came that the saints possessed the kingdom" (Daniel 7:22). And in that day, "The LORD shall be king over all the earth. . . . And there shall be no more utter destruction" (Zechariah 14:9, 11).

NO MORE SEA; NO MORE CURSE

As the apostle of love penned these words, "no more sea" (Revelation 21:1), his joy knew no bounds, for isolated as he was on the penal island of Patmos, the sea only made more real the cruel separation and loneliness that gnawed at his heart. But when God remakes the earth, everything that tells the sad story of sin and sorrow will be obliterated. How often John had heard the sea as it pounded that rocky coast. It spoke to him of the fury of war and commotion, of godless antagonism, of the deep mystery of iniquity. "The wicked are like the troubled sea, when it cannot rest" (Isaiah 57:20). In vision John had beheld a ferocious beast arising from the sea, as a symbol of a great dictator power whose purpose it was to take peace from the earth. But in the earth made new there will be no fury of the tempest, no wreck-strewn shore, but only the calm peace of eternity. Not only will there be a new humanity; there will also be a new geography.

This present world has much more water than land surface; in fact, three-fifths of the earth's surface is covered by oceans. In the days of Noah "were all the foundations of the great deep broken up" (Genesis 7:11). This is what caused the Flood; not merely the downpour of rain. The earth was convulsed, resulting in tremendous physical changes. Oceans seem essential to our present world. They constitute a great system of sanitation as well as a water supply, the clouds being the result of evaporation. But in the new earth, things will be different. "There shall be no more curse," says John (Revelation 22:3). Actually, the earth today suffers under a threefold curse. When Adam sinned, the earth was cursed, and forthwith it brought forth "thorns also and thistles" (Genesis 3:18). Later when the first diabolical crime, the murder of Abel, was committed, the ground suffered another curse; it no longer yielded of its full strength. (See Genesis 4:11, 12). After the Flood, God said, "I will not again curse the ground any more for man's sake" (Genesis 8:21). So the Flood was the final curse upon the earth because of man's sin and corruption.

Many today ridicule the Flood story. But Christ confirmed it. He said that the wicked in Noah's day "knew not until the Flood came, and took them all away" (Matthew 24:39). Evidence piles upon evidence in every land of earth testifying to a worldwide destruction by water. Not only the mighty oceans, but great, yawning canyons and torn, twisted strata stand as tombstones of a buried civilization. God's Word says, "The world that then was, being overflowed with water, perished" (2 Peter 3:6). Only water action could deposit the abundant marine life that we find today in fossil form in mountains fifteen thousand to twenty thousand feet high. The world today is actually a vast cemetery. But when God re-creates it there will be no "leftovers" to remind us of sin.

The new creation

"And he that sat upon the throne said, Behold, I make all things new" (Revelation 21:5). Note that the Word says, "all things new," not "all new things." This earth is not to be destroyed, but to be renewed. It will be an eternal witness of God's great love. This little world, where the Creator Himself suffered humiliation, shame, and death in order to redeem it; this place where His persecuted people have been but strangers and pilgrims; this sin-cursed land that Satan claimed as his own, is to be remade, and then it will be the habitation of the saved.

In that day "the desert shall rejoice, and blossom as the rose," and "the wilderness and the solitary place shall be glad." "Then the eyes of the blind shall be opened, and the ears of the deaf shall be unstopped. Then shall the lame man leap as an hart, and the tongue of the dumb sing" (Isaiah 35:1, 5, 6). This is man's long-lost home; lost through sin, but redeemed through grace. "The first dominion"

(Micah 4:8) will be restored to the human family when God makes all things new. He promises that there will be a "restitution of all things" (Acts 3:21). The New Jerusalem will be the eternal capital of this restored kingdom.

ONLY THE OVERCOMES WILL INHERIT THE KINGDOM

Every citizen of that kingdom will have been tested and tried. But some who have lived on this earth, perchance our neighbors, friends, or even loved ones, will not be there. The apostle reveals who it is that will have missed that inheritance. They are "the fearful, and unbelieving, and the abominable, and murderers, and whoremongers, and sorcerers, and idolaters, and all liars" (Revelation 21:8). The list begins with "the fearful." They could have been with their Savior for eternity, but they were fearful—too afraid to own their Lord. They feared the ridicule of friends. They feared the loss of their social prestige or perhaps their employment, so they hesitated to accept God's message. They were not disreputable sinners; they were not criminals, murderers, adulterers, or drunkards; they were fearful—afraid to do what they knew to be right, so they lost the kingdom. At last they are found outside the kingdom and in the company of the abominable, the sorcerers, and the whoremongers. It takes courage to obey God. It costs something to be on the side of truth, but what a terrible price is paid by those who fail to accept citizenship in the kingdom of God! Sin is always costly.

Another class who find themselves outside the city are the unbelieving—those who think it a mark of scholarship to doubt the Word of God. Nor will that city have a place for whosoever "maketh a lie" (verse 27). Some who would shun to *tell* a lie will not hesitate to *make* a lie. By a glance or a nod a lie can be made. Sometimes lies are classified as "white lies," "black lies," "business lies," "society lies," or "diplomatic lies." But no one who loves lies, tells lies, or works lies will get into that kingdom.

In the twelve foundations in that city wall will be found "the names of the twelve apostles of the Lamb" (verse 14). It is, therefore, not a Jewish city, although many Jews will be there. But they will be

there, not because they are Jews, but because they have been overcomers through the grace of God. Not only are the names of the
apostles engraved on the foundations, but also the names of the
twelve tribes of Israel will be upon the twelve gates. Both dispensa-
tions are thus linked together. The overcomers from all the ages find
entrance there. The city is immense and is built in a perfect square.
John learned the measurements of it—twelve thousand furlongs, or
fifteen hundred miles! Some would ridicule any attempt to interpret
these measurements as literal. If not literal, they are meaningless.
Wonderful spiritual lessons may be brought from these descriptions,
but we must never forget that the earth itself is literal and that its
inhabitants are literal. To attempt to spiritualize this city away
makes the message of the Revelation lose its appeal. God promises
that the citizens of that eternal kingdom "Shall build houses, and
inhabit them; and they shall plant vineyards, and eat the fruit of
them" (Isaiah 65:21). Then why wonder if the city which God has
built and prepared for those that love Him is literal? Heaven is not
a state of mind; it is a glorious place. Jesus said, "I go to prepare a
place for you" (John 14:2).

THE CITY WALL A BLAZE OF GLORY

Mortal eyes have never beheld a city such as this—a city without
slums, without police officers, without law courts, even without
sewers. There is nothing there that defiles; all flashes in the splendor
of the glory of God. Golden streets, gates of pearl, and walls of jasper! It is garnished or adorned with all manner of transparent precious stones, which taken together reflect the colors of the rainbow—the sapphire (sky blue); chalcedony or agate (bluish white);
emerald (vivid green); sardonyx (carnelian or flesh-colored); sardius
(vivid red); chrysolyte (bright yellow); beryl (sea-green); topaz (yel-
lowish green); chrysoprasus (pale green); hyacinth or jacinth (sapphire blue); amethyst (violet). As John beheld this glory in vision, it
was a striking contrast with the dust and dirt of barren Patmos.
Those prophetic pictures were first sent to Christians who knew the
heavy hand of persecution. John was telling them that if they but
held fast their faith, even in the face of death or devils, this Holy

City would be theirs. Paul said, "I reckon that the sufferings of this present time are not worthy to be compared with the glory which shall be revealed in us" (Romans 8:18).

STREETS OF GOLD AND GATES OF PEARL

How lavish is the appearance of this city! Gold, the one thing for which so many men have sold their souls, will be under the feet of the redeemed in that glorious city. And the gates will never close. Ancient cities often had but one gate, which could be closed and guarded at night. But this city has twelve gates, and these will never close, for no enemy can enter that fair land. And the gates are pearls. Pearls are produced by suffering. When a grain of sand works its way into the oyster shell, there seems only one thing for that lowly creature to do. To deny the existence of the sand is futile, for it is there. To rebel is useless. So, slowly and patiently, the oyster begins to build layer upon layer of a plastic, milky substance, which at last covers up the cutting edges of the sand, leaving a lovely coating over all, which hardens to become a beautiful pearl. Thus the trial is conquered and the misfortune turned to blessing. All who enter that fair city will pass through a gate of pearl, a symbol of suffering. By the abundant grace of God they have turned their trials into triumphs; every gnawing sin was covered with the righteousness of Christ.

NO TEMPLE THEREIN

John reported, "I saw no temple therein" (Revelation 21:22). In the temple service of the Hebrews the most prominent feature in the ritual worship was the sacrifice. The temple itself stood for a sacrificial system. In the new heaven and the new earth, sin and sacrifice will be no more. The only thing to remind us of the price of our redemption will be the wounds in our Savior's hands, feet, and side. The redeemed will have unbroken fellowship with the Father and communion with all His creation, and "affliction shall not rise up the second time" (Nahum 1:9). Sin will have come to an end. Only those who are saved will walk in the light of that city. But representatives of every nation will be there.

No hospitals or cemeteries will be needed in that fair land, for "the inhabitants shall not say, I am sick" (Isaiah 33:24). What will it be to live in a land where there will be joy without sorrow, laughter without tears, and life without sickness and death? "God shall wipe away all tears from their eyes; and there shall be no more death, neither sorrow, nor crying, neither shall there be any more pain: for the former things are passed away" (Revelation 21:4).

THE ANIMALS WILL BE DIFFERENT IN NATURE

When God created this earth, He made the animals to be companions to man. But sin came in, and the whole animal kingdom, instead of being affectionate, became quarrelsome and belligerent; the beasts became ferocious. All this, however, will be changed forever in that coming kingdom, for there "the wolf also shall dwell with the lamb, and the leopard shall lie down with the kid; and the calf and the young lion and the fatling together; and a little child shall lead them. And the cow and the bear shall feed; their young ones shall lie down together: and the lion shall eat straw like the ox. . . . They shall not hurt nor destroy in all my holy mountain: for the earth shall be full of the knowledge of the Lord, as the waters cover the sea" (Isaiah 11:6–9).

THE WOUNDS OF SIN HEALED BY THE TREE OF LIFE

When Adam sinned he was denied access to the tree of life. Sin must not be perpetuated. The way was barred by cherubim with a flaming sword. Wounded in soul and bowed under the burden of their sin, our first parents left the Garden of God. But all that was lost will be restored. In the earth made new we will eat of the fruit of the tree of life and drink of the water of life so that we may live forever. (See Revelation 22:1, 12; Genesis 3:22). Such is the prophetic picture of God's perfect provision—perfect fellowship and perfect protection. Redeemed by His grace, we will be His companions throughout eternity.

Our Lord became a member of our human family that He might make us members of His heavenly family. Paul says, "Through him we . . . are no longer exiles, migrants and aliens, excluded from the rights of citizens; but you now share citizenship with the saints—God's own people, consecrated and set apart for himself; and you belong to God's [own] household" (Ephesians 2:18, 19, Amplified Bible). When the redeemed of all ages gather in God's banqueting house, God's Word says that His banner over us will be love. (See Song of Solomon 2:4.) In Revelation 12:5 we read that the Child to be born our Savior is to "rule all nations with a rod of iron." But His rulership will be that of a Shepherd who wipes away "all tears from their eyes" (Revelation 7:17). The rod with which He rules His people is labeled "LOVE."

40. The Conclusion

The great pageant is over. The final curtain has closed. Through scene after scene the prophet has led us, as he pictured Christ and His care for His people. We have witnessed the church passing through crushing conflicts and suffering bitter persecutions, yet always she has lived to triumph over her enemies. Her constant inspiration, that which has continually beckoned her forward, has been the promise of a place at last in the land beyond the sunset. The conviction that her Bridegroom will return has ever been her "blessed hope" (Titus 2:13), the polestar by which the church has steered her steady course.

As the beauties of the new earth and the glories of the Holy City suddenly burst upon us in the closing scenes of this drama, they leave us thrilled but sobered. Now hear these words: "There shall in no wise enter into it anything that defileth: . . . but they which are written in the Lamb's book of life" (Revelation 21:27). It is indeed a *holy* city, for every one of its occupants will be an overcomer. The glorious kingdom of Jesus Christ will be the eternal home of the righteous of all ages.

A FINAL GREETING FROM THE REVEALER

And now the Revealer steps forward, as it were, and, standing in front of the curtain, He says a final word. He is eager to impress us with the fact that the things we have seen and heard are "faithful and true." Abundant blessings are also pronounced upon him "that keepeth the sayings of the prophecy of this book" (Revelation 22:6, 7). The Lord realizes that the message of this book would be unwelcome in some circles and that some would even try to change the words, so He gave us this final word to assure us of its importance. He says, "I Jesus have sent mine angel to testify unto you these things in the churches. . . . For I testify unto every man that heareth the words of the prophecy of this book, If any man shall add unto these things,

God shall add unto him the plagues that are written in this book: and if any man shall take away from the words of the book of this prophecy, God shall take away his part out of the book of life, and out of the Holy City, and from the things which are written in this book" (verses 16–19). Solemn words indeed! This was doubtless a warning to copyists of succeeding centuries to be exceedingly careful not to change a word. But it is also a warning to all interpreters. One who misapplies the message of this book imperils his own soul.

An unsealed book

The Revelation is not a sealed book. A portion of Daniel's prophecy was sealed. He was told to "shut up the words, and seal the book, even to the time of the end" (Daniel 12:4). But John, on the contrary, was told distinctly, "Seal not the sayings of the prophecy of this book: for the time is at hand" (Revelation 20:10). If we had no other evidence than this one statement, it would be sufficient to reveal the weakness and fallacy of the futuristic interpretation. Futurism is that method of interpretation that endeavors to throw these prophecies away off into the future as if they had no message for the church of the centuries. Those who follow this papal error, which was a direct attack on the Protestant Reformation, lose the very purpose of the book. Those who try to make these prophecies apply *after* Christ has returned for His church are unwittingly sealing the "the sayings of the prophecy of this book" (verse 10). The Revelation is not for the future alone; its message is for the whole Christian Era. All the Reformers of the sixteenth century interpreted this prophetic book in the historical method, finding its fulfillment in history.

When mercy's door closes

As Jesus Christ, our exalted High Priest and Judge, concludes His ministry of intercession, He pronounces the sentence of judgment in these most solemn words: "He that is unjust, let him be unjust still: and he which is filthy, let him be filthy still: and he that is righteous, let him be righteous still: and he that his holy, let him be holy still. And, behold, I come quickly; and my reward is with me, to give every man according as his work shall be" (Revelation 22:11, 12).

These momentous words, spoken by "the judge of all the earth" (Genesis 18:25), settle forever the destiny of every soul that has ever lived on this earth. There is no suggestion anywhere in God's Word of a second chance. Nor is there any need for another opportunity. True, not all have been in the same places of opportunity, but in the great judgment every influence that has played any part in the individual's life will be taken into account. "The Lord shall count, when he writeth up the people, that his man was born there" (Psalm 87:6). We will be judged not merely by what we have done, but by what we might have done with the opportunities given us. "Shall not the Judge of all the earth do right?" (Genesis 18:25).

THE FINAL BEATITUDE

Of the seven beatitudes found in the Revelation, this is the final one: "Blessed are they that do his commandments, that they may have right to the tree of life, and may enter in through the gates into the city" (Revelation 22:14). This passage is sometimes translated, "Blessed are those who wash their robes." The reading of the oldest manuscripts, however, is in accordance with the Authorized Version, as is evident from the quotations by early Christian writers who were quoting from older manuscripts that are no longer available to us today. Whichever reading is preferred, the result is the same, for only those who have "washed their robes . . . in the blood of the Lamb" (Revelation 7:14) are able to "do his commandments." Obedience is never a ground of grace, but God's grace is the only ground for our obedience. It was disobedience that shut our first parents out of Eden and barred them from the tree of life. And only through the all-sufficient sacrifice of Christ and a life of submission to God's will can man be reinstated in the Paradise of God and again have access to the tree of life.

THE FINAL INVITATION

"The Spirit and the bride say, Come. And let him that heareth say, Come. And let him that is athirst come. And whosoever will, let him take the water of life freely" (verse Revelation 22:17).

God's last command to Noah, just before the Flood that swept away his generation, was, "Come thou and all thy house into the ark" (Genesis 7:1). A similar appeal is going to all mankind today. How tender is this appeal, and yet how far reaching! Whosoever will may come. Heaven is free; it is a prepared place for a prepared people. Jesus says: "Ye who are wandering, care-worn and weary, come! Share with Me My home of peace and joy and love—a home that will never be invaded by suffering, sorrow, and sin. For you I suffered and bled and died, taking your place in a world of darkness and death that you might share My place in the realms of light and love. Accept My invitation. It is for you. Come! Take all! It is yours 'without money and without price!' And now, having heard My invitation, will you not go and tell someone else?"

The primary mission of the church is not to fight, but to invite others to accept God's love. A bride is dressed in white not that she may fight but that she may be winsome. And Christ's bride "hath made herself ready" (Revelation 19:7) in His righteousness.

LET HIM THAT HEARS SAY, "COME"

The camel caravans that moved through the desert did not always keep close together. But when the leader saw water in the distance, he would wave his arms, calling, "Come! Water!" The next man would do the same, and the next, and the next, until all had heard the news. Having heard the news, the hearer must pass the word on to someone else.

THE THRONE OF GOD AND THE LAMB

From that matchless throne of glory flows the wondrous river of life, and on its verdant banks of green blooms the fadeless tree of life. Those who reach that land of love shall never know hunger or thirst again. And the Good Shepherd Himself will lead His flock to fountains of living water. What joy to exchange the toil-worn garments of our pilgrimage for the beautiful robes of light!

While the glory of God like a molten sea
Bathes the immortal company.

All the wounds of all the wars and all the hurts of hate and sin, will be forever banished when "the Lord bindeth up the breach of his people, and healeth the stroke of their wound" (Isaiah 30:26).

How wonderful to be in the society of heaven! Abraham, Isaac, Jacob, and Joseph; Moses, Isaiah, Daniel, and Job; Esther, Elijah, David, and Ruth; Mary, Peter, Stephen, and Paul—the great and good of all the ages will be there. Beauty beyond comparison, flowers in infinite variety, fruits that never decay, fields of verdant green, music unheard by mortal ears, all combining to make more glorious your homeland and mine, dear friend, if by grace we have prepared ourselves to fellowship with God and holy angels. Soon we will lay down the cross and take the crown. Soon our days of sorrow will be past. Soon we will leave this vale of tears and be with Him whose glory fills creation.

At the end of a hard and toilsome day the aged prophet is seated on the rugged shore of Patmos. As the evening sun dips behind the watery horizon, the whole scene changes into a pageant of gold. In the glory of that spectacle, the hardships of the day are forgotten as for a few moments he lives anew those scenes of wonder he beheld in vision. Before him is another "sea of glass mingled with fire" (Revelation 15:2). By faith he hears again the voices of a great multitude in the paean of praise and victory. The song of creation sung by the elders and angels he has already recorded (see Revelation chapter 4), and also the new song of redemption (see chapter 5). But the mighty song of re-creation and eternal victory fills his heart once more with jubilation. Winding his way back to his hut, he lifts his pen and writes, "And I saw as it were a sea of glass mingled with fire: and them that had gotten the victory over the beast, and over his image, and over his mark, and over the number of his name, stand on the sea of glass, having the harps of God. And they sing the song of Moses the servant of God, and the song of the Lamb, saying, Great and marvelous are thy works, Lord God Almighty; just and true are thy ways, thou King of saints. Who shall not fear thee, O Lord, and glorify thy name? for thou only art holy: for all nations shall come and worship before thee" (Revelation 15:2–4).

Shall we be among them, dear friend? Will you and I join in that anthem of praise? In that wonderland of light the redeemed will contemplate the vast expanse of God's treasures as all the universe is opened for their study. What will it be to follow the Lamb whithersoever He goeth, and wing our tireless flight to worlds afar! How glorious to tell and retell the story of His love and grace! How rich a reward for a few years of heartache and sorrow if we can but revel in the harmonies of heaven and watch entranced the myriads of suns, stars, and systems all circling the throne of Deity! O day of rapture, speed thy dawning! The last recorded words of Jesus are, "Surely I come quickly" (Revelation 22:20). And with the saintly seer of Patmos we respond, "Even so, come, Lord Jesus. The grace of our Lord Jesus Christ be with you all. Amen" (verses 20, 21).

If you found this book helpful, you'll want to read these, too.

DANIEL: A READERS GUIDE
Dr. William H. Shea

The author, a retired associate director of the Biblical Research Institute, guides readers into the history and prophecies in Daniel, revealing the true heart of the book—Jesus!

Paper, 304 pages   0-8163-2077-2   US$16.99

LAST DAY EVENTS
Ellen G. White

A compilation of statements about the end time taken from 65 sources, including published books, manuscript collections, and material never before published.

330 pages

English hardcover   0-8163-1879-4   US$14.99
English paper   0-8163-1901-4   US$6.99
French paper   4-3330-0284-5   US$5.99
Spanish hardcover   0-8163-9524-1   US$12.99
Spanish paper   0-8163-9795-3   US$5.99

GOD CARES, VOLS. 1, 2
C. Mervyn Maxwell

You will discover in volume 1 (Daniel) and volume 2 (Revelation) that prophecy not only fortells the future but also tells us about God's character and how much He cares.

Vol. 1 paper, 320 pages   0-8163-1417-9   US$14.99
Vol. 2 paper, 576 pages   0-8163-1418-7   US$19.99
Set   0-8163-0972-8   US$31.99

Order from your ABC by calling **1-800-765-6955**, or get online and shop our virtual store at **<www.AdventistBookCenter.com>**.

• Read a chapter from your favorite book
• Order online
• Sign up for email notices on new products